AQA GCSE

Spanish

Higher

Silvia Gómez, Christopher Lillington, Leanda Reeves

Published by Pearson Education Limited, 80 Strand, London, WC2R ORL.

www.pearsonschoolsandfecolleges.co.uk

Copies of official specifications for all Pearson qualifications may be found on the website: qualifications.pearson.com

Text © Pearson Education Limited 2024
Edited by Pearson and Newgen
Designed and typeset by Kamae Design
Original illustrations © Pearson Education Limited 2024
Illustrated by Beehive Illustrations (Andrew Pagram, Alan Rowe and Matt Ward) and Johanna Crainmark
Cover design by Kamae Design
Cover photo © Pierre Maheux/Getty Images
Audio recorded at Chatterbox Studios, London, with thanks to Rowan Laxton

Written by Silvia Gómez, Leanda Reeves and Christopher Lillington.
Additional material written by Adam Lamb.

First published 2024

28 27 26 25 24

10 9 8 7 6 5 4 3 2

British Library Cataloguing in Publication Data

A catalogue record for this book is available from the British Library

ISBN 978 1 292 736846

Printed in the UK by Bell & Bain Ltd, Glasgow

Acknowledgements

We would like to thank Silvia Gómez, Leanda Reeves, Christopher Lillington, Adam Lamb, Samantha Alzuria, Cristina Díaz Varela, Christi du Toit, Gillian Eades, Penny Fisher, Luz Kettle, Wendy Law, Ruth Manteca, Fiona Pryce, Kelly Walker, the teams at Newgen and Kamae, and everyone else involved, for their invaluable work in the development of this course. We would also like to thank Rowan Laxton and the team at Chatterbox Studios: Montserrat Roig de Puig, Marina Palomo, Javier Perez, Raquel Gómez, Fran Canals, Mario Mendez Pereiro, Natalia Dominguez Sanudo, Julia Zucchelli Roig and Alex Perez Escamilla. Christopher Lillington would like to thank Daniel Fox and the staff and students at Prince Henry's Grammar School, Otley. Leanda Reeves would like to thank Dan, Sam, Joel and Maya Reeves. Silvia Gómez would like to thank her family, especially her husband, Kut, and her mother, Pilar. Adam Lamb would like to thank his partner Matthew, the Languages Learning Area, and the students of Mossbourne Community Academy.

The authors and publisher would like to thank the following individuals and organisations for permission to reproduce photographs:

123RF: yayayoy 12, golubovy 15, pkazmierczak 31, hansgeel 35, studioaccendo 56, luckybusiness 56, wihtgod 59, kadettmann 59, lenyvavsha 82, lenagh 82, cokemomo 82, manubeach 82, lblinova 82, patrickhastings 83, danielb4nda 83, kaew6566 91, anatoliygleb 93, ferli 109, wavebreakmediamicro 112, uatp2 112, stockbroker 121, Kamchatka 135, moovstock 141, nomadsoul1/ 148, Wavebreak Media Ltd 165, lightwise 166, pitinan 168, sangiao 172, sevalv 188, rawpixel 188, gstockstudio 193, avistock 198, stockbroker 223; **Alamy Images:** Addictive Stock, ADDICTIVE STOCK CREATIVES 8, Rupert Sagar-Musgrave 31, Nicholas Stubbs 31, Richard Bradley 32, Alistair Laming 34, Travelscape Images 34, Rene Wassenbergh 36, Florian Blümm 39, Claude Paris, Associated Press 46, Image Press Agency, NurPhoto SRL 56, Aaron Chown, PA Images 61, Alexander Baluev/ 64, Jose Lucas 69, Photo Media Express/VWPics 74, Cal Sport Media, Cal Sport Media 84, frantic 87, Dennis MacDonald 109, Fernanda Reyes 110, Ingolf Pompe 94 116, Jeffrey Isaac Greenberg 2+/ 127, Jared Milgrim, The Photo Access 135, Marek Poplawski 136, Peter Devlin 144, Juan Fernando Velez 147, Luis Javier Sandoval Alvarado, RGB Ventures 158, Hero Images Inc./ 164, fotoas13 166, Jeffrey Mayer 182, ZUMA, ZUMA Press, Inc 183, Allan Cash Picture Library 193; **Fundación Affinity**: Fundación Affinity 113; **Getty Images:** Pierre Maheux 6, Megan Briggs/Stringer 6, Bruno Bade/Stringer 6, Naomi Baker/Staff 6, Christopher Morris - Corbis/Contributor 6, James Gilbert/Stringer 6, Anna Frank 8, BananaStock 8, Maja Hitij - FIFA/Contributor 11, FG Trade 12, Jacob Wackerhausen 13, Edwin Tan 22, mixetto 25, Thomas Janisch 32, NurPhoto/ Contributor 34, John Elk 39, Laurent KOFFEL/Contributor 56, Carol Yepes 56, Kyodo News/Contributor 61, Mike Marsland/Contributor 61, JackF/ 63, darkovujic 65, triloks 66, Tony Anna Mingardi/Awakening/Contributor 69, Klaus Vedfelt/DigitalVision via Getty Images 77, Yelena Rodriguez Mena 82, Javier Ghersi 82, Inna Dodor 83, andreswd 84, Asia-Pacific Images Studio 85, FG Trade 94, Valeriy_G 94, Tatsiana Volkava 97, Marcos Elihu Castillo Ramirez 98, Edwin Tan 108, SDI Productions 112, izusek 112, David C Tomlinson 116, Photon-Photos 117, Todd Wright 122, NurPhoto/Contributor 135, Debra L Rothenberg/Contributor 135, Ulf Andersen/Contributor 135, Stu Forster/ Staff 135, Ernesto Ryan/Stringer 135, David Ramos/Staff 137, Maximiliano Blanco/Stringer 137, Egoitz Bengoetxea Iguaran 139, LifestyleVisuals 139, CoffeeAndMilk/ 140, Maskot 140, Cavan Images 140, Olga Mosman 142, Thomas Barwick 142, Hispanolistic 143, Dave G Kelly 144, MesquitaFMS 144, Sura Ark 149, SolStock 153, Claudio Sieber 158, Santiago Urquijo 159, Rawpixel 160, peepo 162, Westend61 163, OMAR TORRES/Contributor 169, Imgorthand 171, PeopleImages.com - Yuri A 175, Daisy Daisy 177, DGLimages 179, Tristan Fewings/Stringer 182, Penske Media/Contributor 182, Granger, NYC., GRANGER - Historical Picture Archive 182, Bloomberg / Contributor 182, Anna Moneymaker/Staff 182, Gary Gershoff/Contributor 183, Manuel Arias Duran 185, Alexander Spatari 186, Tony Anderson 186, Dave G Kelly 188, Jesus Calonge 188, RgStudio/ 188, Brothers91/ 191, Grafissimo 192, Valerii Apetroaiei 195, Westend61 198, Hispanolistic 198, pixelheadphoto digitalskillet 200, PixelsEffect 203, New Africa 205, jean meyntjens 216, NBC/Contributor 218, martin-dm 224, M79ICHAEL TRAN/Contributor 225; **Parquemet**: Parquemet 167; **Pearson Education Ltd:** MindStudio 59, Miguel Dominguez Muñoz 68, Gareth Boden 77, Gareth Boden 112, Jon Barlow 125, Jon Barlow 177; **Shutterstock:** Master1305 6, COULANGES 7, ALX1618 9, Gorodenkoff 9, Shutterstock 12, Daniel Hoz 14, NotarYES 15, Stock-Asso 16, Belikova Oksana 16, Csaba Peterdi 17, Carballo 19, Jacob Lund 21, 10topvector 27, SpeedKingz 25, Dm_Cherry 30, Marques 31, cristovao 32, imagestockdesign 34, Kite_rin 35, hlphoto 35, Stefano Ember 37, elRoce 37, Unai Huizi Photography 37, Travel Faery 37, Roberto Sorin 37, Pabkov 37, Lorenza Marzocchi 37, ChiccoDodiFC 40, Ingus Kruklitus 40, Scharfsinn 40, holbox 40, Tamil Selvam 40, Moab Republic 40, Julia-Bogdanova 40, KinoMasterskaya 41, sunsinger 41, kavalenkau 42, Balate Dorin 42, Stefano Ember 42, Morgentau 46, 10topvector 51, Shutterstock 49, Prostock-studio 49, New Africa 56, Shutterstock 58, Artie Medvedev 60, MANDY GODBEHEAR 62, Ground Picture 63, Africa Studio 63, Irma eyewink 66, PeopleImages.com - Yuri A 66, Shutterstock 66, Shutterstock 68, phatymak's studio 68, Mor Levi 68, Robert Kneschke 68, fizkes 71, 4 PM production 71, 10topvector 79, Snowboy 82, Ildi Papp 83, Timolina 86, BAZA Production 88, Maridav 88, Mark Nazh 92, cheapbooks 93, Elena Veselova 96, wavebreakmedia 101, sirtravelalot 101, 10topvector 103, Orange Line Media 106, Rawpixel.com 107, pyzata 107, Iakov Filimonov 109, Bangun Stock Productions 111, gpointstudio 111, SeventyFour/ 112, Perfect Wave 114, Zigres 120, Shutterstock 125, 10topvector 127, Matthieu Berrone 136, Fotos593 136, Alexander Canas Arango 138, AJR_photo 140, Nitiphonphat 141, F8 studio 142, Daniel M Ernst 142, 13ching13/ 144, oscar garces 144, oscar garces 145, Fabio Lamanna 153, 10topvector 155, Globe Guide Media Inc 158, alejojimenezyt 158, Sergey Nivens 165, SpeedKingz 166, addkm 166, Larina Marina 166, 10topvector 179, Image Press Agency/NurPhoto 183, Shutterstock 185, Odua Images 186, Samuel Borges Photography 186, whiteMocca 142, Tracy Whiteside 194, Shutterstock 194, Arlette Lopez 196, panuwat phimpha 198, grafvision 198, John Gomez 198, George Rudy 203, 10topvector 205, Gansstock 215, Moab Republic 217, Zakharova_Elena/ 219, beats1 227, 220, Shutterstock 221, DGLimages 221, Chad Zuber 227, Dragana Gordic 227, Inside Creative House Pressmaster 227, Anna Kutukova 229; **Joaquín Verdej /Undood Argentina**: Joaquín Verdeja / Undood Argentina 168.

Notes from the publisher

Pearson has robust editorial processes, including answer and fact checks, to ensure the accuracy of the content in this publication, and every effort is made to ensure this publication is free of errors. We are, however, only human, and occasionally errors do occur. Pearson is not liable for any misunderstandings that arise as a result of errors in this publication, but it is our priority to ensure that the content is accurate. If you spot an error, please do contact us at resourcescorrections@pearson.com so we can make sure it is corrected.

Contenidos

Módulo 1 ¡Diviértete!

Theme 2: Popular culture
Theme 3: Communication and the world around us

Zona de cultura: El mundo hispanohablante 6
- Talking about Spanish-speaking sports stars
- Using adjectives in Spanish

Unit 1: Mi vida digital 8
- Talking about life online
- Revising the present tense
- Using expressions of frequency

Unit 2: ¡Disfrutamos al máximo! 10
- Talking about sports and free-time activities
- Revising irregular present tense verbs
- Using opinion verbs and expressions

Unit 3: ¿Quedamos? 12
- Arranging to go out
- Using the near future tense
- Listening for preferences

Unit 4: El fin de semana pasado 14
- Saying what you did at the weekend
- Using the preterite tense
- Pronouncing the letter 'c' correctly

Unit 5: ¡Un día fatal! 16
- Talking about days that went wrong
- Using direct object pronouns
- Recognising and using three tenses

Gramática 1 18
Gramática 2 20
Leer y escuchar 22
Prueba oral 24
Prueba escrita 26
Palabras 28

Módulo 2 Viajes

Theme 3: Communication and the world around us
Theme 2: Popular culture

Zona de cultura: ¡Descubre Andalucía! 30
- Using *me gusta(n)* / *me gustaría* + infinitive
- Describing a photo

Unit 1: En ruta 32
- Discussing travel plans
- Using comparatives
- Using *se puede(n)* + infinitive

Unit 2: ¡De fiesta en fiesta! 34
- Talking about festivals in the Spanish-speaking world
- Using the superlative
- Using *if* clauses with the present tense

Unit 3: Mis últimas vacaciones 36
- Saying what you did on holiday
- Using *acabar de* + infinitive
- Using a range of structures to give opinions in the past

Unit 4: ¿Dónde te quedaste? 38
- Describing where you stayed
- Using the imperfect tense
- Giving and spotting positive/negative opinions

Unit 5: Mi aventura por América Latina 40
- Talking about holidays using different tenses
- Using *suelo* + infinitive
- Using strategies to work out meaning

Gramática 1 42
Gramática 2 44
Leer y escuchar 46
Prueba oral 48
Prueba escrita 50
Palabras 52
Repaso de gramática: Módulos 1–2 54

Módulo 3 Mi gente, mi mundo

Theme 1: People and lifestyle, Theme 2: Popular culture
Theme 3: Communication and the world around us

Zona de cultura: ¡No hay dos familias iguales! 56
- Reading about different families
- Using possessive adjectives

Unit 1: Esta es mi gente 58
- Describing people
- Using the present continuous to describe a photo
- Using *ser* for physical descriptions and *estar* for location

Unit 2: Mis famosos favoritos 60
- Talking about your favourite celebrities
- Saying how long you have been doing something
- Using the personal *a*

Unit 3: ¡Amigos para siempre! 62
- Talking about friendships and relationships
- Using reflexive verbs
- Using the pronouns *me* and *te* before a verb

Unit 4: Así soy yo 64
- Talking about your identity and what matters to you
- Using *para* + infinitive
- Listening for gist

Unit 5: Necesito ayuda, ¿qué puedo hacer? 66
- Talking about problems and giving advice
- Using *estar* to express moods
- Using *podrías* and *deberías* + infinitive

Unit 6: Celebraciones 68
- Talking about family celebrations
- Using indirect object pronouns
- Using a range of preterite tense verb forms

Gramática 1 70
Gramática 2 72
Leer y escuchar 74
Prueba oral 76
Prueba escrita 78
Palabras 80

Contenidos

Módulo 4 Mi estilo de vida — Theme 1: People and lifestyle

Zona de cultura: ¡Qué rico! 82
- Learning about typical foods in Spanish-speaking countries
- Using adjectives of nationality

Unit 1: ¿Llevas una vida sana? 84
- Describing healthy daily routines
- Using indefinite adjectives
- Using *tener* + noun

Unit 2: ¿Somos lo que comemos? 86
- Talking about mealtimes and food trends
- Using direct object pronouns
- Practising listening skills

Unit 3: ¡Los tiempos cambian! 88
- Comparing old and new habits
- Using the imperfect tense to say what you used to do
- Using *ya no* + verb

Unit 4: ¡Qué mal estoy! 90
- Talking about illnesses and injuries
- Using reflexive verbs in the preterite tense
- Giving advice using *debes, tienes que* and *necesitas*

Unit 5: Mi salud, de la cabeza a los pies 92
- Making future plans for health and wellbeing
- Using the simple future tense
- Using *if* clauses

Gramática 1 94
Gramática 2 96
Leer y escuchar 98
Prueba oral 100
Prueba escrita 102
Palabras 104

Módulo 5 ¡A clase! — Theme 1: People and lifestyle

Zona de cultura: La vida escolar en España 106
- Learning about schools in Spain
- Using absolute superlatives

Unit 1: Un día en el insti 108
- Talking about a typical day at school
- Using the relative pronouns *que, donde, cuando*
- Translating into English effectively

Unit 2: ¿Qué tal tus estudios? 110
- Talking about your studies
- Using *lo que*
- Talking about the opinions of others

Unit 3: ¿Cómo cambiarías tu instituto? 112
- Talking about how you would change your school
- Using the conditional tense
- Using impersonal verbs with an infinitive

Unit 4: La gente de mi insti 114
- Talking about students and teachers at school
- Using negatives
- Forming questions

Unit 5: El viaje de fin de curso 116
- Describing a school trip in the past
- Using adjectives and adverbs
- Identifying false friends

Gramática 1 118
Gramática 2 120
Leer y escuchar 122
Prueba oral 124
Prueba escrita 126
Palabras 128

Repaso de gramática: Módulos 1–5 130

Módulo 6 Mi barrio y yo — Theme 3: Communication and the world around us

Zona de cultura: En Colombia todo es posible 134
- Finding out about Colombia
- Recognising demonstrative adjectives

Unit 1: Medellín, ciudad inteligente 136
- Describing cities
- Using the perfect tense
- Using prepositions of place for directions

Unit 2: Medellín ahora y antes 138
- Describing how a city or town has changed
- Using demonstrative adjectives for descriptions
- Comparing now and then in the imperfect tense

Unit 3: ¡A comprar! 140
- Describing shopping preferences
- Revising direct object pronouns
- Practising key sounds

Unit 4: ¿Dónde prefieres vivir? 142
- Giving preferences about where you live
- Using the present subjunctive with *cuando*
- Revising comparisons

Unit 5: Un intercambio cultural 144
- Talking about your area
- Using a variety of verb tenses
- Finding different ways to describe future plans

Gramática 1 146
Gramática 2 148
Leer y escuchar 150
Prueba oral 152
Prueba escrita 154
Palabras 156

Módulo 7 Un mundo mejor para todos

Theme 3: Communication and the world around us

Zona de cultura: Espacios naturales maravillosos 158
- Learning about natural wonders of Spanish-speaking countries
- Using pronouns after prepositions

Unit 1: ¡Actúa ya! 160
- Talking about how you help in your community
- Using the imperative
- Using *falta, hace falta, vale la pena, basta*

Unit 2: El planeta en peligro 162
- Talking about climate change
- Using the passive
- Using the imperfect continuous tense

Unit 3: Protegemos el planeta 164
- Talking about actions to help the environment
- Avoiding the passive
- Practising negatives

Unit 4: Nuestro mundo, nuestra responsabilidad 166
- Talking about solutions
- Using the present subjunctive to give opinions
- Translating more complex texts

Unit 5: El futuro está en nuestras manos 168
- Developing effective comprehension skills
- Using *(no) se debería* + infinitive
- Understanding multiple tenses

Gramática 1 170
Gramática 2 172
Leer y escuchar 174
Prueba oral 176
Prueba escrita 178
Palabras 180

Módulo 8 El futuro te espera

Theme 1: People and lifestyle

Zona de cultura: Pioneros latinos 182
- Learning about Latino trailblazers
- Using Spanish stress patterns correctly

Unit 1: Sueños y esperanzas 184
- Talking about plans for the future
- Using *seguir/continuar* + present participle
- Transcribing unfamiliar words

Unit 2: ¡A trabajar! 186
- Talking about getting a job
- Using possessive pronouns
- Using prepositions followed by the infinitive

Unit 3: Un trabajo para todos 188
- Talking about future career intentions
- Using masculine and feminine nouns for jobs
- Using and understanding the suffix *-dad/-idad*

Unit 4: Las lenguas te abren las puertas 190
- Talking about the importance of learning languages
- Using modal verbs
- Using different verb forms

Unit 5: El trabajo antes, ahora ... y mañana 192
- Talking about changes in the world of work
- Understanding more complex texts
- Listening for percentages

Unit 6: El futuro sin límites 194
- Talking about the impact of artificial intelligence
- Using *para que* + present subjunctive
- Working out the infinitive of a conjugated verb

Gramática 1 196
Gramática 2 198
Leer y escuchar 200
Prueba oral 202
Prueba escrita 204
Palabras 206

Repaso de gramática: Módulos 1–8 208

¡A repasar!

Módulo 1 ¡Diviértete! 214
Módulo 2 Viajes 216
Módulo 3 Mi gente, mi mundo 218
Módulo 4 Mi estilo de vida 220
Módulo 5 ¡A clase! 222
Módulo 6 Mi barrio y yo 224
Módulo 7 Un mundo mejor para todos 226
Módulo 8 El futuro te espera 228

Speaking support

Speaking test revision: Conversation questions 230
Speaking test revision: Spanish phonics 232
Speaking test revision: Role play skills 234
Speaking test revision: Photo card task 236
Verb tables 238

Módulo **1**

¡Diviértete!

El mundo hispanohablante

- Talking about Spanish-speaking sports stars
- Using adjectives in Spanish

Escuchar 1 **Look at the map and listen to the information about famous Spanish-speaking sports stars. Fill in the gaps in Spanish to complete the missing details for each person.**

Nombre: Al Horford
Deporte: el **a**
Nacionalidad: dominicano
Vive en: Estados Unidos
Nació: el 3 de junio de 1986
Personalidad: tranquilo y **b**

Nombre: Margarita (Mavi) García
Deporte: el ciclismo
Nacionalidad: española
Vive en: Mallorca (España)
Nació: el 2 de enero de **c**
Personalidad: **d** y práctica

¿Dónde se habla el español?

Years in Spanish are said like a normal number.
1984 *mil novecientos ochenta y cuatro*
2010 *dos mil diez*

Nombre: Gustavo Sánchez Martínez
Deporte: la **e**
Nacionalidad: mexicano
Vive en: México
Nació: el 3 de mayo de 1994
Personalidad: optimista y **f**

Nombre: Valentina Toro
Deporte: el kárate
Nacionalidad: chilena
Vive en: Chile
Nació: el 17 de febrero de **g**
Personalidad: **h** y dedicada

Nombre: Caterine Ibargüen
Deporte: el atletismo
Nacionalidad: colombiana
Vive en: Puerto Rico
Nació: el 12 de **i** de 1984
Personalidad: inteligente y **j**

Nombre: Lionel Messi
Deporte: el fútbol
Nacionalidad: argentino
Vive en: Estados Unidos
Nació: el **k** de junio de 1987
Personalidad: **l** y creativo

Estados Unidos *the United States*

Escuchar 2 **Listen to these young people. For each person, note down their personality and which sports star they relate to. (1–4)**

Hablar 3 **Practise saying these sentences in Spanish, paying close attention to your pronunciation of the vowels. Then, listen to check your pronunciation.**

¿Cómo eres?

1 Me llamo Ana y soy práctica.
2 Me llamo Enrique y creo que soy inteligente.
3 Mi nombre es Isabel y diría que soy divertida.
4 Me llamo Óscar y soy tranquilo y honesto.
5 Me llamo Úrsula y soy una persona buena.

Hablar 4 **In pairs, give two true details and one false detail about one of the Hispanic sports stars from exercise 1. Your partner has to guess the correct person and correct the false information.**

Hace kárate, **vive en** Mallorca y **es** dedicada.

Es Valentina Toro, pero no vive en Mallorca, vive en Chile.

G

Adjectives need to agree with the noun they describe.

divertido	*divertida*	*divertidos*	*divertidas*
interesante	*interesante*	*interesantes*	*interesantes*
social	*social*	*sociales*	*sociales*

El fútbol es divertido. *La natación es aburrida.*
Los deportes de equipo son interesantes.

In Spanish, there are five vowel sounds and the sound of each vowel is always pronounced the same way. Listen and repeat the sounds and words. Pay attention to the vowel sounds.

'a' → *natación, práctica*
'e' → *tenis, interesante*
'i' → *ciclismo, divertido*
'o' → *baloncesto, tranquilo*
'u' → *fútbol, seguro*

When a word contains two vowels, you usually pronounce each one separately: *natación, buena*

Leer 5 **Read the information about Spanish and complete the facts in English.**

¡Hablamos el español!

Más de 500 millones de personas hablan el español y es el idioma oficial de 21 países. También conocido como castellano, el español es el segundo idioma más hablado del mundo, después del chino.

El español es una lengua muy popular para los usuarios del Internet. Más del 7.9% de la población digital prefiere comunicarse en español y en las redes sociales es el segundo idioma más usado.

En México se puede encontrar la mayor población de hablantes nativos de español. Hay más hispanohablantes allí que en otros países latinoamericanos como Colombia, Argentina o Perú.

En Estados Unidos hay muchísimos hablantes nativos de español. En 2060, será el segundo país hispanohablante del mundo después de México y se estima que casi una de cada tres personas hablará español.

Statistics from the *Instituto Cervantes* (2023)

la población *population*

1 Spanish is spoken by more than …
2 There are 21 countries with Spanish as …
3 The highest number of Spanish speakers are in …
4 In 2060, the second highest number of Spanish speakers will live …

Fun Facts about Latin America

1 En Yoro, en Honduras, llueven peces. Se llama *la lluvia de peces*.
2 Hay *delfines rosados* en el río Amazonas.
3 La cascada más grande está en el Parque Nacional Canaima, Venezuela. Se llama *El Salto Ángel*.
4 En Lima, la capital de Perú, se puede ver *la Estatua del Oso de Paddington*.

Can you name the capital cities of the Spanish-speaking countries on the map? Can you find a fun fact about each city/country?

la cascada *waterfall*
peces *fish*

1 Mi vida digital

- Talking about life online
- Revising the present tense
- Using expressions of frequency

Escuchar 1 Listen to and read the texts. Translate the phrases in **bold**. Then copy and complete the table in English. (1–3)

	Activity on phone/ device	Frequency	Daily screen time
Yolanda	listens to music	all the time	2 hours

¿Qué haces con tu móvil?

Vivo en España y utilizo mi móvil todos los días. Todo el tiempo **escucho música** y **a veces mando mensajes**. **Mis amigos y yo sacamos fotos** en Snapchat todos los días. **No tengo ordenador** ni portátil en casa y paso dos horas al día con el móvil.

Vivo en México. A veces uso BeReal o Instagram y mis amigos y yo **siempre subimos vídeos** a YouTube. ¡Me encanta! De vez en cuando **leo noticias**, pero nunca **envío correos electrónicos**. Paso dos o tres horas al día con mi dispositivo.

Soy chilena y **soy adicta a los videojuegos**. **Casi nunca hago compras** por Internet y **nunca llamo a mis amigos** porque **charlo online**. A veces uso apps como TikTok y paso una hora cada noche con mi celular.

el celular *mobile phone (used in Latin America instead of **el móvil**)*

Leer 2 Read the texts again. Pick out six present tense verbs in the 'I' form and write the 'we' form for each one.

Example: *vivo* ⟶ *vivimos*

Hablar 3 In pairs, take turns to ask your partner about what you do online.

- *¿Cuánto tiempo pasas con tu móvil?*
- *Paso ... horas al día con mi móvil.*
- *¿Qué haces con tu móvil? ¿Qué haces con tu ordenador/portátil/ dispositivo?*
- *Todo el tiempo / Muchas veces / A veces ... No tengo ordenador.*

G

Remember how the **present tense** works. Take the infinitive (verb ending in ***-ar***, ***-er*** or ***-ir***, which is **not** conjugated). Remove ***-ar***, ***-er*** or ***-ir*** and add these endings:

	us**ar** (*to use*)	le**er** (*to read*)	sub**ir** (*to upload / to get on / to go up*)
(yo)	us**o**	le**o**	sub**o**
(tú)	us**as**	le**es**	sub**es**
(él/ella/usted)	us**a**	le**e**	sub**e**
(nosotros/as)	us**amos**	le**emos**	sub**imos**
(vosotros/as)	us**áis**	le**éis**	sub**ís**
(ellos/ellas/ustedes)	us**an**	le**en**	sub**en**

Some verbs are irregular in the 'I' form only:
hacer ⟶ ***hago*** (to do/make), *ver* ⟶ ***veo*** (to see/watch).

Page 18

siempre / todo el tiempo / a veces / de vez en cuando / casi nunca / nunca

Siempre *utilizo emoticones.*	I **always** use emojis.
A veces *uso apps.*	**Sometimes** I use apps.
Nunca *grabo vídeos.*	I **never** record videos.

Escuchar 4 **Listen to Pablo and complete the dictation task. Fill in the gaps (1–2) and then write down the whole sentences. (3–5)**

1 Escucho ___ y siempre ___ las redes sociales.
2 A ___ hago ___ y también ___ con mis amigos.
3 ___
4 ___
5 ___

When completing a dictation task, remember to use your phonics knowledge to help you spell words correctly. In exercise 4, focus on the vowel sounds and also listen carefully for different verb endings.

en vivo	*live*
palabras feas	*mean words*

Leer 5 **Read the text and answer the questions in English.**

Los riesgos de la vida digital

Los jóvenes prefieren apps como WhatsApp, Instagram o TikTok para recibir mensajes, compartir imágenes y ver vídeos. También muchos jóvenes juegan a los videojuegos online. Los medios sociales son populares porque son una forma excelente de mantenerse en contacto con los amigos. Muchas personas piensan que el uso excesivo de dispositivos electrónicos es malo. También es peligroso si los jóvenes comparten información privada o sus contraseñas y si tienen muchos seguidores desconocidos.

¿Qué piensan los jóvenes? Aquí hay unas opiniones de unos adolescentes de España.

Las redes sociales son seguras y fáciles de usar. Son buenas para buscar información o comunicarse. El problema es que paso demasiado tiempo delante de la pantalla.
Ana (16 años)

Mis amigos y yo preferimos jugar en vivo a Xbox, pero algunos usuarios gritan o dicen palabras feas.
Diego (17 años)

Creo que navegar en Internet es práctico, pero también es peligroso porque muchas apps no son muy privadas. Mis amigos y yo no jugamos mucho a los videojuegos. Prefiero ver documentales o series en la televisión.
Felipe (18 años)

1 Name three things teenagers do with apps.
2 Why is social media popular?
3 What do many people think is bad?
4 What two things can put young people in danger?
5 Who thinks being online is risky and why?

G Some verbs are **stem-changing** in the present tense.

	jugar (*to play*)	**preferir** (*to prefer*)
(yo)	j**ue**go	pref**ie**ro
(tú)	j**ue**gas	pref**ie**res
(él/ella/usted)	j**ue**ga	pref**ie**re
(nosotros/as)	jugamos	preferimos
(vosotros/as)	jugáis	preferís
(ellos/ellas/ustedes)	j**ue**gan	pref**ie**ren

Use an infinitive after ***preferir*** to say what you **prefer** to do.
***Prefiero** jugar con gafas de realidad virtual.*
I prefer to play with a virtual reality headset.
*¿**Prefieres** ver las telenovelas o las series de televisión?*
Do you prefer to watch soaps or television series?

Page 18

Escuchar 6 **Listen to these young people. Copy and complete the table in English. (1–5)**

	I prefer to ...	I never/don't ...
1	watch programmes on Netflix	watch reality TV programmes

Escribir 7 **Write a post about your hobbies. Explain:**

- what you do online and how often (*Todos los días* ...)
- what you prefer to do and why (*Prefiero* ... *porque* ...)
- the advantages or disadvantages of going online (*El Internet es.... pero...*)

2 ¡Disfrutamos al máximo!

- Talking about sports and free-time activities
- Revising irregular present tense verbs
- Using opinion verbs and expressions

Escuchar 1 **Listen and write the correct letters (a–f) to identify the activity. Add a tick or a cross to show likes or dislikes. (1–5)**

Example: 1 c ✓, b ✗

¿Qué actividades te gusta hacer?

me mola(n) / me chifla(n)	*I love (slang)*

a

El fútbol es mi pasión.

b

No me gusta el baile.

c

Me interesa la natación.

d

El baloncesto es difícil y aburrido.

e

Las películas son interesantes.

f

Me molan las novelas.

Hablar 2 **Talk to your partner about which activities you like and dislike.**

- *¿Qué actividades te gustan o no te gustan? ¿Por qué?*
- *Me gusta **el** fútbol porque es divertid**o**.*
- *Me gustan **los** libros porque son muy relajant**es**.*
- *Odio **la** natación porque es aburrid**a**.*

(No) Me gusta **el**/**la** [tenis/natación]	porque es	divertid**o**/**a**. aburrid**o**/**a** / tont**o**/**a**. difícil/fácil. relajante/mi pasión.
(No) Me gustan **los**/**las** [libros/películas]	porque son	divertid**os**/**as**. aburrid**os**/**as** / tont**os**/**as**. difícil**es**/fácil**es**. relajant**es**/guay.

Si tenemos tiempo, mis amigos y yo	vamos al [gimnasio] vamos a la [piscina]	todos los días. los fines de semana. una vez a la semana. [dos] veces a la semana.
En mi tiempo libre, Si tengo tiempo,	juego al ... hago/leo/bailo ... escucho/veo ... soy miembro de ... voy al/a la ...	
porque me ayuda a	estar en forma. mantenerme en contacto con mis amigos. olvidarme de todo.	

Lots of sports in Spanish are **cognates**. Cognates are words that are the same in both languages: ***el rugby***, ***el hockey***, ***el golf***, ***el judo***, ***el kárate***. Sometimes cognates are very similar to the English words but with spelling differences: ***el tenis***, ***el fútbol***, ***el voleibol***, ***el boxeo***, ***las artes marciales***. Remember that the pronunciation is different too.

Escuchar 3 **Listen to these young people and note down the following information in English (1–5):**

- Activities they like
- Why?

Example:

- *Going to concerts*
- *They can go with friends*

G

Use the verbs ***gustar***, ***encantar*** and ***interesar*** to express an opinion.

Singular	**Plural**
Me encanta el fútbol.	*Me gusta**n** las películas románticas.*
No me interesa nada el baile.	*Me encanta**n** el baloncesto y el ciclismo.*

Remember to change the pronoun:

me *gusta* (**I** like)	***nos*** *gusta* (**we** like)
te *gusta* (**you** like)	***os*** *gusta* (**you** (**pl**) like)
le *gusta* (**he**/**she**/**it** likes)	***les*** *gusta* (**they** like)

Use an **opinion verb** + infinitive to talk about activities:

Me gusta *jugar al baloncesto porque es divertido.*

I like to play/playing basketball because it is fun.

Nos encanta *bailar porque es genial.*

We love to dance/dancing because it is great.

Escuchar 4 **Listen, read and complete the sentences below in English. Then translate two of the texts (*Colombia* and *República Dominicana*) into English.**

¡Los adolescentes latinoamericanos y sus intereses!

Argentina

¿Qué deportes haces?

En mis ratos libres disfruto del deporte porque me ayuda a olvidarme de todo. Juego al baloncesto dos o tres veces a la semana y también me gusta jugar al fútbol.

Colombia

¿Eres aventurero?

Creo que sí porque monto a caballo, hago deportes acuáticos y practico ciclismo. ¡Es guay! Para mí, el deporte es muy importante y me ayuda a estar en forma.

México

¿Qué te gusta hacer en tus ratos libres?

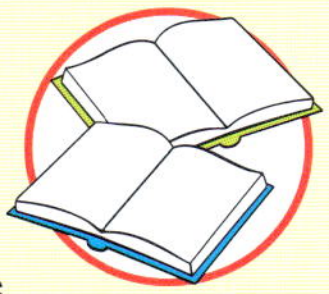

Leo libros y revistas porque son relajantes. Soy aficionado a las novelas de terror. También escucho canciones de reguetón. Son muy buenas.

República Dominicana

¿Eres miembro de un club o equipo?

Soy miembro de un club de natación y voy a la piscina tres veces a la semana. También mis amigos y yo vamos al estadio si tenemos dinero, ya que somos aficionados del Atlético Vega Real, nuestro equipo favorito.

1 In Argentina, the teenager plays basketball … a week.
2 In Mexico, the teenager likes to read …
3 In Colombia, the teenager is adventurous as they …
4 In the Dominican Republic, the teenager is asked if they …

Leer 5 **Read the text about Spanish footballer, Alexia Putellas, and translate the words in purple. Then identify the three correct sentences.**

Alexia Putellas, futbolista española

En su tiempo libre, **le gusta pasar tiempo con su familia** y amigos. Claro que también **le encanta jugar al fútbol, ya que es su pasión** y su vida. **Para ella, los concursos son emocionantes** y divertidos. Ahora es una jugadora de la selección española, pero también **le chifla jugar en un equipo local**. Le encantan el ambiente y la sensación de estar en el campo de fútbol. Promover el deporte femenino es muy importante para animar a más niñas a practicar deporte. Ahora muchas niñas tienen las mismas oportunidades que los niños, pero **es necesario luchar por la igualdad** de todos los equipos femeninos.

1 She doesn't like to spend time with her family.
2 Football is a fun and exciting sport for her.
3 Being on the pitch makes her feel nervous.
4 She no longer plays football for the national team.
5 Promoting women's sport is crucial for encouraging more girls into sport.
6 More girls now have the same opportunities as boys.

Escribir 6 **Write a short paragraph about your free-time activities by answering these questions.**

- ¿Qué actividades haces en tu tiempo libre?
  En mi tiempo libre …
  Si tengo tiempo, …
- ¿Qué te gusta hacer y por qué?
  Me encanta … porque …
- ¿Qué no te gusta hacer y por qué?
  No me gusta nada …, ya que …

G

These verbs are **irregular** and they do **not** follow the normal patterns of regular **-ar**, **-er**, and **-ir** verbs.

	ir (*to go*)	**ser** (*to be*)	**tener** (*to have*)
(yo)	voy	soy	tengo
(tú)	vas	eres	tienes
(él/ella/usted)	va	es	tiene
(nosotros/as)	vamos	somos	tenemos
(vosotros/as)	vais	sois	tenéis
(ellos/ellas/ustedes)	van	son	tienen

Page 19

3 ¿Quedamos?

- Arranging to go out
- Using the near future tense
- Listening for preferences

Leer 1 **Read the text conversation. Select the correct option to complete each sentence in Spanish.**

Gabriel

Diego

¿Qué vamos a hacer este fin de semana? ¿Quieres ir a un concierto el sábado?

Lo siento, el sábado no puedo porque no tengo dinero y tengo que hacer varias cosas. Por la mañana voy a hacer los deberes y por la tarde tengo que limpiar mi habitación.

¡Qué sábado más aburrido! ¿Tienes planes para el domingo? Voy a ir al parque a jugar al fútbol. ¿Quieres venir conmigo?

¡Claro que sí! Sabes que me encanta jugar contigo, pero solo puedo ir por la mañana porque mis padres y yo vamos a salir por la tarde.

Vale. Entonces, ¿a qué hora quedamos el domingo?

¿A las diez y media en la cafetería del parque?

Perfecto. ¡Hasta luego!

¡Guay! Nos vemos el domingo.

1 El sábado Diego no va a **ir a un espectáculo** / **hacer tareas** / **estar en casa**.
2 Diego no puede ir al concierto porque **tiene que salir con sus abuelos** / **tiene planes** / **va a tomar un café**.
3 El domingo Diego y Gabriel van a **hacer deporte** / **ir a un partido** / **ver una película**.
4 Diego y Gabriel van a quedar en el parque **por la mañana** / **el sábado** / **mañana**.

Use the present tense of ***tener*** + ***que*** + infinitive to say what you **have to** do:
Tengo que *salir con mis padres.*
I have to go out with my parents.

No ***tenemos que*** *hacer tareas.*
We don't have to do chores/homework.

G

To talk about what you are going to do, use the **near future tense**. Use the **present tense of *ir*** + ***a*** + infinitive.

voy vas va vamos vais van	a	jugar comer salir

Mis amigos ***van a*** *ver una banda.*
My friends **are going** to see a band.

Page 20

Escuchar 2 **Listen to some friends arranging to go out. For each conversation, identify what they will do (include the verb), when they will go and what time they will meet. (1–5)**

Example: 1 *go to the cinema / tomorrow / 8.30 pm*

Hablar 3 **In pairs, play the trap door game. Secretly select your answers. Then, have your partner read out the text with their choices. Every time they read out a different option to yours, say '*¡Trampilla!*' Restart until your answers match.**

¿Tienes planes?

Sí, tengo planes para el viernes / este fin de semana / la semana que viene / mañana. Primero, voy a hacer los deberes / hacer deporte / jugar a los videojuegos / mandar mensajes a mis amigos. Luego, mis amigos y yo / mis padres y yo / mi mejor amigo y yo / mi mejor amiga y yo vamos a descansar en casa y a ver una telenovela / una película / una serie / un programa de telerrealidad. No voy a ir al centro comercial / al cine / a la cafetería / a la discoteca porque tengo que trabajar / tengo que cuidar a mi perro / tengo que salir con mis padres / tengo que hacer los deberes. ¿Y tú? ¿Qué vas a hacer?

Leer 4 **Read the text and find the phrases below in Spanish.**

Tengo unos planes divertidos con mi novia Martina. Primero vamos a ir al Barrio Palermo en Buenos Aires, donde podemos caminar por las calles, y donde queremos visitar una exposición de arte. También voy a comprar unos libros. ¡Me mola la lectura! El domingo Martina quiere hacer yoga y yo voy a hacer natación. En mi opinión, los deportes ayudan a reducir el estrés. Nos gusta vivir en Buenos Aires porque es una ciudad abierta, donde podemos disfrutar de la vida sin problemas. Yo sé que es un lugar donde puedo seguir mis sueños.

Ana y Martina

1. I have some fun plans
2. first we are going to go to the … neighbourhood
3. where we want to visit an art exhibition
4. sports help to reduce stress
5. it is an open city
6. we can enjoy life

Leer 5 **Read the text again. Select ten different verbs in the text and translate them into English. Remember that any verbs referring to future plans will use an infinitive.**

Example: 1 *Tengo – I have*

Escribir 6 **Write a short text about your plans for next weekend. Adapt the language from exercise 3 and use a range of connectives and persons of the verb.**

Tengo planes para el fin de semana que viene.
- ***Primero****, voy a …*
- ***Luego****, mis amigos y yo vamos a …*
- *Mis amigos van a …,* ***pero*** *yo quiero …*
- *No voy a …* ***porque*** *tengo que …*

G

The verbs ***querer*** (to want) and ***poder*** (to be able to) are both **stem-changing**. They are very useful to talk about plans when they are used with an infinitive.

(yo)	qu**ie**ro	p**ue**do
(tú)	qu**ie**res	p**ue**des
(él/ella/usted)	qu**ie**re	p**ue**de
(nosotros/as)	queremos	podemos
(vosotros/as)	queréis	podéis
(ellos/ellas/ustedes)	qu**ie**ren	p**ue**den

No ***puedo*** *ir al concierto.* **I can't** go to the concert.
Queremos *ver una serie.* We **want** to watch a series.

Escuchar 7 **Listen and read the conversation. Fill in the gaps for both speakers in Spanish. (1–2)**

- *¿Prefieres escuchar música en vivo o en casa?*
- *A mí me encanta escuchar música* **a** *porque creo que el ambiente es mejor con* **b** *personas y es una experiencia estupenda.*
- *¿Prefieres ver las series o las películas?*
- *Prefiero ver* **c** *en casa, pero también a veces voy al cine. Sin embargo, los domingos siempre veo la tele con mi familia. Nos gustan mucho* **d**. *¿Y tú?*
- *Mi pasatiempo favorito es ir al cine. Prefiero ver las películas de* **e** *porque los personajes son* **f** *y tienen historias emocionantes.* **g** *voy a ir al cine para ver una película del director español Almodóvar.*

Remember to contract ***a*** and **el** and also ***de*** and **el**.
Prefiero ir ***al*** *cine.*
I prefer to go to the cinema.
Muchas canciones tratan ***del*** *amor.*
Many songs deal with love.

Hablar 8 **In pairs, use the questions from exercise 7 to talk about your preferences for listening to music and watching films or television programmes.**

Prefiero….
escuchar música en vivo / en casa.
ir al cine / a los conciertos / a los espectáculos.
ver los programas de telerrealidad / los documentales / las telenovelas.

El ambiente La experiencia	es … bueno/a, estupendo/a, malo/a, increíble
Los personajes Los actores Las canciones	son … buenos/as, estupendos/as malos/as interesantes

¿Qué hora es?
What time is it?
Es la una. / Son las dos.
It's one o'clock. / It's two o'clock.
Son las seis y cuarto/media.
It's quarter/half past six.
Son las ocho menos cuarto.
It's quarter to eight.

4 El fin de semana pasado

- Saying what you did at the weekend
- Using the preterite tense
- Pronouncing the letter 'c' correctly

Escuchar 1 **Listen to some young people talking about what they did at the weekend. Write the correct letters (a–j). (1–4)**

Example: 1 *j, e, g*

¿Qué hiciste?

a Jugué a los videojuegos y escuché música.

b Gané un torneo de natación.

c Vi a mi banda favorita en su gira mundial.

d Fui a un restaurante y comí pizza.

e Bebí un café con leche con mi novio.

f Compré una entrada para un partido de fútbol.

g Hablé con mi novio en el parque.

h Escuché un buen pódcast sobre delitos reales.

i Hice un maratón de películas en mi habitación.

j Salí al centro comercial con mi novio.

la gira	*tour*

Leer 2 **Read and translate the statements from exercise 1 into English.**

Example: a *I played videogames and I listened to music.*

Time phrases help us to understand **when** something happens.

ayer	yesterday
la semana pasada	last week
el fin de semana pasado	last weekend
el mes pasado	last month

To translate 'ago' use ***hace***:

Hace *dos días celebré mi cumpleaños.*

Two days **ago**, I celebrated my birthday.

Hace *una semana montamos en bici.*

A week **ago**, we rode bikes.

Hablar 3 **In pairs, read out the statements from exercise 1, adding a <u>time reference</u> and an <u>opinion</u>. Pay particular attention to your pronunciation of the letter *c*.**

Example: a *<u>El sábado pasado</u> jugué a los videojuegos y escuché música. <u>Fue relajante</u>.*

¿Qué tal fue?

Me encantó ... / Me gustó ...	
(porque) fue	genial. estupendo/a. increíble. emocionante. guay.
No me gustó (nada) ...	
(porque) fue	aburrido/a. fatal.

Read and repeat the sounds/words below. The letter ***c*** in Spanish can be pronounced in <u>three</u> different ways:

The **soft *c*** (in Spain it often sounds like 'th' as in 'thin', and in Latin America it sounds like 's' as in 'sit') with vowels ***e*** and ***i***:

cine, natación, centro, hice

The **hard *c*** (as in 'cat') with vowels ***a***, ***o*** and ***u***, and if it comes before a consonant:

canté, música, comí, cuatro, crimen

The ***ch*** sound (as in 'chin') when ***c*** is followed by ***h***:

chico/a, escuché

Now, can you read out these tricky tongue-twisters?

Comí chocolate con churros con Carlos y Cecilia en Cáceres.

Cinco chicos compraron cuatro caramelos y comieron cinco croquetas.

Escuchar 4 **Listen to and read about two Spanish teenagers and their Sundays. Note down all the preterite verbs and create new sentences for five of these verbs.**

Example: *nací – Nací en Liverpool.*

el Rastro	*market*
cualquier otro/a	*any other*
entrenar	*to train*

Los domingos en España son un día muy especial, con una gran variedad de pasatiempos y costumbres que cambian de una región a otra. Normalmente, los domingos son un día de descanso para la mayoría de las personas, pero no es siempre así.

Me encanta el domingo porque es un día importante para descansar y para ver a familiares y amigos. Cuando puedo, me gusta pasar los domingos en casa. Ahora vivo en Madrid, pero nací en un pueblo cerca de Barcelona. El domingo pasado disfruté de una mañana tranquila con mi familia. Preparamos un zumo de naranja natural y luego fuimos al Rastro. ¡Fue increíble! Por la tarde volvimos a casa y vi unos programas nuevos de Netflix en casa con mi madre y mi mascota Sancha, que es una perrita blanca y bonita.

Espero ser tenista en el futuro y los domingos son un día como cualquier otro en la academia de Rafa Nadal en Mallorca. Empiezo en el gimnasio a las ocho y termino a las once cuando voy a la pista de tenis hasta la una y media. Luego como y descanso con mis padres, y a las cuatro tengo que entrenar. El domingo pasado fue la misma rutina de siempre. Fui al gimnasio y entrené. ¡Fue genial! Después mi familia y yo comimos en un restaurante peruano, y luego hice varias horas de tenis. Por la tarde leí y escribí mucho porque tengo muchos deberes de inglés de la academia.

Leer 5 **Read the text from exercise 4 again and note down if the statement refers to Lola (*L*), Omar (*O*) or both (*L+O*).**

1. Sundays are like any other day.
2. Sundays are good for seeing family members and friends.
3. I trained in the gym last Sunday.
4. Last Sunday was relaxing.
5. The evening was spent studying.
6. I saw my family last Sunday.

Hablar 6 **In pairs, have a conversation about Sundays. Use verbs from exercises 1 and 4.**

- *¿Qué haces los domingos normalmente?*
- *¿Y qué hiciste el domingo pasado?*
- *¿Por qué (no) te gustó?*

- *Normalmente … voy/veo/escucho/descanso …*
- *Primero salí … Luego fui a … Finalmente … Comí/Bebí …*
- *(No) Me gustó porque fue …*

Escribir 7 **Translate the text into Spanish.**

Singular or plural of *gustar*?

Adjectival ending for 'boring'?

What tense is this?

Sometimes I don't like weekends because they are boring. Normally I don't have plans, but last weekend was very exciting. On Saturday morning, I went out with my friends. We went to the cinema to celebrate my friend's birthday. In the afternoon, we ate pizza in the shopping centre and then I listened to music and watched videos at home. On Sunday, my brother and I went to the park and we played basketball. Next weekend, I am going to play videogames at home!

G

Use the **preterite tense** to talk about completed actions in the past.

habl**ar** (*to speak*)	sal**ir** (*to go out / to leave*)	com**er** (*to eat*)	**Irregular verbs: ir** (*to go*) **ser** (*to be*)
habl**é**	sal**í**	com**í**	**fui**
habl**aste**	sal**iste**	com**iste**	**fuiste**
habl**ó**	sal**ió**	com**ió**	**fue**
habl**amos**	sal**imos**	com**imos**	**fuimos**
habl**asteis**	sal**isteis**	com**isteis**	**fuisteis**
habl**aron**	sal**ieron**	com**ieron**	**fueron**

Other irregulars in the preterite include:

hacer → ***hice*** (I did/made) *tener* → ***tuve*** (I had) *ver* → ***vi*** (I saw)

Some irregulars have a spelling change in the 'I' form only:

jugar → ***jugué*** (I played) *llegar* → ***llegué*** (I arrived) *sacar* → ***saqué*** (I took)

Page 20

5 ¡Un día fatal!

- Talking about days that went wrong
- Using direct object pronouns
- Recognising and using three tenses

Escuchar 1 **The Sánchez family had a bad day. Listen to what happened and then select the correct answer.**

1 **Emilio** tuvo un día muy malo porque ...
- **a** no comió hamburguesas.
- **b** no encontró la llave del coche.
- **c** perdió el móvil.

2 El día fue horrible para **Sofía** porque ...
- **a** Emilio pasó todo el día delante de la televisión.
- **b** fue al colegio para hablar con el profesor de Javier.
- **c** no compró nada en el centro comercial.

3 **Javier** tuvo un día muy difícil en el colegio porque ...
- **a** no hizo los deberes.
- **b** perdió su mochila en el parque.
- **c** no comió nada.

4 **Monika** no tuvo un día bueno porque ...
- **a** perdió la trompeta.
- **b** no leyó nada.
- **c** se cayó en la cocina.

Escribir 2 **Rewrite the answers to exercise 1 in the <u>first person</u>. Then translate them into English.**

Example: Emilio: Tuve un día muy malo porque perdí el móvil. – I had a very bad day because I lost my mobile.

Leer 3 **Read the text and translate the phrases in bold into English. Then answer the questions below.**

G

Direct object pronouns replace the noun that has just been mentioned and avoid repetition. The pronoun agrees with the noun it replaces. It usually goes before the verb.

	masculine	feminine
singular	lo	la
plural	los	las

*Perdí el **móvil**. **Lo** perdí.* I lost my **mobile**. I lost **it**.
*Leo **libros**. **Los** leo.* I read **books**. I read **them**.

With the near future tense, the direct object pronoun goes at the **end** of the <u>infinitive</u> or **before** the present tense of *ir*. This is the same for other verbs, which take an <u>infinitive</u>.

*No voy a <u>perder**lo**</u>.* I am not going to <u>lose</u> **it**.
*No **lo** voy a <u>perder</u>.* I am not going to <u>lose</u> **it**.

Page 21

¡Una visita al cine fatal!

Soy Carla y vivo en La Paz, Bolivia. Normalmente **no veo películas de terror porque las odio**, pero ayer decidí ir al cine con mi novio para ver una. ¡Qué desastre! Primero, **cuando llegué**, abrí mi mochila para buscar mi teléfono celular y ver las entradas del cine, pero no lo encontré.

Triste y frustrada, regresé a casa para buscarlo. **Más tarde lo encontré en mi habitación**. Fui al cine de nuevo con mi celular, pero **no vimos la película** porque llegué muy tarde, y por lo tanto compré dos entradas para la siguiente sesión. Luego mi novio compró palomitas de maíz, pero la mitad se cayó al suelo. ¡Fue terrible!

Cuando entramos a ver la película, **el sonido no funcionó**, no oí nada, y **tuvimos que esperar media hora**. **Finalmente, vimos la película, pero la odié**. La próxima vez no voy a ver otra película de terror. ¡Prefiero los dibujos animados porque **los puedo ver sin miedo**!

la mochila	*rucksack*
las palomitas de maíz	*popcorn*

1. What did Carla decide to do and who with?
2. How did she realise her phone was lost?
3. How did she feel?
4. What happened to the popcorn?
5. Why did they have to wait half an hour to see the film?
6. What film will she choose in the future and why?

Leer **4** **Read about the disastrous visit and select the correct words to complete the text. Listen to check your answers. Then translate the text into English.**

¿Qué pasó el fin de semana pasado?

Fui / **Fue** a un partido con mi padre porque **le encanta** / **odia** el fútbol. Entramos en **el estadio** / **la tienda** a las tres menos cuarto. El partido **comenzó** / **comienza**, pero mi padre se durmió y mi **jugador** / **juego** favorito se cayó y, por lo tanto, no **puedo** / **pudo** jugar el resto del partido. **Ganamos** / **Perdimos** y volvimos a casa tristes. El sábado próximo no voy a **ir** / **ver** al estadio.

Hablar **5** **Prepare your answers to this role play. Imagine you are talking to your Spanish friend.**

Start your answer with *normalmente*

Remember to use an opinion phrase (like *creo que* or *en mi opinión*) to start your answer

1. Say what you usually do at weekends. (Give two details.)
2. Say what you did last weekend **and** what you lost.
3. Say how often you go to the cinema. (Give one detail.)
4. Say what you think about phones. (Give two details.)
5. Ask your friend a question about free time.

You could start your question with *¿Qué?* or *¿Dónde?*

When you use a **question word**, it is usually followed immediately by the verb.
¿Dónde *juegas al fútbol con tus amigos?*
Where do you play football with your friends?

¿Qué?	*¿Cuándo?*	*¿Cuánto?*
¿Dónde?	*¿Cómo?*	*¿Cuál?*
¿Quién?	*¿Por qué?*	*¿A qué hora?*

Escribir **6** **Write a short text about a disastrous situation (a or b) where you lost something. Use three tenses and a direct object pronoun in your answer. Use the concert text below as a model.**

Normalmente **no me gusta** ir a conciertos, pero el sábado pasado **fui** a un concierto de música pop. ¡Qué desastre! El sonido no funcionó y la voz del cantante fue terrible. No oí nada. También perdí el móvil. Creo que **lo** perdí en el tren y no pude encontrar**lo** en toda la noche. La próxima vez **no voy a ir** a un concierto si es de un grupo que no conozco.

a 

b 

El fin de semana pasado El sábado/domingo pasado La semana pasada	fui/fuimos a ... una fiesta de cumpleaños./un concierto. ver una película de ...	
Sin embargo,	perdí el móvil / la cámara / a mis amig**os**/**as**. mi equipo perdió. el sonido no funcionó. la banda fue horroros**a**.	
Lo/**La**/**Los**/**Las** perdí en	el estadio / la ciudad. el coche. casa.	
La próxima vez El sábado próximo	(no) voy a ir a ... (no) voy a ver ...	porque ... / ya que ...

Look out for negatives such as ***no*** and ***nada***.
No *veo películas de terror.*
I **don't** watch horror films.
No *compró* ***nada***.
He/She **didn't** buy **anything**.
No *voy a ir.*
I'm **not** going to go.

Gramática 1

Verbs in the present tense (Unit 1, page 8)

mandar ver hacer utilizar usar leer pasar sacar grabar subir

Escribir 1 **Choose and conjugate <u>six</u> infinitives from the word cloud to make sentences in the present tense. Use a different person of the verb each time (e.g. I, you, he/she/it …).**

*Example: A veces **mandamos** mensajes.*

Escribir 2 **Translate your sentences (or your partner's) into English.**

*Example: A veces **mandamos** mensajes. – We often send messages.*

Use the **present tense** to say what you do or what you are doing.

	escuch**ar** (*to listen*)	com**er** (*to eat*)	viv**ir** (*to live*)
(yo)	escuch**o**	com**o**	viv**o**
(tú)	escuch**as**	com**es**	viv**es**
(él/ella/usted)	escuch**a**	com**e**	viv**e**
(nosotros/as)	escuch**amos**	com**emos**	viv**imos**
(vosotros/as)	escuch**áis**	com**éis**	viv**ís**
(ellos/ellas/ustedes)	escuch**an**	com**en**	viv**en**

Look out for verbs with an irregular 'I' form only:
hacer (to do/to make): ***hago***, *haces, hace, hacemos, hacéis, hacen*
salir (to go out): ***salgo***, *sales, sale, salimos, salís, salen*
ver (to see/watch): ***veo***, *ves, ve, vemos, veis, ven*
dar (to give): ***doy***, *das, da, damos, dais, dan*
saber (to know): ***sé***, *sabes, sabe, sabemos, sabéis, saben*
coger (to take/catch): ***cojo***, *coges, coge, cogemos, cogéis, cogen*
conocer (to know/meet): ***conozco***, *conoces, conoce, conocemos, conocéis, conocen*

Stem-changing verbs (Unit 1, page 9)

Escuchar 3 **Listen to the text and write down the <u>ten</u> missing verbs. Tick the verbs which are stem-changing.**

Example: 1 *prefieres* ✓

¿Qué **1** hacer en tu tiempo libre? Muchos jóvenes **2** pasar demasiado tiempo en las redes sociales. También algunos jóvenes **3** a los videojuegos todos los días. En mi opinión, las redes sociales **4** ser peligrosas, y por eso **5** usar apps más seguras. Mi hermana **6** a los videojuegos con sus amigos, pero mis amigos y yo **7** mandar mensajes. Nunca **8** vídeos porque soy muy tímido, ¡pero a veces **9** imágenes de mi perro! Creo que **10** dos o tres horas al día con mi móvil.

Verbs with **stem changes** have endings that are formed in the same way as regular present tense verbs.

Stem changes follow different spelling patterns:

u/o ➔ ue	
j<u>u</u>gar ➔ j**ue**go	**p<u>o</u>der** ➔ p**ue**do
j**ue**gas	p**ue**des
j**ue**ga	p**ue**de
jugamos	podemos
jugáis	podéis
j**ue**gan	p**ue**den

e ➔ ie	
pref<u>e</u>rir ➔ pref**ie**ro	**qu<u>e</u>rer** ➔ qu**ie**ro
pref**ie**res	qu**ie**res
pref**ie**re	qu**ie**re
preferimos	queremos
preferís	queréis
pref**ie**ren	qu**ie**ren

Stem-changing verbs can be called '1-2-3-6 verbs' due to there being no stem changes for *nosotros* (4) or *vosotros* (5). They can also be called 'radical changing verbs'.

Opinion verbs (Unit 2, page 10)

Escribir 4

Complete these statements in Spanish by adding your own opinion and reasons. Choose from these opinion verbs: *preferir*, *gustar*, *encantar*, *interesar* or any of the informal opinion verbs.

Example: ***No me gusta*** *jugar al tenis porque* ***es bastante aburrido****.*

1. ___ jugar al tenis porque ___.
2. ___ los libros porque ___.
3. ___ usar apps como TikTok porque ___.
4. ___ el baile porque ___.
5. ___ charlar online porque ___.

Many opinion verbs need **pronouns** and change their endings for **singular** and **plural**:

Me *gust**a** el baloncesto.*	I like basketball. (singular)
*¿**Te** interes**an** el fútbol y el tenis?*	Are you interested in football and tennis? (plural)
*A Miguel **le** encant**an** las películas.*	Miguel loves films.
Nos *gust**a** mucho la natación.*	We really like swimming.
Os *gust**an** los libros.*	You (all) like books.
*No **les** gust**an** los deportes.*	They don't like sports.

There are some popular informal verbs that work in this way too. You won't be tested on them, but you may want to use them for writing or speaking tasks.

molar, chiflar, flipar ⟶ ***Me flipan*** *los programas de telerrealidad.*
I love reality TV.

Verbs added after opinion verbs must be infinitives:
Me encanta leer.
Nos interesa ir a conciertos.
Les gusta ver partidos de fútbol.

Irregular present tense verbs (Unit 2, page 11)

Leer 5

Match the questions to the answers. Then translate each set of questions and answers into English.

1. ¿Qué te gusta hacer en tu tiempo libre?
2. ¿Qué deportes haces?
3. ¿Te gusta jugar al fútbol?
4. ¿Eres miembro de algún club?

a No, porque no tengo tiempo, pero mis hermanos son miembros de un club de tenis que está cerca de nuestra casa.
b Pues, disfruto de muchas actividades deportivas porque soy deportista, pero mi deporte preferido es la natación.
c Me gusta hacer muchas cosas. A veces voy al cine, y los fines de semana mis amigos y yo vamos al centro comercial. Cuando estoy en casa, leo libros o escucho música.
d Sí, creo que es muy divertido. Si puedo, voy a los partidos de mi equipo favorito.

Hablar 6

Read out the messages below. Conjugate the correct infinitive from the word box to complete the sentences in Spanish. Some verbs are used more than once. Then, listen to check your pronunciation.

¿Qué haces en tu tiempo libre?

1. En casa (***I play***) a los videojuegos y (***I have***) muchos seguidores en las redes sociales.
2. Los fines de semana mis amigos y yo (***we go***) al cine, pero en casa, (***we watch***) programas de Netflix.
3. El deporte (***it is***) mi pasión: (***I do***) ciclismo todos los días y (***I am***) muy deportista.
4. No utilizo mucho el móvil porque (***I prefer***) la lectura, pero mis amigos siempre (***they do***) compras por Internet o (***they use***) apps como Snapchat.

tener ser ir usar jugar preferir hacer ver

Ser, ***tener*** and ***ir*** are important irregular verbs in the present tense. Learn them carefully.

Notice that ***ser*** and ***ir*** have no accents in the present tense, even in the *vosotros* form. See verb tables on page 11.

Gramática 2

The near future tense (Unit 3, page 12)

Escribir 1 **Choose the correct form of the verb *ir* to complete the near future sentences. Then translate the sentences into English.**

1 Mi madre **vas** / **vamos** / **va** a tomar un café con su amiga.
2 ¿**Van** / **Vas** / **Voy** a visitar a tus abuelos?
3 Marta y Diego **va** / **van** / **vais** a quedar en el parque el domingo.
4 Creo que **voy** / **vas** / **va** a ir al cine con mi novia esta tarde.
5 Pablo **van** / **va** / **voy** a ver una serie nueva en casa si tiene tiempo.
6 Mis padres y yo **van** / **vais** / **vamos** a ir de compras después de hacer tareas.

The **near future tense** is used to describe what is going to happen and is the most common tense in Spanish for describing future plans.

Remember that this tense consists of three parts: ***ir*** (in the present tense) + ***a*** + infinitive.

(yo)	**Voy a** ver una obra de teatro.
(tú)	**Vas a** bailar mucho.
(él/ella/usted)	**Va a** salir a las tres y media.
(nosotros/as)	**Vamos a** tocar la guitarra.
(vosotros/as)	**Vais a** ir a un espectáculo.
(ellos/ellas/ustedes)	**Van a** relajarse.

Hablar 2 **Read out the sentence starters and complete them using the near future tense.**

1 Mi amigo va a ir al cine, pero yo ...
2 Ayer no hice nada, pero mañana ...
3 Si tengo tiempo, mis amigos y yo ... y también ...
4 Más tarde, mi hermano ...
5 El fin de semana próximo mis padres y yo ...

The preterite tense (Unit 4, page 15)

Escuchar 3 **Listen. Complete and transcribe the sentences about Maya's weekend. (1–4)**

1 El fin de semana pasado ... estupendo porque ... muchas cosas.
2 Primero, mis amigos y yo ... por la tarde y ... a un concierto de mi banda favorita y me ...
3 Luego, ...
4 ... y escuché música ...

Escribir 4 **Write a paragraph about what you did last weekend. Use the sentence starters and pictures below to create your text, using as much detail as you can.**

El sábado pasado ...
Luego ..., pero no ...
Después, mis amigos y yo ...
Finalmente, ...

The **preterite tense** is used to talk about completed actions in the past.

Remember that ***-er*** and ***-ir*** verbs in the preterite have the same endings, which are different to ***-ar*** verbs.

As well as ***ser*** and ***ir***, other common irregulars in the preterite include ***hacer***, ***tener*** and ***ver***.

hacer (*to do/make*)	**tener** (*to have*)	**ver** (*to see/watch*)
hice	tuve	vi
hiciste	tuviste	viste
hizo	tuvo	vio
hicimos	tuvimos	vimos
hicisteis	tuvisteis	visteis
hicieron	tuvieron	vieron

Irregular verbs do not take accents in the preterite.

Some verbs are irregular in the first person singular: *ju**gu**é* (I played), *lle**gu**é* (I arrived), *sa**qu**é* (I took), *to**qu**é* (I played), *cru**c**é* (I crossed), *empe**c**é* (I started).

Some verbs are irregular in the third person singular and plural: *le**y**ó, le**y**eron* (he/she read, they read) *ca**y**ó, ca**y**eron* (he/she fell, they fell), *d**u**rmió, d**u**rmieron* (he/she slept, they slept).

Direct object pronouns (Unit 5, page 16)

Escribir 5 **Fill in the gaps with the correct direct object pronoun.**

1 Me gustan las series. Siempre ___ veo con mi abuelo.
2 El tenis es un deporte bastante popular y me gusta mucho ver___ en la tele.
3 Hay un documental en la televisión esta noche. ___ voy a ver con mi madre.
4 Joel perdió su mochila en el metro, pero su amigo ___ encontró en la estación.
5 Queremos dos entradas para el concierto y ___ vamos a comprar por Internet.
6 En mi opinión, los móviles son importantes porque ___ usamos para hacer muchas cosas.

Leer 6 **Translate the text into English.**

Ayer tuve un día muy malo porque mis amigos trabajaron todo el día, yo no hice nada interesante y perdí el móvil. Creo que lo perdí en casa, pero lo busqué y no lo encontré. Por la mañana hice los deberes y los encontré muy difíciles.

Luego mi padre fue al centro comercial, donde compró unos libros. Los voy a leer el domingo. Mi padre también compró unas revistas, pero son aburridas y, por lo tanto, no voy a leerlas. Mañana quiero tener un día mejor.

Direct object pronouns replace something or someone that has already been mentioned.
Remember to place the direct object pronoun directly before the conjugated verb.

Lo/La tenemos. We have **it**.
No lo/la tenemos. We do not have **it**.

The pronoun should agree with the noun it replaces.
*Me gustan **las** telenovelas.* → ***Las** veo mucho.*
*Me gustan **los** libros.* → ***Los** compro mucho.*

Direct object pronouns can be attached to the infinitive or can be placed before the conjugated verb, regardless of the tense used.
*No pude encontrar**lo**/encontrar**la**.* I could not find **it**.
*No **lo**/**la** pude encontrar.* I could not find **it**.

¡En marcha! (Units 1–5)

Escribir 7 **Copy and complete the text with the correct form of each verb. Use the time markers in purple to help.**

En mi tiempo libre **normalmente** **1 (ir)** al gimnasio o **2 (jugar)** al hockey. En casa, mis hermanos y yo **3 (buscar)** música nueva o **4 (utilizar)** apps en nuestros móviles. **El domingo pasado** **5 (ir)** al estadio y **6 (ver)** un partido de fútbol increíble. **7** ¡**(Ser)** muy divertido! **El fin de semana que viene** mis padres y yo **8 (tomar)** un café y después **9 (ir)** al cine. Normalmente **10 (preferir)** las películas de aventura.

Hablar 8 **In pairs, copy the table and add some more verbs (infinitives or preterite tense) to columns 1, 3 and 4. Use your table to help you ask and answer these questions.**

- *¿Qué te gusta hacer en tu tiempo libre?*
- *¿Qué deportes haces? ¿Por qué?*
- *¿Qué hiciste el fin de semana pasado?*
- *¿Qué vas a hacer el sábado que viene?*

1	2	3	4
Me gusta/encanta ...	Hago ...	Fui/Fuimos al / a la ...	Voy/Vamos a ...
jugar al ...	Juego al ...	Jugué/Jugamos al ...	jugar al ...
ir al / a la ...	porque es ...		ir al / a la ...

Módulo 1

Leer y escuchar

Reading

Leer 1 ***News headlines.*** **You see some newspaper headlines on a Spanish news website. Which headlines match each description? Write the correct letter. (A–E)**

A	Demasiados jóvenes usan sitios web poco apropiados
B	La gente mayor no sabe usar los dispositivos
C	Hoy en día los ordenadores cuestan demasiado
D	Los jóvenes pasan toda la noche en sus dispositivos
E	Muchos padres por fin aprendieron a usar emoticones

1 expensive computers
2 inappropriate websites
3 difficulty using devices

Read the descriptions carefully and don't worry if you don't understand every word. Reading the options in English should help you to pinpoint the key information.

el emoticón	*emoji*
por fin	*finally*

Leer 2 **You receive this email from Raúl about a disastrous weekend. Complete each sentence by writing down the correct letter. (A–C)**

Hoy no tengo nada que hacer. Normalmente, los sábados paso mucho tiempo frente a mis dispositivos. Me gusta usar TikTok para subir vídeos y a veces utilizo apps para ver series. Pero ayer perdí mi móvil en el centro comercial y ahora tengo que usar el móvil de mi madre. No puedo utilizar mis apps. Mañana voy a ir a un concierto en el estadio. No quiero ir porque no puedo grabar el concierto sin mi móvil.

1 Today, Raúl has...
A a little bit of free time.
B no free time.
C nothing to do.

2 He likes...
A spending some time in front of his devices.
B going to the shopping centre.
C uploading videos to TikTok.

3 Yesterday, he...
A lost his mobile phone.
B used his mum's phone.
C used his favourite apps.

4 Raúl...
A went to a concert yesterday.
B cannot record the concert without his mobile phone.
C isn't going to go to the stadium.

Familiarise yourself with the options before going to the text.

Locate different time markers in the text to help rule out options.

Leer 3

My hobbies. **Translate the following sentences into English.**

Do you need to translate the article ('the') here?

After *después de*, translate the infinitive as 'doing'.

1 Mis amigos y yo vamos a subir fotos a las redes sociales.
2 Después de hacer los deberes, vi un documental en la televisión.
3 Mañana, mi amigo Diego quiere ir a un espectáculo de baile.
4 Voy a casa para navegar en Internet porque es divertido.

What is a better way to write 'show of dance' in English?

Be careful to distinguish between ***voy a* + noun** (I'm going to a place) and ***voy a* + infinitive** (I'm going to do something - the near future) when translating into English.

Listening

Escuchar 1

Free time. **You are listening to a Mexican podcast. The guests are talking about technology. Write down the pros and cons of technology for each guest. (A–F)**

A distractions
B contact with others
C safety
D usability
E watching the news online
F buying clothes

	Pros	**Cons**
Emilio		
Paula		

Listen to the whole recording before confirming your answers. Sometimes the second part of the question will be answered before the first.

Escuchar 2

María is talking about free-time activities. How does she feel about each activity? Write down the correct letter (A–F). Answer both parts of the question.

A	fun
B	difficult
C	important
D	practical
E	relaxing
F	boring

Watch out for distractors. For example, they might also mention other people's opinions.

1.1 playing videogames
1.2 playing sports

2.1 going to the cinema
2.2 going to shows

Escuchar 3

You will hear five short sentences. Listen carefully and, using your knowledge of Spanish sounds, write down, in Spanish, exactly what you hear for each sentence. (1–5)

You will hear each sentence three times: the first time as a full sentence, the second time in short sections and the third time as a full sentence again. Check your sentences for correct spelling.

Módulo 1 Prueba oral

Role play

Hablar 1 **Look at the role play card and prepare what you are going to say.**

You are talking to your Cuban friend.
Your teacher will play the part of your friend and will speak first.
You should address your friend as *tú*.
When you see – **?** – you will have to ask a question.
You must include at least one verb in your response to each point.

Task:

1. Say what you think about sport and why. (Give one opinion and one reason.)
2. Say what you are going do next weekend in your free time.
3. **?** Ask your friend a question about music.
4. Give **two** disadvantages of social media.
5. Say something about mobile phones.

Don't forget to give the reason **why**.

Use the near future tense to answer the question

You could use 'Do you like ...?' Remember to use questioning intonation – raising the pitch at the end.

You could use negative adjectives here (e.g. 'dangerous').

Use the word in the task to ensure your point is relevant.

Escuchar 2 **Practise your role play answers. Listen and respond to the questions.**

Escuchar 3 **Now listen to Louie doing the role play task. In English, note down what he says for each of the points on the card, including the question he asks.**

Reading aloud

Hablar 1 **When your teacher/partner asks you, read aloud the following text in Spanish:**

Paso dos horas al día en mi móvil.

Nunca comparto mis contraseñas.

Muchas apps son prácticas, pero a veces algunos usuarios escriben cosas que no son apropiadas.

No me gustan esos comentarios.

Mi padre usa sus dispositivos para ver las noticias.

Voy a usar mi ordenador para hacer mis deberes y jugar a los videojuegos.

Pay close attention to the pronunciation of the underlined words, for example the word contraseñas, which uses the letter 'ñ'.

Remember to pronounce *v* and *b* like a 'b' in English.

Remember that you can correct yourself whilst reading aloud - it is the final, corrected version that counts.

Escuchar 2 **Listen and check your pronunciation.**

Hablar 3 **Listen to the teacher asking four questions that relate to the topic of media and technology. Translate each question into English and prepare your own answers in Spanish. Then listen again and respond to the teacher.**

You will be asked four questions following a read aloud task. You must develop all responses and extend at least two questions using extra sentences and connectives in order to achieve full marks.

Photo card

Escuchar 1 **Look at the two photographs below and read the task. Then listen to Lily describing the photos.**

1 What does Lily say young people do on their phones?
2 Where does she say the group is?
3 What does she say about the teenagers' mood?
4 What does Lily say is happening in the second photo?

Prepare your own description of the photos.
Your teacher will ask you to talk about the content of these photos. You must include at least one detail about each photo.

After you have described the photos, your teacher will then ask you questions related to **Communication and the world around us**.

Remember you **must** describe both photos to score full marks.
Introduce each photo by using *en la primera foto ... en la segunda foto ...*

Describe the people/things you see in the photos. Add details about their location and activities to develop your response.

Hablar 2 **Prepare your own description of the two photos. Then, with a partner, take turns to describe them.**

- *En la primera foto hay ...*
- *En la segunda foto hay ...*

Escuchar 3 **Now listen to Lily responding to the second part of the task card and the questions on media and technology asked by her teacher. Write down the missing words for each gap. (1–10)**

¿Para qué usas el móvil?
Soy **1** a los videojuegos y por eso **2** uso mi móvil y mi ordenador. Mis amigos y yo **3** apps seguras como WhatsApp, y cuando **4** en directo a Xbox **5** usar auriculares.

¿Cómo usaste Internet el fin de semana?
El sábado **6** al baloncesto con mis amigos y luego **7** al estadio para ver un **8** de fútbol. Usé Internet para **9** las entradas. El domingo vi un montón de películas en Netflix **10** mi hermano escuchó un pódcast.

Escuchar 4 **Listen to Lily answering more conversation questions. Note down, in English, the three questions she is asked by the teacher. Next, for each of her answers, note down, in Spanish, three verbs she uses.**

Ensure that you show off your knowledge of different verb conjugations. Don't just answer using the 'I' form.

Hablar 5 **Prepare your own answers to Module 1 questions 1–10 on page 230. Then practise with your partner.**

Módulo 1

Prueba escrita

Translation

Escribir 1

Read the English text and Mohammed's translation of it. Write down the missing word for each gap. (1–8)

In my free time I use my phone all the time. Sometimes I take photos on my mobile. Normally I send emails, but I almost never play videogames. Yesterday I played football with my friends in the park and then we went to the cinema. Next week, my brother and I are going to go to a concert.

En mi tiempo libre **1** mi móvil todo el tiempo. A veces **2** fotos con mi móvil. Normalmente **3** correos electrónicos, pero casi **4** juego a los videojuegos. **5** jugué al fútbol con mis amigos en el **6** y luego fuimos al cine. La **7** semana, mi hermano y yo vamos a **8** a un concierto.

Escribir 2

Translate the sentences into Spanish.

1 If I have free time, I do sport.
2 Next month, I am going to go horse riding.
3 I don't spend much time on my phone because I think it is boring.
4 On Sunday my parents are going to go to a football match.
5 Last weekend, I went swimming with my friends, then we went out.

Be careful with phrases which cannot be translated word for word. How do you translate 'on' when we are talking about a day of the week?

90-Word writing task

Escribir 1

Look at the writing task below. Think about what vocabulary you have learned which you could use in your answer:

- **verbs in the present tense** to talk about activities that you and others do.
- **different persons of the verb** to show what others do.
- **verbs in the preterite tense** to narrate what you did last weekend.
- **near future tense** to say what you are going to do next weekend.

Write down three or four useful phrases that you could use in your answer.

Spend one minute thinking of useful structures you could use. Share and compare your ideas with a partner.

You are writing a blog post about your free time.

Write approximately **90** words in **Spanish**. You must include something about each bullet point.

Mention:

- what you do in your free time
- what you did last weekend with your friends or family
- what you are going to do next weekend

Leer 2 **Read Sam's answer to the ask. Answer questions 1–5 in the coloured shapes.**

1 What sentence starters have been used to introduce each paragraph?

2 What verb form do you need after ***me ayuda a***? Find two other structures in the text that work in the same way.

3 When saying 'my sister and I', what verb form do you need to use? Find one other example of a verb in the text in this form.

4 Use sequencers like ***después*** to give order to events. Find one more sequencer in the text.

5 Use adjectives to show a range of vocabulary. Pick out two other adjectives you can see in the text.

En mi tiempo libre, soy miembro de un club de natación y voy a la piscina dos veces a la semana. Me encanta nadar porque me ayuda a olvidarme de todo. También me gusta leer cuando estoy en casa.

La semana pasada, mi hermana y yo fuimos al cine para ver una película de aventura y después vimos a una banda increíble en un concierto. ¡Fue guay!

El próximo fin de semana creo que voy a ver un documental sobre mi equipo de fútbol favorito con mi madre, y luego vamos a salir a comer.

Leer 3 **Read Sam's text again and answer the questions.**

1 How often does he go swimming?
2 Why does he love swimming?
3 What else does he like doing?
4 What did he do last week? (Give two details.)
5 What is he going to watch this weekend?
6 What else is he going to do and who with?

Escribir 4 **Prepare your own answer to the task.**

- Think about how you can develop your answer for each bullet point.
- Look back at your notes from exercises 1 and 2.
- Look at the 'Challenge checklist' and consider how you can show off your Spanish!
- Write a brief plan and organise your answer into paragraphs.
- Write your answer and then carefully check the accuracy of what you have written.

Challenge checklist	
	✓ Past, present and future time frames ✓ Connectives (e.g. *y, pero, también*) ✓ Time phrases (e.g. *dos veces a la semana*) ✓ Different opinion phrases (e.g. *me encanta, me interesa, prefiero*)
	✓ Different persons of the verb (e.g. *fuimos, vamos a comer*) ✓ Sequencers (e.g. *primero, después, luego*) ✓ A wide range of interesting vocabulary ✓ Reasons and exclamations (e.g. *¡Fue guay!*)
	✓ Phrases with more than one tense (e.g. *creo que voy a ver*) ✓ More complex structures to give reasons (e.g. *porque me ayuda a*) ✓ More varied connectives (e.g. *por lo tanto, cuando*) ✓ Direct object pronouns (e.g. *lo hago porque*)

Módulo

1 Palabras

Key:
bold = this word will appear in higher exams only
* = this word is not on the vocabulary list, but you may use it in your own sentences

El mundo hispanohablante (pages 6–7):

La personalidad	*Personality*
Mi nombre es / Me llamo ...	*My name is / I am called ...*
Soy / Es una persona ...	*I am / He/She is a ... person.*
Soy como ...	*I am like ...*
Soy / Es ...	*I am / He/She is ...*
bueno/a	*good*
divertido/a	*fun, enjoyable*
interesante / optimista	*interesting / optimistic*
positivo/a / **práctico/a**	*positive / practical*
*tímido/a	*shy*
trabajador/a	*hard-working*
optimista	*optimistic*
creativo/a	*creative*
tranquilo/a	*calm*

Mi vida digital (pages 8–9):

¿Qué haces con tu móvil?	*What do you do on your phone?*
¿Qué haces con tu ordenador/portátil/**dispositivo**?	*What do you do on your computer/laptop/device?*
Escucho música	*I listen to music*
Mando / Recibo mensajes	*I send / receive messages*
Leo las noticias	*I read the news*
Envío correos electrónicos	*I send emails*
*Saco fotos / Grabo vídeos	*I take photos / record videos*
Uso apps como ...	*I use apps like ...*
Utilizo las redes sociales	*I use social media*
No tengo ordenador	*I don't have a computer*
Charlo online	*I chat online*
Llamo a mis amigos	*I call my friends*
Hago compras / *llamadas	*I shop / I make calls*
Soy *adicto/a a ...	*I am addicted to ...*
Mis amigos y yo ...	*My friends and I ...*
*sacamos fotos / subimos vídeos	*take photos / upload videos*
no jugamos mucho a los videojuegos	*don't play video games much*
Prefiero / Preferimos / Prefieren ...	*I / We / They prefer (to) ...*
apps como ...	*apps like ...*
compartir/subir imágenes ...	*share/upload images ...*
enviar correos electrónicos	*send emails*
hacer compras por Internet	*shop on the internet*
jugar en vivo a ...	*play ... live*
navegar en Internet	*browse, surf the Internet*
ver vídeos	*watch videos*
ver programas de telerrealidad/**telenovelas**/series	*watch reality TV shows/soaps/series*
¿Cuánto tiempo pasas ...?	*How much time do you spend ...?*
Paso ... horas al día	*I spend ... hours per day*
Siempre / Todo el tiempo	*Always / All the time*
Todos los días / Muchas veces	*Every day / Often*
De vez en cuando	*From time to time*
A veces	*Sometimes*
(**Casi**) Nunca	*(Almost) Never*
Una vez / dos veces a la semana	*Once / twice a week*
Los fines de semana	*At the weekends*

¡Disfrutamos al máximo! (pages 10–11):

¿Qué actividades te gusta hacer?	*What activities do you like doing?*
(No) Me gusta (mucho) ...	*I (don't) (really) like ...*
(No) Me encanta ...	*I (don't) love ...*
(No) Me interesa (nada) ...	*I am (not) interested in ... (at all)*
Odio ...	*I hate ...*
Prefiero / Preferimos ...	*I prefer / We prefer ...*
*... es mi pasión	*... is my passion*
escuchar música/canciones	*listening to music/songs*
ir a conciertos	*going to concerts*
jugar al baloncesto/voleibol	*playing basketball/volleyball*
montar a caballo	*horse riding*
salir con mis amigos	*going out with my friends*
ver películas	*watching films*
leer (libros/novelas de ...)	*reading (... books/novels)*
bailar	*dancing*
(No) Hago muchas actividades	*I (don't) do many activities*
porque es / son ...	*because it is / they are ...*
aburrido/a(s) / difícil(es)	*boring / difficult*
divertido/a(s) / emocionante(s)	*fun / exciting*
fácil(es) / guay	*easy / cool*
relajante(s) / tonto/a(s)	*relaxing / stupid*
¿Qué deportes haces?	*What sports do you do?*
Juego al / a la ...	*I play ...*
Practico / Hago ...	*I practise / I do ...*
(el) baile / ciclismo / deporte	*dance / cycling / sport*
(el) fútbol / baloncesto / tenis	*football / basketball / tennis*
(la) natación	*swimming*
(los) deportes **acuáticos**	*water sports*
¿Qué te gusta hacer en tu tiempo libre?	*What do you like doing in your free time?*
¿Qué actividades haces en tu tiempo libre?	*What activities do you do in your free time?*
En mi tiempo libre ...	*In my free time ...*
Si tengo / tenemos tiempo, ...	*If I / we have time, ...*
Si tengo / tenemos dinero, ...	*If I / we have money, ...*
voy / vamos al/a la ...	*I / we go to the ...*
leo / veo / bailo / escucho ...	*I read / watch / dance / listen to ...*
juego al/a la / hago ...	*I play / do ...*
porque me ayuda a ...	*because it helps me to ...*
estar en forma	*keep fit*
olvidarme de todo	*forget everything*
mantenerme en contacto con ...	*stay in touch with ...*
Soy **aficionado** a ...	*I am a fan of ...*
¿Eres miembro de algún club?	*Are you a member of a club?*
Soy miembro de un equipo	*I am a member of a team*

¿Quedamos? (pages 12–13):

¿Qué vas / vamos a hacer?	*What are you / we going to do?*
Este fin de semana / Primero	*This weekend / First*
Luego	*Later/afterwards*
Por la mañana/tarde ...	*In the morning/afternoon ...*
Por la noche ...	*In the evening / at night*
Quiero / Queremos ...	*I / We want to ...*
Mis amigos y yo vamos a ...	*My friends and I are going to ...*
(No) Voy a ...	*I am (not) going to ...*
descansar / estar en casa	*rest / be at home*
hacer deporte/los deberes	*do sports/homework*
ir al parque/cine	*go to the park/cinema*
ir a un concierto	*go to a concert*
ir a un restaurante	*go to a restaurant*
ir a la piscina	*go to the pool*
limpiar mi habitación	*clean my bedroom*
salir (por la tarde)	*go out (in the afternoon)*
tomar un café	*have a coffee*
mandar mensajes a mis amigos	*send messages to my friends*
hacer tareas	*do chores/homework*
No puedo ...	*I can't ...*
porque tengo que ...	*because I have to ...*
hacer los deberes	*do my homework*
¿Tienes planes?	*Do you have (any) plans?*
(No) Tengo planes para ...	*I (don't) have plans for ...*
hoy / mañana	*today / tomorrow*
este fin de semana	*this weekend*
el viernes/sábado/domingo	*Friday/Saturday/Sunday*
la semana próxima/que viene	*next week*
Estoy libre / No puedo ir	*I am free / I can't come*
Lo siento / ¡Claro que sí!	*I'm sorry / Of course!*
No tengo dinero	*I don't have (any) money*
De acuerdo	*OK*
¿A qué hora quedamos?	*What time shall we meet?*
A las (diez) en (la *cafetería)	*At (ten o'clock) at (the café)*
¿Quedamos a las (cuatro)?	*Shall we meet at (four o'clock)?*
ir al cine / a los espectáculos	*to go to the cinema / to shows*
El ambiente es ...	*The atmosphere is ...*
Los actores son ...	*The actors are ...*
bueno/a(s) / estupendo/a(s) increíble(s) / malo/a(s)	*good / great incredible / bad*

El fin de semana pasado (pages 14–15):

¿Qué hiciste ...?	*What did you do ...?*
El fin de semana pasado / Ayer	*Last weekend / Yesterday*
El sábado/domingo pasado	*Last Saturday/Sunday*
La semana pasada	*Last week*
El mes pasado	*Last month*
Hace ... días	*... days ago*
Hace una semana ...	*A week ago ...*
celebré mi cumpleaños	*I celebrated my birthday*
comí / bebí ...	*I ate / I drank ...*
compré una entrada para un partido de fútbol	*I bought a ticket to a football match*
escuché música	*I listened to music*
no hice mucho	*I didn't do much*
fui a un restaurante	*I went to a restaurant*
fui a un concierto	*I went to a concert*
gané un **torneo** (de natación)	*I won a (swimming) tournament*
me quedé en casa todo el día	*I stayed at home all day*
hablé con mi amigo en el parque	*I spoke to my friend at the park*
salí con mi amigo al centro comercial	*I went out to the shopping centre with my friend*
fui al **gimnasio** y *entrené	*I went to the gym and trained*
jugué a los *videojuegos	*I played video games*
Mi familia y yo ...	*My family and I ...*
comimos en un restaurante (peruano)	*(we) ate at a (Peruvian) restaurant*
fuimos a un concierto	*(we) went to a concert*
salimos a comer	*(we) went out to eat*
¿Qué tal fue?	*How was it?*
Me gustó / Me encantó	*I liked it / I loved it*
No me gustó (nada)	*I didn't like it (at all)*
porque fue ...	*because it was ...*
aburrido/a / emocionante	*boring / exciting*
estupendo/a / guay / fatal	*great / cool / terrible*
¿Qué haces los domingos normalmente?	*What do you normally do on Sundays?*
Normalmente voy al / a la ...	*Normally I go to the ...*
Veo programas de ...	*I watch ... programmes*
Escucho ... / Descanso	*I listen to ... / I rest*

¡Un día fatal! (pages 16–17):

¿Qué pasó el fin de semana pasado?	*What happened last weekend?*
Tuve un día ...	*I had a(n) ... day*
difícil / horrible / **fatal**	*difficult / horrible / awful*
porque ...	*because ...*
comí ... / no comí (nada)	*I ate ... / I didn't eat (anything)*
llegué muy tarde	*I arrived very late*
no hice los deberes	*I didn't do my homework*
pasé todo el día enfrente de la televisión	*I spent all day in front of the television*
me caí	*I fell*
Normalmente ...	*Normally ...*
me gusta ir a conciertos	*I like going to concerts*
no veo películas de ...	*I don't watch ... films*
pero el fin de semana pasado fui/fuimos a ...	*but last weekend I/we went to ...*
un concierto / un partido	*a concert / a match*
ver una película de ...	*watch a ... film*
y ...	*and ...*
la banda fue terrible	*the band was terrible*
mi equipo perdió	*my team lost*
el sonido no funcionó	*the sound didn't work*
Perdí ...	*I lost ...*
el móvil / la mochila / a mis amigos	*my mobile / rucksack, school bag / friends*
Lo/La/Los/Las perdí ...	*I lost it/them ...*
Lo/La/Los/Las encontré ...	*I found it/them ...*
en casa	*at home*
en la ciudad	*in the city*
en el coche	*in the car*
en el estadio	*at the stadium*
¿Qué vas a hacer el fin de semana próximo?	*What are you going to do next weekend?*
El fin de semana próximo	*Next weekend*
La próxima vez	*Next time*
(no) voy a ...	*I am (not) going to ...*
ir al estadio	*go to the stadium*
ver otra película de terror	*watch another horror film*
viajar en ...	*travel by ...*

¡Descubre Andalucía!

- Using *me gusta(n)* / *me gustaría* + infinitive
- Describing a photo

Bienvenidos a Andalucía

Cada año, Andalucía atrae a más de doce millones de turistas extranjeros. Situada en el sur de España, esta región (la segunda más grande del país) tiene más de ochocientos kilómetros de costa, montes y montañas preciosos, dos Parques Nacionales y ciudades históricas como Sevilla, Málaga, Córdoba y Granada.

Un ejemplo famoso de su cultura única es el flamenco, un arte andaluz que incluye el baile, el cante y la música de guitarra.

el flamenco

¿Por qué vienen a Andalucía?

Según un estudio, los turistas visitan Andalucía por muchos motivos distintos.

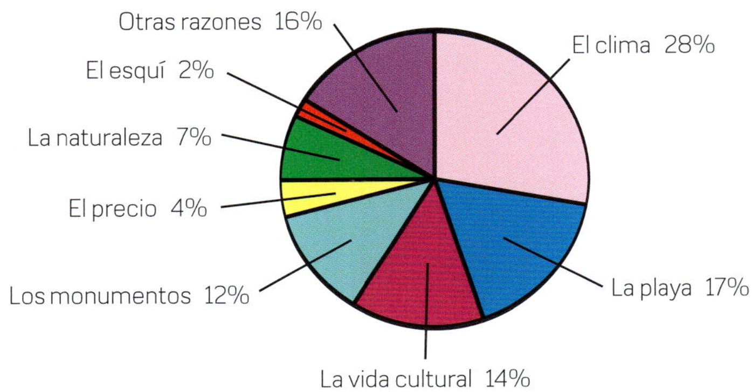

Leer 1 **Read the text above. Find the Spanish for the following phrases.**

1 foreign tourists
2 the second biggest in the country
3 beautiful hills and mountains
4 historic cities
5 according to a study
6 for many different reasons
7 the cultural life
8 the price

En la foto A la izquierda A la derecha En el centro Al fondo	hay	un bosque. una torre. un río. una playa. un barco. agua. vistas bonitas. muchos árboles/animales/edificios. muchas casas/montañas/personas.
Está(n) en		el campo. la montaña. la costa. un pueblo. una ciudad.
Es		bonito/a. histórico/a. precioso/a. hermoso/a. tranquilo/a. interesante.

Hace	sol		frío	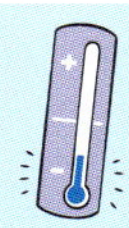
	viento		buen tiempo	
	calor	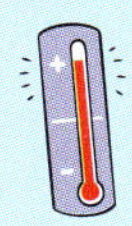	mal tiempo	
	Llueve		Nieva	

Así es Andalucía

conocido por	*known for*	***el bosque***	*forest, wood*
el paisaje	*landscape*	***la marisma***	*marsh*

A El Rocío

¿Dónde? El Parque Nacional de Doñana

Tipo de destino pueblo pequeño

Conocido por el turismo verde
el paisaje hermoso

Tiene ecosistemas diferentes como bosques y marismas
varias especies de pájaros y otros animales

Ideal para apreciar la naturaleza
estar al aire libre
montar a caballo

Flamencos y caballos

C Pradollano

¿Dónde? Sierra Nevada

Tipo de destino estación de esquí

Conocido por las vistas bonitas de la montaña

Tiene tiendas y hoteles
escuelas de esquí

Ideal para hacer esquí
hacer snowboard
hacer ciclismo de montaña

La estación de esquí

B Sevilla

¿Dónde? A orillas del río Guadalquivir

Tipo de destino ciudad histórica

Conocido por las procesiones de Semana Santa

Tiene edificios antiguos
más de 2.000 años de historia

Ideal para ver un espectáculo de flamenco
caminar por el centro
hacer turismo

La Torre del Oro

D Estepona

¿Dónde? La Costa del Sol

Tipo de destino ciudad costera

Conocido por las diecisiete playas

Tiene más de 20 kilómetros de costa y un parque acuático al lado del mar

Ideal para tomar el sol y nadar
descansar
hacer deportes acuáticos

La playa

Escuchar 2 **Read the information about the <u>four</u> destinations and then listen. Which one would you recommend for each person? (1–8)**

> Spanish sometimes uses *hacer* where English uses the verb 'to go'.
> What do these phrases mean?
> *hacer ciclismo* *hacer esquí*
> *hacer natación* *hacer turismo*

Hablar 3 **In pairs, talk about the <u>four</u> destinations. Which ones would you (not) like to visit?**

- *¿Te gusta**ría** visitar <u>Sevilla</u>?*
- *Sí, me gusta**ría** visitar ... porque me gust**a** la historia / porque me gust**an** los edificios antiguos.*
  *También me gust**a** <u>hacer turismo</u>. Finalmente, me gusta**ría** ver <u>un espectáculo de flamenco</u>. ¿Y a ti? ¿Te gusta**ría** visitar ... ?*
- *No, no me gusta**ría** visitar ... porque no ...*

> **G**
> To say what you like, use:
> ***Me gusta(n)*** + *el*/*la*/*los*/*las* + noun
> To say what you like to do/doing, use:
> ***Me gusta*** + <u>infinitive</u>
> To say what you would like to do, use:
> ***Me gustaría*** + <u>infinitive</u>
> Page 42

Escuchar 4 **Listen to Mariam. Which destination (A–D) is she describing? Which <u>two</u> things does she mention which are <u>not</u> in the photo?**

Escribir 5 **Write a description of <u>one</u> of the photos from exercise 2. Then read it out to your partner.**

> In these photos, focus on the setting rather than what people are doing. Use:
> ***hay*** (there is/are) to say what/who is in the photo
> ***es*** (he/she/it is) to describe someone or something
> ***está*** (he/she/it is) to talk about location.

1 En ruta

- Discussing travel plans
- Using comparatives
- Using se *puede(n)* + infinitive

Escuchar 1 **Match each question to the correct section of this holiday planning website. Then listen and write down the <u>five</u> correct letters (a–v) for each person. (1–4)**

1 ¿**Adónde** te gustaría ir de vacaciones?
2 ¿**Cuándo** te gustaría ir?
3 ¿**Qué tipo** de destino te gustaría visitar?
4 ¿**Con quién** te gustaría viajar?
5 ¿**Qué** te gustaría hacer?

G

Use these **impersonal verb phrases** to say 'you/one can ...':

Se puede *<u>visitar</u> la capital.* (singular noun)
Se pueden *<u>sacar</u> fotos.* (plural noun)

Page 42

Continente
- **a** África
- **b** Asia
- **c** Europa
- **d** América Latina

Zona
- **e** costa
- **f** campo
- **g** ciudad
- **h** montaña

Viajeros
- **i** solo/a
- **j** pareja
- **k** grupo de amigos
- **l** familia

Estación
- **m** primavera
- **n** verano
- **o** otoño
- **p** invierno

Actividades

q  hacer deportes de aventura

r  hacer turismo

s  ir de compras

t  disfrutar de la vida cultural

u  tomar el sol

v  probar platos típicos

Leer 2 **Read these holiday recommendations. Write the correct destination for each question.**

La Habana (Cuba)
La Habana Vieja es la parte antigua de la ciudad, donde se puede pasear por las calles y descubrir la arquitectura única con sus edificios de colores vivos. Además, se puede hacer un viaje en uno de los famosos coches clásicos.

Lanzarote (Islas Canarias)
En Lanzarote hay más de cien playas donde se pueden hacer castillos de arena, disfrutar del buen clima y descansar. Una atracción muy popular es el Parque Nacional de Timanfaya, donde se puede apreciar el paisaje volcánico, ¡y montar a camello!

Baños de Agua Santa (Ecuador)
Situado a los pies de un volcán, el pueblo de Baños es ideal para hacer deportes de aventura como el ciclismo de montaña y el rafting. También se pueden probar productos locales como la bebida de caña de azúcar. Para los niños hay un parque temático: El Bosque Encantado.

Where can you ...

1 ride a camel?
2 ride in a classic car?
3 go to a theme park?
4 take advantage of the good weather?
5 discover unique architecture?
6 try the local drink?

Hablar 3 **In pairs, take turns to ask and answer the <u>five</u> questions from exercise 1.**

- *¿Adónde te gustaría ir de vacaciones?*
- *Me gustaría ir a <u>América Latina</u>.*
- *¿...?*

Me gustaría Quisiera Se pued**e**	ir a ... disfrutar de la vida cultural. pasear por las calles. ver una obra de teatro.
Me gustaría Quisiera Se pued**en**	sacar fotos [del paisaje]. hacer castillos de arena. probar platos típicos.

Leer 4 **Read the opinions about how people prefer to travel. Fill in the gaps with the correct word from the blue word box below. Then translate the phrases in bold into English.**

¿Cómo te gustaría viajar?

Me gustaría viajar en **1** porque **es más seguro que** el barco y hay muchas tiendas en el aeropuerto donde se puede ir de compras antes del vuelo. ***Carlos***

Quisiera viajar por la ciudad a **2** porque me gusta hacer ejercicio, **es más saludable que** coger el metro y es gratis. También, para el medio ambiente **es mejor que** viajar en coche. Además, siempre hay mucho tráfico, ¡y muchas obras! ***Luis***

Me gustaría coger el **3** porque vivo cerca de la estación. **Es más cómodo que** el autobús para distancias largas, aunque **no es tan rápido como** el avión. También se pueden hacer otras cosas durante el viaje. Sin embargo, actualmente hay muchas huelgas y muchos retrasos. ***Bea***

No me gusta viajar en autobús porque la otra gente me molesta – prefiero viajar sola. Me gustaría ir en **4** porque siempre tengo una maleta enorme, y por eso **es más práctico que** el transporte público. ***Irene***

Me gustaría ir en **5**, ya que me encanta el mar y no aguanto los aviones. ¡Qué miedo! **Es menos caro que** el tren, aunque también **es más lento**. ***Jesús***

el retraso *delay*

avión tren
barco autobús
pie coche

ir/viajar ***en*** *[avión]*
coger ***el*** *[avión]*
Note: ir ***a*** pie

Leer 5 **Read the texts again.** Who ...

1 says there are lots of strikes?
2 mentions travelling by bus or underground?
3 can't stand aeroplanes?
4 lives near the train station?
5 likes to go shopping before a flight?
6 always has an enormous suitcase?

G

Use a 'comparative sandwich' with an adjective or adverb.

más ... ***que*** ... more ... than ...
menos ... ***que*** ... less ... than ...
tan ... ***como*** ... as ... as ...

El tren es ***más*** *rápido* ***que*** *el barco.*
The train is **faster than** the boat.

These comparatives are irregular:
mejor/peor que ... better/worse than ...
mayor/menor que ... bigger/smaller than ...

Page 43

Escuchar 6 **Listen. Copy and complete the table in English. (1–6)**

	Preference	Reason	Disadvantage
1	train	quicker than ...	much more ...

Escribir 7 **Write a paragraph about where you would like to go on holiday and how you would like to travel.**

Me gustaría ir a América Latina con mi familia en verano porque ...

Creo que me gustaría visitar La Habana porque hay ... donde se puede(n) ...

También se puede(n) ...

Me gustaría viajar en ... / coger el ... porque ...

Además, es más/menos ... que ...

No me gustaría viajar en ..., porque ...

Me gustaría Quisiera	ir/viajar en coger el	autobús/coche/avión/metro/barco/tren	
porque es	más	caro/barato/económico	que ...
	menos	rápido/lento/saludable	que ...
	tan	cómodo/práctico/seguro	como ...
	mejor/peor [para el medioambiente]		que ...
porque hay	mucho tráfico. mucha gente.	muchos retrasos/problemas. muchas obras/huelgas.	
porque	me gusta hacer ejercicio. se pueden hacer otras cosas. siempre tengo muchas maletas. no aguanto [los aviones]. la otra gente me molesta.		

2 ¡De fiesta en fiesta!

- Talking about festivals in the Spanish-speaking world
- Using the superlative
- Using *if* clauses with the present tense

Escuchar **1** **Listen and read. Translate the superlative phrases in purple into English.**

Una fiesta para todos

Son una parte esencial de las tradiciones y costumbres de un país. Muchas tienen una importancia histórica o religiosa. Te hacen sentir orgulloso de tu cultura, son populares entre los turistas, ¡y son muy divertidas! Aquí recomendamos cuatro de **las mejores fiestas** del mundo hispanohablante.

Si te gusta el ruido, ...

hay que ir a **las Fallas de Valencia** donde se puede disfrutar de la música, los desfiles y **los fuegos artificiales más ruidosos**. Sin embargo, **el momento más emocionante** es cuando queman las enormes figuras de cartón y madera.

del 15 al 19 de marzo

Si eres muy aventurero, ...

hay que ir a **la fiesta más popular** de España (¡y **la más peligrosa**!), **los Sanfermines**. Cada mañana, **las personas más locas** participan en el encierro donde corren delante de los toros. También hay corridas de toros.

del 7 al 14 de julio

Si te interesa la historia, ...

hay que viajar a Cuzco, en Perú, donde organizan un espectáculo especial para representar **la Fiesta del Sol**, el festival inca que coincide con **el día más corto** del año. Es quizás una de **las fiestas menos conocidas, pero más históricas**.

24 de junio

Si quieres divertirte al máximo, ...

hay que participar en **la Tomatina**, **la fiesta más divertida** del mundo. Los participantes tiran miles de tomates en una batalla animada. (¡Pero es **la peor opción** si no aguantas los tomates!)

último miércoles de agosto

orgulloso/a	*proud*
el encierro	*running of the bulls*

Leer **2** **Read the text again and write the phrases in Spanish. Then choose one of the festivals and translate the text into English.**

1 they burn
2 they run
3 they throw
4 they organise
5 they make you feel
6 they participate

Use complex structures such as ***si*** (if) clauses and ***hay que*** (you must) + infinitive.
***Si** te gusta el ruido, **hay que** ir a ...*
If you like noise, **you must** go to ...

Escuchar **3** **Look at the pronunciation box on page 35. Then listen and fill in the gaps with the correct word in Spanish.**

Cada año en abril o mayo, en **1** celebran la Feria de Abril, donde **2**, bailan y **3** instrumentos por las **4**. Mucha gente **5** ropa tradicional y ve desfiles como el 'Paseo de **6**.' Si te gusta el pescado, hay que **7** el plato más típico y **8** de la fiesta: el pescaíto frito.

G

Use the **superlative** to talk about the biggest, the most popular, the best etc.
el/la/los/las + noun + ***más/menos*** + adjective
Sometimes the noun is omitted:

***el** [plato] **más** rico*	the **tastiest** [dish]
***las** [fiestas] **menos** populares*	the **least** popular [festivals]

Note these irregular superlatives:

el/la/los/las	*mejor(es)*	*peor(es)*	*mayor(es)*	*menor(es)*
the	best	worst	biggest	smallest

Page 43

Hablar 4 **In pairs, take turns to give your opinion of different festivals.**

- *En tu opinión, ¿cuál es la fiesta más divertida/interesante/histórica/loca (etc.)?*
- *Para mí, la fiesta más ... es la Feria de Abril porque llevan/comen ... (etc.)*
- *¿Cuándo es la Feria de Abril?*
- *Es ... Y en tu opinión, ¿cuál es la fiesta más ...?*
- *Para mí, la fiesta más ... es...*
- *¿Por qué son importantes las fiestas?*
- *Creo que las fiestas son importantes porque... ¿Y tú ?*

Remember that ***ll*** has a similar sound to 'y' in English. Listen and repeat the words.
***ll**evan* *las Fa**ll**as* *orgu**ll**oso*

son	animadas/divertidas/ emocionantes/populares
tienen	una importancia económica/ histórica/religiosa
te hacen sentir orgulloso/a de	tu cultura las costumbres de tu país

Escribir 5 **Translate this text into Spanish.**

Superlatives – take care with word order.

el Carnaval

Hay que + infinitive

One of the liveliest festivals is Carnival, which they celebrate in February or March in lots of Spanish-speaking countries. If you visit Latin America, you must go to Oruro in Bolivia, where you can try the tastiest dishes. Also, you can see the best parades where lots of people wear a fancy-dress costume.

Look back at Unit 1.

un disfraz

Escuchar 6 **Listen to and read the dialogue. Look at the menu and then answer the questions in English.**

Mustafa e Isatere están en Sevilla y quieren tomar tapas.

- *Quisiera una mesa para dos personas, por favor.*
- *Sí, señora. ¿Prefiere dentro o fuera?*
- *Fuera, por favor, hace buen tiempo hoy.*
- *Muy bien. Aquí tiene la carta. ¿Qué van a tomar?*
- *Vamos a pedir tapas. Queremos pan con tomate, pescaíto frito y tortilla española, por favor.*
- *¿Y para beber?*
- *Una botella de agua para compartir.*

****

- *¡Camarero! La cuenta, por favor.*
- *Sí, señora. Aquí tiene.*

****

1. Where do they want to sit and why?
2. Which three tapas do they order?
3. Why do they only order one drink?
4. What is the very last thing she asks for?
5. Which four main courses are on the menu?

Hablar 7 **In pairs, make up your own dialogue by changing the underlined words/phrases from exercise 6. Choose from the menu or use any other food vocabulary you have learned.**

Quisiera	una mesa para ... personas. la carta. la cuenta.
Voy a / Vamos a	pedir ... / tomar ...

3 Mis últimas vacaciones

- Saying what you did on holiday
- Using *acabar de* + infinitive
- Using a range of structures to give opinions in the past

Escuchar 1 **Read the texts and then listen. For each person, correct the mistake and write down the two opinions you hear in English. (1–4)**

¿Qué tal tus últimas vacaciones?

1 Acabo de visitar Cartagena donde pasé una semana en casa de mis abuelos.
2 Acabo de volver de San Juan donde pasé quince días.
3 Acabo de regresar de Vigo donde pasé una semana con mi pareja.
4 Mi familia y yo acabamos de ir a Bilbao donde pasamos la Nochevieja.

quince días *a fortnight*

Use a variety of structures to give opinions about activities in the past:

(No) Me/Nos gustó Me/Nos encantó	*Fue ... genial. increíble.*
Lo pasé ... bien/mal/fatal.	*¡Qué ... desastre! suerte!*

G

To say that you have just done something, use the present tense of ***acabar de*** + infinitive.

***Acabo de** volver de España.*
I have just returned from Spain.

***Acabamos de** visitar Sevilla.*
We have just visited Seville.

Page 44

Hablar 2 **In pairs, take turns to read out the text. Pay attention to *j*, *ge*, *gi* and *h*.**

Acabo de visitar **Gij**ón donde pasé una semana con mi **h**ermano. Via**j**amos en tren y fue **ge**nial. El primer día tomé el sol porque **h**izo buen tiempo.
Sin embargo, al día siguiente **h**izo viento, y por lo tanto decidimos **h**acer windsurf. ¡Qué risa!
Lo me**j**or fue cuando visitamos el parque temático, pero lo peor fue cuando de**j**é mi relo**j** en el **h**otel.

Remember that ***j***, ***ge*** and ***gi*** are pronounced like a stronger version of 'h' in English. However, the Spanish ***h*** is silent.

Escuchar 3 **Listen to check your pronunciation. Then translate the underlined phrases in exercise 2 into English.**

Escuchar 4 **Listen. Copy and complete the table in English. (1–4)**

	Transport	Weather	Best thing	Worst thing
1				

G

*¿Qué fue **lo mejor/peor** de tu visita?*
Lo + **adjective** means 'the ... thing'.
Lo bueno/malo The good/bad thing
Lo mejor/peor The best/worst thing

Page 44

El primer día ... Al día siguiente ... El último día ... Lo peor fue cuando ...
comí algo malo y vomité. me puse enferm**o**/**a**.

dejé perdí rompí	mi bolsa mi reloj	mi cámara mi pasaporte	mi maleta mi tarjeta de crédito	mis llaves
en	el aeropuerto.	la playa.	el autobús.	la estación.
¿Qué tiempo hizo?	Hizo	buen tiempo / mal tiempo. calor/frío/sol/viento.		
	Llovió.			

Hablar 5 **In pairs, describe a recent trip. Use the underlined phrases from exercise 2 and the vocabulary from exercise 4 to help you.**

- *¿Qué tal tus últimas vacaciones?*
- *Acabo de visitar ... donde pasé ... con ... Viajé en ... Fue ...*
- *¿Qué hiciste?*
- *El primer día ... porque ... Al día siguiente ...*
- *¿Qué fue lo mejor de tus vacaciones?*
- *Lo mejor fue cuando ..., pero lo peor ...*

Leer 6 **Read the text and select the correct photo for each gap. Then copy and complete the sentences below in English.**

Un día de excursión por Málaga

Iñaki Sánchez

Mi novio y yo acabamos de pasar tres días en Málaga, la ciudad más hermosa de la región. El primer día decidimos comprar billetes para el autobús turístico porque se puede subir y bajar durante todo el día.

Por la mañana, dimos un paseo por el centro histórico. Empezamos en **a**, dos de los lugares más antiguos donde se pueden apreciar las vistas increíbles de la ciudad.

Por la tarde, mi novio visitó **b** porque es un aficionado al fútbol, pero yo fui al **c**, ya que prefiero la naturaleza. Me encantó. Después, fuimos al **d** donde compramos pan, jamón y queso para hacer bocadillos frescos. ¡Qué ricos!

Al día siguiente hizo mucho calor, y por eso fuimos a **e** donde jugamos al voleibol en la arena y nadé en el mar. Más tarde, compré recuerdos en un centro comercial, pero lo peor fue cuando perdí mis bolsas ¡y todas mis compras!

Finalmente, lo mejor fue cuando asistimos a un espectáculo de flamenco por la noche. Fue una experiencia estupenda.

dar un paseo	*to go for a walk*
asistir a	*to attend*

1. According to Iñaki, Málaga is the ...
2. They decided to buy bus tour tickets because you can ...
3. From the castle you can appreciate ...
4. They bought bread, ...
5. They played volleyball on ...
6. The worst thing was when he ...
7. The best thing was when they ...

Escribir 7 **Write a text about a recent trip (real or imaginary). Include the following information:**

- where you have just been, with whom and for how long
- how you travelled
- your opinion of the trip
- what the weather was like
- what you did
- the best/worst thing about your trip.

Use **time phrases** and **sequencers** to help structure your text.

por la mañana	*primero*
por la tarde	*luego*
por la noche	*más tarde*
	finalmente

4 ¿Dónde te quedaste?

- Describing where you stayed
- Using the imperfect tense
- Giving and spotting positive/negative opinions

Leer 1 **Read these accommodation reviews. Identify the <u>two</u> correct pictures for each person. What do the phrases in purple mean?**

la ubicación	*location*	***quedarse***	*to stay*
alquilar	*to rent/hire*	***decepcionante***	*disappointing*

Ubicación ★★★★★ **Instalaciones** ★★★★

En mayo, me quedé en un camping con mi novia. **Estaba** cerca de la playa y **tenía** vistas preciosas al mar. También **había** acceso gratis a la piscina al aire libre. Sin embargo, **no era** posible cargar el coche eléctrico allí. ***Ricardo Salas***

Ubicación ★★ **Instalaciones** ★★★★★

En marzo, mi familia y yo alquilamos un apartamento de lujo en el centro de la ciudad. La cocina **era** muy moderna y las camas **eran** cómodas. **Estaba** cerca de los restaurantes, los cines, etc., pero por la noche **había** mucha gente en la calle, ¡y mucho ruido! ***Marcos Navarro***

Ubicación ★★★★ **Instalaciones** ★★

En agosto, nos quedamos en un hotel de tres estrellas en un barrio en las afueras. Por un lado, **era** bastante económico y todo **estaba** muy limpio. Por otro lado, el desayuno **no estaba** incluido y las habitaciones **no tenían ni** teléfono **ni** televisión. **Tampoco había** gimnasio en el hotel. ¡Qué decepcionante! ***Águeda Rubio***

a

b

c

d

e

f

Leer 2 **Read the text and fill in the gaps with the correct word from the box.**

Acabamos de pasar **1** días en Murcia donde nos **2** en un pueblo en el campo. **3** una casa cerca del **4**, pero no me gustó. El dueño no era nada agradable y el pueblo era demasiado **5** porque estaba lejos de todo. El salón y los dormitorios eran muy **6**, y no había jardín ni ducha. Mi madre tuvo que **7** porque el baño estaba muy sucio, la calefacción no funcionaba y la ventana estaba rota. ¡ **8** desastre!

pe**que**ños	bos**que**	**que**jarse
quince	Al**qui**lamos	
tran**qui**lo	**Qué**	**que**damos

Hablar 3 **Look at the pronunciation box on page 39. Then read out the completed text.**

Escuchar 4 **Listen to the text from exercise 2 to check your pronunciation. Then translate the text into English.**

G

The **imperfect tense** is used for describing things in the past.
Estaba *en el campo y* ***tenía*** *un restaurante.*
It was in the country(side) and **it had** a restaurant.

	est**ar** (*to be*)	ten**er** (*to have*)
(yo)	est**aba**	ten**ía**
(tú)	est**abas**	ten**ías**
(él/ella/usted)	est**aba**	ten**ía**
(nosotros/as)	est**ábamos**	ten**íamos**
(vosotros/as)	est**abais**	ten**íais**
(ellos/ellas/ustedes)	est**aban**	ten**ían**

-er / ***-ir*** **verbs** have the same endings.
Verbs which are irregular in the imperfect include
ser (to be) → ***era*** (it was)
The imperfect tense of ***hay*** (there is/are) is ***había*** (there was/were).

Page 44

Use ***era*** (*ser*) for describing something in the past.
El baño ***era*** *pequeño.* The bathroom **was** small.

Use ***estaba*** (*estar*) for talking about a location or a temporary state in the past.
Estaba *cerca de la playa.* **It was** near the beach.
La ducha ***estaba*** *rota.* The shower **was** broken.

Note:
No *tenía* ***ni*** ~~*un*~~ *bar* ***ni*** ~~*una*~~ *piscina.* It didn't have a bar or a pool.
Tampoco *tenía* ~~*un*~~ *ascensor.* Nor did it have a lift.

Escuchar 5 **Listen and write positive (P), negative (N) or positive and negative (P+N) for each person. Then listen again and note down <u>three</u> other details in English. (1–5)**

¿Dónde te quedaste?

Remember that ***qu*** is pronounced like 'k' in English. The ***u*** is always silent.
When pronouncing ***que*** ('keh') and ***qui*** ('key'), take care to avoid saying 'kw' (as in 'question' or 'quick').

Escribir 6 **Use your imagination to write a review for a holiday website.**

En <u>mayo</u> me quedé en <u>una casa</u> en ...
Estaba ... Tenía ... y ...
Por un lado, era ... y ...
Por otro lado, no tenía ni ... ni ...
(No) Me gustó porque ...

Add variety by giving both positive and negative opinions.
Lo bueno/malo era que (era/tenía) ...
The good/bad thing was that (it was/it had) ...

Use phrases such as *sin embargo* (however), *en cambio* (on the other hand) and *por un lado, ... por otro lado, ...* (on one hand, ... on the other hand, ...).

When listening/reading, pay attention to adjectives.
Don't jump to conclusions – do these suggest positive or negative opinions?
No *era nada caro.* ***Tampoco*** *era bonito.* *Era* ***demasiado*** *tranquilo.*

El hotel ...	El camping ...	El apartamento ...	La casa ...		
era	bastante muy demasiado	moderno/a. pequeño/a. barato/a. cómodo/a. decepcionante.	antiguo/a. grande. caro/a. viejo/a. agradable.	Tenía No tenía (ni ... ni ...)	(un) baño. (un) gimnasio. (un) jardín. (un) restaurante. (una) cocina. (una) piscina. mucho espacio. mucho ruido. mucha gente. vistas al mar.
estaba	en el centro	en las afueras	cerca/lejos de	También había Tampoco había	
	limpio/a.	sucio/a.			
La ducha	La ventana	La cama	estaba roto/a.		
El gimnasio	La recepción		estaba cerrado/a.		
El ascensor	La calefacción	La luz	no funcionaba.		

Leer 7 **Read the text and choose the correct option for each question.**

Alojamientos con carácter

Aquí descubrimos dos de los lugares más únicos para quedarse en Sudamérica.

Palacio de Sal (Bolivia). No es un palacio verdadero, ¡pero sí que está construido de sal! Las habitaciones, las paredes, las camas, las sillas… casi todo está hecho de sal. Fue el primer hotel de sal del mundo y tiene vistas preciosas del salar de Uyuni. Además, su restaurante tiene un menú regional con una gran variedad de platos.

El Palacio de Sal es un hotel de lujo y quedarse allí está lejos de ser la opción más barata. Sin embargo, es la opción más única.

Isla Flotante de los Uros (Perú). Si quieres disfrutar de las hermosas vistas del Lago Titicaca y te interesa el turismo verde, una opción ideal es quedarse en casa de una familia local en una isla flotante. Es mucho más divertido que un hotel porque hay que viajar en barco para llegar a la isla.

Mucha gente elige la opción con el desayuno incluido. Se puede pagar un costo adicional para cenar allí, también.

el salar	*salt flat*
elegir	*to choose*

1 The *Palacio de Sal* is...
  a a real palace.
  b the only 'salt hotel' in the world.
  c built almost entirely from salt.

2 The *Palacio de Sal* is...
  a a cheap option.
  b far from Uyuni.
  c a unique place to stay.

3 On Lake Titicaca, it is more fun to stay...
  a in a hotel.
  b with a local family.
  c on a boat.

4 You have to pay extra for...
  a travelling to the island.
  b breakfast.
  c dinner.

5 Mi aventura por América Latina

- Talking about holidays using different tenses
- Using *suelo* + infinitive
- Using strategies to work out meaning

Leer 1 **Read the text and complete the statements.**

Soy Víctor y vivo en Tenerife. Normalmente paso las vacaciones en casa donde suelo ver películas en mi tableta. No suelo ir de vacaciones al extranjero, pero mi hermano y yo solemos ir a la playa. Sin embargo, acabo de ganar un concurso y el premio es increíble, ¡una excursión en grupo por México! Voy a escribir un blog para describir mis aventuras.

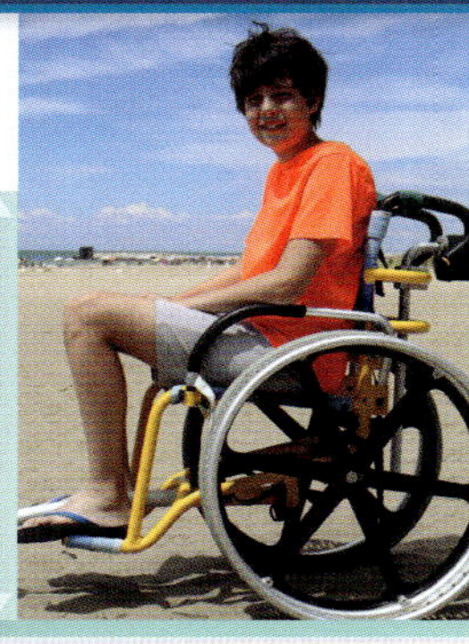

1 Víctor usually spends the holidays ... where he ...
2 He doesn't tend to ...
3 He has just ...
4 He is going to ...

G

To say what you tend to do or usually do, you can use ***soler*** + infinitive.

Suelo *ir de vacaciones.*
I tend to / I usually go on holiday.

Soler is a stem-changing verb.

Page 45

Escuchar 2 **Listen to and read the blog. Then put the photos in the order in which they are mentioned.**

Mi aventura por México

Día 4

Llegué a la capital hace tres días. El primer día estaba cansado después del vuelo, pero al día siguiente decidí visitar Xochimilco donde hice una excursión en barco y escuché la música tradicional de los mariachis. Mañana voy a visitar el Museo Frida Kahlo, 'la Casa Azul', donde nació.

Día 8

Me encantó Oaxaca. La ciudad estaba llena de colores y olores, y el centro era fácil de visitar en silla de ruedas. Primero, fuimos a un cementerio decorado con flores para el Día de los Muertos, que celebran en México el 1 y 2 de noviembre. Pero lo mejor fue cuando vimos los desfiles por la calle. Conocí a mucha gente agradable y aprendí mucho sobre esta tradición.

Día 11

Ayer probé *papadzules*, un plato tradicional con tortillas de maíz, huevo duro y una salsa especial. ¡Qué rico! Hoy vamos a ir a las ruinas de Chichén Itzá, el sitio arqueológico maya más famoso.

Día 14

Chichén Itzá fue increíble. Tenía buen acceso para personas con discapacidad y saqué muchas fotos del Templo de Kukulcán, una pirámide enorme. Ayer nadé en un cenote en forma de corazón, solo me costó cien pesos. Desafortunadamente, mañana va a ser el último día de mi visita a México. ¡No quiero despedirme!

el cenote *a water-filled sinkhole*
pesos *pesos (Mexican currency)*

Leer 3 **Read the blog again and write the Spanish for the following phrases.**

Present	**Imperfect**
1 which they celebrate	5 I was tired
2 I don't want to say goodbye!	6 it was full of colours and smells
Preterite	**Near future**
3 where she was born	7 I am going to visit
4 I met lots of nice people	8 it is going to be

Use **the four Cs** to help you work out the meaning of words which you can't remember or don't know.

Clues	(e.g. the glossary box, photos)
Cognates	(e.g. *las ruinas, arqueológico*)
Context	(e.g. 'It had good access for people with ______')
Common sense	(e.g. How might he feel after the flight?)

Escuchar **4** **Listen and for each person write down:**

- **what they are talking about (a–f)**
- **which tense they use (present / preterite / imperfect / near future). (1–6)**

a cost
b food
c festivals
d travel
e accommodation
f shopping

G

Use the **present tense** to say what you normally do.

Veo *películas.*	**I watch** films.
Suelo *ir a la playa.*	**I tend to** go to the beach.

Use the **preterite tense** to say what you did, to talk about the weather and to give opinions in the past.

Probé *un plato típico.*	**I tried** a typical dish.
Me gustó *porque* ***hizo*** *sol.*	**I liked it** because **it was** sunny.

Use the **imperfect tense** to describe something in the past.

Tenía *una piscina.*	**It had** a swimming pool.

Use the **near future tense** to say what you are going to do.

Voy a sacar *fotos.*	**I'm going to take** photos.

Page 45

Leer **5** **Read the text and write the correct form of each verb in brackets. Remember that you may need the preterite or imperfect tense when talking about the past. Then listen to check your answers.**

En verano yo **1 (soler)** ir al parque donde **2 (montar)** en bici o **3 (jugar)** al fútbol. También, mis amigas y yo **4 (ir)** a la piscina a veces.

Sin embargo, el verano pasado yo **5 (ir)** de vacaciones a Buenos Aires, la capital de Argentina. El primer día **6 (pasear)** por la Plaza de Mayo donde **7 (sacar)** fotos de la Casa Rosada. Luego, por la noche, **8 (disfrutar)** de un espectáculo de tango (un tipo de baile y música) en el Café Tortoni, el café más antiguo de la ciudad. Me encantó, pero después **9 (estar)** muy cansada.

Por un lado, lo mejor fue cuando **10 (visitar)** la Bombonera, el estadio de Boca Juniors. ¡Qué guay! Por otro lado, desafortunadamente, no **11 (ver)** un partido porque **12 (ser)** demasiado caro.

El año próximo, **13 (pasar)** dos semanas en un camping con mi familia. Mi hermana y yo **14 (alquilar)** bicicletas y creo que **15 (ser)** muy relajante.

Hablar **6** **In pairs, take turns to ask and answer questions about your holidays.**

- *¿Qué sueles hacer en verano?*
- *¿Adónde fuiste de vacaciones el año pasado?*
- *¿Qué hiciste el primer día/el último día?*
- *¿Qué fue lo mejor/lo peor de tus vacaciones?*
- *¿Cómo era el pueblo/la ciudad?*
- *¿Adónde vas a ir de vacaciones el año próximo?*
- *¿Qué vas a hacer allí?*

En las vacaciones En verano	suelo	jugar … hacer … ir …		
	normalmente	juego … hago … voy …		
Hace [dos] años El verano pasado	fui	de vacaciones a … a un parque temático. al mercado / a la playa.		
El primer día Al día siguiente El último día Por la mañana Por la tarde Por la noche Lo mejor/lo peor fue cuando	hice	una excursión [en barco]. turismo.		
	vi	un partido. los edificios. una exposición [de arte].		
	aprendí [mucho sobre] … conocí a [mucha gente] … decidí [ir a] … probé [un plato típico] …	compré … llegué … nadé en … visité …		
Costó/Costaron … euros/pesos.				
El año próximo El año que viene	voy a vamos a	ir … pasar …	hacer … alquilar …	ver … viajar …

Escribir **7** **Write a text about your holidays (real or imaginary). Use the present, preterite, imperfect and near future tenses.**

Gramática 1

Me gusta(n) / Me gustaría (Zona de cultura, page 31)

Escuchar 1 **Listen and write down the phrase which should replace each beep in the sentence (*me gusta*, *me gustan* or *me gustaría*). Listen out for clues such as singular/plural nouns, infinitive verbs and time phrases. (1–8)**

Example: 1 ***Me gusta*** *(mucho el paisaje hermoso de la región).*

Escribir 2 **Translate these sentences into Spanish.**

Example: 1 *Me gustaría ir a un parque acuático porque …*

1 I would like to go to a water park because I like swimming.
2 I really like animals and therefore I would like to go horse riding.
3 When it is sunny, I like doing water sports.
4 I don't like going to the beach because I don't like the sand.
5 I love birds and trees and therefore I would like to walk through the forest.
6 I would like to visit Seville because I love to go sightseeing.

To say what you like, use:
Me gusta + ***el***/***la*** + singular noun
Me gustan + ***los***/***las*** + plural noun
Me gusta el *campo, pero* ***no me gustan los*** *animales.*
I like the countryside, but **I don't like** animals.

You must use the definite article (***el***/***la***/***los***/***las***) when giving an opinion about a noun.

To say what you like to do/doing, use:
Me gusta + infinitive
Me gusta *mucho tomar el sol.*
I really **like** to sunbathe/sunbathing.

To say what you would like to do, use the conditional tense of the verb ***gustar***.
Me gustaría + infinitive
En el futuro ***me gustaría*** *visitar Andalucía.*
In the future **I would like** to visit Andalusia.

Verbs such as ***encantar*** and ***interesar*** work in a similar way.
Me encantaría *visitar Alicante.*
I would love to visit Alicante.

Se puede(n) + infinitive (Unit 1, page 32)

Escribir 3 **Look at this webpage and write eight sentences about what you can do in Córdoba. Try to use a different infinitive verb in each sentence (e.g. *ver*, *probar*, *apreciar* …).**

Example: 1 ***Se pueden*** *descubrir los jardines del Alcázar.*

¿Cómo se puede disfrutar al máximo de una visita a Córdoba?

el Puente Romano y la Torre de la Calahorra

los patios típicos llenos de flores

la Mezquita-Catedral

- la Mezquita-Catedral
- los platos tradicionales
- el barrio judío
- los patios típicos
- el Puente Romano y la Torre de la Calahorra
- los jardines del Alcázar
- el Palacio de Viana
- los Baños Árabes

Use these **impersonal verb phrases** to say 'you/one can …':
Se puede + infinitive + singular noun
Se pueden + infinitive + plural noun
Se puede *visitar el museo, pero no* ***se pueden*** *sacar fotos.*
You can visit the museum but **you can't** take photos.

Where the verb is not directly followed by a noun, use ***se puede*** + infinitive.
Se puede *pasear por las calles.*

Where there are two or more nouns, use ***se pueden*** + infinitive.
Se pueden *apreciar el parque y el río.*

Comparatives (Unit 1, page 33)

Leer 4 **Translate these puzzles into English to work out each person's preference.**

1 Marc prefers to travel by ... **2** Eva would prefer to visit ...

El tren es **más** rápido **que** el barco.
Sin embargo, el tren es **tan** caro **como** el autobús y **menos** cómodo **que** el avión.
El coche es **menos** seguro **que** el avión y también es más lento.
Además, los retrasos en el aeropuerto son **menos** frecuentes **que** en la estación de tren.
Marc

Me gustaría ir a la costa, pero es **más** caro **que** ir al campo.
También, las vistas en el campo son **más** bonitas **que** en la costa.
En la capital las tiendas son **mejores que** en el campo, pero la capital es menos tranquila.
Para mí, el precio y el paisaje son **más** importantes **que** las compras.
Eva

Escribir 5 **Use exercise 4 to write <u>three</u> comparison sentences of your own. Extra challenge: try to write your own puzzle using comparatives.**

Use a 'comparative sandwich' with an adjective or adverb.

***más** ... **que** ...*	more ... than ...
***menos** ... **que** ...*	less ... than ...
***tan** ... **como** ...*	as ... as ...

*La costa es **más** bonita **que** la ciudad.*
The coast is **prettier than** the city.

These comparatives are irregular:

***mejor que** ...*	better than ...
***peor que** ...*	worse than ...
***mayor que** ...*	bigger than ...
***menor que** ...*	smaller than ...

*Granada es **mejor que** Madrid para hacer turismo.*
Granada is **better than** Madrid for sightseeing.

The adjective must agree with the first noun mentioned. However, when used to compare two <u>infinitives</u>, it doesn't agree.

*<u>Visitar</u> la capital es **tan** caro **como** <u>ir</u> al extranjero.*
Visiting the capital is **as** expensive **as** going abroad.

Superlatives (Unit 2, page 34)

Escribir 6 **Read the grammar box on page 34 and then write the jumbled words below in the correct order to form superlative sentences. Translate each one into English.**

Example: 1 *El plato más rico es la paella. / La paella es el plato más rico.*
The tastiest dish is paella. / Paella is the tastiest dish.

1 la | más | plato | rico | paella | es | el
2 la | es | batalla | peligrosa | la | más | Tomatina
3 ciudad | hermosa | es | la | Córdoba | más
4 costumbres | las | fiestas | más | las | interesantes | son
5 la | importante | la | aspecto | más | ropa | es | de | el | fiesta

Hablar 7 **In pairs, discuss these results of a survey in Spanish. Remember to make adjectives agree.**

- *¿Cuál es <u>la ciudad</u> / <u>el plato</u> / <u>la fiesta</u> / <u>el aspecto</u> más ...?*
- *<u>El plato</u> más <u>rico</u> es ...*
- *<u>La ciudad</u> más <u>histórica</u> es ...*

- *¿Cuál es <u>la mejor ciudad</u> / <u>el peor aspecto</u>?*
- *<u>La mejor ciudad</u> es ...*

City	Festival
• Most historic – Cádiz • Most beautiful – Granada • Most interesting – Valencia • Best – Sevilla	• Most fun – La Feria de Abril • Oldest – Las Fallas • Most well known – La Tomatina • Best – El Día de los Muertos
Dish	**Aspect (of the festival)**
• Tastiest – pan con tomate • Most typical – pescaíto frito • Most famous – paella • Best – tortilla	• Most important – the music • Most popular – the food • Best – the parade • Worst – the noise

Gramática 2

Acabar de + infinitive (Unit 3, page 36)

Escuchar 1

Read the grammar box on page 36 and listen to people talking about what they have just done. Write down the letter of the picture (a–f) and the form of *acabar* which is mentioned. Then identify the correct person of the verb in English. (1–6)

Example: 1 *d – acabáis – you (plural)*

a 

b 

c 

d 

e 

f 

Lo + adjective (Unit 3, page 36)

Hablar 2

Read the grammar box on page 36. In pairs, take turns to build sentences. Your partner then translates your sentence into English.

Lo	bueno malo mejor peor increíble divertido	es que	se puede descansar hay fuegos artificiales hay mucha gente la comida es muy rica	en el aeropuerto. en el autobús. en el estadio. en el mar. en el mercado. en la calle. en la fiesta. en la playa.
		fue cuando	dejé mi pasaporte perdí mis llaves compramos recuerdos vimos un espectáculo	

The imperfect tense (Unit 4, page 38)

Escribir 3

Rewrite these sentences using the imperfect tense.

Example: 1 *La ciudad era moderna y …*

1 La ciudad es moderna y tiene muchos restaurantes.
2 El camping está cerca de la playa y es muy económico.
3 Las habitaciones son modernas, pero no tienen mucho espacio.
4 Las camas están rotas y la luz no funciona.
5 No hay ducha, pero el dueño es agradable.
6 No podemos ir al museo porque no tenemos tiempo.

Leer 4

Translate this text into English.

El hotel era caro, pero no tenía ni piscina ni gimnasio. Los jardines eran decepcionantes y había mucho ruido por la noche. Tenía vistas preciosas, pero las ventanas estaban sucias. Un día hacía mucho frío, pero la calefacción no funcionaba. Queríamos cambiar de habitación, pero no había habitaciones libres.

cambiar *to change*

The **imperfect tense** is used for describing things in the past and for what you used to do.
Estaba *en el campo y* ***había*** *un restaurante.*
It was in the country and **there was** a restaurant.

	est**ar** (*to be*)	ten**er** (*to have*)
(yo)	est**aba**	ten**ía**
(tú)	est**abas**	ten**ías**
(él/ella/usted)	est**aba**	ten**ía**
(nosotros/as)	est**ábamos**	ten**íamos**
(vosotros/as)	est**abais**	ten**íais**
(ellos/ellas/ustedes)	est**aban**	ten**ían**

-er / ***-ir*** **verbs** have the same endings.

Irregular verbs:
ser (to be) → ***era***, ***eras***, etc.
ir (to go) → ***iba***, ***ibas***, etc.
ver (to see/watch) → ***veía***, ***veías***, etc.

Soler + infinitive (Unit 5, page 40)

Escribir **5** **Rewrite these sentences. Replace the underlined verbs with the correct form of *soler* (in the present tense) followed by the infinitive. Then translate the sentences into English.**

Example: 1 *Mi padre* ***suele*** *montar en bici los fines de semana.*
My dad ***tends to*** *ride /* ***usually*** *rides his bike at weekends.*

1 Mi padre monta en bici los fines de semana.
2 Cuando hace buen tiempo, salgo con mis amigos.
3 David, ¿adónde vas de vacaciones en verano?
4 Mi mejor amiga y yo compramos ropa en el mercado.
5 Mi abuelo ve los desfiles, pero mi abuela juega al golf.
6 No aprenden nada porque es muy aburrido.

To say what you tend to do or usually do, you can use ***soler*** + infinitive.
Suelo *ir de compras.*
I tend to / I usually go shopping.
Soler is a stem-changing verb.

(yo)	s**ue**lo
(tú)	s**ue**les
(él/ella/usted)	s**ue**le
(nosotros/as)	solemos
(vosotros/as)	soléis
(ellos/ellas/ustedes)	s**ue**len

Using different tenses (Unit 5, page 40)

Leer **6** **Select the correct verb to complete each question. Then translate each question into English. Refer to the grammar box below to help you.**

1 ¿Adónde **ibas** / **fuiste** / **vas a ir** de vacaciones hace dos años?
2 ¿Qué **vas a hacer** / **hiciste** / **haces** en verano cuando no llueve?
3 ¿Con quién **íbamos** / **fuimos** / **vamos a ir** a la fiesta la semana próxima?
4 ¿Cómo **es** / **era** / **va a ser** tu ciudad en el pasado?
5 ¿A qué hora **llegó** / **llegaba** / **llega** el tren ayer?
6 ¿Por qué no **van a visitar** / **visitaban** / **visitaron** el parque temático mañana?
7 ¿Cuándo **fuiste** / **ibas** / **vas** de compras normalmente?
8 ¿Cuántos dormitorios **tenía** / **tuvo** / **va a tener** la casa que alquilaste?
9 ¿Qué platos **vas a decidir** / **decidiste** / **decides** probar en tus últimas vacaciones?
10 ¿**Vas a estar** / **Estás** / **Estabas** cansado cuando llegaste a Argentina?

¡En marcha! (Units 1–5)

Escuchar **7** **Listen and fill in the gaps with the correct word(s) in Spanish.**

a mucho las fiestas, y por eso **b** ir de vacaciones a España. Mi familia y yo **c** visitar Valencia, una ciudad preciosa donde **d** ver **e** fuegos artificiales. Fueron maravillosos. En cambio, **f** fue cuando perdí mi cámara. **g** mucha gente en el centro de la ciudad y las calles **h** llenas de turistas.
En el futuro, **i** asistir a la fiesta de los Sanfermines. En mi opinión, es **j** las Fallas, ¡aunque también es la fiesta **k**! Creo que **l** guay.

Tense	Used to talk about ...	Examples
Present	what you normally **do** what something **is like**	**Veo** películas. **Suelo** ir al cine. **Hace** sol. **Hay** vistas bonitas.
Preterite	what you **did** **opinions** in the past the **weather** in the past	**Probé** platos típicos. **Me gustó** porque **fue** genial. **Hizo** frío y **llovió**.
Imperfect	**descriptions** in the past what you **used to** do	**Era** moderno. **Tenía** una piscina.
Near future	what you **are going to do**	**Voy a sacar** fotos.

Hablar **8** **Look back at exercise 7. In pairs, take turns to read the whole text, paying attention to pronunciation. Then find five examples of the different grammar points covered on pages 42–45. Copy and translate, into English, the phrase where each one is used.**

Example: ***Me gustan*** *mucho las fiestas. –* ***I*** *really* ***like*** *festivals.*

Leer y escuchar

Reading

Leer 1

Festivals. **Read this travel-guide article about the Tomatina festival.**

Miles de personas llegan al pueblo de todas partes del mundo para vivir la Tomatina, la fiesta más divertida de España donde tiran tomates. Para participar, hay diferentes tipos de entradas, por ejemplo, con transporte incluido o con paella y bebida incluidas. Mucha gente también compra una camiseta como recuerdo.

El día de la fiesta, los trenes siempre están llenos de gente y puede ser muy caro dejar el coche en el centro. Por eso, la mejor opción es tomar el autobús.

Suele hacer calor y es una buena idea llevar ropa vieja. Hay que llevar gafas de natación para proteger los ojos. Además, es más seguro guardar tu móvil, tu cámara y otros objetos personales en una ***taquilla***.

las gafas	*glasses, goggles*
los ojos	*eyes*
guardar	*keep, store*

1 Complete the sentences below. Write the correct letter, **A**, **B** or **C**, for each question.

(i) People arrive from all over ...
A the town.
B Spain.
C the world.

(ii) As well as their ticket, lots of people also buy ...
A something to eat.
B something to drink.
C something to wear.

(iii) It can cost a lot of money if you travel to the festival ...
A by train.
B by car.
C by bus.

(iv) It's advisable to wear ...
A warm clothing.
B old clothing.
C summer clothing.

2 Which of these is the best translation of the word ***taquilla***? Write the correct letter, **A**, **B** or **C**.
A locker **B** car park **C** information desk

Leer 2

Holidays. **Read a blog post on how holidays have changed. What does the blog say about these changes? For each question:**

Write **P** for something that happened **in the past**.

Write **N** for something that is happening **now**.

Write **F** for something that is going to happen **in the future**.

A mucha gente le gusta descansar durante las vacaciones. Sin embargo, hoy en día es más caro que antes viajar al extranjero y por eso más personas pasan las vacaciones en el país donde viven.

Los precios de los vuelos suelen ser más caros que en el pasado. Hace unos años era más fácil comprar un vuelo barato para ver a familiares que viven en el extranjero.

Hace diez años era más popular ir en coche a la costa. Creo que más gente va a coger el tren porque es mejor para el medioambiente.

familiares	*family members*

1 more expensive holiday prices
2 holidays at home
3 cheaper cost of visiting family abroad
4 use of the train

Look out for different words that mean the same thing in the text to help locate the answer.

Leer 3

***Festivals.* Translate the following sentences into English.**

1 Queremos ir a una fiesta en España el próximo año.
2 Me gusta la comida típica y por eso probé las tapas.
3 La ciudad era hermosa con muchas calles históricas.
4 Acabo de ver el espectáculo de fuegos artificiales.

When translating, pay attention to differences in word order. Remember that adjectives usually follow the noun in Spanish but come before it in English.

Listening

Escuchar 1

***Tourism.* You and your classmates have just arrived at a hotel in Spain and are talking about what you can do. What does the tour guide say you can do? Write down A if only statement A is correct; B if only statement B is correct, or A+B if both statements are correct. (1–4)**

1 Today is a good day for ...
  A sunbathing on the beach.
  B visiting museums.

2 This weekend ...
  A you cannot go shopping.
  B you can try local food.

3 As well as appreciating the architecture, you should ...
  A go to the parades.
  B watch the fireworks.

4 At the moment, you cannot get to the city centre ...
  A by underground.
  B by bus.

Escuchar 2

***Hotels.* Marcos is talking about accommodation. Write down the answer to the questions (1–4) in English.**

1 In what type of hotel did Marcos stay?
2 What does Marcos say about the hotel's location?
3 What problem did Marcos have?
4 What was Marcos's favourite thing about the hotel?

For 'type', listen out for an adjective describing the hotel.

Listen to the full extract – you are listening for details about Marcos's hotel and not other hotels.

Several positive things will be mentioned – listen out for the 'best' thing.

Ensure you state the problem and not the action Marcos took to sort out the problem.

Escuchar 3

You will hear five short sentences. Listen carefully and, using your knowledge of Spanish sounds, write down, in Spanish, exactly what you hear for each sentence.

You will hear each sentence three times: the first time as a full sentence, the second time in short sections and the third time as a full sentence again. Check your sentences for spelling.

Escuchar 4

You listen to a hotel review on a Spanish podcast. Answer the questions in English.

1 What type of accommodation did the reviewer stay in?
2 Where was the hotel located?
3 What was the problem with the room?
4 What are the reviewer's plans for next summer?

Prueba oral

Role play

Hablar 1 **Look at the role play card and prepare what you are going to say.**

You are talking to your Argentinian friend.
Your teacher will play the part of your friend and will speak first.
You should address your friend as *tú*.
When you see this – **?** – you will have to ask a question.
You must include at least one verb in your response to each point.

Task:

1. Say what transport you prefer and why. (Give one opinion and one reason.)
2. Say what you did during the holidays last year.
3. Say what is good about holidays. (Give two details.)
4. **?** Ask your friend a question about festivals.
5. Say what type of accommodation you prefer, and why.

Don't forget to say why.

Think about which tense you need to use.

Ensure you give two positives.

A good way to ask a question is to ask someone if they like something.

Introduce your answer with 'I prefer'.

Hablar 2 **Practise your role play answers. Listen and respond to the questions.**

Escuchar 3 **Now listen to Clara doing the role play task. In English, note down what she says for each of the points on the card, including the question the friend asks.**

Reading aloud

Hablar 1 **When your teacher/partner asks you, read aloud the following text in Spanish, paying particular attention to the underlined letters.**

En todas las regiones de España hay muchas fiestas maravillosas.

En junio, voy a viajar a Alicante.

Allí celebran la fiesta de las Hogueras de San Juan.

La ciudad va a estar llena de gente que llega de todo el país.

Quiero descubrir esta costumbre con orígenes religiosos.

También hay figuras enormes que queman en las calles.

Take extra care with how you pronounce:
- *ll*
- *qui, que*
- *j, ge, gi*
- *h* (remember that *h* is silent in Spanish)

Escuchar 2 **Listen and check your pronunciation.**

Hablar 3 **Listen to the teacher asking four questions that relate to travel and tourism. Translate each question into English and prepare your own answers in Spanish. Then listen again and respond to the teacher.**

Remember to use the question you are asked to help you start your responses. Aim for 2–3 sentences per question to ensure you have sufficient development.

Photo card

Escuchar 1 **Look at the two photographs below and read the task. Then listen to Anna describing the photos.**

1 Where does Anna say the family is in the first photo?
2 How does Anna describe the weather?
3 Where does Anna say the people are in the second photo?
4 What does she say she thinks they are going to do?

Prepare your own description of the photos.

Your teacher will ask you to talk about the content of these photos. You must include at least <u>one</u> detail about each photo.

After you have described the photos, your teacher will then ask you questions related to **Communication and the world around us**.

Remember, you **must** describe both photos to score full marks. Introduce each photo by using *en la primera foto … en la segunda foto …*

Remember to use *estar* to describe location.

Hablar 2 **Prepare your own description of the two photos. Then, with a partner, take turns to describe them.**

- *En la primera foto hay …*
- *En la segunda foto hay …*

Escuchar 3 **Now listen to Anna responding to the second part of the task card and the questions on Communication and the world around us asked by her teacher. Write down the missing word for each gap. (1–9)**

¿Cómo prefieres pasar las vacaciones?
Prefiero pasar las **1** en otro país porque pienso que mi país **2** ser muy aburrido. Me gusta **3** viajar con mis padres, pero en el futuro me encantaría ir de vacaciones con mis amigos porque son más **4** que mis padres.

¿Qué hiciste durante las vacaciones de verano?
Durante las vacaciones de verano, fui de vacaciones a España con mis padres. **5** en avión porque es el transporte más **6** para ir a España y se puede descansar durante el **7**. Vimos muchos monumentos históricos pero también **8** el sol en la playa. Lo mejor fue cuando **9** la comida típica de España.

Escuchar 4 **Listen to Anna answering more conversation questions. Note down, in English, the <u>three</u> questions she is asked by the teacher. Next, for each of her answers, note down how she gives opinions.**

Hablar 5 **Prepare your own answers to Module 2 questions 1–10 on page 230. Then practise with your partner.**

Use verbs which are followed by the infinitive to show your ability to use more sophisticated language.

You can give positives and negatives to help extend your answers.

Módulo 2

Prueba escrita

Translation

Escribir 1

Read the English text and Kai's translation of it. Write down the missing word for each gap.

Last year I went to Spain by train. I stayed at my cousin's house in the centre. The house was very clean and it had views of the historic centre. I have just uploaded the photos. I am going to go to a festival. At the festival, one can see a dance show in the theatre.

El año pasado, **1** a España en tren. Me **2** en la casa **3** mi primo en el centro. La casa **4** muy limpia y **5** vistas al centro histórico. Acabo de **6** las fotos. Voy a **7** a una fiesta. En la fiesta, se puede **8** un espectáculo de baile en el teatro.

Escribir 2

Translate these sentences into Spanish.

1 Yesterday, I went to the city centre by underground.
2 I am going to stay at my cousin's apartment in the countryside.
3 One can use the swimming pool, but I don't like swimming.
4 The worst thing was that the hotel did not have a gym.
5 We have just uploaded the photos.

When translating phrases such as 'my cousin's house', rephrase these as 'the house of my cousin' to translate accurately into Spanish.

90-Word writing task

Escribir 1

Look at the writing task and then, for each bullet point:

1 Think about what vocabulary you have learned that you could use in your answer. For example:
- **nouns** and **verbs** to say what there is / what tourists can do
- language for **narrating a story** about what you did
- how to explain where you **would like to go** and **why**.

2 Write down three or four ideas for what you could write about.
3 Write down which tense(s) you will need to use in your answer.

Spend one minute thinking of useful structures you could use. Share and compare your ideas with a partner.

You are writing an article about festivals and tourism in your area.

Write approximately **90** words in **Spanish**. You must include something about each bullet point.

Mention:
- what attractions there are for tourists in your area
- what you did in the summer holidays last year
- somewhere you would like to visit in the future.

Leer 2 **Read Alex's answer to the task. Answer questions 1–5 in the coloured shapes.**

1 This is an example of **complex language**. What does it mean? Find three more examples from the text.

2 This word shows a **variety of vocabulary**. What does it mean? Find two more examples.

3 Which **tense** is this? What other examples can you find? Does he use any other tenses?

4 How could he **avoid repetition** by using a synonym here?

5 Which connective could you use here to form an **extended sentence**? What other connectives does he use?

Mi pueblo es bonito pero es pequeño. No hay mucho para los turistas. Sin embargo, si te gusta la historia hay que pasear por las calles antiguas. También hay un bosque. Podemos apreciar la naturaleza.

Acabo de pasar una semana en España. Lo mejor fue cuando fuimos a la playa y jugué en la arena con mi hermano, pero el hotel era decepcionante porque no tenía ni piscina ni gimnasio.

Creo que me gustaría ir a Australia y disfrutar del buen clima. También, me gustaría descubrir el paisaje bonito.

¡Hasta luego!

Alex

Leer 3 **Read Alex's answer again. Copy and complete the sentences.**

1 In Alex's town there is a … where you can …
2 He has just …
3 He liked it when they …
4 He wasn't impressed with the … because …
5 Australia has … and …, in his opinion.

Escribir 4 **Prepare your own answer to the task.**

- Think about how you can develop your answer for each bullet point.
- Look back at your notes from exercises 1 and 2.
- Look at the 'Challenge checklist' and consider how you can show off your Spanish!
- Write a brief plan and organise your answer into paragraphs.
- Write your answer and then carefully check the accuracy of what you have written.

Challenge checklist	
	✓ Some extended sentences ✓ Connectives / time phrases / sequencers ✓ Different opinion phrases ✓ Past, present and future time frames
	✓ Negatives (e.g. *no tenía ni … ni …*) ✓ Different persons of the verb ✓ More varied opinions (e.g. exclamations) ✓ A wider range of tenses (e.g. imperfect)
	✓ Phrases with more than one tense (e.g. *Creo que me gustaría …*) ✓ Positive/negative phrases (e.g. *lo peor fue cuando …*) ✓ Verbs with an infinitive (e.g. *acabo de / hay que / se puede(n)* + infinitive) ✓ Complex language (e.g. comparatives, superlatives, *si* + present tense)

Módulo 2

Palabras

Key:
bold = this word will appear in higher exams only
* = this word is not on the vocabulary list, but you may use it in your own sentences

¡Descubre Andalucía! (pages 30–31):

Describe la foto	*Describe the photo*
Hace ...	*It is ...*
sol / calor / frío / viento	*sunny / hot / cold / windy*
Hace buen/mal tiempo	*It is good/bad weather*
Llueve / *Nieva	*It is raining / It is snowing*
En la foto ...	*In the photo ...*
a la izquierda / a la derecha	*on the left / on the right*
en el centro / al **fondo**	*in the centre / in the background*
hay ...	*there is / there are ...*
un bosque / un río	*a forest / a river*
un barco / una **torre**	*a boat / a tower*
una playa / agua	*a beach / water*
vistas bonitas	*beautiful views*
muchos árboles/animales	*lots of trees/animals*
muchas casas/personas	*lots of houses/people*
Está(n) en ...	*It is / They are in ...*
el campo / la costa	*the countryside / the coast*
un pueblo / una ciudad	*a small town / a city*
¿Te gustaría visitar ...?	*Would you like to visit ...?*
(No) Me gustaría visitar ... porque ...	*I would (not) like to visit ... because ...*
(no) me gusta la historia	*I (don't) like history*
(no) me gustan los edificios antiguos	*I (don't) like old buildings*
los montes (**preciosos**)	*(beautiful) hills*
los caballos / los pájaros	*horses / birds*
los turistas (extranjeros)	*(foreign) tourists*
las tiendas / los *monumentos	*shops / monuments*
el paisaje hermoso	*beautiful landscape*
el turismo (verde)	*(green) tourism*
la escuela de *esquí / el parque **acuático**	*ski school / water park*
Me gusta / Me gustaría ...	*I like to / I would like to ...*
caminar / descansar	*walk / rest, relax*
*hacer ciclismo (de montaña)	*go cycling (mountain biking)*
montar a caballo	*go horse riding*
tomar el sol	*sunbathe*
ver un espectáculo de flamenco	*watch a flamenco show*
apreciar la naturaleza	*appreciate nature*
estar al aire libre	*be outside*
hacer turismo	*go sightseeing*
hacer **natación** / nadar	*go swimming / swim*

En ruta (pages 32–33):

¿Adónde te gustaría ir de vacaciones?	*Where would you like to go on holiday?*
Me gustaría ir (de vacaciones) a ...	*I would like to go (on holiday) to ...*
¿Cuándo te gustaría ir?	*When would you like to go?*
Me gustaría ir (de vacaciones) ...	*I would like to go (on holiday) ...*
en primavera / en verano	*in spring / in summer*
en otoño / en invierno	*in autumn / in winter*
al campo / a la ciudad	*to the countryside / to the city*
a la costa / a la montaña	*to the coast / to the mountains*
¿Con quién te gustaría ir?	*Who would you like to go with?*
Me gustaría ir con ...	*I would like to go with ...*
mi familia	*my family*
mi pareja / mis amigos/as	*my partner / my friends*
Me gustaría ir **solo/a**	*I would like to go alone*
¿Qué se puede hacer?	*What can you do?*
Se puede(n) ...	*You/One can ...*
Quisiera / Me gustaría ...	*I would like to ...*
disfrutar de la vida cultural	*enjoy the cultural life*
hacer deportes de **aventura**	*do adventure sports*
ir al cine	*go to the cinema*
ir de compras	*go shopping*
pasear por las calles	*walk through the streets*
ver una **obra** de teatro	*watch a play*
apreciar el paisaje	*appreciate the landscape*
hacer castillos de **arena**	*build sandcastles*
descubrir la arquitectura	*discover the architecture*
probar platos típicos	*try typical dishes*
sacar fotos	*take photos*
¿Cómo te gustaría viajar?	*How would you like to travel?*
Me gustaría / Quisiera ...	*I would like to ...*
viajar en / coger el ...	*travel by / take the ...*
autobús / avión / barco	*bus / plane / boat*
coche / metro / tren	*car / underground / train*
ir a pie	*go on foot*
porque ...	*because ...*
es más/menos ... que ...	*it's more/less ... than ...*
es tan ... como ...	*it's as ... as ...*
barato / caro	*cheap / expensive*
cómodo / **económico**	*comfortable / inexpensive*
lento / rápido	*slow / fast*
seguro / práctico	*safe, secure / practical*
es mejor/peor que ...	*it's better/worse than ...*
me gusta hacer ejercicio	*I like doing exercise*
la otra gente me molesta	*other people annoy me*
no aguanto (los aviones)	*I can't stand (aeroplanes)*
hay ...	*there is/are ...*
retrasos / **obras** / **huelgas**	*delays / roadworks / strikes*
mucho tráfico / mucha gente	*lots of traffic / people*

¡De fiesta en fiesta! (pages 34–35):

Las fiestas	*Festivals*
Si te gusta/interesa ...	*If you like / are interested in ...*
hay que ...	*you/one must ...*
ver las Fallas	*see the Fallas*
ir a la Tomatina	*go to the Tomatina*
las costumbres / los desfiles	*customs / parades*
los *festivales / las fiestas	*festivals*
los fuegos artificiales / las tradiciones	*fireworks / traditions*
las corridas	*bullfights*
El/La/Los/Las más / menos ...	*The most / least ...*
conocido/a(s) / divertido/a(s)	*well-known / fun*
emocionante(s) / histórico/a(s)	*exciting / historic*
interesante(s) / animado/a(s)	*interesting / lively*
peligroso/a(s) / popular(es)	*dangerous / popular*
rico/a(s) / típico/a(s)	*rich, tasty / typical*
mayor / menor	*biggest / smallest*
mejor / peor	*best / worst*
Cada año/mañana ...	*Every year/morning ...*
queman / participan	*they burn / participate*
corren (delante de los toros)	*they run (in front of the bulls)*
organizan / tiran	*they organise / throw*
celebran / bailan	*they celebrate / dance*
llevan / comen	*they wear / eat*

¿Qué van a tomar?	*What are you going to have?*
Quisiera ...	*I would like ...*
la carta / la cuenta	*the menu / the bill*
una mesa para ... personas	*a table for ... people*
dentro / **fuera**	*inside / outside*
Voy/Vamos a pedir/tomar ...	*I/We are going to order/have ...*
arroz / pollo / pescado	*rice / chicken / fish*
una hamburguesa	*a hamburger*
una ensalada *mixta	*a mixed salad*
paella / los tomates	*paella / tomatoes*
*una tortilla española	*a Spanish omelette*
patatas fritas	*chips*
una botella de agua (para compartir)	*a bottle of water (to share)*

Mis últimas vacaciones (pages 36–37):

¿Qué tal tus últimas vacaciones?	*How was your last holiday?*
Acabo/Acabamos de ...	*I/We have just ...*
volver/**regresar** de	*come back / returned from*
visitar / ir a	*visited / been to*
Viajé/Viajamos en ...	*I/We travelled by ...*
donde pasé/pasamos ...	*where I/we spent ...*
el fin de semana / una semana	*the weekend / a week*
cinco días / la Nochevieja	*five days / New Year's Eve*
Me/Nos gustó/encantó	*I/We liked/loved it*
Fue genial/estupendo	*It was great/amazing*
Lo pasé bien/mal/**fatal**	*I had a good/bad/terrible time*
¿Qué hiciste?	*What did you do?*
Por la mañana/tarde ...	*In the morning/afternoon ...*
Por la noche...	*In the evening / at night ...*
compré / decidí	*I bought / I decided to*
encontré / fui (de compras)	*I found / I went (shopping)*
jugué / **asistí** a	*I played / I attended*
di un paseo / vi	*I went for a walk / I saw*

¿Qué tiempo hizo?	*What was the weather like?*
Hizo buen/mal tiempo	*It was good/bad weather*
Hizo calor/frío/sol/viento	*It was hot/cold/sunny/windy*
Llovió	*It rained*
¿Qué fue lo mejor/peor de tu visita?	*What was the best/worst thing about your visit?*
El primer/último día ...	*The first/last day ...*
Al día siguiente ...	*The next day ...*
Lo bueno/malo fue cuando ...	*The good/bad thing was when ...*
comí algo malo y *vomité	*I ate something bad and vomited*
me puse enfermo/a	*I became ill*
tuvimos que (volver a casa)	*we had to (go back home)*
dejé / perdí / rompí	*I left / lost / broke*
mi bolsa / mi cámara / mi reloj	*my bag / camera / watch*
mi maleta / tarjeta de *crédito	*my suitcase / credit card*
*mi pasaporte / mis **llaves**	*my passport / keys*

¿Dónde te quedaste? (pages 38–39):

El alojamiento	*Accommodation*
¿Dónde te quedaste?	*Where did you stay?*
Me quedé en ...	*I stayed in ...*
Nos quedamos en ...	*We stayed in ...*
Alquilé / **Alquilamos** ...	*I / We rented ...*
*un apartamento / una casa	*an apartment / a house*
una habitación / un coche	*a room / a car*
Tenía / No tenía ...	*It had / It didn't have ...*
Había / No había ...	*There was/were / There wasn't/ weren't ...*
No tenía **ni ... ni ...**	*It didn't have either ... or ...*
(un) baño / jardín	*a bathroom / garden*
(un) restaurante	*a restaurant*
(una) cocina / piscina	*a kitchen / pool*
vistas al mar / mucho ruido	*sea views / lots of noise*
El **ascensor** / La *ducha / La luz ...	*The lift / shower / light ...*
La cama / La **calefacción** ...	*The bed / heating ...*
La televisión / La ventana ...	*The TV / window ...*

estaba roto/a	*was broken*
no funcionaba	*didn't work*
El gimnasio / La recepción	*The gym / reception*
estaba cerrado/a	*was closed*
Era (muy/bastante/demasiado) ...	*It was (very/quite/too) ...*
agradable / **decepcionante**	*pleasant / disappointing*
tranquilo/a / moderno/a	*calm, relaxed / modern*
antiguo/a / viejo/a	*old*
Estaba ...	*It was ...*
cerca de / lejos de	*near (to) / far from*
en las afueras	*in the outskirts, suburbs*
limpio/a / sucio/a	*clean / dirty*
(No) Me gustó porque ...	*I (didn't like) liked it because ...*
el dueño (no) era (nada) agradable	*the owner was (not) pleasant (at all)*
*Por un lado / Por otro lado...	*On one hand/the other hand ...*
En cambio ...	*On the other hand / Whereas ...*
Sin embargo ...	*However ...*

Mi aventura por América Latina (pages 40–41):

¿Qué sueles hacer en verano?	*What do you tend to do in summer?*
Suelo / **Solemos** (ir al extranjero)	*I / We tend to (go abroad)*
¿Adónde fuiste de vacaciones el año pasado?	*Where did you go on holiday last year?*
El verano pasado ...	*Last summer ...*
Hace ... días/meses/años ...	*... days/months/years ago ...*
fui de vacaciones a ...	*I went on holiday to ...*
Lo mejor/peor fue cuando ...	*The best/worst thing was when ...*
aprendí (mucho) sobre ...	*I learned (a lot) about ...*
conocí a ...	*I met ...*
decidí (visitar ...) / llegué	*I decided (to visit) / I arrived*

fui a un parque temático	*I went to a theme park*
vi un partido / una **exposición**	*I watched a game / saw an exhibition*
visité / **hice turismo**	*I visited / I went sightseeing*
probé un plato típico	*I tried a typical dish*
Costó/Costaron ... euros	*It/They cost ... euros*
¿Adónde vas a ir?	*Where are you going?*
El año próximo / que viene ...	*Next year ...*
voy a / vamos a ...	*I am / We are going to ...*
ir a / pasar ...	*go to / spend ...*
hacer / ver / visitar ...	*do / see/watch / visit ...*
Va a ser ...	*It is going to be ...*

Repaso de gramática

Different types of verbs in the present tense (Pages 8, 9, 11 and 13)

Escribir **1** **Copy and complete the table according to how each verb behaves in the present tense. Then write each verb in the 'I' form of the present tense.**

Regular verbs	Stem-changing verbs	Irregular verbs	Verbs with irregular 'I' form only
	querer (quiero)		

~~querer~~ visitar subir poder ser salir montar ir
preferir leer hacer jugar ver soler escribir tener

Escribir **2** **Complete the sentences with the correct form of the present tense of the verbs in brackets. Use exercise 1 to help you. Then translate each sentence into English.**

1 En las vacaciones (*do*) mucho deporte porque me encanta.
2 Mis amigas y yo (*go*) al parque, donde (*play*) al fútbol. (*Are*) muy deportistas.
3 Sin embargo, cuando (*is*) frío, mi hermano David (*prefers*) quedarse en casa.
4 David (*reads*) muchas novelas y también (*watches*) películas en su dormitorio.
5 Yo nunca (*watch*) películas en casa porque el sonido (*is*) mejor en el cine.
6 A veces, mi hermana y yo (*visit*) a nuestros abuelos cuando (*have*) tiempo.
7 Mi abuela (*has*) un móvil nuevo. Le gusta grabar vídeos y luego los (*uploads*) a YouTube.
8 Mis padres (*ride*) en bici porque (*are*) miembros de un club de ciclismo.

To conjugate a verb accurately, always consider:
1 the **tense**
2 the **person** of the verb
3 the **type** of verb

In this task, all verbs are in the present tense.
Look for clues in the sentences to work out the **person** of the verb.

Talking about the past (Pages 15 and 38)

Leer **3** **Read this text and write down at least <u>ten</u> preterite tense verbs in Spanish. Translate each verb into English and then write down the infinitive form.**

Example: visitamos – we visited (visitar)

Hace seis meses visitamos Perú, donde descubrimos la Fiesta del Sol, un festival inca muy antiguo. Lo mejor fue cuando asistimos al espectáculo especial que organizaron para celebrar el día más corto del año. ¡Qué bonito! También probé muchos platos típicos de la región e hice turismo con mis padres. Desafortunadamente, cuando volvimos a España, mi madre dejó su maleta en el aeropuerto y luego yo perdí mi cámara durante el vuelo. Finalmente, rompieron la silla de ruedas de mi padre. Sin embargo, disfruté mucho de la visita.

Escribir **4** **Rewrite the following story in the past, changing each verb to the correct form of the preterite tense or the imperfect tense. Then translate the new version into English.**

Por la mañana **voy** al centro de la ciudad. **Viajo** en metro, pero **no me gusta** porque **está** muy sucio. Cuando **llego** al centro, **quedo** con mis amigos. Primero, **visitamos** mi tienda favorita para comprar un nuevo videojuego. Desafortunadamente, la tienda no **tiene** mucha variedad y por eso no **compro** nada. Por la tarde **vamos** al estadio, donde **vemos** un partido. **Hay** mucha gente y el ambiente **es** increíble. ¡Y lo mejor **es** cuando mi equipo **gana** el partido!

Remember that some verbs have a spelling change in the 'I' form of the **preterite tense**.
Also, the 'we' form of regular ***-ar*** and ***-ir*** verbs is identical in the **present** and **preterite tenses**.

Using different tenses (Pages 12, 15, 38 and 41)

Leer 5

In each set of verbs below, one verb is in a different tense than the others. Write the odd one out and explain why it is different. Then translate that verb into English.

Example: 1 *voy (present tense; the others are preterite tense) – I go / I am going*

1	fui	comí	voy	compré	**4** son	tienen	comieron	suben
2	voy a ir	vamos	vas a ser	van a ver	**5** perdió	compró	juego	hizo
3	tenía	canta	manda	juega	**6** era	había	estaba	va a usar

Verbs and phrases followed by the infinitive (Pages 13, 31, 32, 34, 36 and 40)

Leer 6

Translate this text into English.

No **suelo** ir al extranjero porque no **me gusta** viajar en avión, pero **acabo de** pasar una semana en Salamanca, donde vi una obra de teatro. Salamanca es una ciudad preciosa que es conocida por su Plaza Mayor, donde **se puede** tomar un café. Si te gusta la arquitectura, **hay que** dar un paseo por las calles del barrio histórico donde **se pueden** apreciar los edificios antiguos. **Me gustaría** regresar en el futuro porque **quiero** visitar la Catedral Vieja. Además, **quisiera** ver la universidad.

Escribir 7

Translate these sentences into Spanish. Use the purple phrases from exercise 6 and the verbs in the box below to help you.

1 You must visit Mexico, where you can enjoy the good climate.
2 I tend to travel by train because you can do other things during the journey.
3 Tomorrow I want to look for a watch and so I would like to go to the shopping centre.
4 We have just celebrated my birthday in Jaén and next year I would like to spend a week there.

pasar buscar hacer visitar viajar ir disfrutar de celebrar

The verbs in **purple** are always followed by the infinitive.
For phrases like ***soler*** and ***acabar de***, use the correct person of the verb.
Also remember:
Se puede + infinitive + singular noun
Se pueden + infinitive + plural noun

Comparatives and superlatives (Pages 7, 33 and 34)

Leer 8

Translate these sentences into English. Then write C (comparative) or S (superlative) next to each one.

1 Compro ropa por Internet ya que es más rápido que en las tiendas.
2 Los campings suelen ser menos caros que los hoteles.
3 Para mí, Ecuador es el país más hermoso de Sudamérica.
4 No aguanto jugar con mi móvil porque la pantalla no es tan grande como la pantalla de mi portátil.
5 Alquilamos un apartamento porque fue la opción menos cara.
6 El peor problema en la capital es el tráfico.

Escribir 9

Write sentences using at least two of the options from each purple shape below to give your opinion using both the comparative and the superlative.

Example: 1 *El fútbol es **más** divertido **que** la natación, pero el tenis es **el** deporte **más** divertido.*
*La natación es **menos** divertida **que** el tenis, pero el fútbol es **el** deporte **menos** divertido.*

1 el fútbol el tenis la natación
(sport, fun)

2 las series los documentales las telenovelas
(programmes, interesting)

3 la lectura el ciclismo el baile
(activity, expensive)

4 la paella la tortilla española el pan con tomate
(dish, tasty)

¡No hay dos familias iguales!

- Reading about different families
- Using possessive adjectives

¡Feliz Día Internacional de la Familia!

¿Sabes que el *Día Internacional de la Familia* se celebra el 15 de mayo todos los años? Descubre a tres jóvenes hablando de sus familias. ¿Reconoces a las familias famosas que mencionan?

1

Gemelos Javi y Paco: **Nuestra familia** es numerosa y multicultural como la familia de Cesc Fàbregas. **Nuestro padrastro** y **nuestra madre** se casaron hace cinco años en una boda civil y ¡ahora somos siete! Adoramos el fútbol, especialmente cuando nuestra madre juega con nosotros.

2

Itzan: **Mi padre** es cantante y está de gira con frecuencia. **Mis hermanos** pequeños me molestan mucho cuando mi padre no está, pero el bebé es un ángel. Siempre quiere besar a todos. ¡Somos semejantes a la familia de Ricky Martin!

3

Luz: Me llevo muy bien con **mi madrastra** y **mi hermanastra**. Nos encanta pasar tiempo juntas y yo sé que siempre puedo confiar en ellas. Compartimos todo. **Mi abuelo** dice que somos como la actriz Salma Hayek y **su hija**.

el padrastro	*stepdad*
la hermanastra	*stepsister*
estar de gira	*be on tour*
la familia homoparental	*same-sex (parent) family*

Leer 1 **Read and match the correct text (a–d) to the family profiles (1–3). There is one text too many. Then make notes in English about all the family members mentioned in purple by Javi, Paco, Itzan and Luz.**

¿Quién es mi familia?

a Mi padre viaja mucho por su trabajo. En mi opinión, tener que cuidar siempre de mis hermanos es duro. Me molesta porque hacen mucho ruido y son un poco tontos.

b Puedo hablar con mi hermanastra y no tenemos secretos. Es sensible y alegre. Aunque no vivo con ella, nos vemos casi todos los días.

c Tengo una familia homoparental. Aunque soy hija única, hay mucho amor en mi familia. Siempre tenemos muchos amigos en casa.

d Mi hermano nació el mismo día que yo. Hay muchos miembros en mi familia y somos una familia muy activa, ¡no somos perezosos!

¿Qué otras familias famosas conoces?

Escuchar 2

Listen and select the correct word to complete each sentence. Then translate the completed sentences into English.

1 Su **primo** / **tío** / **abuelo** vive en México.
2 Nuestra **hija** / **prima** / **tía** es una actriz famosa.
3 Mi **hermanastro** / **hermanastra** / **hermano** está en Sevilla de vacaciones.
4 La hermana de mi **madre** / **padre** / **abuela** es mi tía.
5 Es el coche de su **madrastra** / **padrastro** / **primo**.

Spanish doesn't use apostrophes in the same way as English.

*El hermano **de mi madre** es mi tío.*
My mum's brother is my uncle.

*La hija **de mi tía** es mi prima.*
My aunt's daughter is my cousin.

*Es el coche **de mi padrastro**.*
It's **my stepdad's** car.

Escribir 3

Translate the phrases for family members into Spanish.

1 my sisters
2 her father
3 our grandparents
4 their children
5 your (plural) families
6 our cousin (female)
7 her brothers and sisters
8 your (singular) parents

G

Most **possessive adjectives** have two forms, singular and plural.

	singular	**plural**
my	mi	mis
your	tu	tus
his/her/its	su	sus
our	nuestro/a	nuestros/as
your (plural)	vuestro/a	vuestros/as
their	su	sus

In addition, *nuestro* (our) and *vuestro* (your, plural) also have masculine and feminine forms:

nuestro hermano — our brother
nuestras hermanas — our sisters

Page 70

Hablar 4

Look at the pronunciation box. Read this phrase out in pairs to practise the *v*, *j*, *ge-*, *gi-* and silent *h* sounds. Then listen to check your pronunciation.

Jorge y Hugo son los hijos gemelos de Germán y Virginia.

el gemelo *twin*

Remember:
- the Spanish ***h*** is silent
- ***v*** is pronounced the same as ***b***
- ***j***, ***ge*** and ***gi*** are pronounced like a stronger version of the English 'h'. However the Spanish ***h*** is silent

Escuchar 5

Listen and fill in the gaps with the correct word from the box. Read out the text to practise pronunciation. Then translate the text into English.

Las familias **1** de hoy son muy **2** y complejas porque hay muchos tipos y formas de familia. A veces, **3** generaciones viven **4**, lo que significa que abuelos, padres e **5** viven en el mismo **6**. En **7**, la familia es muy importante para la cultura hispanohablante. Los hispanohablantes **8** las tradiciones y costumbres familiares. Les gusta estar **9** para celebrar los cumpleaños, las bodas, las fiestas culturales y la Navidad con alegría. La religión es **10** importante para muchas familias del mundo hispanohablante.

todavía	varias	hijos
general	juntas	juntos
diversas	valoran	hogar
hispanohablantes		

1 Esta es mi gente

- Describing people
- Using the present continuous to describe a photo
- Using *ser* for physical descriptions and *estar* for location

Escuchar 1 Listen and read. What do the words in **bold** mean? Then translate text number 2 into English. (1–2)

¿Qué están haciendo?

1 Aquí hay una foto de mi familia: mis padres, mi abuela y mi hermano menor están al fondo, en el jardín. Mi abuelo y mi hermana **están sonriendo**. Mi abuelo **está cocinando** y mi hermana **está mirando** y **ayudando**. Mis padres y mi abuela **están hablando** y mi padre **está tocando** la guitarra. **Estamos celebrando** mi cumpleaños. ¿Y yo? ¿Dónde estoy? ¡**Estoy sacando** la foto para mandarla a mis tíos!

2 Aquí hay una foto de mis padres y mis dos hermanos. Están en la cocina. Mientras **están tomando** el desayuno, mi hermana **está haciendo** sus deberes en la tableta y **bebiendo** zumo. Mi madre **está comiendo** y **mandando** un mensaje. Mi hermano **está escuchando** música en el móvil y **charlando** con sus amigos en Snapchat. Mi padre **está trabajando** en el ordenador y **leyendo** correos electrónicos.

Escuchar 2 Listen. Copy and complete the table in English. (1–5)

	People in the photo	Where they are	What they are doing
1	2 younger brothers	in their bedroom	

el pastel *cake*

Hablar 3 Look at the photo. Imagine this is your family. In pairs, describe the following in Spanish:

- *¿Quién está en la foto?*
- *¿Dónde están?*
- *¿Qué están haciendo?*

Aquí hay una foto de	mi padre. mi madre. mis padres. mi herman**o**/**a**. mis herman**os**/**as**. mi abuel**o**/**a**. mis abuel**os**/**as**.
Está(n)	en casa / en la cocina / en el salón / en el jardín.
Está(n)	jugando/cocinando/charlando/sonriendo. bebiendo/comiendo/leyendo. haciendo/viendo/sacando ...

G

The **present continuous tense** is used to describe what people are doing, for example in a photo.
Use the present tense of ***estar*** + **present participle**.

To form the present participle, remove the ***-ar***, ***-er***, ***-ir*** from the infinitive and add the endings ***-ando*** (for ***-ar*** verbs) or ***-iendo*** (for ***-er*** and ***-ir*** verbs).

	estar (*to be*)	**present participle** ('-*ing*' form)
(yo)	estoy	
(tú)	estás	
(él/ella/usted)	está	jug**ando**
(nosotros/as)	estamos	com**iendo**
(vosotros/as)	estáis	escrib**iendo**
(ellos/as/ustedes)	están	

Note these irregular present participles:
leer → ***leyendo*** (reading)
sonreír → ***sonriendo*** (smiling)

Page 70

G

Use the verb ***estar*** for talking about **location**.
Estoy/Están *en el jardín.*
I am / They are in the garden.

Use the verb ***ser*** when talking about **physical description**.
Soy/Es *moren**o**/**a**.*
I am / He/She is dark-haired.

Page 70

Leer 4 **Read the texts and answer the questions in English. Then practise reading out Nina's description.**

¿A quién te pareces?

Ayesha

Tengo el pelo negro, largo y los ojos marrones. A veces llevo el pelo con trenzas. Soy bastante alta y delgada. No me parezco a nadie de mi familia porque soy adoptada. Mi mejor amigo lleva gafas y es más alto que yo.

Nina

Tengo los ojos verdes y el pelo largo y castaño. Me parezco a mi padre porque tenemos los mismos ojos y los dos somos bajos, aunque yo soy más baja que él. Tengo dos hermanas menores.

Marcus

Soy alto y moreno. Tengo el pelo corto y negro. No me parezco nada a mis dos hermanos porque nuestras madres son diferentes. Sin embargo, mi hermana menor se parece a mi padre porque los dos son rubios y tienen la misma boca. ¡Es una niña muy guapa!

1 Who has siblings with different mothers?
2 Who does not look like anyone in their family?
3 Who is shorter than their father?
4 Who is adopted?
5 In what way does Marcus' younger sister look like their father? (Give two details.)
6 Who looks more like their father? Why?

castaño	*brown*
las trenzas	*braids*
me parezco a	*I look like*
se parece a	*he/she looks like*
la misma boca	*the same mouth*

Hablar 5 **In pairs, talk about what you look like.**

- *¿Cómo eres?*
- *Soy …*
- *¿De qué color tienes los ojos?*
- *Tengo los ojos …*
- *¿Cómo tienes el pelo?*
- *Tengo el pelo …*
- *¿A quién te pareces de tu familia? ¿Por qué?*
- *Me parezco a … porque los dos / las dos tenemos …*

Soy/Es [muy/bastante]	alt**o**/**a**. baj**o**/**a**. moren**o**/**a**. rubi**o**/**a**.	
Tengo/Tiene el pelo	largo. corto. castaño. rubio. negro. rizado.	
Llevo/Lleva	gafas. trenzas.	
Tengo/Tiene los ojos	marron**es**. azul**es**. verd**es**.	
Mi herman**o**/**a** es más/menos	alt**o**/**a** baj**o**/**a** gord**o**/**a** delgad**o**/**a**	que yo.
Me parezco a Se parece a	mi [padre]	porque … **los**/**las** dos somos/son … **los**/**las** dos tenemos/tienen [la misma boca] / [los mismos ojos].
No me parezco a	nadie de mi familia	porque soy adoptad**o**/**a**.

Escuchar 6 **Listen and write down the details in English. (1–3) Then correct the errors in sentences a–c.**

- People in the family
- Physical description of the family member

¿Cómo es tu familia?

a Mi familia es **numerosa**.
b Mi familia es **multicultural**.
c Mis padres **se casaron** hace dos años.

la familia monoparental	*single-parent family*

Escribir 7 **Choose one of the families on page 56, or another famous family you know.**

Write about it as if it were yours. Then read it out to your partner. Your partner guesses who the family is. Include:

- who the family members are
- physical descriptions.

Adjectives in Spanish usually come after the noun and 'agree' with the noun in gender and number (singular/plural). Adjectives referring to eyes and hair are always masculine.

*Soy alt**o**/**a**.* *Somos alt**os**/**as**.*
*Tengo el pelo cort**o**.* *Tengo los ojos verd**es**.*

2 Mis famosos favoritos

- Talking about your favourite celebrities
- Saying how long you have been doing something
- Using the personal *a*

Escuchar 1 **Read and complete the messages by writing the correct letter for each person. Listen to check your answers. Then translate sentences 1–4 into Spanish.**

¿A qué famosos sigues en las redes sociales?

Diego: Soy aficionado a los videojuegos de acción. Los juego **desde hace mucho tiempo**. Por eso …

Salima: Me interesa actuar y cantar. Hago actuaciones en el colegio **desde hace un mes**. Por eso …

Chloe: Me interesa el mundo de la belleza y la moda. Por eso …

1 … sigo a mis cantantes y actores favoritos para aprender y mejorar mi talento. Muchas personas famosas usan su plataforma para promover cambios positivos en el mundo.

2 … sigo a *streamers* en Twitch **desde hace dos años**. Mucha gente piensa que son una mala influencia para los jóvenes, pero yo creo que son divertidos.

3 … sigo *vlogs* de rutinas, estilo de vida y moda **desde hace un año**. Sigo a mis *influencers* famosas favoritas porque tienen buenos consejos sobre las tendencias.

1 I've been doing acting for two years.
2 Many famous people promote positive change in the world.
3 They have been a bad influence for young people for a long time.
4 I follow lifestyle, beauty and fashion vlogs.

Escuchar 2 **Listen. For each person (Julia, David, Gema or Roberto), write down in English (1-4):**

- who or what they follow
- for how long
- why? (Give two reasons.)

en vivo	*live*

Hablar 3 **In pairs, talk about the celebrities you follow on social media.**

- *¿A qué personas famosas sigues en las redes sociales?*
- *Sigo a cantantes/actores/deportistas como…*
  porque soy aficionado(a) a la música / a la moda / al deporte.
- *¿Desde hace cuánto tiempo?*
- *Desde hace un año / meses / (mucho) tiempo.*
- *¿Por qué te gusta(n)?*
- *Me gusta porque tiene éxito / es un buen modelo a seguir.*

G

To say how long you have been doing something, use ***desde hace*** + period of time and the **present tense** of the verb.

Sigo *a streamers en Twitch* ***desde hace*** *dos años.*
I have been following streamers on Twitch **for** two years.

Notice that ***seguir*** is a stem-changing verb in the present tense (*sigo, sigues*, etc.).

Page 71

Escuchar 4 **Listen and fill in the gaps. Then translate the text into English.**

Bad Bunny, estrella mundial del *trap* latino
Sigo al cantante latino Bad Bunny desde hace muchos años porque **1** sus dificultades y **2** conseguir el éxito en su carrera. **3** desde cero y **4** en un supermercado. Con su imagen, **5** las reglas del estilo rap. Además, es trabajador, tiene un gran corazón y parece una buena persona porque ayuda a otras personas. En el pasado, **6** dinero a seguidores que sufren a causa de la pobreza. En mi opinión es la voz de una nueva generación. ***Susana***

G

Use the **personal *a*** when the object of the verb is a person.
Sigo ***a*** *esta persona famosa desde hace mucho tiempo.*
I have followed this famous person for a long time.

Do **not** use it when the object is **not** a person.
Veo vídeos sobre mis deportistas favoritos.
I watch videos about my favourite sports stars.

Page 71

Leer 5 **Read the comments about role models. Find <u>six</u> verbs in the preterite and translate them into English. Then answer the questions.**

¿Quién es tu persona famosa favorita?

1 Malek

Mi persona famosa favorita es el deportista Lionel Messi. Lo sigo porque ganó ocho veces el Premio Balón de Oro y jugó en muchos partidos importantes para su equipo. Cuando era pequeño, superó problemas de salud. Pienso que tiene mucho talento y un estilo único. Ayuda a los niños enfermos a tener las mismas oportunidades.

Lionel Messi

2 Lena

Mi personalidad favorita es Anya Taylor-Joy. En mi opinión es una actriz joven y guapa. Actuó en su primera película importante cuando tenía 19 años, donde demostró su enorme talento para los papeles complicados. Ganó muchos premios en una serie famosa. Me gusta porque es una actriz muy buena. También la sigo en las redes sociales porque tiene una imagen diferente a otras actrices de su generación y es un buen modelo a seguir.

Anya Taylor-Joy

Use the **preterite tense** to talk about completed actions in the past.
Remember to add an <u>accent</u> and to stress the last syllable in the third person singular for *-ar* verbs. Otherwise it could be confused with the present tense:
gano (I win)
ganó (he/she won)

Remember to pay attention to grammatical agreement when using **direct object pronouns** to replace the noun.
Lo *sigo.* — I follow **him**.
La *sigo.* — I follow **her**.

1 What are two of Messi's achievements that Malek mentions?
2 What are the reasons Malek likes Messi? (Give <u>two</u> details.)
3 What information does Lena give about her favourite famous person? (Give <u>two</u> details.)
4 Why does Lena follow Anya Taylor-Joy?

Escuchar 6 **Read the sentences below and decide if each one is an advantage or disadvantage of being a celebrity. Then listen and note down which <u>two</u> opinions each person mentions. Note down <u>one</u> extra opinion for each person. (1–4)**

a Recibes muchos comentarios negativos
b Puedes animar a otras personas con tus historias
c Puedes ser víctima de ciberacoso por parte de tus seguidores
d Tienes mucha influencia en las tendencias y en la moda
e Puedes sufrir problemas de salud mental
f La presión de la vida pública puede causar mucho estrés
g Puedes usar tu fama para promover cambios positivos
h Ganas mucho dinero y puedes tener una vida de lujo

la campaña *campaign*
la falta *lack*

Escribir 7 **Write about your favourite celebrity. Include:**

- who your favourite famous person is
- what they are like and why you follow them
- details of their life and achievements
- the advantages and disadvantages of being a celebrity.

Marcus Rashford **ganó** un premio porque **ayudó** a muchos niños de familias pobres a tener suficiente comida en el instituto.

Mi persona famosa favorita es ... porque es ...	fuerte/trabajador(a)/guapo/a.
Sigo (a) ... en las redes sociales	desde hace ... meses / un año / (mucho) tiempo.
Lo/**La** sigo porque Pienso/Creo que	tiene mucho talento / éxito / una vida de lujo. es un buen modelo a seguir. apoya / ayuda a otras personas.
El año pasado / Hace dos años / En ...	ganó / actuó en... / jugó en ... / dio dinero a... / ayudó a...

3 ¡Amigos para siempre!

- Talking about friendships and relationships
- Using reflexive verbs
- Using the pronouns *me* and *te* before a verb

Escuchar 1 **Listen to and read the texts. Translate the phrases in purple into English. Then write if the activities mentioned refer to the near future (NF) or the preterite (P). (1–6)**

¿Cómo es tu relación con tus amigos?

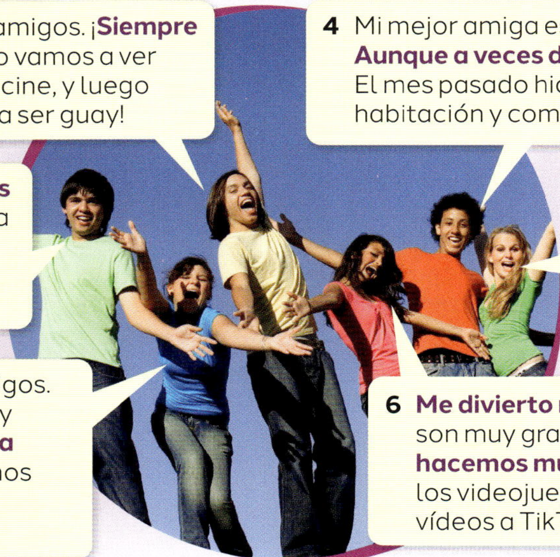

1 **Me llevo muy bien con** mis amigos. ¡**Siempre estamos juntos**! El domingo vamos a ver una película de terror en el cine, y luego vamos a tomar un café. ¡Va a ser guay!

2 Mis mejores amigos y yo **nos llevamos muy bien**. Mañana vamos a jugar un partido de fútbol contra un equipo rival. ¡Vamos a ganar!

3 Me llevo genial con mis amigos. **Tenemos mucho en común** y **puedo contar con ellos para todo**. El sábado pasado vimos a nuestra banda de música favorita. ¡Fue increíble!

4 Mi mejor amiga es divertida, alegre y positiva. **Aunque a veces discutimos, tengo confianza en ella**. El mes pasado hicimos un maratón de películas en mi habitación y comimos caramelos. ¡Fue muy relajante!

5 La amistad es muy importante para mí. Mis amigos y yo **tenemos los mismos intereses**, por eso nos llevamos genial. El viernes vamos a montar en bici. ¡Va a ser divertido!

6 **Me divierto mucho** con mis amigos porque son muy graciosos. Casi nunca nos peleamos y **hacemos muchas cosas juntos**. Ayer jugamos a los videojuegos, escuchamos música y subimos vídeos a TikTok. ¡Fue guay!

contar con	*to count on*
la película de terror	*a horror film*

Escuchar 2 **Listen. Copy and complete the table for each person in English. (1–4)**

Two details about their friendship	Two activities mentioned	Future or past activity?

Hablar 3 **In pairs, answer these questions.**

- *¿Cómo es tu relación con tus amigos?*
- *¿Qué hiciste con tus amigos el fin de semana pasado?*
- *¿Qué vas a hacer con tus amigos el próximo fin de semana?*

Me llevo bien/genial con	mi mejor amigo/a mis amigos/as
porque	es divertido/a. son divertidos/as. puedo contar con él/ella/ellos/ellas para todo. me conoce(n) bien. tengo confianza en él/ella/ellos/ellas.
Me divierto con mis amigos/as porque	hacemos muchas cosas juntos/as. me río mucho con ellos/ellas.
Mi mejor amigo/a y yo Mis amigos/as y yo	nos llevamos bien/genial/superbién
porque	tenemos los mismos intereses. tenemos mucho en común. hacemos muchas cosas juntos/as. nos divertimos mucho. siempre estamos juntos/as.
A veces / (Casi) Nunca / Siempre	discutimos / nos peleamos.

G

Some verbs for describing relationships are **reflexive** in Spanish.

	llevarse (*to get on*)
(yo)	**me** llevo
(tú)	**te** llevas
(él/ella/usted)	**se** lleva
(nosotros/as)	**nos** llevamos
(vosotros/as)	**os** lleváis
(ellos/ellas/ustedes)	**se** llevan

Verbs like this include:
pelearse
divertirse (ie)
sentirse (ie)
reírse (i)
(the last three are stem-changing)

Page 72

Check page 20 in the Module 1 grammar section for more on the preterite and near future tenses.

Leer 4 **Read the texts and answer the questions. Then translate what Lorena says into English.**

¿Cómo es un buen amigo?

Lorena
Para mí, la amistad es muy importante. Pienso que la amiga ideal es alegre, te acepta como eres, no te critica y sabe perdonarte. Además, es fiel, te escucha cuando tienes problemas y puede guardar un secreto. Con una amiga de verdad puedes ser tú misma, sin miedo. Por ejemplo, mi mejor amiga siempre me apoya. La semana pasada, me dio buenos consejos para resolver un problema con mi novio. Tiene buen carácter, es ambiciosa y no es perezosa. Somos amigas desde niñas. Por eso me conoce bien y me ayuda en todo. Puedo confiar en ella totalmente y me siento feliz en su compañía.

Adrián
En mi opinión, los buenos amigos te comprenden y te apoyan en lo bueno y en lo malo. Creo que los amigos verdaderos también te respetan. Mis mejores amigos son muy importantes para mí porque siempre puedo contar con ellos cuando tengo problemas. Son muy comprensivos, me ayudan mucho y tengo confianza en ellos. También son graciosos y me hacen reír, ¡nos divertimos mucho juntos! Por eso nos llevamos genial.

Who says that a good friend …

1 supports you in good and bad moments?
2 is loyal?
3 knows how to forgive you?
4 helps when you have problems?
5 accepts you the way you are?
6 understands you and respects you?

Escribir 5 **Translate these sentences into Spanish.**

1 My best friend understands me and supports me.
2 An ideal friend respects you and never criticises you.
3 My friend knows me well and accepts me the way I am.
4 A good friend listens to you and always gives you good advice.
5 A good friend helps you with everything.
6 My best friend makes me laugh.

Remember to put the pronouns ***me*** and ***te*** before the conjugated verb.
me *escucha* — he/she listens **to me**
te *ayuda* — he/she helps **you**

Escuchar 6 **Listen to Santi describing his best friend, Rafa, and note down <u>four</u> details about their friendship and <u>one</u> detail about how his friend helped him.**

Escribir 7 **Write a paragraph about friends and friendship. Then read it out to your partner. Include:**

- ¿Cómo es tu mejor amigo/a físicamente y de carácter?
  Es alto/a, moreno/a … También es comprensivo/fiel … Se llama …
- ¿Desde cuándo sois amigos? *Somos amigos desde hace … años.*
- ¿Cómo es un buen amigo?
- ¿Cómo te ayuda tu mejor amigo/a?
- ¿Qué actividades hiciste la semana pasada con tu mejor amigo/a?

Para mí, En mi opinión, Creo que	un buen amig**o** una buen**a** amig**a**	me/te escucha y me/te comprende. me/te ayuda cuando tengo/tienes problemas. me/te apoya en todo / en lo bueno y en lo malo. me/te conoce bien y me/te respeta. me/te da buenos consejos. me acepta como soy / te acepta como eres. me/te hace reír. no me/te critica.
Mi mejor amig**o**/**a**		
La semana pasada	fuimos	al cine / al polideportivo / al centro comercial / a una fiesta.
	vimos	una película.
	jugamos	a los videojuegos.
	montamos	en bici.
	ayudé a mi mejor amig**o**/**a**	con un problema con su novi**o**/**a** / a estudiar para un examen / resolver un problema.

4 Así soy yo

- Talking about your identity and what matters to you
- Using *para* + infinitive
- Listening for gist

Escuchar 1 **Listen and write the letters of the categories mentioned for each person. (1–5) Then choose your own categories from the list to create your 'identity pizza' toppings.**

¡Mi identidad es única!

¡Todos somos diferentes!

los Juegos Olímpicos	*the Olympic Games*

¿Cómo eres? ¿Cómo es tu identidad?

a mi personalidad **b** mi género / mi sexo **c** mis intereses

¿Qué es lo más importante para ti?

d mi familia **e** mi educación **f** la amistad **g** mi religión

¿Qué cosas te preocupan?

h las cosas que me importan o me preocupan:

el amor, la paz, el planeta, mis derechos, mi cultura / mis raíces

¿Cuáles son tus sueños?

i mis sueños

Leer 2 **Match the questions to the answers to create a dialogue.**

1 ¿Cómo eres?
2 ¿Qué pronombre usas?
3 ¿Qué es lo más importante para ti?
4 ¿Qué cosas te preocupan?
5 ¿Cuál es tu sueño?

a **Para mí, lo más importante es** mi familia y mi educación. Mi familia porque me da cariño y mi educación porque es clave para mi futuro.

b **Mi sueño es** luchar por un mundo mejor porque **pienso que** los derechos de los animales son muy importantes. Quiero fundar una empresa verde.

c **Soy** optimista y social. No soy vago. Además, **pienso que soy** trabajador y responsable.

d **Me preocupan** mis derechos. **Creo que es necesario** conseguir la paz. Además, estoy a favor de la acción climática.

e **Uso el pronombre** 'él'. Tengo amigos que usan el pronombre 'elle', y no 'él' o 'ella'. También se puede usar el pronombre 'ellx.'

Hablar 3 **In pairs, use the questions and bold phrases in exercise 2 to make up your own dialogue.**

Soy		trabajador(a). serio/a. perezoso/a. responsable. abierto/a. vago/a. social. optimista.
Uso el pronombre		él/ella/elle/ellx.
Para mí, lo más importante	es	mi familia/educación/identidad. mi cultura/mi religión/la amistad.
	son	mis amigos/intereses/sueños.
Me interesa(n) Me preocupa(n)		el futuro del mundo. la protección del planeta / la paz. mis derechos / los derechos de los animales.
Mi sueño es Mi objetivo es		tener (mucho) dinero/éxito. ser rico/a. ser jefe/a. luchar por un mundo mejor.

Listen for gist. Remember that you don't need to understand every phrase or sentence. Instead, focus on important pieces of information without details.

Try to pick up keywords, intonation and other clues to guess the overall meaning or topic of the passage.

Leer 4 **Read the texts. Decide if the opinions about technology and social media are positive (P), negative (N) or both (P+N). Then write down <u>five</u> advantages and disadvantages of social media in Spanish.**

Mi identidad en línea. ¿Qué importancia tiene la tecnología en tu vida?

La tecnología es clave en mi vida porque la uso cada día. Pienso que las redes sociales son esenciales para organizar mi vida social. Las uso para jugar y charlar con mis amigos. Ayer las usé para buscar información sobre mi trabajo ideal y mis derechos. Me interesa mi futuro y uso las redes sociales para estar en contacto con gente con mucha experiencia. ¡Es guay! ***Tarik***

Creo que las redes sociales son una gran distracción para los jóvenes porque las usan todo el tiempo y no duermen bien. Pienso que hay que tener cuidado porque también pueden ser peligrosas. No debes compartir tus datos personales ni tu contraseña. Además, no toda la información en Internet es verdadera. Eso me preocupa mucho. ***Marta***

Uso la tecnología a diario para estudiar, aprender y ver películas. Aunque las redes sociales son buenas para expresarse y divertirse, no todo es positivo porque también causan acoso debido a la presión de grupo. Para mí, la mejor red es TikTok. La usé hace dos días para compartir fotos, mensajes y vídeos y también para buscar información. Me interesan las noticias y la música. ***Laia***

Creo que las redes sociales son útiles para comunicarse y hacer amigos. Para mí, no son una pérdida de tiempo porque suelo usarlas para participar en la comunidad y en la sociedad en general. También, muchos famosos las usan para mandar mensajes positivos a sus seguidores. ***Rosario***

Ventajas	Desventajas
son esenciales	son una gran distracción

tener cuidado	*to be careful*
la pérdida de tiempo	*a waste of time*

Escuchar 5 **Listen. For each bullet point, note down <u>two</u> details for each speaker. (1–6)**

- advantages of social media
- disadvantages of social media

G

Use ***para*** to mean '**for …-ing**' or '**in order to**'.
It is always followed by an <u>infinitive</u> if you are using a verb.
La tecnología es importante para *<u>estar</u> en contacto.*
Technology is important **for** being in touch.
*Las uso **para** <u>compartir</u> fotos.*
I use them **in order to** <u>share</u> photos.

Page 73

Hablar 6 **In pairs, practise saying the words ending in *-ión*. Remember to pronounce the words ending in *-ción* with a soft *c*. Listen to check your pronunciation.**

adicción, discriminación, opinión, información, comunicación, protección, presión, relación

Hablar 7 **In pairs, practise the questions and answers in the grid about technology and social media. Then write a paragraph with your own opinions. You can look at exercise 4 for more ideas.**

G

Interesar and ***preocupar*** are used in the same way as ***gustar*** and ***encantar***. They are used in the third person singular and plural forms.

Page 72

¿Qué piensas de la tecnología y las redes sociales?

¿Para qué usaste la tecnología la semana pasada?

¿Qué es lo bueno/malo de las redes sociales?

Creo que Pienso que	es/son … útil(es)/ importante(es) para	estar en contacto con … buscar información sobre … compartir vídeos …
Me interesa(n)	mi futuro. la música. mis derechos. las noticias.	
La(s) usé para Usé [TikTok] para	escuchar/ver / charlar con / jugar a …	
Lo bueno es que puedes	divertirte/expresarte / comunicarte con …	
Lo malo es que causan	problemas para dormir. acoso/adicción/presión.	

5 Necesito ayuda, ¿qué puedo hacer?

- Talking about problems and giving advice
- Using *estar* to express moods
- Using *podrías* and *deberías* + infinitive

Leer 1 **Read the texts. What do the phrases in purple mean in English?**

www.problemasyconflictos.com

Tengo 15 años y mi problema es que no me relaciono con nadie y **me siento diferente**. **Solo soy feliz** cuando estoy con mi madre. **Tengo vergüenza** y me siento muy mal cuando tengo que ir al instituto. Pienso que todos **se ríen de mí**. ¿Qué puedo hacer? **Virginia**

No me llevo bien con mi padre y **discuto mucho con él**. Es muy negativo y **siempre está enojado**. **Nunca está contento** con mi comportamiento y, cuando cometo algún error, no me perdona. Tampoco me apoya cuando necesito ayuda y siempre me critica. ¿Cómo puedo mejorar mi relación con él? **Roberto**

Mi hermano menor no tiene amigos desde hace dos años. **Se siente solo** y **está muy triste**. No sale nunca. Está todo el tiempo en su cuarto viendo la televisión, jugando a los videojuegos y usando las redes sociales. **Estoy muy preocupado** porque veo que sufre soledad.¿Cómo puedo ayudarle? **Diego**

¡Ayuda! No me llevo bien con mi mejor amiga. Sale con un chico desde hace un mes y ahora **nunca se relaciona conmigo**. Ignora todos mis mensajes y no me invitó a su cumpleaños. Soy soltera y **estoy muy sola y triste**. **Laura**

Watch out for negatives like ***nunca***, ***nada***, ***nadie*** and ***tampoco***. Sometimes the negative comes after the verb as a 'sandwich' with ***no*** before the verb. Other times it comes at the beginning of the whole sentence.

No *me relaciono con* ***nadie***.	I **don't** interact with **anyone**.
No *sale* ***nada***.	He/She **doesn't** go out **at all**.
Nunca *se relaciona conmigo*.	He/She **never** interacts with me.
Tampoco *me apoya*.	**Nor** does he/she support me.

G Use the verb ***estar*** when talking about **feelings**, **emotions** and **mood**.

Estoy *contento/a*. **I'm** happy.
Está *enojado/a*. **He/She is** angry.

Page 73

Leer 2 **Read and match each piece of advice to the correct photo.**

a

b

c

d
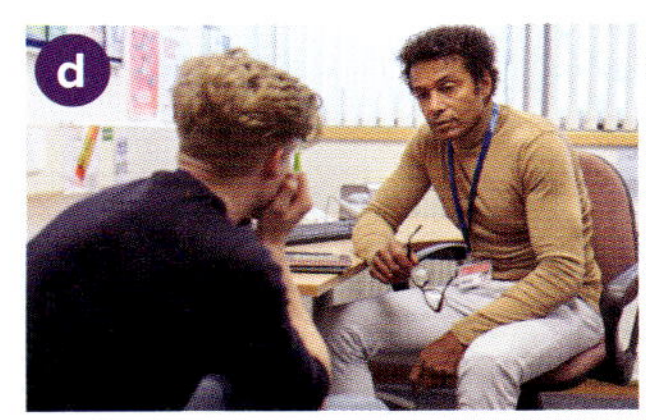

1 **Deberías** buscar ayuda profesional. Tienes que ser fuerte. Poco a poco **podrías** cambiar cómo te sientes y encontrar amigos.

2 **Podrías** sentarte para hablar con él en un ambiente tranquilo. **Deberías** explicarle cómo te sientes y tus deseos de llevarte mejor con él.

3 **Podrías** hablar con ella cara a cara. La comunicación en persona es importante. **Deberías** expresar tus sentimientos sobre la situación.

4 **Deberías** ayudarle a cambiar de costumbres. **Podrías** organizar actividades divertidas fuera de casa y pasar tiempo juntos.

Hablar 3 **Choose one person from exercise 1 and read out the problem to your partner. Your partner then chooses two pieces of advice to give you, using exercise 2 for help.**

G Use ***deberías*** (you should) and ***podrías*** (you could) followed by the infinitive to give advice or suggestions.

Deberías *buscar ayuda profesional*.
You should seek professional help.
Podrías *explicarle cómo te sientes*.
You could explain to him/her how you feel.

Escuchar 4

Read the survey results. Then listen and write the two problems each person mentions. (1–5)

La voz de los jóvenes

¿Cuáles son los principales puntos de conflicto y de preocupación para los jóvenes de hoy? Aquí tienes el resultado de un informe con la lista de problemas que sufren:

1. Problemas con los estudios
2. Las relaciones con los amigos y los novios / las novias
3. El acoso en la escuela y/o por Internet
4. La obsesión con el aspecto físico y el cuerpo
5. Problemas en las relaciones familiares
6. La presión social o de grupo
7. La adicción a las redes sociales
8. El futuro del planeta
9. La violencia en el hogar
10. La discriminación

Leer 5

Read the texts and complete the sentences below in English.

Consejos de un experto

El acoso por Internet es un problema serio que afecta a muchos jóvenes. Si eres víctima de acoso online, es importante hablar con alguien de confianza, como tus padres, un buen amigo o un profesor. Además, es necesario tomar medidas para proteger tu privacidad en la red y no compartir nunca información personal online ni tu contraseña porque te pueden robar tu identidad.

El uso excesivo y sin control de la tecnología y las redes sociales puede causar adicción entre los jóvenes, lo que puede tener efectos negativos en su salud física y emocional. Los jóvenes que sufren este problema pasan mucho tiempo pensando en el móvil y en las redes sociales, mirando y enviando mensajes. Como consecuencia, no estudian ni hacen los deberes y se pelean con sus padres. Para evitar esto, es importante limitar el tiempo online y crear nuevas costumbres.

1. If you are being bullied online, it is important …
2. Examples of people who can help you are …
3. The advice given is to take measures to … and never to …
4. Young people who experience this problem …
5. Two consequences of this problem are …
6. Two pieces of advice to avoid this are … and …

Escuchar 6

Listen and fill in the gaps with the correct word(s) in Spanish. Practise reading out the text to a partner. Then translate the text into English.

Problema

No **a** bien con mis padres y **b** relación es bastante mala. **c** mucho con ellos porque son demasiado estrictos, entonces en mi casa no hay buen ambiente familiar. Nunca **d**, tampoco me entienden y siempre me están criticando. **e** que mis amigos son una mala influencia y no les gusta su comportamiento. Me siento mal y **f** muy triste.

Consejo

Deberías hablar con ellos para explicarles cómo te sientes. Podrías expresar tus sentimientos sobre la situación. Si esto no funciona, deberías **g** ayuda profesional para **h** a tu familia. Con el tiempo todo es posible.

- reflexive verb (a)
- *te* and *me* pronouns (d)
- stem-changing verb (e)
- possessive adjective (b)
- *estar* with mood (f)
- verb in the infinitive (g, h)

el ambiente familiar *family atmosphere*

Escribir 7

Write an imaginary problem in Spanish for an online forum. Then write the advice received, using exercises 1 and 2 for ideas.

6 Celebraciones

- Talking about family celebrations
- Using indirect object pronouns
- Using a range of preterite tense verb forms

Escuchar 1 **Listen and read. For each person write down in English:**

a the special occasion **b** where they went **c** one thing they did

Anoche fui a la cama muy tarde porque fue **Nochevieja**. Fuimos a casa de mis tíos y nos cocinaron una cena muy rica. Después, a las doce, salimos a la calle donde vimos los fuegos artificiales. ¡Y claro que tomamos doce uvas para tener suerte durante todo el año!

Ayer fue el día de San David, y por eso fue **el santo de mi hermanito** (porque se llama David). Le preparé su desayuno favorito, le dimos unos regalitos y luego todos fuimos al cine juntos. También le diseñé una tarjeta especial.

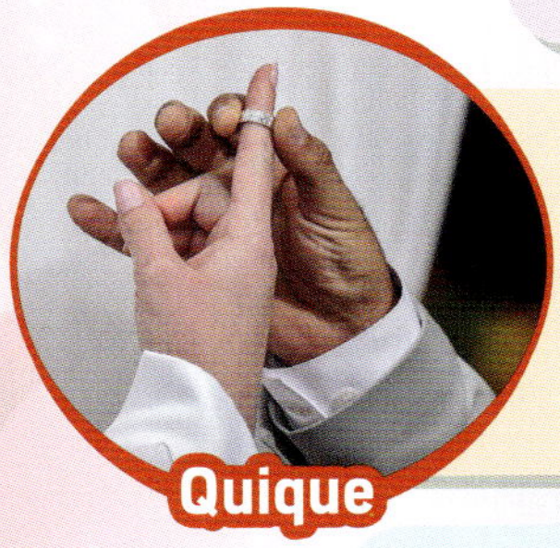

El domingo fui a la sinagoga para **la boda de mi vecina**. Los novios intercambiaron anillos de oro y luego el novio rompió un vaso en el suelo (una costumbre de las bodas judías). Más tarde, en la fiesta, levantamos a los novios, ¡mientras estaban sentados en sus sillas!

Anoche toda la familia se reunió para una ocasión muy especial: **las bodas de oro de mis abuelos**. Les organicé una fiesta sorpresa en un restaurante chino para celebrar los cincuenta años de matrimonio y a mi abuelita le regalamos un vestido. Le encantó.

el santo	*saint's day / name day*
el/la vecino/a	*neighbour*

Leer 2 **Read the texts again. Find the Spanish for the phrases below.**

1 I designed a special card for him
2 we gave my grandma a dress as a gift
3 whilst they were seated
4 we went out into the street
5 I organised a surprise party for them
6 they cooked us a very tasty meal
7 we gave him some little gifts
8 (they) exchanged gold rings

G

Direct object pronouns (*me, te, lo, la, nos, os, los, las*) replace a person or thing which has already been mentioned. They usually come before the verb.

*Rompió **el vaso**. **Lo** rompió.* He broke the glass. He broke **it**.

Indirect object pronouns (*me, te, le, nos, os, les*) are used where the English pronoun may use a preposition such as 'to' or 'for'.

***Le** di un regalo.* I gave **him/her** a gift. / I gave a gift **to him/her**.

***Nos** cocinó la cena.* He/She cooked **us** dinner. / He/She cooked dinner **for us**.

Find more information on direct and indirect object pronouns in Modules 3 (p.61) and 4 (p.86).

Leer 3 **Complete each column with three preterite tense verbs from the texts. Then translate one text into English.**

I	he/she/it	we	they
compre			

The suffix *-**ito**/-**ita*** can be added to some nouns to mean 'little', or to express affection.
If the word ends in *-o/-a*, remove it first.
*un regal**ito*** (a little gift) *mi abuel**ita*** (my gran)

Escuchar 4 **Listen and write positive (P), negative (N) or positive and negative (P+N) for each heading. Then listen again and write down <u>three</u> other details in English. (1–4)**

1 **a** the day **b** the gifts
2 **a** the venues **b** the food
3 **a** the fireworks **b** the party
4 **a** the surprise **b** the gifts

Hablar 5 **In pairs, talk about a recent special occasion. Add opinions.**

- *<u>En junio</u> fue <u>mi</u>… / <u>la boda de mi</u>…*
- *¿Adónde fuiste?*
- *Fuimos a… Fue…*
- *¿Qué recibiste? / ¿Qué le regalaste?*
- *Recibí… / Le regalé…*

Ayer Anoche En [abril]	fui fuimos	a un restaurante a la sinagoga a la mezquita	a un hotel a la iglesia al templo
para celebrar porque fue		mi (santo) Nochevieja el Día del Padre / el Día de la Madre	la boda de… el cumpleaños de…
Soy / Es Fui a una boda		católic**o**/**a**. cristian**o**/**a**. musulm**án**/musulm**ana**.	judí**o**/**a**. civil
Mi madre/padre me compró / regaló Mis amigos me compraron / regalaron También recibí		ropa. vino. flores.	caramelos. un diario. un librito.
Le(s) di / cociné / compré / organicé / preparé / regalé…			

Leer 6 **Read the text and write the correct letter for each gap. Then correct the factual mistakes in the statements below.**

Celebrando en casa y en la calle

En los países hispanohablantes, muchas de las celebraciones más importantes tienen un carácter religioso.

En marzo o abril, **1** destaca por sus desfiles donde un grupo de personas lleva 'pasos', imágenes de madera con escenas religiosas. **Andan despacio** porque los pasos son muy pesados, y son acompañados por bandas musicales. Es una ocasión seria porque **nos recuerda la muerte de Jesús**, aunque también expresa **la alegría que los católicos sienten** por su resurrección.

El 24 de diciembre es **2**, cuando las familias suelen reunirse para una cena especial. A medianoche, mucha gente va a la iglesia. Al día siguiente es **3**, cuando celebramos el nacimiento del bebé Jesús. Pasamos el día **con nuestros familiares** y los niños juegan con **sus nuevos juguetes**. En algunas partes de Sudamérica es común ir a la playa ya que es verano.

Sin duda, una fecha clave es el 6 de enero, **4**, cuando celebramos la llegada de los tres Reyes Magos a Belén. Quizás la parte más divertida es **la noche anterior**, el 5 de enero, cuando hay un desfile animado por el pueblo. Tres personas, llevando un disfraz de 'rey', pasan por las calles y **tiran caramelos que los niños recogen**.

un paso

los Reyes Magos

pesado/a	*heavy*
destacar por	*to stand out because of*
quizás	*perhaps/maybe*

A el día de Navidad
B el día de Reyes
C Semana Santa
D Nochebuena

1 The *pasos* (religious images) are made of gold.
2 Easter parades take place in silence.
3 On Christmas Eve families have breakfast together.
4 On Christmas Day many people go to church at midnight.
5 In Spain, many people spend Christmas on the beach.
6 The 'Three Kings' throw little toys for children to pick up.

Hablar 7 **Read the text again and translate the phrases in bold into English. Then, in pairs, read aloud <u>one</u> paragraph, paying attention to stress patterns.**

Escribir 8 **Write a paragraph about a recent family celebration. Mention:**

- which occasion you celebrated / when
- what you did / where you went
- what gifts/cards you gave/received
- why family celebrations are important.

Use **correct stress patterns** when reading aloud. Stress any vowel with a written accent *(be<u>bé</u>)*.
For other words, stress:
- the second-to-last syllable of words ending in a **vowel** / ***n*** / ***s*** *(ma<u>de</u>ra, <u>pa</u>sos)*
- the final syllable of all other words *(a<u>bril</u>, dis<u>fraz</u>)*

Gramática 1

Possessive adjectives (Zona de cultura, page 57)

Escribir 1 **Read the grammar box on page 57. Use the prompts to fill in the gaps with the correct possessive adjective. Then translate the sentences into English.**

Example: 1 <u>*Nuestros*</u> *padres no son famosos.* <u>*Our*</u> *parents are not famous.*

1 ___ padres no son famosos. (*our*)
2 ¿Qué te gusta hacer con ___ hermanos? (*your, singular*)
3 ¿Cómo es ___ familia? (*your, plural*)
4 ___ familia es pequeña. (*our*)
5 ___ abuelos viven en México. (*her*)
6 Alejandra y Sergio son ___ tíos. (*my*)
7 Valeria, ¿cómo es ___ familia? (*your, singular*)
8 ___ hermano mayor se llama Javier. (*his*)

The present continuous tense (Unit 1, page 58)

Escuchar 2 **Read the grammar box on page 58. Listen to <u>six</u> sentences about what people are doing. Write down the letter of the correct picture. Listen again and write down the present continuous form you hear. Then translate the sentences into English. (1–6)**

Example: 1 *c – está cocinando – he's cooking*

a

b

c

d
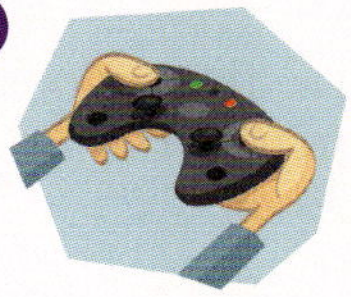
e

f

Ser and *estar* (Unit 1, page 58)

Escribir 3 **Complete each sentence with the correct form of *ser* or *estar*. Then translate them into English.**

1 En esta foto, mis tíos y mis primos ___ en el jardín de su casa.
2 Tengo el pelo largo y ___ bastante baja.
3 Mi hermana mayor ___ rubia y tiene los ojos azules.
4 En la foto, hay una familia que ___ en el salón de su casa viendo una película.
5 Aquí, mi familia y yo ___ en la cocina comiendo.
6 En la foto, yo ___ en el instituto con mis amigos.
7 Mis padres ___ altos y morenos.
8 No me parezco nada a mis hermanos. Ellos y yo ___ muy diferentes.

The verbs ***ser*** and ***estar*** mean 'to be' but are used to express different things in Spanish. ***Ser*** has an irregular pattern in the present tense. Remember that the first person of ***estar*** is also irregular.

Use ***ser*** + <u>adjective</u> for descriptions.

Mi tía ***es*** <u>*alta*</u> *y* <u>*simpática*</u>. My aunt **is** <u>tall</u> and <u>nice</u>.
Mis primos ***son*** <u>*bajos*</u>. My cousins **are** <u>short</u>.

Use ***estar*** when talking about location.

El perro ***está*** *en el jardín.* The dog **is** in the garden.

You also use ***estar*** to talk about feelings, emotions and your mood.

Estoy *contento/a.* **I'm** happy.
Está *triste.* **He/She is** sad.

Can you complete the missing verbs in this table?

	ser (*to be*)	**estar** (*to be*)	**tener** (*to have*)
(yo)	**soy**	4	7
(tú)	1	est**ás**	8
(él/ella/usted)	2	est**á**	ti**e**n**e**
(nosotros/as)	**somos**	5	9
(vosotros/as)	**sois**	6	ten**éis**
(ellos/ellas/ustedes)	3	est**án**	ti**e**n**en**

Hablar 4 **In pairs, imagine this is a photo of your family. Create a dialogue using the questions and the prompts provided in the table. Make up the details for the eyes and remember to make the adjectives agree.**

- *¿Quiénes son las personas de la foto?*
- *Las personas de la foto son …*
- *¿Dónde está/están en la foto?*
- *Está/Están en …*
- *¿Qué está haciendo tu padre/madre/hermano …?*
- *Mi padre está …*
- *¿Cómo tiene el pelo tu padre/madre/hermano …?*
- *Tiene el pelo …*
- *¿De qué color tiene los ojos?*
- *Tiene los ojos …*

People	Actions
mi hermano/a menor/mayor … mi padre / mi madre …	escuchar/comer/beber/hacer/hablar/trabajar/ sonreír/mandar/hablar/charlar/jugar …

Desde hace + period of time (Unit 2, page 60)

Escuchar 5 **Listen to six people talking about different activities. Correct the underlined words in the Spanish sentences. (1–6)**

Example: 1 *pop / Spotify*

1 Escucho música rap desde hace tres años en YouTube.
2 Toco el violín desde hace cinco meses.
3 Mis amigos y yo seguimos canales de ciencias desde hace un año en el insti.
4 Mi hermano sigue a *streamers* como Shakira y Bizarrap desde hace semanas.
5 Mis padres hacen *podcasts* sobre política desde hace años.
6 Mi prima es aficionada al fútbol desde hace poco tiempo.

los canales	*channels*

To say how long you've been doing something use ***desde hace*** + period of time and the **present tense** of the verb.

Escucho *reguetón* ***desde hace*** *dos años.*

I've listened to/been listening to reguetón **for** two years.

Remember that when you are translating, the equivalent in English for ***desde hace*** is 'for' + amount of time. This structure can go either at the end of the whole sentence or at the very beginning, before the verb. e.g. *Desde hace dos años escucho reguetón.*

Escribir 6 **Translate the following sentences into Spanish.**

1 My friend has been listening to music channels on TikTok for months.
2 My sisters have been following famous singers and celebrities for two years.
3 He has played the piano for seven years.
4 I have been a basketball fan for a long time.

Personal *a* (Unit 2, page 60)

Escribir 7 **Refer to the grammar box on page 60. Read the sentences and identify the ones that need a personal *a* and write them out in full. Then create your own four sentences: two that need a personal *a*, and two that don't.**

1 Admiro mi abuela porque es una persona optimista.
2 Sigo canales de viajes desde hace un mes porque son interesantes.
3 Sigo mis cantantes favoritos en YouTube desde hace mucho tiempo.
4 Admiro Marcus Rashford porque es un buen modelo a seguir.
5 Sigo videotutoriales de cocina para aprender a cocinar platos ricos desde hace un año.
6 Sigo mi youtubero favorito porque sus sesiones de videojuegos en vivo son emocionantes.

Gramática 2

Reflexive verbs for relationships (Unit 3, page 62)

Some verbs for describing relationships are **reflexive** in Spanish. Watch out for those that are also stem-changing in the present tense, such as ***sentirse***.

Present tense	**pelearse** (*to argue/fight*)	**sentirse** → ie (*to feel*)
(yo)	**me** peleo	**me** siento
(tú)	**te** peleas	**te** sientes
(él/ella/usted)	**se** pelea	**se** siente
(nosotros/as)	**nos** peleamos	**nos** sentimos
(vosotros/as)	**os** peleáis	**os** sentís
(ellos/ellas/ustedes)	**se** pelean	**se** sienten

Other reflexive verbs include:
llevarse (to get on)
relacionarse (con) (to relate to / interact with)
casarse (con) (to get married to)
separarse (to separate)
reírse → i (to laugh)
divertirse → ie (to have fun)

Escribir 1

Translate these sentences into Spanish.

Example: 1 *Mi padre y yo no nos ...*

1. My father and I don't get on well and we argue a lot.
2. I get on very well with my best friend. We never argue.
3. I relax with my family when I go on holiday.
4. I feel good when I'm with my friends because we have a lot of fun.
5. Friendship is important for me and I relate well to all my friends.
6. I have a lot of fun with my friends because we laugh a lot when we are together.

Verbs of opinion: *me interesa(n) / me preocupa(n)* (Unit 4, page 65)

Escribir 2

Use the prompts to fill in the gaps with the verb and pronoun. Check for clues such as singular/plural nouns. Then translate the sentences into English.

Example: 1

1. Me preocupa la falta de paz en nuestro mundo. (*yo, preocupar*)
2. A los jóvenes ___ ___ las redes sociales porque son divertidas. (*ellos, interesar*)
3. ¿___ ___ tu educación? (*tú, importar*)
4. A mi hermano ___ ___ mucho el futuro de nuestro planeta. (*él, preocupar*)
5. ¿___ ___ los problemas del mundo? (*vosotros, importar*)
6. A los padres y a los profesores ___ ___ el acoso y la adicción a las redes sociales. (*ellos, preocupar*)

To say what interests you or worries you, use ***interesar***, ***preocupar*** or ***importar***.

These verbs work like ***gustar/encantar*** and use singular/plural forms, and the definite article (or a possessive adjective like *mi/mis*).

*Me interesa **la** lectura.*
I'm interested in reading.

*Me importan **los** derechos de los animales.*
I'm worried about animal rights.

*Me interesa**n** **la** música **y** **el** deporte.*
I'm interested in music and sport.

Remember to add '***a***' when talking about someone else like your brother, sister or friend.
***A** mi hermana **le** preocupa la situación.*
My sister is worried about the situation.

Remember to change the **pronoun**:

me *interesa*	***nos*** *interesa*
te *interesa*	***os*** *interesa*
le *interesa*	***les*** *interesa*

Para + infinitive (Unit 4, page 65)

Escribir 3 **Refer to the grammar box on page 65. Then translate these sentences into Spanish.**

Example: 1 *Las redes sociales son buenas para ...*

1 Social media is good for communicating with other people.
2 I use social media to follow famous people.
3 Some people use social media to send negative messages.
4 Yesterday I used Snapchat to watch funny videos with my friends.
5 Some people use social media to present a false image.
6 I think social media is good for reading and seeing what's happening in the world.

Estar to express feelings, emotions and moods (Unit 5, page 66)

Escribir 4 **Write the <u>six</u> short sentences contained in the word box to reveal the full conjugation of *estar* in the present tense. Write down the letter of the matching picture and then translate each sentence into English.**

Example: estoy contento – c – I am happy

a

b

c

d

e

f

estoy contenta
estás triste
está enojado
estamos cansados
estáis enamorados
están nerviosos

¡En marcha! (Units 1–5)

Escuchar 5 **Read the text and fill in the gaps. Then listen to check your answers.**

Problemas y conflictos

a **1** tímido y nuevo en el instituto, por eso no **2** amigos. Siempre estoy aburrido y triste. ¿Qué puedo hacer?

b Estoy muy cansado porque no puedo dormir por la noche desde **3** meses. Paso horas en las redes sociales, ¡son mi vida!

c Algunos estudiantes del instituto **4** ignoran, dicen cosas malas sobre mí y se ríen cuando me ven. ¡Ayuda, por favor!

d **5** muy triste porque me **6** el futuro de nuestro planeta. Hay muchos problemas serios. ¿Cómo puedo ayudar?

e A mi madre **7** preocupa mi actitud. Siempre **8** enojada conmigo y me grita todo el tiempo. ¿Cómo puedo llevarme bien con ella?

f Ahora no estudio ni hago los deberes porque siempre estoy **9** a los videojuegos. **10** peleo con mis padres porque ¡no están nada contentos con mi actitud!

Reading

Leer 1

Problems and advice. **Read this article about the main problems facing young people. Answer the questions in English.**

Antes, muchos jóvenes no usaban tanto las redes sociales porque no tenían móviles. Sin embargo, hoy en día la mayoría tiene su propio móvil y las usa más, lo que está causando un aumento del acoso en las escuelas y online. Además, la situación es más seria ahora porque los jóvenes no quieren hablar con sus profesores para resolver sus problemas.

¿Qué podrías hacer si eres víctima del acoso? Lo más importante es hablar con alguien de confianza, por ejemplo, con tus padres o con un buen amigo. Todos los profesores deberían explicarte cómo puedes conseguir ayuda profesional. Uno de los expertos que te puede ayudar es un ***orientador*** o psicólogo.

un aumento *an increase*

1 What change in the use of technology is causing an increase in bullying?
2 What else is making the problem worse nowadays?
3 What is the most important thing to do if you are a victim of bullying?
4 What should teachers do to help you?
5 What is a ***orientador***?
A an activity **B** a person **C** a place

Be careful – questions that contain 'most' or 'biggest' will always have similar, plausible distractors. Make sure you pick 'the most' or 'the biggest' as your answer.

This is an example of an 'inference' question. It requires you to look at the **context** of the rest of the sentence to help you work out the meaning of a word you haven't seen before.

Leer 2

Celebrity culture. **You see a blog post where four people talk about celebrities. What opinion do they express?**

Write down **P** for a positive opinion.
Write down **N** for a negative opinion.
Write down **P+N** for a positive and negative opinion.

Vicente
Sigo al cantante Álvaro Soler desde hace tres años en Instagram. Ayuda mucho a nuevos artistas, por eso me parece que es un buen modelo de comportamiento.

Fátima
Salma Paralluelo nació en España en el 2003. La razón principal por la cual creo que es una buena influencia es porque está cambiando la imagen del fútbol.

Paula
Aunque muchos deportistas usan Internet para promover cambios positivos en el mundo, hay algunos deportistas que dan una mala imagen por cómo se comportan en su vida privada. Beben demasiado o se pelean con otras personas.

Juan
Hay jóvenes que no saben que muchos blogs no son reales. En mi opinión, hay demasiados influencers que crean una imagen completamente falsa de su vida.

la razón *the reason*

Read the whole sentence before deciding if something is positive, negative, or positive and negative. Information later on in the sentence might change your mind.

Leer 3

Personal problems. **Translate the following sentences into English.**

Pay close attention to the person of the verb.

1 En la clase de la próxima semana, vamos a charlar sobre nuestros problemas.
2 Después de tener muchos problemas personales, mi amigo buscó ayuda profesional.
3 No veo a mis amigos desde hace mucho tiempo.
4 Si hablas con alguien cara a cara, podrías cambiar cómo te sientes.
5 Mis amigos están organizando una fiesta para promover cambios positivos en el instituto.

English word order is different for adjectives and nouns. Ensure you use the correct word order in your translation.

How do you translate '*desde hace*' + present tense into English?

Watch out for accents that change the meaning of words.

Think about how to translate this sentence into English to avoid a word-for-word translation.

Listening

Escuchar 1

A radio interview. **The presenter is talking about items that are going to be on today's show. What does the presenter say? Write down the correct letter.**

1 The parents think that …
 A it's important to discuss issues with their children.
 B famous people's bad behaviour has a negative impact.
 C many famous people have family problems.

2 The young person believes …
 A most celebrities behave well.
 B social media is addictive / all celebrities use social media.
 C some celebrities give good advice.

3 Listeners will share their opinions on the consequences of …
 A social media use.
 B a lack of a private life.
 C poor behaviour.

4 The show will start with a chat about …
 A the world of cinema.
 B global problems.
 C positive internet use.

During the reading time before you hear the recording, ensure you read the options presented carefully. Think about vocabulary you might hear that could point you to the correct answer.

Escuchar 2

Relationships. **Two Spanish people give their views on relationships. Answer the questions in English.**

1 What does the first speaker want to do in the future?
2 What makes it easier to solve family problems?
3 What does the speaker want?
4 Why does the speaker have problems with her parents?

Check the question word being used and always ensure your response answers the question you are asked.

Escuchar 3

You will hear <u>five</u> short sentences. Listen carefully and, using your knowledge of Spanish sounds, write down in Spanish exactly what you hear for each sentence.

You will hear each sentence three times: the first time as a full sentence, the second time in short sections and the third time as a full sentence again. Check your sentences for correct spelling.

Módulo 3

Prueba oral

Role play

Hablar 1 **Look at the role play card and prepare what you are going to say.**

You are talking to your Spanish friend about friendship and free time.
Your teacher will play the part of your friend and will speak first.
You should address your friend as *tú*.
When you see this – **?** – you will have to ask a question.
You must include at least one verb in your response to each point.

Task:

1. Say what you did yesterday with your friends. (Give two details.)
2. Say who your favourite celebrity is and why. (Say who and give one reason.)
3. Say what your relationship is like with your friends and why. (Give one opinion and one reason.)
4. Give an opinion about cinema.
5. **?** Ask your friend a question about free-time activities.

Remember to use the preterite tense.

This is a two-part task – don't forget to give the reason!

Use a reflexive verb to describe the relationship, and don't forget to say why.

An opinion could be any positive or negative adjective, such as 'boring', 'fun', 'exciting' …

You could ask your friend what they do in their free time.

Hablar 2 **Practise your role play answers. Listen and respond to the questions.**

Escuchar 3 **Now listen to Max doing the role play task. In English, note down what he says for each of the points on the card, including the question he asks.**

Reading aloud

Hablar 1 **When your teacher/partner asks you, read aloud the following text in Spanish:**

Hay muchos famosos que tienen cuentas en las redes sociales.

Algunas cuentas no son apropiadas.

Había un vídeo de un actor que le gritó a un seguidor.

Al día siguiente, muchas personas compartieron el vídeo.

Sin embargo, hay historias positivas.

Deberías ver la página que creó un cantante para apoyar a jóvenes sin familia.

Pay particular attention to *ce* and *ci*, which start with a 'th' sound.

Remember that *h* in Spanish is silent.

Remember, you can correct yourself whilst reading aloud – it is the final, corrected version that counts.

Escuchar 2 **Listen and check your pronunciation.**

Hablar 3 **Listen to the teacher asking four questions that relate to the topic of identity and relationships with others. Translate each question into English and prepare your own answers in Spanish. Then listen again and respond to the teacher.**

When answering a question, aim for 2–3 sentences per question to ensure you have sufficient development.

Photo card

Escuchar 1 **Look at the two photographs below and read the task. Then listen to Joanna describing the photos.**

1. What does Joanna think the relationship is between the two men?
2. What is one of the men doing?
3. How does Joanna describe the mood of one of the men?
4. What does she say the people are doing in the second photo?

Prepare your own description of the photos.

Your teacher will ask you to talk about the content of these photos. You must include at least one detail about each photo.

After you have described the photos, your teacher will then ask you questions related to **People and lifestyle**.

Remember, you **must** describe both pictures to score full marks. Introduce each photo by using *en la primera foto … en la segunda foto …* to signpost this to an examiner.

Use the present continuous or present tense to say what people are doing.

Hablar 2 **Prepare your own description of the two photos. Then, with a partner, take turns to describe them.**

- *En la primera foto hay …*
- *En la segunda foto hay …*

Escuchar 3 **Now listen to Joanna responding to the second part of the task card and the questions on People and lifestyle. Write down the missing word for each gap. (1–9)**

¿Cómo es un buen amigo o una buena amiga?
Un buen amigo **1** escucharte si tienes problemas. Un buen amigo **2** ser alegre o podría ser **3**, pero creo que la cosa **4** importante es que un buen amigo te escucha y **5** te critica.

¿Qué hiciste para ayudar a un amigo o a una amiga en el pasado?
El **6** pasado, mi amiga Beth discutió con sus **7** porque no les gusta su **8** porque dicen que su novia es **9** y nunca ayuda en casa. Por eso, fuimos a un restaurante **10** comer y hablar sobre el problema.

Escuchar 4 **Listen to Joanna answering more conversation questions. Note down, in English, the <u>three</u> questions she is asked by the teacher. Next, write down the expressions used by Joanna that take the infinitive.**

Hablar 5 **Prepare your own answers to Module 3 questions 1–10 on page 230. Then practise with your partner.**

For questions asking for your opinion, give both sides of the argument to extend your response.

Talk about what other people think to show off your knowledge of verbs and to extend your responses.

Prueba escrita

Translation

Escribir 1

Read the English text and Ahmed's translation of it. Write down the missing word for each gap. (1–8)

I'm interested in searching for information on social media. I am using TikTok to watch videos of famous people. I have known my best friend for ten years. We get on well, but sometimes we fight. If you have problems with your friends, you could talk face-to-face.

Me **1** buscar información en las redes sociales. **2** usando TikTok **3** ver vídeos de los famosos. Conozco **4** mi mejor amiga **5** hace diez años. **6** llevamos bien, pero a veces nos **7**. Si tienes problemas con tus amigos, **8** hablar cara a cara con ellos.

Escribir 2

Translate these sentences into Spanish.

1 Yesterday, I used Facebook to search for information.
2 You should talk to a friend if you have a problem.
3 My brother is using social media, but I prefer to read.
4 I have listened to classical music for three years.
5 My friends and I get on well because we have lots in common.

If you can replace 'to' in a sentence with 'in order to', you must use *para* + infinitive.

90-Word writing task

Escribir 1

Look at the writing task below. Think about the vocabulary you have learned that you could use in your answer:

- **verbs in the present tense** that you could use to talk about activities that you and others do
- **different persons of the verb** to show what others do
- **verbs in the preterite tense** to narrate what you did to help a friend
- **the near future tense** to say what you are going to do this weekend.

Write down three or four ideas for what you could write about.

Write down which tenses you will need to use in your answer for each bullet point.

Spend one minute thinking of useful vocabulary and structures you could use.

Share and compare your ideas with a partner.

You are writing an email to a Spanish friend about technology and relationships.

Write approximately **90** words in **Spanish**. You must include something about each bullet point.

Mention:
- what you usually use technology for
- something you did recently to help a friend
- your plans with your friends or family this weekend.

Leer 2 **Read Zoe's answer to the task. Answer questions 1–5 in the coloured shapes.**

1 Which form of the verb follows *para*? Find three other structures in the text that work in the same way.

2 Remember to use the personal *a* when the object of a verb is a person. Find one further example of the personal *a* in the text.

3 Remember to use the correct reflexive pronoun. Find one more example of a reflexive verb in the text.

4 Contrast two different tenses to show off your knowledge of tenses. How does Zoe do this in her answer for bullet point 2?

5 Use *deberías* + infinitive to give an opinion on what you should do. How does Zoe justify the opinion she gives here?

Suelo usar la tecnología para seguir a los famosos en las redes sociales. Me interesa ver los vídeos que publican sobre sus vidas, pero lo negativo es que a veces los famosos pueden ser malos modelos de comportamiento.

La última vez que vi a mi mejor amiga tuve un problema y nos peleamos. Discutimos sobre el colegio. Sin embargo normalmente puedo contar con ella para todo.

El próximo fin de semana, voy a ir a la costa con mi familia. Creo que deberías pasar tiempo con tu familia porque es importante comunicarte con tus familiares.

Leer 3 **Read Zoe's text again and finish the sentences.**

1 Zoe usually uses technology to …
2 Zoe is interested in …
3 The negative thing is that …
4 Zoe had a problem with her friend and …
5 Normally, she can …
6 Next weekend, Zoe is going …

Escribir 4 **Prepare your own answer to the task.**

- Think about how you can develop your answer for each bullet point.
- Look back at your notes from exercises 1 and 2.
- Look at the 'Challenge checklist' and consider how you can show off your Spanish!
- Write a brief plan and organise your answer into paragraphs.
- Write your answer and then carefully check the accuracy of what you have written.

Challenge checklist

	✓ Past, present and future time frames ✓ Connectives / time phrases / sequencers ✓ Different opinion phrases (e.g. *me interesa, me encanta*)
	✓ Different persons of the verb (e.g. *pueden ser, discutimos*) ✓ A wide range of interesting vocabulary (e.g. *comportamiento, familiares*) ✓ Reflexive verbs to talk about relationships ✓ A variety of structures (e.g. *para* + infinitive)
	✓ Positive/negative phrases (e.g. *lo negativo es que …*) ✓ Phrases with more than one tense ✓ Verbs with an infinitive (e.g. *suelo, puedo, deberías, podrías* + infinitive) ✓ Complex structures (e.g. *la última vez que …*)

Palabras

Key:
bold = this word will appear in higher exams only
* = this word is not on the vocabulary list, but you may use it in your own sentences

¡No hay dos familias iguales! (pages 56–57):

¿Quién es mi familia?	*Who is my family?*
mi(s) / tu(s)	*my / your*
su(s)	*his/her/their*
nuestro/a(s) / vuestro/a(s)	*our / your*
el padre / el padrastro	*father / stepfather*
la madre / la madrastra	*mother / stepmother*
el hermano / el *hermanastro	*brother / stepbrother*
la hermana / la *hermanastra	*sister / stepsister*
el primo / la prima	*(male) cousin / (female) cousin*
los padres / los hermanos	*parents / siblings*
el hijo (único) / la hija (única)	*(only) son / (only) daughter*
el abuelo / la abuela	*grandfather / grandmother*
los abuelos / los *gemelos	*grandparents / twins*
el tío / la tía	*uncle / aunt*
el bebé	*baby*
los miembros de la familia	*members of the family*

Esta es mi gente (pages 58–59):

¿Quién está en la foto?	*Who is in the photo?*
Aquí hay una foto de ...	*Here is a photo of ...*
¿Dónde están?	*Where are they?*
Está / Están ...	*He/She is / They are ...*
en el jardín	*in the garden*
en el salón	*in the living room*
en casa / en la cocina	*at home / in the kitchen*
en su habitación	*in his/her/their room*
al **fondo**	*in the background*
¿Qué están haciendo?	*What are they doing?*
Estoy / Estamos ...	*I am / We are ...*
Está / Están ...	*He/She is / They are ...*
bebiendo / **charlando**	*drinking / chatting*
cocinando / comiendo	*cooking / eating*
escuchando (música) / hablando	*listening (to music) / talking*
haciendo / jugando	*doing / playing*
leyendo / mandando (un mensaje)	*reading / sending (a message)*
sacando (fotos) / sonriendo	*taking (photos) / smiling*
trabajando / viendo	*working / watching*
¿A quién te pareces?	*Who are you like?*
¿Cómo eres?	*What are you like?*
Soy / Es ...	*I am / He/She is ...*
(bastante) alto/a / bajo/a	*(quite) tall / short*
gordo/a	*fat*
moreno/a	*dark-haired, tanned*
rubio/a	*blonde*
más alto/a que yo	*taller than me*
más bajo/a que él/ella	*shorter than him/her*
Somos / Son ...	*We are / They are ...*
bajos/as	*short*
delgados/as	*thin, slim*
¿De qué color tienes los ojos?	*What colour are your eyes?*
¿Cómo tienes el pelo?	*What is your hair like?*
Tengo / Tenemos ...	*I have / We have ...*
Tiene(n) ...	*He/She has / They have ...*
el pelo ...	*... hair*
*castaño / negro	*brown / black*
*rizado / rubio	*curly / blonde*
largo / corto	*long / short*
los ojos ...	*... eyes*
azules / marrones / verdes	*blue / brown / green*
la misma **boca**	*the same mouth*
Llevo / Lleva gafas	*I wear / He/She wears glasses*
¿A quién te pareces de tu familia?	*Who are you like in your family?*
(No) Me parezco (nada) a ...	*I am (not at all) like ...*
(No) Se parece a ...	*He/She is (not) like ...*
nadie de mi/su familia	*anyone in my/his/her family*
mis dos hermanos	*my two siblings*

Mis famosos favoritos (pages 60–61):

¿A qué famosos sigues en las redes sociales?	*Which celebrities do you follow on social media?*
Sigo ...	*I follow ...*
a actores / cantantes latinos	*actors / Latin singers*
a **deportistas**	*sportspeople*
canales de cocina/videojuegos	*cooking/video-games channels*
*vlogs de ...	*... vlogs*
*rutinas / **estilo** de vida / moda	*routines / lifestyle / fashion*
¿**Desde hace** cuánto tiempo?	*For how long?*
Desde hace ...	*For ...*
un mes/año	*a month/year*
meses / (mucho) tiempo	*months / a long time*
¿Por qué te gusta?	*Why do you like it?*
Me gusta porque ...	*I like it because ...*
aprendo mucho	*I learn a lot*
la música es mi vida	*music is my life*
los vídeos son divertidos/ útiles/*virales	*the videos are fun/ useful/viral*
soy **aficionado/a**	*I am a fan ...*
al deporte	*of sport*
a la música **latina**	*of Latin music*
¿Quién es tu persona famosa favorita?	*Who is your favourite celebrity?*
Mi persona famosa favorita es ...	*My favourite celebrity is ...*
Lo/La sigo porque ...	*I follow him/her because he/she ...*
es guapo(a)	*is good-looking*
es fuerte/trabajador(a)	*is strong/hardworking*
tiene mucho **talento**/éxito	*is very talented/successful*
es un buen modelo de comportamiento	*is a good role model*
apoya a otras personas	*supports other people*
da mensajes positivos a ...	*sends positive messages to ...*
El año pasado / Hace dos años ...	*Last year / Two years ago he/she ...*
ganó / **actuó** en...	*won / acted in ...*
jugó en ...	*played in ...*
ayudó a...	*helped ...*

¡Amigos para siempre! (pages 62–63):

¿Cómo es tu relación con tus amigos?	*What is your relationship with your friends like?*
¿Te llevas bien con tus amigos?	*Do you get on well with your friends?*
(No) Me llevo bien con …	*I (don't) get on well with …*
Me divierto mucho con …	*I have lots of fun with …*
Mi mejor amigo/a y yo …	*My best friend and I …*
nos llevamos genial	*get on really well/great*
nos divertimos mucho **juntos/as**	*have lots of fun together*
porque …	*because …*
hacemos muchas cosas **juntos/as**	*we do lots of things together*
puedo **confiar** en él/ella *totalmente	*I can trust him/her totally*
siempre estamos **juntos**	*we are always together*
casi nunca nos peleamos	*we hardly ever fight*
puedo **contar** con él/ella/ ellos/ellas (para todo)	*I can count on him/her/ them (for everything)*
compartimos intereses	*we share interests*

¿Cómo es un buen amigo?	*What is a good friend like?*
¿Cómo te ayuda tu mejor amigo/a?	*How does your best friend help you?*
Mi mejor amigo/a …	*My best friend …*
Un buen amigo / Una buena amiga …	*A good friend …*
te **comprende**	*understands you*
te conoce bien	*knows you well*
te hace **reír**	*makes you laugh*
te respeta / es **fiel**	*respects you / is loyal*
me acepta como soy	*accepts me as I am*
te acepta como eres	*accepts you as you are*
te ayuda cuando tienes problemas	*helps you when you have problems*
te apoya en lo bueno y en lo malo	*supports you in the good and the bad*
te da buenos consejos	*gives you good advice*
no te critica	*does not criticise you*
puede guardar un **secreto**	*can keep a secret*
nunca te dice mentiras	*never tells you lies*

Así soy yo (pages 64–65):

¿Cómo eres?	*What are you like?*
¿Qué es **lo** más importante para ti?	*What is the most import thing to you?*
Para mí, **lo** más importante es/ son …	*For me, the most important thing is …*
mi familia / mi educación	*my family / my education*
la amistad / mi religión	*friendship / my religion*
Las cosas que me interesan/ preocupan son …	*The things that interest/worry me are …*
el amor / la **paz** / mi cultura	*love / peace / my culture*
mis **derechos** / mi identidad	*my rights / my identity*
el futuro del mundo/**planeta**	*the future of the world/planet*
¿Cuáles son tus sueños?	*What are your dreams?*
Mi *objetivo/sueño es …	*My objective/dream is to …*
En el futuro voy a …	*In the future I am going to …*
ser jefe/a (de una compañía)	*be a/the boss (of a company)*
ser rico/a / tener éxito	*be wealthy / be successful*
luchar por un mundo mejor	*fight for a better world*

¿Qué importancia tiene la tecnología en tu vida?	*How important is technology in your life?*
¿Qué es **lo** bueno/**lo** malo de las redes sociales?	*What is the good/bad thing about social media?*
Lo bueno / malo es que …	*The good/bad thing is that …*
causan *adicción/presión/ acoso	*it causes addiction/pressure/ bullying*
causan problemas para dormir	*it causes sleeping problems*
son una gran *distracción	*it is a big distraction*
Las redes sociales son buenas/ útiles para …	*Social media is good/ useful for …*
compartir fotos/vídeos/ideas	*sharing photos/videos/ideas*
buscar información sobre …	*searching for information about …*
estar en contacto con tus amigos	*being in touch with your friends*
participar en la comunidad	*participating in the community*
*expresarse	*expressing yourself*
charlar con …	*chatting with ..*
escuchar / ver …	*listening to / watching …*

Necesito ayuda, ¿qué hago? (pages 66–67):

¿Qué puedo hacer?	*What can I do?*
Mi problema es que …	*My problem is that …*
me siento / estoy …	*I feel / I am …*
diferente / triste / solo/a	*different / sad / alone*
no **me relaciono** con nadie	*I don't interact with anyone*
es muy negativo/a	*he/she is very negative*
me peleo mucho con él/ella	*I fight with him/her a lot*
se ríen de mí	*they laugh at me*
siempre me critica	*he/she is always criticising me*

Deberías / Podrías …	*You should / You could …*
Es importante/necesario …	*It is important/necessary to …*
*limitar el tiempo online	*limit your time online*
organizar actividades	*organise activities*
apoyar a tu familia	*support your family*
buscar ayuda **profesional**	*seek professional help*
expresar tus sentimientos	*express your feelings*
hablar con él/ella/ellos/ ellas **cara a cara**	*speak to him/her/them face to face*

Celebraciones (pages 68–69)

¿Adónde fuiste?	*Where did you go?*
Ayer / Anoche / En [abril]	*Yesterday / Last night / In [April]*
Fui / fuimos	*I went / we went*
a un restaurante/hotel	*to a restaurant/hotel*
a la sinagoga / a la iglesia / a la mezquita / al templo	*to the synagogue / to the church / to the mosque/ to the temple*
para celebrar	*to celebrate*
Nochevieja / el cumpleaños de…	*New Year's Eve / the birthday of…*
el santo / la boda de …	*the saint's day / the wedding of …*
Soy católico/a / cristiano/a / judío/a / musulmán/musulmana	*I'm Catholic / Christian / Jewish / Muslim*

¿Qué recibiste? / ¿Qué le regalaste?	*What did you receive? / What did you give?*
Mi madre/padre me compró/ **regaló** …	*My mother/father bought me/ gave me …*
Mis amigos me compraron / **regalaron** …	*My friends bought me/gave me …*
ropa / caramelos / vino / un **diario** / flores / un *librito	*clothes / sweets / wine / a diary / flowers / a little book*
Le(s) di / **cociné** / compré / organicé / preparé / **regalé** …	*I gave / cooked / bought / organised / prepared / gave him/her/them …*

¡Qué rico!

- Learning about typical foods in Spanish-speaking countries
- Using adjectives of nationality

¡A comer!

La diversidad cultural y geográfica en los países hispanohablantes ofrece muchas opciones de comida rica. De hecho, la comida es muy importante en la cultura de Sudamérica y España. Descubre los platos más conocidos y las bebidas más típicas.

Para el desayuno ...

A las ocho de la mañana

Los chilaquiles son el desayuno **mexicano** más rico, hecho con tortillas de maíz, huevos, queso, tomates y crema.

Beber el té que contiene hojas de *yerba mate* es la costumbre social **argentina** más típica. El mate es una bebida buena.

Para la comida ...

A las dos de la tarde

La paella es el plato **español** de arroz más famoso. Hay muchos tipos: de verduras, carne o pescado. ¡Qué rico!

Los tamales son un plato popular de Sudamérica. Es tradición comer los tamales **cubanos** en las fiestas familiares. Tienen maíz, verduras y carne.

Para la merienda ...

A las cinco y media de la tarde

El chocolate caliente con churros es la merienda **española** más típica, especialmente en invierno. ¡No es muy sano!

El choclo con queso es una comida típica **peruana**. Los ingredientes sencillos son maíz, queso y sal.

Para la cena ...

A las nueve de la noche

El choripán es el bocadillo **argentino** más típico. Tiene pan, carne y salsa chimichurri.

El pastel de choclo es un plato típico **chileno** hecho con maíz. Los chilenos lo comen especialmente en verano. Puede ser dulce o salado.

las tortillas de maíz	*corn (maize) tortillas*
la merienda	*afternoon snack, tea*
la salsa chimichurri	*Chimichurri sauce*
salado/a	*savoury*

Leer **1** **Read the texts and look at the photos. Note down the key food ingredients mentioned for each dish in English.**

Example: Los chilaquiles – tortillas, eggs, cheese, tomatoes, cream

Escribir **2** **Read the texts again. Copy and complete the sentences in Spanish with the country each dish comes from.**

¿De qué país es cada plato?

Example: La paella **es** de ...
Los chilaquiles **son** de ...

México	España	Perú
Chile	Argentina	Cuba

Escribir **3** **Copy and complete the table with the countries from exercise 2. Then write the corresponding adjectives of nationality.**

Country	People
Mexico	los mexicanos

G

Adjectives of nationality do not start with a capital letter in Spanish, unlike countries, which do.
Like all adjectives, they must agree with the noun.
Adjectives of nationality ending in a vowel usually follow the regular pattern:

chilen**o**	chilen**a**	chilen**os**	chilen**as**

Those ending in a consonant follow an irregular pattern:

ending in **-l**	español	español**a**	español**es**	español**as**
ending in **-s**	inglés	ingles**a**	ingles**es**	ingles**as**

Adjectives of nationality can be used to form nouns:
los españoles – Spanish people

Page 94

Escuchar 4 **Listen to some young people talking about food and drink they would like to try. Copy and complete the table in English. (1–3)**

	Food/Drink	Photo	Country	Opinion
1				

la horchata · las arepas · el agua de Jamaica

a

b

Hablar 5 **In pairs, talk about which dish and which drink you would like to try.**

¿Qué plato y qué bebida te gustaría probar?

- *¿Qué plato te gustaría probar?*
- *Me gustaría probar el pastel de choclo porque parece rico y me gustan los pasteles.*
  Sin embargo, no me gustaría probar ... porque no me gusta(n) ...
- *¿Qué bebida te gustaría probar?*
- *...*

c

el pastel	*cake*

Leer 6 **Translate the text into English and then take turns to read it out with your partner. Pay attention to the letters in purple. Then listen to check your pronunciation.**

Bebidas típicas

El champurrado

El **ch**ampu**rr**ado es una de las bebidas más tradi**ci**onales de la **co**cina mexi**ca**na. Los mexi**ca**nos lo toman muy **ca**liente, y po**r** eso es ideal pa**r**a bebe**r**lo en invie**r**no, **cu**ando ha**ce** mucho frío. Pa**r**a ha**ce**rlo de mane**r**a tradi**ci**onal, ne**ce**sitas agua, **ch**o**co**late, ha**r**ina de maíz, azú**car** y **ca**nela.

la harina de maíz	*corn flour*
la canela	*cinnamon*

Hablar 7 **Mystery words. Write <u>two</u> words from the list. Can your partner guess them? Respond *'No, no es correcto'* or *'Sí, es correcto'*. Then close your book and say a word from the list for your partner to transcribe.**

La palabra misteriosa

churros con chocolate · caliente · choripán · choclo con queso · cocina · agua de Jamaica · chilaquiles · arepas · Cuba · horchata · rico · champurrado · azúcar · tradicional

Use these phrases to make your guess:
Pienso que / Creo que / Diría que / Me parece que la palabra misteriosa es ...

- ***ch*** is pronounced like 'ch' in 'chat'
- ***r*** is a soft 'r' pronounced by lightly touching your tongue against the back of your front teeth
- ***rr*** (or ***r*** at the start of a word) has a stronger, rolled sound – a bit like an engine revving!
- ***ce*** and ***ci*** are pronounced like 'th' in 'think' in most of Spain
- ***ca***, ***co*** and ***cu*** are pronounced like 'k', similar to the English word 'cake'

1 ¿Llevas una vida sana?

- Describing healthy daily routines
- Using indefinite adjectives
- Using *tener* + noun

Escuchar 1 **Listen to and read the text. Translate the phrases in purple. Then copy and complete the sentences in English.**

Una rutina sana

Admiro a la atleta venezolana Lisbeli Vera. Me gustaría ser una atleta profesional como ella. Por eso tengo una rutina sana y cuido mi dieta, pero no hago régimen. Por la mañana **me levanto** temprano, a las seis y media. Primero hago diez minutos de ejercicio para empezar el día con energía.

'Lisbeli es mi inspiración en mi vida diaria.'

'Me siento feliz cuando corro.'

Luego **me lavo** y **me visto**. A las siete **tomo un desayuno ligero** porque no tengo mucha hambre. **Normalmente como a la una**. **Suelo comer** una ensalada de tomate y huevo o un bocadillo de jamón y una manzana. **Siempre llevo** una botella de agua para cuando tengo sed porque es la bebida más sana.

Después de terminar las clases, **voy** directamente al estadio para entrenarme. Me entreno de lunes a sábado, aun si llueve. **Antes de empezar a correr**, suelo comer chocolate negro, sin leche. Cuando corro me divierto mucho. **Vuelvo** a casa cansada pero feliz. Nunca fumo cigarrillos y no bebo alcohol.

Mi cena consiste en verduras con pollo o pescado. Evito comer mucha grasa. Por la noche **descanso un poco**. Antes de acostarme, **suelo hacer** meditación para cuidar mi salud mental. Finalmente, **me acuesto** a las diez y media de la noche. ¡Siempre tengo mucho sueño y duermo bien! ***Gabriela***

venezolano/a *Venezuelan*

1. Gabriela would like to be …
2. After getting up in the morning, she …
3. Gabriela's breakfast is … because …
4. She trains … to … even …
5. When she returns home, she is …
6. She usually meditates in order to …
7. She goes to bed at …
8. At the end of the day she's always … and …

G

The expressions ***después de*** and ***antes de*** can be followed by a verb or a noun. When followed by a verb, use the infinitive:

Antes de comer	Before eating
Después de terminar	After finishing

For reflexive verbs, add the correct **reflexive pronoun** to the infinitive:

*Antes de vestir**me***	Before getting (**myself**) dressed
*Después de lavar**te***	After washing (**yourself**)

When followed by a masculine singular noun, remember that ***de* + *el* = *del***.

*Después **del** desayuno*	After breakfast
Antes de la cena	Before dinner

Page 94

Escuchar 2 **Listen. Write the correct time for each person and what they do in English. (1–8)**

Example: 1 *have breakfast – 7.30*

Use ***a* + *la*/*las*** + time to say what time you do something.
*Me levanto **a las** siete menos cuarto de la mañana.*
I get up **at** quarter to seven in the morning.
*Me acuesto **a las** diez y cuarto de la noche.*
I go to bed **at** quarter past ten at night.
Use ***tomar el desayuno* / *la comida* / *la cena*** for 'to have breakfast/lunch/dinner'.

Escribir 3 **Translate the sentences into Spanish.**

1. In summer I'm thirsty.
2. In the morning I'm not very hungry.
3. In the afternoon I'm very sleepy.
4. At night I'm very cold.
5. During the day I'm very hot.
6. I'm always right.

The verb ***tener*** (to have) is sometimes used with a noun where English uses the verb 'to be':

Tengo mucha hambre.	I am very hungry.
Tengo sed.	I am thirsty.
Tienes razón.	You are right.
Tener cuidado	To be careful.
Tengo sueño.	I am sleepy.
Tengo calor/frío.	I am hot/cold.

Escuchar 4

Listen to Quique and Ricardo talking about their typical weekend. Write down the following information for each person in English. (1–2)

- what they do at the weekend (Give two details.)
- two healthy habits
- two unhealthy habits

fumar	*to smoke*
beber alcohol	*to drink alcohol*
el humo	*smoke*
el olor	*smell*

Escuchar 5

Listen again and write down at least four examples of indefinite adjectives and nouns that Quique and Ricardo use. Then translate them into English.

Example:
algunos fines de semana – some weekends

G

Like all adjectives, **indefinite adjectives** agree in number and gender with the noun they modify, except ***cada***, which is invariable. They always come before the noun.

*algun**os**/**as*** (some)	*much**os**/**as*** (many/a lot of)
*mism**os**/**as*** (same)	*demasiad**os**/**as*** (too many)
*otr**os**/**as*** (other)	*tod**os**/**as*** (all/every)

*Tod**os**/**as*** is followed by ***los**/**las***.
*Hago ejercicio **todos los** días.* I exercise **every day**.

Page 95

Hablar 6

In pairs, talk about your routine and habits.

- *¿Cómo es tu día típico?*
- *¿Qué costumbres sanas tienes?*
- *¿Tienes costumbres no saludables?*

- *Durante la semana ..., pero algunos fines de semana ...*
- *Me levanto/acuesto temprano, ...*
- *Pues, todas las tardes ...*

Siempre / A veces / Nunca Todos los días / Algunos fines de semana Todas las tardes / Algunas noches Primero / Luego Durante la semana Finalmente	me levanto me acuesto ceno tomo el desayuno hago deporte	tarde. temprano. a las [nueve]. a la misma hora.

Antes de Después de	levantarme tomar el desayuno comer/beber terminar las clases volver a casa	tomo como bebo	demasiadas bebidas con azúcar. [mucha] agua. algunos/muchos pasteles. algunas/muchas verduras. chocolate/fruta/una naranja/una manzana.
Si tengo hambre, Si tengo sed,			

Escribir 7

Rewrite this article about Kai as if you were the person being interviewed. Then change some details and write five sentences about your own routine.

*Example: Kai **se despierta** muy temprano.* → ***Me despierto** muy tarde.*

Durante la semana, Kai se despierta muy temprano, a las seis y media. Mientras toma el desayuno, mira los mensajes para estar en contacto con sus amigos. Luego va al colegio. Durante el camino escucha música. Come a la una. ¡Siempre tiene mucha hambre!

Por la tarde vuelve a casa y cena a las siete. Después de hacer los deberes, descansa un rato con su familia. Finalmente, se acuesta a las diez porque tiene mucho sueño.

Remember that
- some present tense verbs are irregular in the first person:
  tener → *tengo* *estar* → *estoy*
- you have to change the **pronoun** and **ending** in reflexive verbs:
  se** levant**a → ***me** levant**o***
- you have to change **possessive adjectives**:
  ***su** casa* → ***mi** casa*

2 ¿Somos lo que comemos?

- Talking about mealtimes and food trends
- Using direct object pronouns
- Practising listening skills

Escuchar 1 **Listen to Cecilia talking about her breakfast, lunch and dinner. For each point, write down the following information:**

- meal time
- food and drink
- any extra details

Hablar 2 **In pairs, imagine you are from Spain or Chile. Take turns to discuss mealtimes. Use the information to help you.**

Los horarios de las comidas en el mundo hispanohablante

- *¿De qué nacionalidad eres?*
- *Soy …*
- *¿A qué hora tomas el desayuno?*
- *Normalmente **lo** tomo a las …*
- *¿A qué hora tomas la cena?*
- *Generalmente **la** tomo entre las … y las …*

Tomo …	Soy de España 	Soy de Chile 
el desayuno	8.00 – 10.00	7.00 – 9.00
la comida	13.00 – 14.00	14.00 – 15.00
la cena	21.00 – 22.30	20.30 – 22.15

En Chile toman ***la once*** entre las cinco de la tarde y las nueve de la noche.
Es una mezcla de la tradición inglesa del 'té de las cinco' y la tradición española de la merienda.
Los españoles toman la cena a las nueve o las diez de la noche. Sin embargo, los británicos la toman a las seis o las siete de la tarde.

la mezcla *mixture*

G

Direct object pronouns replace the noun that has already been mentioned and avoid repetition. The pronoun agrees with the noun it replaces.

English	Spanish
me	me
you (singular)	te
him/her/it	**lo**/**la**
us	nos
you (plural)	os
them	**los**/**las**

Direct object pronouns:

- go before a conjugated verb.
  ***Lo** comen.* They eat **it**.
- go after a negative word.
  *No **la** toman.* They don't have **it**.
- are attached to the end of an infinitive.
  *Te recomiendo probar**los**.*
  I recommend you try **them**.

Page 96

Leer 3 **Translate the text into English.**

La comida en España y Sudamérica es muy rica y diversa. En general, consiste en una gran variedad de ingredientes frescos como frutas y verduras.
La gente los compra en los mercados y suele prepararlos según la tradición familiar. Además, cada país tiene sus propios platos dulces. En México, la dieta típica consiste en alimentos como maíz, carne y pollo. A los españoles les encanta el pescado y lo comen con frecuencia. Sin embargo, como en otros lugares del mundo, la gente sigue diferentes tipos de dietas según cada gusto. Algunas personas eligen una dieta vegetariana o vegana porque la prefieren.

Leer **4** **Read Guadalupe's food blog post and answer the questions in English.**

www.comidasricas.mx

¿Comer en la calle? ¡Buena idea!

comiendo una quesadilla

La comida callejera en los países hispanohablantes es muy rica y está llena de color. Hay una gran variedad de opciones para disfrutar porque cada país tiene sus platos callejeros únicos. Te recomiendo probarlos en los puestos de comida mientras visitas las calles de cada ciudad. Por ejemplo, en mi país, México, se pueden encontrar *tacos de carne*, *quesadillas* y mucho más. A los mexicanos nos encanta comer en la calle, sobre todo para la cena, porque nos ayuda a ahorrar dinero y suele ser más barato y también es más rápido que comer en un restaurante.

En Argentina, hay que probar *los choripanes* (pan con chorizo). Los argentinos están orgullosos de su plato típico: *el asado de carne*. Cuando fui a España el verano pasado, probé las tapas típicas, que eran muy buenas. Las recomiendo. El pan con tomate, un poco de aceite y jamón estaba muy rico. ¿Te gustaría probarlo? ***Guadalupe Ríos***

la comida callejera	*street food*
el puesto de comida	*food stall*
el asado de carne	*roast meat*
el aceite	*oil*

1. How does Guadalupe describe street food in Spanish-speaking countries?
2. Why are there so many options to enjoy?
3. What does Guadalupe recommend you do and when?
4. What nationality is Guadalupe?
5. What does she say about the people in her country?
6. How do Argentinians feel about their typical dish?

Escuchar **5** **Listen to Claudia talking about her diet. Identify the four correct statements. Then listen again and correct the four incorrect statements.**

el cerebro *brain*

1. Claudia's diet includes fish and eggs.
2. She mentions that eggs are good for your brain.
3. She looks after her health.
4. She likes sweets, and usually has them for dessert.
5. She says that a healthy diet can help prevent illnesses.
6. She has a big breakfast.
7. Her main meal of the day is lunch.
8. She's usually very hungry in the evening.

To identify correct statements, look at each one and decide whether:
1. it gives information that doesn't quite match what you hear. (not correct!)
2. it is talking about something which is simply not mentioned. (not correct!)

Hablar **6** **In pairs, talk about your diet and what you eat.**

- *¿Cómo es tu dieta?*
- *¿Qué hay que hacer para tener una dieta sana?*

(No) Tengo una dieta sana/ equilibrada	porque	soy vegetariano/a. soy vegano/a. a veces como comida rápida/ no saludable. como demasiados pasteles/caramelos.
Mi desayuno/comida/cena consiste en		un plato de ... verduras/carne/ensalada.
Para tener una dieta sana/ saludable	(no) hay que (no) se necesita (no) hace falta	comer comida tradicional/fresca/ rápida. tomar demasiadas bebidas con azúcar. tener cuidado con la dieta.
Es importante tener una dieta sana para		no tener sobrepeso. no sufrir enfermedades.

G These **impersonal verbs** are followed by the infinitive:

hay que	you/one must
se necesita	you/one needs to
hace falta	you/one needs to

Hay que tener una dieta equilibrada.
One must have a balanced diet.

Page 96

Escribir **7** **Find out about a diet or dish from the Spanish-speaking world and write about it.**

- *Es un pastel / un plato típico / una bebida ... Se llama ...*
- *Otros platos típicos de México son ...*
- *Me gustaría probarlo/la/los/las porque ...*
- *La dieta de Chile consiste en ... Normalmente los chilenos comen ...*

3 ¡Los tiempos cambian!

- Comparing old and new habits
- Using the imperfect tense to say what you used to do
- Using *ya no* + verb

Escuchar **1** **Listen and read. Find ten imperfect tense verbs and translate them into English. (1–2)**

Mi vida antes y ahora

Cuando era más pequeño, tenía una dieta sana y equilibrada. También era muy activo y por la mañana me levantaba temprano. Iba a la piscina tres veces a la semana, salía al parque a jugar y montaba en bici cada día. ¡Tenía mucha energía y me gustaban las actividades deportivas! Por el contrario, ahora no hago nada para estar en forma y la comida rápida es mi favorita. Como hamburguesas y patatas fritas, porque ¡siempre tengo hambre! Ya no bebo agua porque prefiero las bebidas con azúcar. En vez de estar al aire libre, estoy sentado en mi cuarto, triste y aburrido. **Roberto**

Antes no tenía energía. Todos los días comía comida poco saludable y bebía demasiado café. Por eso siempre estaba cansada y enferma. Me acostaba tarde porque veía mis series favoritas y, por la mañana, tenía mucho sueño. ¡Necesitaba cambiar de costumbres! Ahora solo como comida sana y fresca, y bebo agua natural. Además, voy al gimnasio a diario para estar en forma. Mi vida actual es más sana y ¡me siento mucho mejor! **Esmeralda**

en vez de *instead of*

Leer **2** **Read the texts again and write the correct name for each question. Then translate Esmeralda's text into English.**

Who ...

1. used to have a very active life?
2. was always tired and sick?
3. was always on the move?
4. only drinks water?
5. is always indoors?
6. doesn't do anything to keep fit?

Escuchar **3** **Listen and fill in the gaps with the correct verb. Then practise reading out the text with a partner.**

Antes no **1** una vida sana. **2** las verduras y el pescado porque **3** asquerosos. Mi dieta no era equilibrada: **4** bastante pan, hamburguesas, arroz, demasiadas patatas fritas y alguna manzana de vez en cuando. Además, me encantaban los pasteles y los caramelos. También me **5** muy tarde. Por eso, al día siguiente **6** siempre cansada. Nunca **7** al gimnasio. Pero un día decidí cambiar mis costumbres no saludables. Ahora **8** más mi dieta y como la mitad de pan y patatas fritas que antes. Ya no **9** comida dulce porque **10** el azúcar. Tengo cuidado con la cantidad de azúcar que tomo a diario ¡y tengo menos estrés! ***Valeria***

G

You have already seen the **imperfect tense** for describing things in the past. It is also used for saying what you used to do.

*Antes **me acostaba** tarde.* Before, **I used to go to bed** late.

	jugar *(to play)*	**comer** *(to eat)*	**salir** *(to go out)*
(yo)	jug**aba**	com**ía**	sal**ía**
(tú)	jug**abas**	com**ías**	sal**ías**
(él/ella/usted)	jug**aba**	com**ía**	sal**ía**
(nosotros/as)	jug**ábamos**	com**íamos**	sal**íamos**
(vosotros/as)	jug**abais**	com**íais**	sal**íais**
(ellos/ellas/ustedes)	jug**aban**	com**ían**	sal**ían**

***-er/-ir* verbs** have the same endings.

Reflexive verbs follow the pattern in the table above: ***me*** *levant**aba***

Only three verbs are irregular in the imperfect tense:

ser (to be) → ***era***, ***eras***, etc.
ir (to go) → ***iba***, ***ibas***, etc.
ver (to see/watch) → ***veía***, ***veías***, etc.

Page 95

Use ***ya no*** + **verb** to talk about what you no longer do or what no longer happens.

Ya no como *comida rápida.* **I no longer eat** fast food.

Escribir 4 **Translate the text into Spanish.**

When I was 8 years old, I never watched television at night because I used to go to bed early at the same time every night. I never had stress. However, now I go to bed later as I have a mobile phone to watch the Spanish series that I like. When I was younger, I used to play more, whereas now I have to do homework and I no longer go to the park to run. Also, before, I used to sleep better and I had a balanced and healthy diet. I had more energy, but now some days I am very sleepy, and I eat too many cakes.

Imperfect tense

Present tense

Ya no + verb

Look back at page 85.

Nationalities – look back at page 82.

Expression with *tener*

Escribir 5 **Write a paragraph about your lifestyle. Mention the things you used to do before, in contrast to what you do now. Include four old habits and four new ones.**

Antes		(no) me levantaba/acostaba	temprano/tarde.
Cuando	era más pequeño/a era más joven tenía [diez] años	(no) tenía una dieta	sana/saludable.
		(no) comía comida	sana/saludable.
		(no) hacía	(mucho/suficiente) ejercicio/deporte.
		(no) tenía	(mucha) energía / (mucho) estrés.
		(no) dormía	bien / mal.
		(no) jugaba/iba/veía ...	
Sin embargo, ahora		me levanto/acuesto ...	
		(ya no) tengo una dieta ...	
		(ya no) como comida ...	
		(no) hago (mucho/suficiente) ...	
		(no) tengo (mucha) energía.	
		(ya no) duermo ...	
		(ya no) juego/voy/veo ...	

Leer 6 **Match the questions with Carlos's replies to find out how his life has changed.**

Cuando era más joven

1 ¿Cómo era tu vida cuando tenías seis años?
2 ¿Qué te gustaba comer y beber?
3 ¿Qué hacías en tu tiempo libre cuando eras pequeño?
4 ¿Cómo eras antes?

Ahora

5 ¿Cómo es tu vida ahora?
6 ¿Qué te gusta comer y beber?
7 ¿Qué haces en tu tiempo libre?
8 ¿Cómo eres ahora?

a Era muy activo y tenía mucha energía. No tenía estrés.
b Me gusta comer comida sana, pero a veces también como pasteles.
c Me acostaba muy pronto y me levantaba muy temprano también.
d Soy bastante activo, pero a veces estoy muy cansado y tengo sueño.
e Me gustaba comer comida dulce cuando tenía hambre y bebía un vaso de leche caliente.
f Hago deporte, voy al cine, escucho música y juego a los videojuegos.
g Jugaba todo el tiempo. También iba al parque y montaba en bicicleta.
h Ya no me levanto temprano como antes. Me acuesto más tarde también.

Carlos

Hablar 7 **In pairs, use the questions from exercise 6 and the vocabulary from exercise 5 to talk about your life when you were a child and now.**

4 ¡Qué mal estoy!

- Talking about illnesses and injuries
- Using reflexive verbs in the preterite tense
- Giving advice using *debes, tienes que* and *necesitas*

Escuchar 1 **Look at the labels for the parts of the body. Listen and use this vocabulary to fill in the gaps in the text with the correct word(s).**

relajarse	*to relax*
visualizar	*to visualise*
la relajación	*relaxation*

Una sesión de relajación

Para comenzar es importante relajarse.

Podemos encontrar una silla cómoda y sentarnos. Primero, empezamos con **1** abiertos y después los cerramos. Es necesario respirar profundo con **2** cerrada, y mantener **3** sobre **4**. Luego, tenemos que poner nuestra atención en **5** derecho e intentar sentirlo. Al mismo tiempo, vamos a intentar visualizarlo con una luz suave.

Después, subimos por **6** derecha y bajamos por la otra hasta el pie izquierdo. Hay que poner atención en cómo se siente cada parte. Ahora empezamos a subir y sentimos **7** y también las manos. Por último, llegamos a **8**, donde sentimos la piel, la boca y **9**. Finalmente, abrimos los ojos. ¿Cómo te sientes después de dos minutos de relajación?

Leer 2 **Read about the different problems and write the correct picture letter for each one.**

me rompí	*I broke*
me corté	*I cut*

1. ¡Estoy fatal! Me duele mucho la cabeza. Me siento débil. Estoy muy enfermo.
2. La semana pasada me rompí el brazo y la pierna cuando me caí de la bici. ¡Qué dolor!
3. Ayer pasé todo el día en la playa y me quemé la piel. ¡Me duele mucho todo el cuerpo! ¡Ay!
4. Estaba preparando la cena y me corté el dedo por accidente. Había mucha sangre. ¡Qué mal!
5. Tengo heridas en los pies porque mis nuevos zapatos son demasiado pequeños. Afortunadamente, no es grave.
6. Ayer comí demasiados pasteles y caramelos y hoy me duelen mucho los dientes.

G

Use the **preterite tense** to say what happened to you.

For reflexive verbs such as *romperse, quemarse* and *cortarse*, put the correct reflexive pronoun before the verb and use the **definite article**.

In English we say 'my leg', but Spanish uses 'the leg'.

***Me** rompí **el** brazo.* I broke **my** arm.

With *caerse* you have to use a **preposition**.

*La semana pasada me caí **de** la bici.*
*Me caí **en** el parque.*

a

b

c

d

e

f

Hablar 3 **In pairs, take turns to choose and read out a problem from exercise 2. Then give advice to help with the problem. Listen to check your pronunciation.**

Debes Tienes que También necesitas	descansar y dormir. ir al médico/hospital. comprar medicinas en la farmacia. quedarte en la cama. beber/tomar agua. evitar el sol. pedir cita con el médico.

Hablar 4 **In pairs, practise reading out the words in the pronunciation box.**

Listen and repeat the sounds and words.
ca – *caí, descansar, cabeza, caramelos, caminar*
co – *comidas, médico, cómoda, costumbre, copa, consumo*
cu – *cultural, cubano, cumpleaños*
cu + vowel – *cuerpo, cuidar, cuidado, cuatro, cuál, me acuesto*

Escuchar 5 **Listen and write the details in English. (1–8)**

- the part of the body that hurts
- the reason

Estoy enfermo/a Me siento mal No me siento bien	porque tengo	dolor de [cabeza]. una herida [en los pies]. el pie roto / la pierna rota.
Me/Te/Le	duele(n)	los pies/ojos.
Ayer La semana pasada	me rompí me quemé me corté	el brazo/pie. la pierna/piel.
Me caí	de la bici / en el parque / en la calle.	

¿Desde cuándo?	
Desde	ayer / esta mañana/tarde. la semana pasada. el [sábado] pasado. el fin de semana pasado.
¿Desde hace cuánto tiempo?	
Desde hace	un día. una hora/semana. más de [dos días].

Escribir 6 **Translate these sentences into Spanish.**

1 I burnt my hand in the kitchen last week. It hurts a lot now.
2 I've had a headache since this morning and I'm not well.
3 I fell off my bike yesterday and now my arm hurts a lot.
4 My mouth has been hurting since Monday.
5 On Sunday I fell in the street. Fortunately, it's not serious.
6 I'm ill. My whole body aches a lot and I feel weak. I need to stay in bed.

G

Doler (to hurt) is a stem-changing verb. It works like ***gustar***.

Te *duel**en** los pies.*	Your feet hurt.
*A mi hermano **le** duel**en** los ojos.*	My brother's eyes ache.

Use ***tengo dolor de*** followed by the part of the body that hurts. Don't use the definite article.
Tengo dolor de cabeza.
My head hurts. / I have a headache.

Page 96

Escuchar 7 **Listen and complete the table in English. Listen again and write down the reason in English. (1–4)**

	What hurts?	What is the advice given?
1	head	go to the hospital immediately / it's urgent

Reason: 1 *fell in the park (yesterday)*

Escuchar 8 **Listen and read. Then create your own dialogue by replacing the underlined words.**

- *¡Ay! ¡Qué mal estoy! Estoy enfermo.*
- *¿Por qué? ¿Qué te pasa?*
- *Tengo <u>dolor de garganta</u>. Además, me duele <u>todo el cuerpo</u>.*
- *¿Desde cuándo estás enfermo/a?*
- *Desde <u>ayer</u>.*
- *Bueno, creo que tienes que <u>quedarte en la cama</u> y también necesitas <u>descansar</u>.*
- *Vale, gracias. Voy a <u>acostarme</u> ahora.*

5 Mi salud, de la cabeza a los pies

- Making future plans for health and wellbeing
- Using the simple future tense
- Using *if* clauses

Leer 1 **Francisco is considering how he will improve his lifestyle. Complete sentences 1–6 with logical future outcomes (a–h). Then listen and compare your answers with Francisco's.**

¿Cómo **cambiarás** tu estilo de vida?

> The simple future tense is used in *if* clauses to say what will happen.
> *Si* + **present** + **simple future**:
> *Si* ***me acuesto*** *más pronto,* ***no estaré*** *cansado/a al día siguiente.*
> If **I go to bed** earlier, **I will not be** tired the next day.

1 Si dejo de comer comida rápida o no saludable, ...

2 Si bebo agua en vez de bebidas con azúcar, ...

3 Si reduzco el tiempo que paso en las redes sociales por la noche, ...

4 Si cada noche duermo al menos ocho horas, ...

5 Si practico más deporte y doy paseos, ...

6 Si practico la meditación, ...

a me sentiré más feliz y tendré menos estrés.
b mi salud física y mental mejorarán.
c mi cuerpo se sentirá mejor.
d evitaré los cambios de humor.
e dormiré mejor y estaré menos cansado.
f no tendré hambre todo el tiempo y evitaré el sobrepeso.
g mis niveles de energía aumentarán.
h me levantaré con más energía al día siguiente.

Escuchar 2 **Listen to these young people talking about their lifestyle. (1–4) For each person write down in English:**

- one bad habit they have
- two things they'll do to improve their lifestyle.

tomar drogas *to take drugs*

Escribir 3 **Translate these sentences into Spanish.**

1. If I do more sport, I will have more energy.
2. If I don't use my mobile at night, I'll sleep better.
3. If I practise meditation, I'll look after my mental health.
4. If I stop eating fast food, I'll have a more balanced diet.
5. If I go to bed earlier, I won't be tired in the morning.
6. If I drink water and have an active life, I will feel happier and avoid mood changes.
7. If I don't smoke, I will feel healthier.

Hablar 4 **In pairs, take turns practising *if* clauses. Start the sentence with an *if* clause. Your partner completes it with a positive outcome.**

- *Si dejo de comer comida no saludable, ...*
- *... tu cuerpo se sentirá mejor.*

G

Use the **simple future tense** to say what you will do or what will happen.
To form the simple future, add the following endings to the infinitive:

	evitar (*to avoid*)
(yo)	evitar**é**
(tú)	evitar**ás**
(él/ella/usted)	evitar**á**
(nosotros/as)	evitar**emos**
(vosotros/as)	evitar**éis**
(ellos/ellas/ustedes)	evitar**án**

Some verbs have an **irregular stem** in the simple future. They include:

tener → ***tendr****é* (I will have)
poner → ***pondr****é* (I will put)
venir → ***vendr****é* (I will come)
hacer → ***har****é* (I will do/make)
decir → ***dir****é* (I will say)
poder → ***podr****é* (I will be able to)
salir → ***saldr****é* (I will go out)
saber → ***sabr****é* (I will know)
querer → ***querr****é* (I will want)

Page 97

Leer 5 **Read Ramiro's lifestyle blog. Answer the questions in English. Then read the text again and write down the verbs that appear in the present, imperfect, preterite and simple future tenses.**

www.mividasana.net

¿Tienes poca energía porque te acuestas tarde? ¿Sobrevives con un montón de café? Yo antes también era como tú. Siempre estaba cansado y no tenía una dieta equilibrada porque no comía comida saludable. Además, me sentía triste porque no cuidaba mi salud mental. Un día decidí cambiar mis malas costumbres, dejé de beber café y mi vida y mi salud empezaron a mejorar. Por eso me gustaría darte algunos consejos.

Si reduces la cantidad de pasteles y comida rápida o no saludable que comes, no tendrás hambre todo el tiempo. ¡Tendrás más energía y evitarás el sobrepeso! Además, si dejas de beber café, te sentirás mejor. Si usas menos el móvil durante la noche, no tendrás sueño al día siguiente. Si evitas fumar y no bebes alcohol, estarás mucho más sano. Yo personalmente no fumo y nunca tomaré drogas. Finalmente, si practicas la meditación tu mente te lo agradecerá. Si sigues estos consejos, mantendrás un estilo de vida más sano y tu salud física y mental mejorarán.

1 What does Ramiro say about his health in the past? (Mention two things.)
2 How did he feel back then? (Give one detail.)
3 When did his life and health start to improve?
4 How will you have more energy, be less hungry and avoid obesity?
5 What will allow you to be less tired?
6 What will happen if you avoid smoking and don't drink alcohol?

Remember that:
- the **present tense** is used to talk about what you normally do: *como, tengo, voy* …
- the **imperfect tense** is used to talk about what you used to do: *estaba, tenía* …
- the **preterite tense** is used to talk about what you did in the past: *empecé, dejé* …
- the **simple future tense** is used to talk about what you will do: *iré, comeré* …

Escuchar 6 **Listen to Tenoch talking about his health and wellbeing. Choose the correct option for each sentence below. (1–6)**

1 Tenoch used to drink **milk** / **cold drinks** / **hot drinks** when he was 11 years old.
2 Sometimes he feels very tired because he **drinks too much coffee** / **studies for his exams** / **doesn't have enough energy**.
3 Now he normally goes to bed **before 10 p.m.** / **before 11 p.m.** / **after 11 p.m.**
4 Tenoch says he will **smoke and drink** / **be more active** / **spend more time in his room** in the future.
5 To sleep better, Tenoch will **reduce his screen time** / **switch off his mobile after 10 p.m.** / **not be addicted to technology**.
6 He thinks it's important to **stay in touch with nature** / **ask for help** / **share how you feel**.

apagar *to switch off*

Hablar 7 **In pairs, take turns to ask and answer questions about your lifestyle.**

- *¿Cómo era tu estilo de vida antes?*
- *Y ahora, ¿cómo te sientes? ¿Tienes malas costumbres?*
- *¿Qué harás para mejorar tu salud y evitar problemas en el futuro?*

Escribir 8 **Write about your lifestyle and the things you will do to improve it.**

- What your life used to be like
- What unhealthy habits you have
- What you will do to change or improve
- How you will feel if …

Cuando era más joven, … / Antes …
Mi problema ahora es que …
Ahora … / Además, siempre …
Para cambiar esta mala costumbre … / Para mejorar mi dieta / mi salud / mi salud mental en el futuro …
Si hago más ejercicio, tendré … / me sentiré … / estaré …

Gramática 1

Adjectives of nationality (Zona de cultura, page 82)

Escribir 1

Read the grammar box on page 82. Complete the words in the table with the missing letters.

	singular		plural	
country	**masculine**	**feminine**	**masculine**	**feminine**
México	mexican **1**	mexicana	mexican **6**	mexican **11**
España	español	español **3**	español **7**	español **12**
Perú	peruan **2**	peruana	peruan **8**	peruan **13**
Colombia	colombiano	colombian **4**	colombian **9**	colombianas
Inglaterra	inglés	ingles **5**	ingles **10**	ingles **14**

peruano *Peruvian*

Escribir 2

Rewrite these sentences using the adjectives of nationality in brackets. Make sure that the endings agree with the nouns. Then translate the sentences into English, using the Spanish names for each dish.

1 *La paella* es una comida **(español)**.
2 *El choclo con queso* es un plato **(peruano)**.
3 A mis amigas **(argentino)** les encanta beber *mate*.
4 La comida **(sudamericano)** es rica y diversa.
5 Los **(mexicano)** comen muchas *quesadillas* y *chilaquiles*.
6 A los **(inglés)** les gusta la comida **(español)**.
7 Me gustaría probar la comida típica **(chileno)**.
8 ¿Cuáles son los platos **(español)** y **(cubano)** más típicos?

Adjectives of nationality can be used to form nouns by adding the **definite article**.
Los *cubanos* (Cubans)
Los *ingleses* (English people)

Después de and *antes de* + infinitive (Unit 1, page 84)

Escuchar 3

Read the grammar box on page 84. Listen to Ricardo and Marisol talking about their daily routine. Correct the underlined part of the sentences in Spanish. Then translate the sentences into English. (1–6)

Example: 1 *Me lavo los dientes y me pongo el uniforme después del desayuno.*
I clean my teeth and I put on my uniform after breakfast.

1 Me lavo los dientes y me pongo el uniforme después de levantarme.
2 Antes de coger el autobús, mando mensajes a mis amigos.
3 Suelo ir al gimnasio después del colegio.
4 Siempre hago los deberes antes de la cena.
5 Por la tarde ceno después de llegar a casa.
6 Por la noche descanso y escucho música después de acostarme.

Ricardo

Marisol

Escribir 4

Translate these sentences into Spanish.

1 Before breakfast, I get dressed to go to school.
2 I do exercise after getting up to start the day with energy.
3 I rest at home after finishing school.
4 My brother and I have dinner after returning home.
5 Normally I do my homework before dinner.
6 My sister reads online and listens to music before going to bed.

Indefinite adjectives (Unit 1, page 85)

singular		plural	
masculine	**feminine**	**masculine**	**feminine**
alg**ún** día	algun**a** vez	algun**os** sábados	algun**as** personas
otr**o** deporte	otr**a** comida	otr**os** ejercicios	otr**as** costumbres
el mism**o** lugar	la mism**a** hora	los mism**os** intereses	las mism**as** cosas
demasiad**o** tiempc	demasiad**a** sal	demasiad**os** exámenes	demasiad**as** fiestas
tod**o** el día	tod**a** la noche	tod**os** los fines de semana	tod**as** las semanas
much**o** dinero	much**a** suerte	much**os** jóvenes	much**as** escuelas

Cada (each) always stays the same. ***Varios/ Varias*** (several) is only used in the plural.

Remember that **indefinite adjectives** always come before the noun.
Ningún/ Ninguna is normally only used in the singular form, except for emphasis.

ningún día (not any day) — ***ninguna persona*** (nobody/not anyone)
*No tengo **ningunas** ganas de ir.* — I don't have any interest in going.

Leer 5 **Choose the correct indefinite adjective phrase for each sentence. Then translate each one into English. Remember to check if the noun is masculine/feminine and singular/plural.**

1. Voy al gimnasio **todas las** / **todos los** / **algunos** tardes.
2. No hago deporte **cada** / **todo el** / **ningún** día.
3. **Algunos** / **Algunas** / **Ninguna** mañanas no tomo el desayuno porque no tengo tiempo.
4. Mi amigo come **mucha** / **demasiadas** / **muchos** patatas fritas y **otras** / **mucha** / **varios** comidas poco saludables.
5. **Toda la** / **Cada** / **Alguna** mañana tomo el desayuno **al mismo** / **a otra** / **a la misma** hora.
6. Mis amigos y yo montamos en bicicleta **demasiados** / **varias** / **algunos** fines de semana.

Imperfect tense (Unit 3, page 88)

Escribir 6 **Read the grammar box on page 88. Complete these sentences with the imperfect tense of the verbs in brackets. Then translate the sentences into English.**

1. ¿Cómo **(ser)** tu rutina por la mañana antes?
2. Antes, **(levantarse, yo)** temprano cada día y **(acostarse, yo)** a la misma hora cada noche.
3. Antes, mis amigos y yo **(ir)** al parque y **(dar)** un paseo todas las tardes después de terminar el colegio.
4. Antes, mi hermano mayor **(fumar)** cigarrillos todos los días y no **(tener)** una vida sana.
5. ¿Qué **(hacer, tú)** cuando **(tener, tú)** diez años?
6. Antes, **(tener, yo)** una vida muy activa porque cada semana **(hacer, yo)** natación, **(montar, yo)** en bici y **(jugar, yo)** al fútbol en el parque.

Hablar 7 **In pairs, take turns to ask and answer questions about your routine now and when you were in primary school. Add extra details to develop your answers, such as *cada día, por la tarde, después de terminar el instituto/la escuela …***

Example: *Ahora, tengo una dieta sana. Sin embargo, cuando tenía ocho años comía muchos pasteles y chocolate.*

Present tense	Imperfect tense
¿Cómo es tu dieta ahora?	¿Qué comías antes?
¿Qué haces en tu tiempo libre ahora?	¿Qué hacías en tu tiempo libre antes?
¿Qué haces después del colegio?	¿Qué hacías después de la escuela?
¿A qué hora te acuestas?	¿A qué hora te acostabas?

Gramática 2

Direct object pronouns (Unit 3, page 86)

La ropa vieja

Escribir **1** **Read the grammar box on page 86. How many sentences can you complete with the correct direct object pronoun? Listen and check your answers. (1–6) Then translate the sentences into English.**

me te lo/la nos os los/las

1 Me encanta la *ropa vieja*. ___ como con frecuencia.
2 Cristina, me gustaría invitar ___ a mi fiesta de cumpleaños el miercoles próximo.
3 Mi padre ___ ayuda a cocinar su plato de carne favorito porque ___ hace muy rico.
4 Antes tomaba muchas bebidas con azúcar, pero ya no ___ bebo.
5 Nuestros amigos mexicanos ___ llevaron a visitar los mercados típicos de frutas y verduras.
6 Luis y Ana, voy a llevar ___ a los mejores restaurantes de la ciudad para disfrutar de la comida.

More impersonal verbs + infinitive: *hay que / hace falta / se necesita* (Unit 3, page 87)

Escribir **2** **Read the grammar box on page 87. Write <u>two</u> sentences for each of the questions on the right using the language from the boxes below. Try to include an opinion. Then read your sentences out in pairs.**

Example: 1 ***Para*** *tener una vida sana,* ***pienso que*** *se necesita evitar fumar* ***porque*** *es malo para la salud.*

1 ¿Qué hay que hacer para tener una vida sana?

2 ¿Qué hace falta comer para tener una dieta sana?

3 ¿Qué se necesita hacer para mantenerse en forma?

hay que hace falta se necesita	evitar (+ infinitive / + noun) comer/tomar hacer/cuidar dormir/descansar	fumar / beber alcohol deporte regularmente verduras/frutas comida sana/fresca/no saludable	demasiad**a** sal / demasiad**o** azúcar demasiad**os** caramelos suficientes horas cada noche usar el móvil demasiado la salud mental / la dieta / el cuerpo

Me duele(n) (Unit 4, page 91)

Escribir **3** **Read the grammar box on page 91. Write an indirect object pronoun from the word box, to match the person in brackets, and the correct form of *doler*. Check for clues, such as singular/plural parts of the body. Then match the <u>two</u> halves of each statement/question and translate them into English.**

Example: 1 ***Me duele*** *mucho la piel porque ayer fui a la playa y me quemé la espalda.*

me te le nos os les

1 ___ ___ ***(I)*** mucho **la piel** porque …
2 ¿Qué **parte** del cuerpo ***(You)*** ___ ___ exactamente?
3 ***(I)*** ___ ___ **las manos** y **la pierna derecha** desde hace dos días porque …
4 ***(You)*** ___ ___ **los ojos** porque …
5 ***(I)*** ___ ___ **la lengua** desde hace un día porque …
6 A mi hermana ***(She)*** ___ ___ mucho **los pies** porque …

a … me caí de la bici y me hice mucho daño.
b ¿Qué hiciste y qué comiste ayer?
c … el otro día caminó muchas horas.
d … ayer fui a la playa y me quemé la espalda.
e … bebí agua demasiado caliente. ¡Ay! ¡Qué dolor de boca tengo!
f … ayer pasaste mucho tiempo delante de la pantalla del ordenador.

The simple future tense (Unit 5, page 92)

Escribir 4 **Read the grammar box on page 92. Complete Santiago's action plan for better health with the correct form of the simple future tense of the verbs in the word box. Then translate the verbs into English.**

Example: 1 *cambiaré – I will change*

Santiago Valverde

Para estar sano y evitar problemas de salud en el futuro, ...

acostarse hacer comer salir cuidar dormir tomar tener poder cambiar

1 ___ todas mis malas costumbres.
2 ___ una dieta sana y equilibrada con muchos alimentos frescos.
3 ___ deporte todas las semanas y ___ una vida activa para aumentar mis niveles de energía.
4 No ___ drogas porque tienen demasiados riesgos para la salud.
5 No ___ demasiado tarde por las noches. ___ al menos ocho horas cada noche.
6 Mi hermano y yo ___ nuestra salud mental con sesiones de meditación para reducir el estrés.
7 Mis padres ___ ayudarme si tengo problemas.
8 Mis amigos y yo ___ a dar un paseo cada fin de semana.

Using a range of tenses: present, imperfect, preterite, simple future (Unit 5, page 93)

Escuchar 5 **Listen and fill in the gaps with the correct word(s) in Spanish.**

Antes **1** una persona activa, **2** un estilo de vida sano y **3** mucho ejercicio. Sin embargo, **4** de hacerlo hace un año y ahora **5** demasiado tarde. El médico **6** que si dejo de comer tantos pasteles y comida no saludable y **7** alimentos frescos, **8** mejor y mis niveles de energía **9**. Por eso, **10** mi dieta.

Alejandra

Hablar 6 **Read out this passage in pairs, paying attention to pronunciation. Write down the verbs and classify them according to their tense: imperfect, preterite, present or simple future. Then translate them into English.**

En el pasado mi tío nunca hacía deporte, no dormía bien y siempre estaba de mal humor. También tenía sobrepeso y muchos problemas de salud porque fumaba cada día. El médico le recomendó hacer régimen y cambiar su estilo de vida. Entonces comenzó a ir al gimnasio cada semana y dejó de fumar. Ahora le gusta pasear, está más contento y se siente mucho mejor. En el futuro hará meditación para cuidar su mente, dará más paseos por el campo y montará en bicicleta.

Francisco

¡En marcha! (Units 1-5)

Escribir 7 **Translate Mark's text into Spanish.**

Imperfect tense · Direct object pronoun · Present tense · Indefinite adjectives · Preterite tense · Simple future tense

In the past I was not an active person because I liked to spend hours sitting in my room. I used to play a lot of video games, I went to bed late every night and I was always very sleepy during the day. Although I didn't smoke or drink alcohol, I didn't have a healthy diet because I ate fast food. I ate it all the time! I decided to change my lifestyle. Now I am no longer tired because I sleep well. If I exercise every week and eat a balanced diet, I will avoid health problems in the future, like obesity. I will also look after my mental health to be happier. ***Mark***

Leer y escuchar

Reading

Leer 1

Daily routine. **Read Sara's post about her daily routine. Complete the sentences below. Write the correct letter, A, B or C, for each question.**

Mucha gente tiene una rutina diaria que no cambia, pero, por el contrario, mi rutina diaria suele cambiar y depende del día de la semana. Normalmente me despierto a las siete menos cuarto para coger el autobús. Sin embargo, ayer fue martes y, como todos los martes, tengo que levantarme más temprano, a las seis y media, para preparar el desayuno para ayudar a mi madre. Lo que me molesta es que no puedo reunirme con mis amigos antes de llegar al colegio. Es una lástima.

la rutina *routine*
reunirse *to meet up*

1 Sara has ...
A a fixed routine.
B a variable daily routine.
C no daily routine.

2 Sara most often wakes up at ...
A 6.45am.
B 7.15am.
C 6.30am.

3 Yesterday, Sara ...
A prepared for school.
B got up later.
C got up earlier.

4 What annoys Sara about Tuesdays is that she ...
A has to prepare breakfast.
B can't meet friends before school.
C gets up early.

Leer 2

Mental and physical health. **Read Marcos's email to Alba about life at school. Answer the following questions in English.**

¡Hola, Alba!

No duermo bien desde hace más de una semana y, para decirte la verdad, debido a esto en este momento me siento bastante triste en el colegio. Antes estaba contento en el instituto pero ahora la presión de los exámenes me pone nervioso. Es imposible estudiar en clase y ayer después de clases lloré. No es normal para mí. Lo que más me molesta es que nunca veo a mis amigos y tampoco salgo con ellos porque tengo que estudiar.

Aunque discuto con mis profesores, si hablo con ellos, puede ser algo positivo porque mi instituto tiene servicios de salud mental y mis profesores siempre me escuchan.

Marcos

la verdad *truth*
llorar *to cry*

Use time markers to locate information that proves/disproves an option.

1 What is worrying about Marcos's current sleeping pattern?
2 How is it making him feel at school?
3 Why is Marcos currently feeling anxious?
4 What was surprising that happened yesterday after class?
5 What are the advantages of Marcos speaking to his teachers? (Give two details.)

Use question words to guide you to your answer: 'how' often points you towards an adjective, a mode of transport or adverb; 'what' may suggest a noun or verb; 'why' indicates a reason.

Leer 3 ***Food*. Translate these sentences into English.**

How does this best translate into English? *(del extranjero)*

Watch out for opinions that don't translate word-for-word into English. *(tengo la intención de)*

A mi padre le encanta probar diferentes tipos de comida del extranjero.

Mis amigos y yo solemos ir a restaurantes en nuestro tiempo libre.

El fin de semana pasado, mis padres decidieron tomar tapas en el nuevo mercado.

En el futuro, tengo la intención de probar más platos de otros países.

Quiero unos churros con chocolate porque me encanta la comida dulce.

What would sound more natural than 'take tapas' in English? *(tomar tapas)*

Take care not to skip important words such as *más, muy, mucho, poco, bastante* and *nunca*. *(más)*

Listening

Escuchar 1 ***Healthy living*. Carla is talking about her lifestyle choices. Listen and complete the sentences. Answer both parts of the question. (1–2)**

1 When Carla was young, she used to …
- **A** eat fruit.
- **B** not eat fast food.
- **C** eat too much fast food.

Two years ago, she decided to …
- **A** do more physical activity.
- **B** change her diet.
- **C** stop doing sport.

2 Carla …
- **A** likes basketball.
- **B** used to like football.
- **C** plays football every weekend.

She has just …
- **A** had a rest.
- **B** recovered from an injury.
- **C** broken her arm.

Escuchar 2 ***Food*. Karima is talking about her family's eating habits. Answer the questions in English.**

1. What does Karima's sister normally eat for breakfast?
2. What is her sister going to eat tomorrow for breakfast?
3. Where are the family going to go to on Thursday?
4. Why will more people have a vegan diet in the future?

Listen carefully for common distractors: negatives, 'more', 'less', 'best', 'worst'. Do they change any of your possible options?

Escuchar 3 **You will hear <u>five</u> short sentences. Listen carefully and, using your knowledge of Spanish sounds, write down in Spanish exactly what you hear for each sentence.**

Listen to the whole extract before confirming your answers.

Módulo 4

Prueba oral

Role play

Escribir 1 **Look at the role play card and prepare what you are going to say.**

You are talking to your Spanish friend.
Your teacher will play the part of your friend and will speak first.
You should address your friend as *tú*.
When you see this – **?** – you will have to ask a question.
You must include at least one verb in your response to each point.

Task:

1 Say where you do exercise. (Give one detail.)
2 Say what you ate last night. (Give two details.)
3 Say what you think about doing exercise and why. (Give one opinion and one reason.)
4 **?** Ask your friend a question about sport.
5 Give two disadvantages of fast food.

Remember to use the preposition *en* to mean 'in'/'at'/'on' + location.

Don't forget to raise your intonation to make what you say sound like a question.

Which tense do you need here?

Ensure you answer both parts of the task.

You could use adjectives such as 'expensive'.

Escuchar 2 **Practise what you have prepared. Then, using your notes, listen and respond to the teacher.**

Escuchar 3 **Now listen to Priya doing the role play task. In English, note down what she says for each of the points on the card, including the question she asks.**

Reading aloud

Hablar 1 **Look at this task. With a partner, read aloud the six sentences, paying attention to the underlined letters.**

Hoy día, los expertos recomiendan llevar una vida sana.
Es importante no comer comida con altos niveles de azúcar.
Afortunadamente, mi familia y yo solemos practicar deporte.
Para cuidar tu salud mental, debes hablar con otras personas.
En el futuro, me encantaría descansar más.
Así podré reducir el estrés.

Remember: *ll* is pronounced like 'y' in English; *v* is pronounced like 'b' in English.

Be careful of *e* (pronounced '*eh*' in Spanish).

Escuchar 2 **Listen and check your pronunciation.**

Hablar 3 **Listen to the teacher asking four questions that relate to the topic of healthy living and lifestyle. Translate each question into English and prepare your own answers in Spanish. Then listen again and respond to the teacher.**

Change the verb form in each question you are asked from the second person (*tú*) to the first person (*yo*) to ensure your answers apply to you.

Photo card

Escuchar **1** **Look at the photos below and read the first part of the task card. Then listen to Harry describing the photos.**

1 How does Harry describe the appearance of the people in the first photo?
2 Where does he say the people are in the first photo?
3 What does he say the people are doing in the first photo?
4 How does Harry describe the appearance of the people in the second photo?
5 What does he say the people are doing in the second photo?

Prepare your own description of the photos. Your teacher will ask you to talk about the content of these photos. You must include one detail about each photo.

After you have described the photos, your teacher will then ask you questions related to **People and lifestyle**.

Hablar **2** **Prepare your own description of the two photos. Then, with a partner, take turns to describe them.**

- *En la primera foto hay ...*
- *En la segunda foto hay ...*

Use ***estar*** to describe location and with the present continuous tense to say what people are doing. Use ***ser*** for physical description and professions.

Escuchar **3** **Now listen to Harry responding to the second part of the task card and the conversation questions asked by his teacher. Write down the questions in Spanish, then translate them into English.**

Escuchar **4** **Listen to Harry answering the conversation questions again. Answer the questions in English.**

1 Why does Harry do exercise?
2 When does he normally play football?
3 What does football help him to do?
4 What did Harry have for breakfast?
5 Why does Harry say he eats breakfast?
6 What did he eat for his evening meal?

Escuchar **5** **The teacher asks Harry the question: '*¿Qué puedes hacer para tener una mejor salud mental?*' Note down what Harry used to do in the past and what he now does to have better mental health.**

Escuchar **6** **The teacher then asks Harry the question: '*¿Qué cambios quieres hacer en el futuro para ser más feliz?*' Note down:**

1 the <u>two</u> changes he wants to make
2 the reason why he wants to make them.

Hablar **7** **Prepare your own answers to Module 4 questions 1–10 on page 230. Then practise with your partner.**

Prueba escrita

Translation

Escribir 1

Read the English text and Annabelle's translation of it. Then, write down the word for each gap in the Spanish translation.

You have to keep in shape in order to lead a healthy life.

On weekends, my friends and I usually run in our local park.

The most difficult thing is eating healthily.

I am Argentinian and before I used to eat too much meat.

I no longer eat as much meat as in the past and I am going to drink less coffee in the future.

Tienes **1** mantenerte en forma para llevar una vida sana.

Los fines de semana mis amigos y yo **2** correr en nuestro parque local.

Lo más difícil es **3** saludablemente.

Soy **4** y antes **5** demasiada carne.

Ya no **6** tanta carne como en el pasado y **7** a beber menos café en el futuro.

Check the subject of the verb carefully to ensure you use the correct form of the verb.

Escribir 2

Translate the following text into Spanish.

You must stay in shape in order to be healthy.

On Tuesdays, my football team usually plays in the park.

The most difficult thing is to not eat unhealthily.

My family and I used to eat lots of sugar but we no longer eat it.

Also, we are going to follow a vegan diet.

Watch out for expressions such as 'football team' that must be translated as 'team of football'.

Para can be used to mean 'for' or 'in order to'.

150-Word writing task

Escribir 1

Look at this writing task and then, for each bullet point, consider:

- what examples of **complex language** you could use to impress the examiner
- how you could use a **variety of vocabulary** to avoid repetition
- **which tense(s)** you will need to use in your answer.

You decide to write a blog about your mental and physical wellbeing.

Write approximately **150** words in **Spanish**. You must write something about both bullet points:

- why a healthy lifestyle is important to you
- what you will do in order to stay healthy and happy in the future.

Leer 2

Read Thomas's answer to the task. Answer the questions in the coloured shapes.

Para mí es muy importante llevar una vida sana porque hay ventajas para el cuerpo y para la mente. Creo que una vida sana consiste en comer bien y hacer ejercicio. Algunas personas intentan evitar la carne y dicen que es mejor para la salud si eres vegano. En el pasado comía mucha carne, pero ya no la como. Además, suelo practicar deporte. Lo bueno es que te ayuda a olvidar la presión del instituto. Lo negativo es el riesgo de tener accidentes. El mes pasado, cuando jugaba al fútbol, tuve un accidente y me rompí el brazo, pero ahora estoy mejor.

Para mantenerme feliz y sano en el futuro, quisiera pasar más tiempo con mis amigos porque siempre me escuchan cuando tengo problemas. Además, tengo la intención de mejorar mi dieta. Me encantan las verduras, y por eso, intentaré comer más.

1 Look for opportunities to use direct object pronouns. Which noun does this direct object pronoun refer back to?

2 Use *lo* + adjective (the ___ thing) as an alternative way to give an opinion. Find one more example from the text.

3 Combine different tenses to build complex sentences. Which tenses are used in this sentence?

4 Use frequency expressions with verbs to say how often you do something. Which other frequency expressions do you know?

5 Which tense is this? How would you translate it? What other tense could you use here?

Leer 3

Read Thomas's answer again and answer the questions in English.

1. According to Thomas, what makes a healthy lifestyle? (Give two details.)
2. What did he use to do that he now does not do?
3. What does he say is the benefit of playing sport?
4. What happened to Thomas last month? (Give two details.)
5. What would he like to do in the future in order to be happy and healthy? (Give three details.)

Escribir 4

Prepare your own answer to the task.

- Think about how you can develop your answer for each bullet point.
- Look back at your notes from exercises 1 and 2.
- Look at the 'Challenge checklist' and consider how you can show off your Spanish!
- Write a brief plan and organise your answer into paragraphs.
- Write your answer and then carefully check the accuracy of what you have written.

Challenge checklist	
	✓ Connectives / sequencers / expressions of frequency ✓ Extended sentences ✓ Past, present and future time frames
	✓ A wider range of tenses (e.g. simple future, imperfect) ✓ *ya no* + present to say what you no longer do (e.g. *ya no bebo refrescos* …) ✓ Other people's opinions (e.g. *mi familia prefiere* …, *mi amiga piensa que* …)
	✓ Direct object pronouns (e.g. *Me gustan las verduras. Las como todos los días.*) ✓ Complex structures (e.g. *suelo* + infinitive, *lo* + adjective, *si* clauses) ✓ Contrast between the imperfect and *pero ahora* + present to say what you now do.

Módulo 4

Palabras

Key:
bold = this word will appear in higher exams only
* = this word is not on the vocabulary list, but you may use it in your own sentences

¡Qué rico! (pages 82–83):

Para …	*For …*
el desayuno / la comida	*breakfast / lunch*
*la merienda / la cena	*afternoon snack / dinner*
una comida típica	*a typical meal*
un plato popular	*a popular dish*
El/La … es de …	*… is from …*
Los/Las … son de …	*… are from …*
España / México / Perú	*Spain / Mexico / Peru*
Chile / Argentina / Cuba / Sudamérica	*Chile / Argentina / Cuba / South America*
argentino/a / chileno/a	*Argentinian / Chilean*
colombiano/a / cubano/a	*Colombian / Cuban*
español(a) / inglés/inglesa	*Spanish / English*
mexicano/a / *peruano/a	*Mexican / Peruvian*
*venezolano/a	*Venezuelan*
¿En qué consiste(n)?	*What is it / are they made of?*
Está hecho/a con …	*It is made with …*
Están hechos/as con …	*They are made with …*
Consiste(n) en …	*It consists / They consist of …*
verduras/carne/pollo	*vegetables/meat/chicken*
pescado/**arroz**/*queso	*fish/rice/cheese*
¿Qué comida o bebida te gustaría probar?	*What food or drink would you like to try?*
Me gustaría probar (la paella).	*I would like to try (paella).*
Porque …	*Because …*
parece rico/a	*it looks tasty*
es (muy) sano/a.	*it is (very) healthy.*
tiene muchos **beneficios** para la salud	*it has lots of health benefits*
¡A comer!	*Let's eat!*
*¡Buen provecho!	*Enjoy your meal!*

¿Llevas una vida sana? (pages 84–85):

¿Cómo es un día típico?	*What is a typical day like?*
Por la mañana/tarde/noche …	*In the morning/afternoon/night …*
Durante el día/la semana …	*During the day/week …*
El fin de semana …	*At the weekend …*
Los domingos …	*On Sundays …*
Todos los días / fines de semana	*Every day/weekend*
Algunos días / fines de semana	*Some days/weekends*
Antes de / **Después de** …	*Before / After …*
hacer los deberes	*doing homework*
levantarme / vestirme	*getting up / getting dressed*
terminar las clases	*finishing classes*
tomar el desayuno	*having breakfast*
volver a casa / **acostarme**	*returning home / going to bed*
¿Qué costumbres sanas tienes?	*What healthy habits do you have?*
Duermo (bien) / Entreno	*I sleep (well) / I train*
Hago diez minutos de ejercicio.	*I do ten minutes of exercise.*
Llevo una botella de agua.	*I carry a bottle of water.*
Me levanto / **Me acuesto** …	*I get up / I go to bed …*
a las … / a la misma hora	*at … (o'clock) / at the same time*
tarde / temprano	*late / early*
Me lavo / Me visto	*I have a wash / I get dressed*
Suelo hacer *meditación	*I usually do meditation*
Como / Ceno a las …	*I eat / I have dinner at …*
Tomo un desayuno ligero.	*I have a light breakfast.*
Evito comer mucha grasa.	*I avoid eating lots of fat.*
No bebo **alcohol**.	*I don't drink alcohol.*
Nunca fumo **cigarrillos**.	*I never smoke cigarettes.*
Odio el olor del **humo**.	*I hate the smell of smoke.*
Tengo / Tienes / Tiene …	*I am / you are / he/she is …*
sed/hambre	*thirsty/hungry*
sueño/calor/frío	*sleepy/hot/cold*
Si tengo hambre/sed, …	*If I'm hungry/thirsty, …*
tomo / como / bebo …	*I have/eat/drink …*
un huevo / una manzana	*an egg / an apple*
algunos/muchos dulces	*some/lots of sweets*
algunas/muchas verduras	*some/lots of vegetables*
chocolate/fruta/ensalada	*chocolate/fruit/salad*
demasiadas bebidas (con azúcar)	*too many (sugary/soft) drinks*

¿Somos lo que comemos? (pages 86–87):

¿A qué hora tomas …	*What time do you have …*
el desayuno / la comida? la cena?	*breakfast/lunch? dinner?*
Normalmente lo/la tomo …	*Normally I have it …*
entre las … y las …	*between … and …*
¿Te gustaría probarlos/las?	*Would you like to try them?*
Te recomiendo …	*I recommend …*
Hay que probar …	*You have to try …*
Es un *postre / una bebida …	*It is a … dessert/drink.*
rico/a / típico/a.	*tasty/typical*
Me gustaría probarlo/la / probarlos/las …	*I would like to try it/them …*
porque parece (n) …	*because it looks/they look …*
¿Cómo es tu dieta?	*What is your diet like?*
(No) Tengo una dieta sana / equilibrada porque …	*I (don't) have a healthy / balanced diet because …*
soy vegano/a / vegetariano/a	*I am vegan/vegetarian*
como comida sana / no **saludable** / rápida	*I eat healthy / unhealthy / fast food*
como demasiados *dulces/ *pasteles/caramelos	*I eat too many sweet things / cakes / sweets*
Mi desayuno/comida/cena **consiste en** un plato de …	*My breakfast/lunch/dinner consists of a plate of …*
¿Qué hay que hacer para tener una dieta sana?	*What do you have to do to have a healthy diet?*
Hay que / Se necesita …	*You have to / need to …*
Hace falta …	*It is necessary to …*
comer una dieta equilibrada	*eat a balanced diet*
tener cuidado con la **cantidad** de **aceite** que tomas	*be careful with the amount of oil you have*
el **cerebro** / el **sobrepeso**	*brain / excess weight*
los **alimentos** frescos	*fresh foods*
las enfermedades	*illnesses*

¡Los tiempos cambian! (pages 88–89):

¿Cómo eras antes?	*What were you like before?*
Cuando era pequeño/a ...	*When I was little*
Cuando era más joven ...	*When I was younger ...*
Antes / Cuando tenía ... años, ...	*Before / When I was ... years old, ...*
dormía bien/mal	*I slept well/badly*
(no) jugaba / iba / veía	*I (didn't) play / go / watch*
me levantaba / **me acostaba** ...	*I got up / I went to bed ...*
temprano/**pronto** / tarde	*early / late*
(no) era muy activo/a.	*I was (not) very active.*
(no) tenía ...	*I had / I didn't have ...*
(mucha) energía	*(lots of) energy*
estrés	*stress*
una dieta/vida sana	*a healthy diet/life*
(nunca) iba al gimnasio	*I (never) went to the gym*

¿Qué te gustaba comer y beber?	*What did you like to eat and drink?*
Solía comer / beber ...	*I usually ate / drank ...*
(No) Comía ...	*I ate / I didn't eat ...*
Bebía demasiado café.	*I drank too much coffee.*
Me encantaba la comida dulce.	*I loved sweet food.*
Me gustaba comer *dulces.	*I liked eating sweet things.*

¿Qué hacías en tu tiempo libre cuando eras pequeño/a?	*What did you do in your free time when you were little?*
(No) Hacía (mucho/suficiente) ejercicio/deporte.	*I did / didn't do (lots of/enough) exercise/sports.*
(No) Iba a la piscina (tres veces a la semana).	*I went / didn't go to the pool (three times a week).*
(No) Montaba en bici (cada día).	*I rode / didn't ride my bike (every day).*
(No) Jugaba ...	*I played / didn't play ...*
(Siempre) Estaba cansado/a y enfermo/a.	*I was (always) tired and sick.*

¿Cómo es tu vida ahora?	*What is your life like now?*
Cuido más mi dieta.	*I look after my diet more.*
Me siento mucho mejor.	*I feel a lot better.*
Soy bastante activo/a.	*I am quite active.*
No / **Ya no** ...	*I don't / no longer ...*
hago ejercicio/deporte	*do exercise/sports*
hago nada para estar en forma	*do anything to stay in shape*
como / bebo / juego / voy / veo ...	*eat / drink / play / go / see ...*
(No) Como comida rápida / poco **saludable**.	*I (don't) eat fast/unhealthy food.*
Prefiero las bebidas con azúcar.	*I prefer sugary drinks.*
(No) Hago ejercicio/deporte.	*I (don't) do exercise/sports.*
(No) Voy al gimnasio/cine.	*I (don't) go to the gym/cinema.*

¡Qué mal estoy! (pages 90–91):

¿Qué te pasa?	*What's the matter with you?*
Me / te / le duele(n) ...	*My / your / his/her ... hurt(s)*
el **brazo** / el pie	*arm / foot*
la **boca** / la mano	*mouth / hand*
la cabeza / la **pierna**	*head / leg*
los ojos / los pies	*eyes / feet*
los dientes / (todo) el cuerpo	*teeth / (whole) body*
Estoy (muy) enfermo/a.	*I am (very) sick.*
Me siento (muy) mal / débil.	*I feel (very) unwell / weak.*
No me siento bien porque tengo ...	*I don't feel well because I have ...*
dolor de cabeza	*a headache*
una **herida** grave	*a (serious) injury*
Ayer / La semana pasada ...	*Yesterday / Last week ...*
me rompí / **me corté** ...	*I broke my / I cut my ...*
me quemé ...	*I burned my ...*
la pierna/piel	*leg/skin*
me caí de la bici	*I fell from my bike*

¿Desde cuándo estás así?	*Since when have you been like this?*
desde ...	*since ...*
ayer	*yesterday*
esta mañana/tarde	*this morning/afternoon*
la semana pasada	*last week*
el [sábado] pasado.	*last [Saturday]*
el fin de semana pasado	*last weekend*
desde hace una hora / más de (dos días)	*for an hour / more than (two days)*
Debes / Necesitas ...	*You must / You need to ...*
Tienes que ...	*You have to ...*
quedarte en la cama / en casa	*stay in bed / at home*
descansar/dormir	*rest/sleep*
comprar medicinas	*buy medicine*
evitar el sol	*avoid the sun*
ir al médico/hospital	*go to the doctor's/hospital*
pedir **cita** con el médico	*ask for a doctor's appointment*

Mi salud, de la cabeza a los pies (pages 92–93):

¿Cómo cambiarás tu estilo de vida?	*How will you change your lifestyle?*
Si dejo de comer/beber/fumar, ...	*If I stop eating/drinking/smoking, ...*
Si duermo (al menos ocho horas), ...	*If I sleep (at least eight hours), ...*
Si practico más deporte, ...	*If I practise more sport, ...*
Si tengo (una vida más activa), ...	*If I have (a more active life), ...*
me sentiré más feliz	*I will be happier*
mi salud física/**mental** mejorará	*my physical/mental health will improve*
dormiré mejor	*I will sleep better*
me levantaré con más energía	*I will wake up with more energy*
estaré menos cansado/a	*I will be less tired*
evitaré el **sobrepeso**	*I will avoid being overweight*
tendré menos estrés	*I will have less stress*

¿Qué harás para mejorar tu salud en el futuro?	*What will you do to improve your health in the future?*
Para cambiar esta mala costumbre, ...	*To change this bad habit, ...*
reduciré la **cantidad** de ... que tomo/bebo/como a diario	*I will reduce the daily amount of ... I have/drink/eat*
Para mejorar mi dieta/salud ...	*To improve my diet/health ...*
dormiré más tiempo	*I will sleep longer*
apagaré el móvil	*I will turn off my mobile*
iré (al gimnasio)	*I will go (to the gym)*
evitaré beber alcohol y fumar	*I will avoid drinking alcohol and smoking*
empezaré a practicar deporte	*I will start practising sport*
Nunca tomaré drogas.	*I will never take drugs.*

Módulo 5 **¡A clase!**

La vida escolar en España

- Learning about schools in Spain
- Using absolute superlatives

¿Lo sabías?

A los doce años, los alumnos españoles dejan la escuela primaria y empiezan la Educación Secundaria Obligatoria (ESO). Luego, a la edad de dieciséis años, hay dos opciones si quieren continuar con los estudios: hacer el Bachillerato (equivalente a los *A-Levels* en el Reino Unido) o hacer un ciclo de Formación Profesional.

¿En qué curso estás?

Estoy en ...
1º (*primero*) de ESO.
2º (*segundo*) de ESO.
3º (*tercero*) de ESO.
4º (*cuarto*) de ESO.
1º (*primero*) de Bachillerato.
2º (*segundo*) de Bachillerato.

El curso escolar

El curso escolar comienza en la segunda o tercera semana de septiembre y termina en junio. Los alumnos suelen tener dos semanas para las vacaciones de Navidad, otra semana para Semana Santa – ¡y casi doce semanas de vacaciones en verano!

El día escolar

Mientras que la mayoría de los alumnos va al instituto por la mañana, en algunos institutos se puede asistir a clases por la noche. El Bachillerato nocturno se ofrece a los adultos y a los mayores de dieciséis años que tienen trabajo o que son deportistas o músicos de alto nivel. Sus clases no terminan hasta las diez de la noche, ¡o incluso más tarde!

El uniforme

En el pasado, el uniforme escolar era obligatorio en muchas escuelas privadas (por ejemplo, una camisa, una corbata, una chaqueta o un jersey y un pantalón o una falda con zapatos). Ahora, es más común en las escuelas públicas también, aunque todavía hay muchos colegios donde los alumnos pueden decidir lo que llevan: una camiseta, un vestido, ropa deportiva ...

Las clases

En muchos institutos hay seis clases por día. En general, los alumnos llaman a los profesores por su nombre, no por su apellido.

la vida escolar	*school life*
la escuela pública	*state school*

Leer 1 **Read the text above about schools in Spain and answer the questions in English.**

1 What do Spanish children do at the age of 12?
2 How many weeks do the school holidays last in total?
3 Which four groups of people can do the *Bachillerato nocturno*?
4 How has the situation regarding school uniform changed? (Give three details.)
5 Write down four differences between schools in Spain and schools in the UK.

In most of Spain, ***ce***, ***ci*** and ***z*** are pronounced like 'th' in the English word 'think'. In parts of southern Spain and in Latin America, they are pronounced like 's' in 'sun'. Listen and repeat.
*do**ce*** *vaca**ci**ones* *empe**z**ar*

Escribir 2 **Read the text again and write down the Spanish for the following phrases. Then take turns to read out the Spanish phrases, taking extra care with how you pronounce *ce*, *ci* and *z*.**

1 they begin compulsory secondary education
2 there are two options
3 do a vocational training course
4 the school year starts
5 12 weeks of holidays
6 is offered to adults and over-16s
7 (they) can decide what they wear

Escuchar 3 **Listen to some teenagers talking about their school. Then copy and complete the table in English. (1–4)**

	Country	School year starts	School year ends	What they wear for school
1				

Remember to use the correct word order and to make adjectives agree with the noun.
*Llevo un**a** camis**a** blanc**a** y un**os** zapat**os** negr**os**.*

However, where a colour adjective is followed by ***claro*** (light) or ***oscuro*** (dark), the **masculine** singular form is used.
*Llevo un**a** camis**a** roj**o** **claro** y un**os** zapat**os** verde **oscuro**.*

Según las cifras del Ministerio de Educación y Formación Profesional (2023), en España, más de ocho millones de alumnos asisten a uno de los 28.000 centros educativos.

- El 67 por ciento asiste a un colegio público (financiado por el Estado).
- El 25 por ciento asiste a un colegio 'concertado' (donde el Estado paga la mitad de los gastos y las familias también contribuyen dinero).
- El 8 por ciento asiste a un colegio privado (financiado por las familias de los alumnos).

Nombre del colegio:	**Colegio Guzmán Miraflores**
Tipo de instituto:	concertado
Instalaciones:	edificio moderno con aulas y laboratorios grandes
Instalaciones deportivas:	dos gimnasios, campos deportivos
Uniforme escolar:	jersey azul oscuro, camiseta blanca, pantalón o falda gris

un colegio concertado *a privately owned school which receives some State funding*

Leer 4 **Read these opinions about life at *Colegio Guzmán Miraflores*. Which aspect is each pupil describing (a–f)? Is their opinion positive (P), negative (N) or positive and negative (P+N)?**

1 Cuesta muchísimo dinero viajar a mi colegio – es carísimo. ***Clara***

2 Los bocadillos son riquísimos y muy baratos. Por otro lado, hay poca variedad. ***Natalia***

3 La directora es alegre y tiene buen sentido del humor. Mi profesora de historia es buenísima – siempre aprendemos mucho en sus clases. ***Samuel***

4 Creo que la falda es feísima, aunque la chaqueta es bastante cómoda. ***Isabel***

5 Acaban de construir un gimnasio nuevo – es increíble. No suelo trabajar en la biblioteca porque hay mucho ruido. ***Andrés***

6 Estudio francés desde hace cinco años pero es aburridísimo y lo odio cuando tenemos que hacer diálogos. Me gustaría aprender una lengua más fácil. ***Karim***

G

To say 'really [good]', 'extremely [expensive]', etc., use the **absolute superlative**.

Add **-ísimo/a** to the end of the adjective, and make it agree.

*Es facil**ísimo/a**.*
It is **extremely easy**.

If the adjective ends in a vowel, remove it before adding the ending.

*Son buen**ísimos/as**.*
They are **really good**.

Page 118

a El uniforme	**d** Las clases
b Las instalaciones	**e** La comida
c La gente	**f** El precio

Hablar 5 **In pairs, talk about your school using the questions below. Include some examples of the absolute superlative. Use vocabulary from the word box and the texts above to help you.**

- *¿Cómo se llama tu instituto?*
- *Mi instituto se llama ... y está en ...*
  Es un instituto público con más de mil alumnos.
- *¿Qué ropa llevas en el insti?*
- *Llevo una camisa blanca, ... y ... En mi opinión, es ...*
- *¿Cómo son las instalaciones?*
- *Hay muchos laboratorios modernísimos y ... Además, hay ...*
- *¿Cómo es el director / la directora?*
- *En mi opinión, el director / la directora es ...*
- *¿Te gusta la comida de tu insti?*
- *Sí, me gusta / No, no me gusta porque ...*

bueno/a(s)	malo/a(s)
moderno/a(s)	viejo/a(s)
caro/a(s)	barato/a(s)
cómodo/a(s)	incómodo/a(s)
bonito/a(s)	feo/a(s)
divertido/a(s)	aburrido/a(s)
excelente(s)	decepcionante(s)

1 Un día en el insti

- Talking about a typical day at school
- Using the relative pronouns *que, donde, cuando*
- Translating into English effectively

Polo y Santiago, Coahuila (México)

Escuchar 1 **Listen and read. Select the three correct statements below. Then translate the phrases in purple into English.**

¿Cómo vas al insti?

Normalmente voy al insti a pie con mi amigo Santiago, **que vive en la misma calle** que yo. Sin embargo, cuando llueve o hace frío, vengo en autobús.

¿Cómo es tu día escolar?

Las clases empiezan a las siete menos cuarto de la mañana y por eso salgo de casa a las seis. ¡Es muy temprano! Cada clase dura una hora y hay un recreo a las diez. Normalmente las clases terminan a las dos y media de la tarde. Sin embargo, en este momento hace muchísimo calor, **que puede ser peligroso para la salud**, ya que las temperaturas alcanzan los cuarenta grados a la sombra. Por lo tanto, actualmente solo asistimos al insti por la mañana y luego a las once volvemos a casa, **donde continuamos con las clases a distancia**.

¿Qué sueles hacer a la hora de comer?

Mi amigo Santiago va a la cantina, **donde compra algo para comer**, pero a mí no me gusta nada la comida **que venden allí**. Por eso traigo un bocadillo de casa. A veces voy a la nueva biblioteca **que acaban de construir**, pero en general salgo al patio, **donde mis amigos y yo jugamos al baloncesto**.

¿Qué día de la semana prefieres?

Prefiero los martes, **cuando tengo actividades extraescolares** después del insti, y también los miércoles, **cuando tenemos todas mis asignaturas favoritas**. Me gustan más las clases **donde trabajamos en equipo**, como la educación física.

extraescolar(es) *extracurricular*

1. Polo lives near his friend Santiago.
2. His lessons begin at 7.15 a.m.
3. His school is currently closed because of the heat.
4. Polo buys something to eat in the school canteen.
5. He generally spends lunchtime outdoors.
6. He has all his favourite lessons on Wednesdays.

G

Use the **relative pronouns** ***que*** (that/which/who), ***donde*** (where) or ***cuando*** (when) to give more information about the noun you are talking about.

*Voy con mi amigo, **que** se llama Álex.*
I go with my friend, **who** is called Alex.
*Salgo al patio, **donde** juego al fútbol.*
I go out to the playground, **where** I play football.

Page 118

Escuchar 2 **Listen to Clari. Which question is she answering? Write down the correct letter. Then listen again and note down two details in English for each answer. (1–6)**

- **a** ¿Cómo vas al instituto por la mañana?
- **b** ¿A qué hora empiezan las clases?
- **c** ¿Cuánto tiempo dura cada clase?
- **d** ¿Qué haces en el recreo?
- **e** ¿Dónde sueles comer?
- **f** ¿Qué haces después del insti?

In the present tense, some verbs are irregular in the '**I**' form only. They include:

hacer	→	*ha**g**o* (I do/make)
venir	→	*ven**g**o* (I come)
poner	→	*pon**g**o* (I put)
tener	→	*tra**ig**o* (I bring)
salir	→	*sal**g**o* (I go out/leave)
conocer	→	*cono**zc**o* (I know/meet)

Hablar 3 **In pairs, take turns to ask and answer the six questions from exercise 2.**

- *¿Cómo vas al instituto por la mañana?*
- *Normalmente voy al insti (en autobús) porque …*

Voy al insti **a** pie / **en** [bici].
Las clases empiezan a las …
Las clases terminan a las …
Cada clase dura …

Leer 4 **Read the texts and write the correct name for each question. Then translate Raquel's text into English.**

la bandera	*flag*
las artes escénicas	*performing arts*

¿Qué actividades extraescolares haces?

Soy muy deportista y llevo dos años jugando al voleibol con el equipo de mi insti. Los lunes a la hora de comer ayudo con la radio escolar. Me encanta porque te da la oportunidad de desarrollar tus talentos y hacer nuevos amigos. Acabo de ganar un premio por un programa, donde hice una entrevista a la directora.

Mi pasión es el medioambiente y mi amiga Mónica y yo llevamos tres años participando en el proyecto 'Ecoescuela' después del insti. Estoy orgulloso de nuestro trabajo porque el año pasado conseguimos la 'Bandera Verde'. La semana pasada organizamos un concurso para celebrar el Día de la Biodiversidad.

¡Me encantan las artes escénicas! Soy miembro del club de teatro y toco en la orquesta del insti. Además, llevo seis meses asistiendo a clases de baile urbano, que es muy popular en nuestro insti, y anoche hicimos un espectáculo. En mi opinión, hacer actividades extraescolares te da más confianza y te permite aprender cosas nuevas.

Who …

1 recently organised a competition?
2 recently won a prize?
3 is proud of their work?
4 says these activities give you more confidence?
5 interviewed the headteacher?
6 plays an instrument?

When translating into English, remember that some phrases do not translate word for word. Spanish often uses the word ***de*** to give more information about a noun.

la hora ***de*** *comer*	lunchtime
el equipo ***de*** *natación*	the swimming team
el club ***de*** *teatro*	the drama club

Escuchar 5 **Listen to some students talking about their extracurricular activities. Copy and complete the table in English. (1–4)**

	Activity	How long?	Opinion (two details)	Recent success
1				

G

To say how long you have been doing something, use the present tense of ***llevar*** + time period + the **present participle**.

Llevo *dos años* ***jugando*** *al fútbol.*
I've been playing football for two years.

You can also use the present tense of a verb + ***desde hace*** + time period.

Juego al fútbol ***desde hace*** *dos años.*
I've been playing football for two years.

Page 119

Hablar 6 **In pairs, take turns to ask and answer the following questions.**

- *¿Qué actividades extraescolares haces?*
- *¿Cuánto tiempo llevas haciendo / participando en / jugando al/a la …?*
- *¿Por qué te gusta esta actividad?*
- *¿Qué hiciste recientemente con el club/equipo?*

Escribir 7 **Write a text about your extracurricular activities. Answer the questions from exercise 6 and look at the texts in exercise 4 for ideas.**

Mi pasión es … y llevo … *meses/años* *…*
También, soy miembro del *club/equipo* *de …*

Soy miembro del club/equipo de …	
Llevo [tres] meses / [dos] años	asistiendo a … jugando al/a la … participando en … tocando …
Te permite Te anima a Te ayuda a	aprender cosas nuevas. desarrollar tus talentos. hacer nuevos amigos.
Te da	la oportunidad de … más confianza. un sentimiento de éxito.
Te hace sentir orgulloso/a. Te quita el estrés.	

2 ¿Qué tal tus estudios?

- Talking about your studies
- Using *lo que*
- Talking about the opinions of others

Escuchar 1

Listen and write the following information in English for each person: (1–5)

- the two subjects they mention
- their opinion of each subject

En Perú, hay más de 20.000 escuelas bilingües donde los alumnos tienen clases en español y también en una de las 48 lenguas originarias (por ejemplo, *el quechua*).

Este sistema ayuda a conservar la identidad cultural, aunque lo malo es que hay una falta de profesores con conocimientos de ambos idiomas.

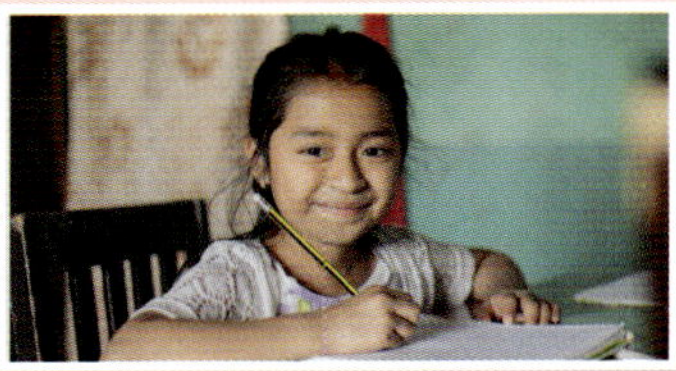

Prefiero Odio Me encanta (No) Me gusta	**el** alemán **el** dibujo **el** español **el** francés **el** teatro **la** educación física	**la** geografía **la** historia **la** informática **la** literatura **la** música **la** religión **la** tecnología	porque (no) es	aburrid**o**/**a**(s). complicad**o**/**a**(s). difícil(es). divertid**o**/**a**(s). dur**o**/**a**(s). fácil(es). importante(s).
Prefiero Odio Me encanta**n** (No) Me gusta**n**	**los** idiomas **las** ciencias **las** matemáticas		porque (no) son	imposible(s). interesante(s). pesad**o**/**a**(s). práctic**o**/**a**(s). sencill**o**/**a**(s). útil(es).

la lengua originaria *indigenous language*

Leer 2

Complete the sentences with the correct subject in Spanish. Remember to include the definite article (*el/la/los/las*). Then translate the phrases in bold into English.

1 **Mi asignatura favorita es** ___ porque me gusta aprender sobre lo que ocurrió en el pasado.

2 **Me interesa** la naturaleza, y por lo tanto me encantan ___.

3 **Hago mucho esfuerzo en** ___ y mi profesor dice que pinto muy bien.

4 **Lo que más me gusta es** ___ y dedico mucho tiempo a leer novelas.

5 **Me cuesta mucho** resolver problemas con los números, y por eso **no aguanto** ___.

6 **Mi pasión es** ___ y llevo tres años tocando el teclado en una banda.

7 **Lo que menos me gusta es** ___ porque **no entiendo** lo que dice mi profesor cuando habla en inglés.

decir (dice) *to say (he/she says)*

G

Use ***lo que*** to mean 'what' when you are not asking a question.

***Lo que** más me gusta es …*
What I like most is …

*No entiendo **lo que** dice.*
I don't understand **what** he/she says.

Page 119

The four consonants in the word **C**a**R**o**L**i**N**a are the only ones that can be written as double letters in Spanish.

abburrido

Take extra care with cognates.

diffícil *impossible*

The only exceptions are some words taken from other languages (e.g. *el jazz*).

Hablar 3

In pairs, give your opinion about the subjects you study. Use phrases from exercise 2 to extend your answers.

- *¿Cuál es tu asignatura favorita?*
- *Prefiero …, ya que es/son … Además, me encanta(n) … porque …*
- *¿Qué otras asignaturas te gustan?*
- *También, me gusta(n) …, ya que …*
- *¿Y qué asignaturas no te gustan?*
- *Odio / No me gusta(n) nada / No aguanto … porque …*

Leer **4** **Read the texts. Then copy and complete the sentences in English.**

Amalia

A mis amigas Raquel y Rosa les gusta mucho la religión, pero mi asignatura favorita es la educación física porque me encanta correr. Sin embargo, odio la informática. La profesora nos pone deberes el martes y luego tenemos que entregarlos el miércoles. No es justo. Mañana tengo una prueba de historia. ¡Qué pesado! Siempre hago un esfuerzo, pero me cuesta recordar todas las fechas. Esta noche repasaré mucho porque quiero aprobar.

Diego

Lo que más me gusta es el teatro. En el pasado no tenía mucha confianza en mí mismo, pero ya no tengo miedo de actuar en escena cuando hacemos una obra de teatro. A mi amigo Ricardo le gustan las matemáticas, pero a mí me cuesta resolver los problemas más complicados. ¡Es durísimo! En abril tengo otro examen de alemán. Para sacar buenas notas, aprenderé de mis errores y participaré más en clase. ¡No quiero volver a suspender!

entregar	*to hand in*
volver a (+ infin)	*to (do) again*

1 Amalia's favourite subject is … because …
2 She hates … because the teacher …
3 In history, she finds it hard to …
4 Tonight she will … because …
5 In the past, Diego …
6 He is no longer scared of …
7 Ricardo likes …, but Diego finds it hard to …
8 To get good marks, he will …

G

For verbs like ***gustar***, ***encantar*** and ***interesar***, change the **pronoun** according to who you are talking about.

me *gusta(n)* ***nos*** *gusta(n)*
te *gusta(n)* ***os*** *gusta(n)*
le *gusta(n)* ***les*** *gusta(n)*

Remember to use the word ***a*** with these verbs when mentioning another person and include the **definite article** (***el***/***la***/***los***/***las***) when giving an opinion of a noun.

A *mi amigo le gusta* ***el*** *alemán, pero no le gustan* ***las*** *ciencias.*
My friend likes German, but he doesn't like science.

Page 119

Hablar **5** **In pairs, read out one of the texts from exercise 4, paying attention to the letters *r* and *rr*.**

r is pronounced by touching your tongue against the back of your front teeth.
rr (or ***r*** at the start of a word) has a stronger, rolled sound.

Escuchar **6** **Listen to some students talking about what they will do to succeed. Copy and complete the table in English. (1–6)**

¿Qué harás para tener éxito?

	Subject	Will …	Why?
1	English	participate more …	

Para …
aprobar mis exámenes, …
mejorar mi nivel, …
sacar buenas/mejores notas, …
tener éxito en la prueba, …

aprenderé de mis errores.
asistiré a clases de repaso.
participaré más en clase.
dedicaré más tiempo a repasar.
preguntaré al profe si no entiendo.

Escribir **7** **Translate this text into Spanish.**

I prefer practical subjects because they are more fun than languages. I have been studying drama for three years. I'm interested in music and my teacher says that I sing well. My best friend likes history, but I think that it's extremely difficult to remember the dates. Tonight I will revise lots because I have a test next week.

Remember to include *el*/*la*/*los*/*las*.

Use a comparative 'sandwich' around the adjective.

Use *llevo* + time period + present participle, or present tense + *desde hace* + time period.

Decir (to say/tell) is a stem-changing verb.

3 ¿Cómo cambiarías tu instituto?

- Talking about how you would change your school
- Using the conditional tense
- Using impersonal verbs with an infinitive

Leer 1 **Read how these students would improve their school and match each text (1–6) to the most appropriate opinion below (a–f). Then translate the seven conditional tense verbs in bold into English.**

¿Qué harías para mejorar tu instituto?

1

Organizaría una campaña para luchar contra el acoso.

2

Mejoraría la calidad y la variedad de la comida.

3

Permitiría el uso de los móviles en clase.

4

Reduciría el precio del uniforme.

5

Ofrecería más actividades extraescolares.

6

Construiría un nuevo gimnasio e **instalaría** una piscina.

Lo malo de mi instituto es que ...

a tenemos que gastar mucho dinero en la chaqueta y la corbata – son carísimas.

b las instalaciones deportivas son viejas, están en mal estado y huelen mal.

c los bocadillos son malísimos y hay pocas opciones para los vegetarianos.

d no hay muchas oportunidades deportivas o artísticas después del insti.

e las reglas son demasiado estrictas. Por ejemplo, los móviles están prohibidos.

f ciertos alumnos son violentos y amenazan o pegan a los demás.

Escuchar 2 **Listen to check your answers to exercise 1. Then write down one additional change that each person would make to improve their school in English. (1–6)**

abriría	cambiaría	dejaría
compraría	vendería	aumentaría

G

Use the **conditional tense** to say what you would do.
You already know *me gustaría* (I would like).

To form the conditional, add the imperfect tense endings of ***-er/-ir*** verbs to the infinitive.

	cambiar (*to change*)
(yo)	cambiar**ía**
(tú)	cambiar**ías**
(él/ella/usted)	cambiar**ía**
(nosotros/as)	cambiar**íamos**
(vosotros/as)	cambiar**íais**
(ellos/ellas/ustedes)	cambiar**ían**

Cambiaría *el uniforme.* — **I would change** the uniform.

Some verbs have an **irregular stem** in both the simple future and conditional tense, including:

tener → ***tendr****ía* (I would have)
hacer → ***har****ía* (I would do/make)
poder → ***podr****ía* (I would be able to / I could)
poner → ***pondr****ía* (I would put)

The conditional of *hay* (there is/are) is ***habría*** (there would be).

Page 120

Hablar **3**

In pairs, discuss what you would change in your school.

- *¿Qué es lo malo de tu instituto?*
- *Lo malo de mi insti es que las instalaciones son … Además, (no) hay mucho/a(s) …*
- *¿Qué harías para mejorar tu instituto?*
- *Primero, pintaría la biblioteca. Luego, … Finalmente, …*

Escuchar **4**

Read the list of school rules and fill in the gaps using the correct word from the word box. Then listen to Daniel and write down which three rules he would change and why.

IES López Blanco

Reglas para los alumnos de secundaria

a Hay que asistir a todas las clases y ___ a tiempo.
b Se debe ___ a los otros alumnos y a los profesores.
c No se permite ___ a los servicios sin el permiso del profesor.
d Hay que ___ limpio el patio y no tirar basura al suelo.
e Está prohibido ___ dispositivos electrónicos personales.
f Hay que ___ sentado durante la clase.
g No se debe ___ ni beber en las aulas (excepto agua).

G

These **impersonal verbs** are followed by the infinitive:

hay que	you/one must
(no) se debe	you/one must (not)
(no) se permite	you are (not) allowed to
está prohibido	it is forbidden (to)

No se debe *comer en clase.*
You mustn't eat in class.

quedarse	comer	~~asistir~~	mantener
respetar	traer	llegar	ir

estar de acuerdo con *to agree with*

Escribir **5**

Write a text about what you would change in your school. Mention:

- what you don't like about your school — *Lo malo de mi insti es que … Además, …*
- how you would improve your school — *Para mejorar mi instituto, primero … Luego, …*
- a school rule that you disagree with — *En mi insti no se permite / hay que …*
- why you disagree with it — *No estoy de acuerdo con esta norma porque …*
- how you would change the rule. — *Permitiría a los alumnos [comer/usar/ir …]*

Leer **6**

Read the text and select the correct option for each question.

Programa de educación con perros para combatir el acoso escolar

Respétame es el nombre de un programa desarrollado por la Fundación Affinity y la escuela Lleó XIII de Barcelona para reducir el acoso escolar. Durante doce semanas, los alumnos asisten a sesiones especiales durante el día escolar donde hacen actividades distintas con los perros de terapia. Aprenden el respeto, la cooperación y la buena comunicación.

Muchos perros diferentes participan en los ejercicios – grandes y pequeños, algunos más rápidos en aprender y otros más lentos. Los alumnos aprenden que todos los perros – y todas las personas – tienen puntos fuertes y débiles, pero que todos son buenos en algo. El programa les enseña la importancia de aceptar las diferencias y de trabajar en equipo para resolver problemas, y que no es necesario gritar o amenazar para conseguir lo que quieres cuando sientes frustración.

el perro de terapia *therapy dog*

1 The programme has been developed to reduce **animal cruelty** / **bullying** / **stress**.
2 The sessions take place **after school** / **at weekends** / **during the school day**.
3 Some of the dogs **finish the exercises** / **run** / **learn** more quickly than others.
4 Pupils learn that everyone has different **strengths** / **interests** / **problems**.
5 You don't need to shout or threaten to **get what you want** / **explain what you need** / **describe how you feel**.

4 La gente de mi insti

- Talking about students and teachers at school
- Using negatives
- Forming questions

Leer 1 **Write down your answers to this survey to find out what sort of student you are. Then translate the <u>seven</u> negative sentences into English.**

Example: *No llevo ni libros ni bolígrafos al insti.*
I don't take either books or pens to school.

¿Qué tipo de alumno eres?

1 ¿Cómo te preparas para el día escolar?
- **a** Todas las noches preparo mi mochila antes de acostarme.
- **b** Suelo recordar lo que necesito, aunque no siempre.
- **c** No llevo ni libros ni bolígrafos al insti.

2 ¿Cuándo sueles llegar al insti por la mañana?
- **a** Siempre llego temprano.
- **b** Suelo llegar a tiempo, pero depende del día.
- **c** Nunca llego a tiempo.

3 ¿Qué haces si te pierdes una clase?
- **a** No me pierdo ninguna clase.
- **b** Pregunto a un compañero lo que perdí.
- **c** No hago nada.

4 ¿Cuánto tiempo pasas repasando para las pruebas?
- **a** Paso dos o tres horas repasando.
- **b** Paso media hora repasando, si tengo tiempo.
- **c** No repaso para las pruebas.

5 ¿Dónde sueles hacer los deberes?
- **a** Los hago en casa o en la biblioteca.
- **b** Los hago en el autobús o en la cantina.
- **c** No los hago jamás.

6 ¿Aprendes mucho en clase? ¿Por qué (no)?
- **a** Sí, ya que siempre escucho al profe y hago todas las tareas.
- **b** Normalmente, sí, pero a veces hablo con mis compañeros.
- **c** No, porque no escucho a nadie y tampoco hago las tareas.

Tus respuestas

- Mayoría de **a** — Siempre eres ambicioso(a), trabajador(a) e independiente. Tienes ganas de tener éxito.
- Mayoría de **b** — A veces eres un(a) estudiante responsable, pero podrías hacer más esfuerzo para sacar buenas notas.
- Mayoría de **c** — Necesitas una actitud más positiva y seria si quieres aprobar los exámenes.

Escuchar 2 **Listen to Yoli answering the survey. Write down the <u>six</u> letters and her reason for each answer in English. Note that she sometimes uses different words to express the answer given. (1–6)**

Hablar 3 **In pairs, take turns to ask and answer the survey in exercise 1. Extend your answers by giving reasons.**

(No) Soy	muy bastante demasiado	perezoso/a. trabajador(a). responsable.	
(No) Es		aburrido/a. importante.	
Me levanto Salgo de casa		temprano. tarde.	
(No) Tengo	tiempo.	ganas (de ...).	
(No) Quiero	aprender. aprobar.	escuchar. estudiar.	hablar. repasar.

What do the <u>six</u> **question words** in exercise 1 mean?

For 'yes/no' questions, simply use question marks (when writing) or correct intonation (when speaking) to turn the statement into a question.

Aprendes mucho en clase.	You learn a lot in class.
¿Aprendes mucho en clase?	Do you learn a lot in class?

G

Many **negative** expressions form a 'sandwich' around the verb:

***No** hago **nada**.*	I **don't** do **anything**.
***No** escucho a **nadie**.*	I **don't** listen to **anyone**.
***No** estudio **ni** dibujo **ni** teatro.*	I **don't** study **either** art **or** drama.
***No** falto a **ninguna** clase.*	I **don't** miss **a single** lesson.

Nunca/jamás (never) can go <u>before</u> or <u>after</u> the verb. When used after, add ***no*** before the verb.

***Nunca** leo. / **No** leo **nunca**.*	I **never** read.

Tampoco (neither/nor) usually goes before the verb.

***Tampoco** repaso.*	I **don't** revise **either**.

Page 120

Leer 4

Read the <u>ten</u> statements below. For each one, decide whether you think it refers to (a) the perfect student, (b) the ideal teacher or (c) both.

¿Cómo sería un alumno perfecto / una alumna perfecta?

¿Cómo sería tu profesor(a) ideal?

Use ***sino*** to say 'but rather'.
Mi profe ideal no sería estricto, ***sino*** *tolerante.*
My ideal teacher wouldn't be strict, **but rather** tolerant.

1 No nos pondría demasiados deberes.
2 Tendría un buen sentido del humor.
3 Nos dejaría usar el móvil en clase.
4 Escucharía al/a la profe con cuidado.
5 No sería estricto/a, sino tolerante.
6 Haría mucho esfuerzo para sacar buenas notas.
7 Crearía un buen ambiente para los alumnos.
8 Siempre entregaría los deberes a tiempo.
9 Nos dejaría expresar nuestra personalidad.
10 Nunca llegaría tarde a clase.

Escuchar 5

Listen and fill in the gaps. Pay particular attention to the pronunciation of the letters *ñ* and *u*.

Me llamo Lucas. Suelo sacar buenas notas porque soy trabajador y nunca llego tarde por la **1**. Sin embargo, mi **2** Begoña no tiene una actitud positiva hacia los estudios y su comportamiento es malísimo. Es muy vaga, nunca se calla y hace los deberes en el **3** – ¡si los hace!

Me llevo bien con mi profesor de **4** porque me da consejos para mejorar mi trabajo y nos deja escuchar música en clase. Por otro lado, no aguanto a la **5** Núñez, mi profe de **6**, porque no estoy de acuerdo con su manera de enseñar. Sus clases son aburridas y nos trata como a niños **7**. Mi profesor ideal sería comprensivo, nunca se pondría enojado y no gritaría a nadie. Tampoco nos pondría demasiadas **8** ni nos castigaría.

¿Y cómo sería el alumno perfecto? En mi opinión, **9** mucho, pero también haría mucho deporte. Es importante tener una vida equilibrada para cuidar la **10** física y mental.

vago/a	*lazy*
comprensivo/a	*understanding*

Leer 6

Read the text from exercise 5 again. Next, using the names in the box below, write down who each picture refers to. Then read out the whole text with your partner.

Example: a – Begoña

The letter ***ñ*** is pronounced 'n-y', as in the English word 'canyon'. The letter ***u*** is a short, crisp sound, which is pronounced with your lips rounded and pushing forward.

Lucas
Begoña
Señora Núñez
El profesor de dibujo
El profesor ideal
El alumno perfecto

Escribir 7

Write a text about your teachers and what your perfect teacher would be like.

- *Me llevo bien con mi profesor(a) de ... porque ...*
- *Sin embargo, no me gusta mi ..., ya que ...*
- *Mi profesor(a) ideal sería/tendría ...*
- *También nos dejaría ... Nunca ...*

5 El viaje de fin de curso

- Describing a school trip in the past
- Using adjectives and adverbs
- Identifying false friends

Escuchar 1 **Listen and read. Then answer the questions below in English.**

Noticias

Viaje de fin de curso 4° ESO

Nuestros alumnos acaban de disfrutar de un gran viaje de fin de curso a Valencia. Yolanda Marzo, alumna de 4° C, nos cuenta qué tal fue la visita.

El viaje a Valencia que hicimos **recientemente** fue increíble. El primer día visitamos el Parque Natural de la Albufera donde dimos un paseo en barco. **Normalmente** no me interesa la naturaleza, pero este lugar me encantó.

Por la noche, asistimos a una clase de cocina donde aprendimos a preparar la paella, el plato de arroz tradicional de Valencia. **Históricamente**, era un plato de carne, pero ahora mucha gente escoge otras variedades. Luego la comimos – ¡estaba riquísima!

El segundo día hicimos windsurf en la playa. Hizo muy buen tiempo, pero el único problema era que el mar estaba muy frío. **Desafortunadamente**, mi amigo Esteban perdió su reloj en la arena. ¡Qué mala suerte!

El tercer día fue **totalmente** distinto – hizo mal tiempo y llovió el día entero. **Afortunadamente**, no importó porque visitamos L'Oceanogràfic. Fue muy emocionante.

Finalmente, el último día fuimos al parque temático Terra Mítica. No había mucha gente, y por eso las colas no eran largas. También bebimos horchata, la bebida típica que se bebe en verano. Sin embargo, nuestro director bebió demasiada horchata, y vomitó **inmediatamente** cuando se montó en Titánide, una montaña rusa divertidísima. ¡Qué vergüenza!

El viaje fue una experiencia **verdaderamente** única y me gustaría volver algún día.

Yolanda

¡Qué vergüenza! *How embarrassing!*

L'Oceanogràfic

Terra Mítica

1. What did they do at *la Albufera*?
2. What does Yolanda tell us about paella? (Give three details.)
3. What didn't she like about going windsurfing?
4. What did her friend Esteban do?
5. Why didn't it matter when it rained?
6. Why was the headteacher sick?

En muchos países hispanohablantes, los alumnos hacen **un viaje de fin de curso** con los compañeros de clase cuando terminan los estudios de secundaria.

Normalmente los padres tienen que pagar el costo total, pero en algunos países el gobierno lo paga. En Buenos Aires (Argentina), los alumnos pueden hacer un viaje de tres noches sin pagar nada.

Leer 2 **Read the text again and write down the adverbs ending in *-mente* that have a similar meaning to the following adverbs.**

1. en el pasado
2. por último
3. en general
4. completamente
5. hace poco
6. realmente
7. enseguida
8. por suerte

Look out for '**false friends**' – words that look or sound like an English word but have a different meaning.

What do these words from the text in exercise 1 mean?

asistir	*cola*	*emocionante*
arena	*importar*	*largo*

Escuchar 3 **Yolanda's teacher is talking about the trip from exercise 1 but gets some of the facts wrong. Listen and write down the numbers of the four correct statements, based on the information given in the text. (1–8)**

G

Adverbs are used to say when, where or how something is done.

In English, many adverbs end in '-ly'.

In Spanish, add -***mente*** to the **feminine** form of the adjective.

rápido → *rápida* → *rápida**mente*** (quickly)
fácil → *fácil* → *fácil**mente*** (easily)

Page 121

Leer 4 **Read the text from exercise 1 again. Copy and complete the table for each of the underlined adjectives.**

	Shortened form? (Y/N)	English meaning
gran	Y	great

G

Adjectives must agree with the noun they are describing and usually follow the noun.
una bebida típica — a **typical** drink

Some adjectives come before the noun. These include:
mucho/a (much/a lot) ***poco/a*** (little/few)
próximo/a (next) ***último/a*** (last/latest)

Some adjectives have a shortened form when used before a **masculine** singular noun:
primero → ***primer*** *tercero* → ***tercer*** *alguno* → ***algún***
bueno → ***buen*** *malo* → ***mal*** *ninguno* → ***ningún***

The meaning of certain adjectives depends on their position:
*el **único** problema* (the **only** problem)
*un lugar **único*** (a **unique** place)

When used before a masculine or feminine singular noun, ***grande*** shortens to ***gran*** and means 'great'. When used after a noun, it means 'big' or 'large'.
*una **gran** persona* (a **great** person)
*un museo **grande*** (a **big** museum)

Page 121

Escribir 5 **Read the text below. Look at the words in brackets and write the correct form of each adjective or adverb ending in *-mente*.**

El Lago Nahuel Huapi, Argentina

1 (reciente) mis compañeros y yo hicimos un viaje de fin de curso a Bariloche, la ciudad más **2 (visitado)** de la Patagonia, que se puede alcanzar **3 (fácil)** en tren, avión o autobús. En invierno hace frío, pero **4 (actual)** hace muy **5 (bueno)** tiempo.

El **6 (primero)** día llegamos al hotel y luego salimos **7 (rápido)** para visitar el parque nacional, donde disfrutamos de las vistas **8 (maravilloso)** de las montañas, los bosques y los lagos y respiramos el aire puro. ¡**9 (seguro)** no hay **10 (ninguno)** lugar más hermoso en el mundo!

Cada día hicimos actividades distintas: excursiones por la ciudad, actividades acuáticas en el lago, ciclismo de montaña, etc. ¡Y la **11 (último)** noche aun tuvimos una fiesta de disfraces! Fue inolvidable y, más que nada, fue una **12 (grande)** oportunidad para celebrar con los amigos el fin de nuestros estudios.

aun *even*

Hablar 6 **In pairs, talk about a school trip using the questions below.**

- *¿Adónde fuiste?*
- *¿Cómo era (el pueblo / la ciudad)?*
- *¿Visitaste algún lugar de interés?*
- *¿Qué otras actividades hiciste?*
- *¿Tuviste algún problema?*
- *¿Qué tiempo hizo?*
- *¿Te gustaría volver en el futuro?*
- *¿Cuál es tu opinión de los viajes escolares?*

Escribir 7 **Use your imagination to write about an end-of-year school trip to Barcelona. Use the texts above and this trip itinerary to help you.**

Viaje de fin de curso a Barcelona

	mañana	tarde/noche
Día 1	Paseo a pie (Barrio Gótico)	Visita cultural (Sagrada Familia)
Día 2	Actividades acuáticas/ deportivas (playa)	Espectáculo de agua, música y luces (Fuente Mágica)
Día 3	Excursión al parque temático (PortAventura)	
Día 4	Visita cultural (Museo Picasso)	Compras (centro comercial)

Remember to use:
- the **preterite tense** to say what you did, what happened, what the weather was like and to give your opinion in the past.
- the **imperfect tense** to describe things in the past or say what something used to be like.

Try to use a variety of verb forms (e.g. I, he/she, we/they, etc.).

Gramática 1

Absolute superlatives (Zona de cultura, page 107)

Escribir 1

Complete the sentences below with the absolute superlative form of the adjectives in brackets. Then translate the sentences into English.

Example: 1 *Las instalaciones son **malísimas** y ...*
The facilities are really bad and ...

1. Las instalaciones son **(malo)** y el gimnasio es **(viejo)**.
2. Mi insti es **(popular)** porque los alumnos sacan notas **(bueno)**.
3. El servicio en la cantina es **(lento)**, aunque sirven platos **(rico)**.
4. La hora de comer es **(corto)**, pero hay muchas actividades **(divertido)**.
5. Mi uniforme escolar es **(caro)** y la camisa es **(feo)**.
6. Las matemáticas son **(útil)**, pero los exámenes son **(duro)**.
7. Mi profesora de historia es **(listo)**. También es **(simpático)**.
8. Estaba **(cansado)** porque el viaje era **(largo)**.

To say 'really [good], 'extremely [expensive]', use the **absolute superlative**.
Add ***-ísimo/a*** to the end of the adjective, and make it agree.

If the adjective ends in a vowel, remove it before adding the ending.
***La** historia es divertid**ísima**.*
***Los** profes son buen**ísimos**.*

Some adjectives have a spelling change to preserve the sound.

*rico → riqu**ísimo***
*largo → largu**ísimo***

Only the ***-ísimo*** part of the word has an accent:
*difícil → dificil**ísimo***

You can only use the absolute superlative if it would also make sense to use ***muy*** or ***bastante*** before the adjective.

grande ✓ *famoso* ✓ *difícil* ✓
favorito ✗ *tercero* ✗ *otro* ✗

Relative pronouns *que, donde, cuando* (Unit 1, page 108)

Escribir 2

Write eight sentences using a phrase or word from each box. Make sure that your sentences are logical, paying attention to verb endings and tenses. Then translate them into English.

Example: 1 *Voy al insti con Sonia que es mi mejor amiga.*
I go to school with Sonia, who is my best friend.

1. Voy al insti con Sonia ...
2. Fuimos al gimnasio ...
3. Soy muy artística y prefiero los días ...
4. Hay muchos alumnos ...
5. No me interesa nada la novela ...
6. Tenemos una piscina enorme ...
7. Me encanta la nueva falda ...
8. Tengo tres meses de vacaciones, ...

que ...
donde ...
cuando ...

estamos leyendo en este momento.
no escuchan al profe en clase.
acabas de comprar.
jugamos al baloncesto.
se puede nadar después del insti.
tengo dibujo y teatro.
es mi mejor amiga.
llega el verano. ¡Qué guay!

Use ***que*** (that/which/who), ***donde*** (where) or ***cuando*** (when) to give more information about the noun you are talking about.

*Voy con una amiga **que** se llama Ana.*	I go with a friend, **who** is called Ana.
*Salgo al patio, **donde** juego al tenis.*	I go out to the playground, **where** I play tennis.
*Prefiero los días **cuando** tenemos teatro.*	I prefer days **when** we have drama.

You must use the word ***que***, even where it is optional in English.
*Me encantó la película **que** vimos ayer.* I loved the film **(that)** we saw yesterday.

Don't confuse relative pronouns with the question words (or 'interrogatives') ***qué***, ***dónde*** and ***cuándo***, which always have a written accent.
*¿**Qué** haces con el dinero **que** recibes?* **What** do you do with the money **(that)** you receive?

Llevar + present participle (Unit 1, page 109)

Hablar 3 **In pairs, take turns to ask and answer questions using the pictures below. Give opinions to develop your answers.**

- For pictures 1–3, use the *tú* (you singular) and *yo* (I) forms.
- For pictures 4–6, use the *vosotros* (you plural) and *nosotros* (we) forms.

Example:

- *¿Cuánto tiempo llevas **tocando** la guitarra?*
- *Llevo más de cinco años **tocando** la guitarra. Es muy difícil.*

To say how long you have been doing something, use the present tense of ***llevar*** + time period + the **present participle**.
*¿Cuánto tiempo **llevas esperando**?*
How long **have you been waiting**?

To form the present participle, remove the ***-ar***, ***-er*** or ***-ir*** from the infinitive and add ***-ando***, ***-iendo*** or ***-iendo***.

Irregular present participles include:
leer → *le**y**endo*
dormir → *d**u**rmiendo*
servir → *s**i**rviendo*

You can also use the present tense of a verb + ***desde hace*** + time period as an alternative. See page 109.

un minuto	un día	un mes
un año	una hora	una semana

Use ***más de*** (more than) + a number to refer to the time period.

1 
more than 5 years

2 
4 hours

3 
2 days

4 
nearly 6 months

5 
3 weeks

6 
more than 20 minutes

Lo que (Unit 2, page 110)

Leer 4 **Read the grammar box on page 110 and translate these texts into English.**

1 Lo que más me gusta es la comida en mi insti. Me encanta lo que sirven en la cantina, pero lo que no entiendo es el precio – es altísimo. ***Paula***

2 No sé lo que quiero estudiar el año próximo. Lo que me gustaría hacer es ir a un instituto diferente, ya que no me gusta lo que tenemos que llevar – el uniforme no es muy cómodo. ***Rafa***

3 Lo que hacemos en las clases de teatro suele ser divertido, pero lo que menos me gusta es que hay alumnos en mi clase que no hacen lo que dice el profesor. ***Arturo***

Talking about the opinions of others (Unit 2, page 111)

Escuchar 5 **Read the grammar box on page 111. Listen to Fernando and write down what he says in Spanish, taking care to spot the correct pronoun (*me/te/le/nos/os/les*). Then write down who each sentence is referring to. (1–6)**

Example: 1 *Nos encantan los deportes. (we)*

Escribir 6 **Write six sentences of your own in which you describe/ask about the opinions of others. Use Fernando's examples from exercise 5 to help you. Where appropriate, justify the opinions by adding reasons.**

Example: 1 *A mi hermano le interesan los idiomas porque son útiles.*

Gramática 2

Conditional tense (Unit 3, page 112)

Escribir **1** **Read what Santi's ideal school would be like. Write out the sentences, changing the verbs in brackets to the conditional tense. Look at the context to identify the correct person of the verb.**

1 En mi insti ideal **(haber)** cuatro recreos al día.
2 Las clases **(empezar)** a las diez.
3 Mis amigos y yo **(poder)** jugar a los videojuegos en clase.
4 Yo no **(hacer)** mis deberes, pero mis profes no **(decir)** nada.
5 Solo **(tener)** mis asignaturas favoritas.
6 Mi amigo Iván **(ser)** el director y nos **(permitir)** dormir en clase.
7 ¡Mis amigos y yo no **(aprender)** nada!
8 ¿Y tú? ¿**(Venir)** a mi instituto ideal?

Use the **conditional tense** to say what you would do. To form the conditional, add the imperfect tense endings of **-er/-ir** verbs to the infinitive:

*cambiar**ía***	I would change
*cambiar**ías***	you (singular) would change
*cambiar**ía***	he/she/it would change
*cambiar**íamos***	we would change
*cambiar**íais***	you (plural) would change
*cambiar**ían***	they would change

Some verbs have an **irregular stem** in both the simple future and conditional tenses, but the endings are the same as for regular verbs:

decir → ***dir**ía* (I would say/tell)
tener → ***tendr**ía* (I would have)
hacer → ***har**ía* (I would do/make)
poder → ***podr**ía* (I would be able to / I could)
poner → ***pondr**ía* (I would put)
querer → ***querr**ía* (I would want)
saber → ***sabr**ía* (I would know)
salir → ***saldr**ía* (I would go out)
venir → ***vendr**ía* (I would come)

The conditional of *hay* (there is/are – from the verb *haber*) is ***habría*** (there would be).

Escribir **2** **Read what Eva doesn't like about her school. In Spanish, write a list of six things you think she would do to improve it. Use the verbs in the word box to help you.**

Example: 1 *Permitiría las zapatillas de deporte.*

I don't like my school. You can't wear t-shirts and mobile phones are banned. I think the rules are stupid. The library is too small, there aren't enough computers and the books are all really old. Also, the teachers are too strict and the headteacher is awful. Worst of all, the gym is falling apart, the food is very expensive and the uniform is uncomfortable. ***Eva***

cambiar comprar construir mejorar permitir poner reducir

Negatives (Unit 4, page 114)

Leer **3** **Read the grammar box on page 114. Select the correct negative word for each sentence below. Then translate each sentence into English.**

1 No voy al insti con **no** / **nadie** / **nunca**, voy sola.
2 Mi profesor de ciencias no hace **tampoco** / **nada** / **ni** para ayudarme.
3 ¿Por qué **ningún** / **nada** / **no** hiciste los deberes?
4 **No** / **Nada** / **Nadie** hablo inglés y **nada** / **nadie** / **tampoco** lo entiendo.
5 **Nadie** / **Nada** / **Nunca** voy a la biblioteca después del insti.
6 No hago **ninguna** / **ni** / **no** actividad extraescolar.
7 No estudio ni historia **jamás** / **nada** / **ni** geografía.
8 **No** / **Nada** / **Nunca** toco nunca en la orquesta.

Adverbs ending in *-mente* (Unit 5, page 116)

Escribir **4** **Translate the texts (1–3) into Spanish. Use the adjectives in the word box to help you form the correct adverb.**

1 **Normally**, I play basketball **regularly**. However, I **rarely** go swimming, **especially** in winter because it rains **daily**.

2 **Recently**, I went to Spain with my class. **Generally**, I understand **perfectly**, but **unfortunately** they spoke very **quickly**!

3 The town was **truly** beautiful but **totally** different.

total diario desafortunado
especial general normal perfecto rápido
raro reciente regular verdadero

Adverbs are used to say when, where or how something is done.
In English, many adverbs end in '-ly'.
In Spanish, add -***mente*** to the **feminine** form of the adjective.
rápido → *rápida* → *rápida**mente*** (quickly)
normal → *normal* → *normal**mente*** (normally)

If the adjective has a written accent, the corresponding adverb does too. Compare the two examples above.

Some adverbs don't end in *-mente*. These include:

bien (well)	*mal* (badly)	*mucho* (a lot)	*poco* (a little)
aquí (here)	*allí* (there)	*siempre* (always)	*a menudo* (often)

The spelling and position of adjectives (Unit 5, page 117)

Escribir **5** **Read the grammar box on page 117. Rewrite the sentences below by using the adjectives in brackets to describe each noun. Think carefully about the spelling and position of the adjectives.**

Example: 1 *Hice **una excursión divertida** con **mi buen amigo** del insti, Tomás.*

1 Hice **una excursión** con **mi amigo** del insti, Tomás. (***fun*** / ***good***)
2 Fuimos a **una ciudad** con **un castillo**. (***big*** / ***old***)
3 Nos quedamos en **un hotel** con **un restaurante**. (***small*** / ***cheap***)
4 **El día** fue genial porque descubrimos **la arquitectura**. (***first*** / ***unique***)
5 Luego, visitamos **un museo** dedicado a **un artista**. (***interesting*** / ***great***)
6 **El problema** era que no había **tiendas**. (***only*** / ***many***)
7 **La primera noche** fuimos a ver **la película** de mi actor favorito. (***third*** / ***latest***)

¡En marcha! (Units 1–5)

Escuchar **6** **Listen and write down the correct word(s) for each gap in Spanish. Then translate the text into English.**

No me gustan las normas escolares porque no se **1** usar el móvil en clase. **2** me gustan las matemáticas, ya que **3** hacemos en clase es **4**. Mi amigo Javier y yo preferimos las asignaturas prácticas y por eso **5** los viernes cuando tenemos teatro. ¡Lo **6** todos los días, pero **7** estudiar otras asignaturas también! Llevamos dos años **8** al club de teatro y Javier es un actor **9**. En las vacaciones de Semana Santa fuimos a Madrid, **10** participamos en un concurso. No ganamos **11**, pero fue una **12** experiencia.

Hablar **7** **In pairs, take turns to read out the whole text from exercise 6, paying attention to pronunciation.**

Leer y escuchar

Reading

Leer 1

My studies. **Read Amira's social media post about what she enjoys studying. Answer the following questions in English.**

Me gusta estudiar matemáticas porque sé que es muy útil. Sin embargo, prefiero las asignaturas como las ciencias donde no tenemos que quedarnos sentados durante la clase entera. El problema es que me cuesta aprender cuando los otros alumnos están haciendo tanto ruido en clase – nunca se callan. A veces es muy difícil estudiar en clase y, por eso, creo que van a suspender sus exámenes, pero yo quiero aprobarlos y sacar buenas notas.

Mi profesor favorito es mi profesor de música. Siempre tiene **una sonrisa** en la cara y es una persona alegre con un buen sentido del humor.

quedarse sentado/a *to stay seated*

1 Why does Amira prefer subjects like science?
2 What stops her from making good progress in lessons?
3 What does Amira think will happen to her friends?
4 How does Amira describe the personality of her favourite teacher?

Leer 2

Which of these is the best translation of the words *una sonrisa*? Write the correct letter, A, B or C.

A a mask **B** a smile **C** a frown

Leer 3

Going back to school. **Read this article about the cost of preparing for the new school year in Spain. Complete the sentences on the following page. Write the correct letter, A, B or C, for each question.**

el cuaderno *exercise book*

Para muchas familias, la vuelta al colegio es uno de los momentos más caros del año. Antes del comienzo de las clases hay que comprar cuadernos, bolígrafos y otras cosas para el colegio. La ropa también representa un gasto grande, especialmente si se debe comprar uniforme con el nombre del instituto.

Lo que cuesta más dinero son los libros de texto, que pueden costar más de doscientos euros por alumno. Es otro gasto para los padres, excepto en algunas partes de España donde el gobierno de la región los compra.

Los gastos no paran cuando las clases empiezan, claro. Si los niños quieren participar en un club después del instituto, las actividades gratis son poco comunes. Y para los alumnos que viven lejos del instituto, tampoco es barato el transporte.

Read the text carefully. A single word can change the meaning of a phrase or a sentence.

Why is this word relevant for question 3?

When used before an adjective, ***poco*** means 'not very'.

Remember that ***tampoco*** is a negative word.

1 For many families, the return to school ...
A is an expensive time of year.
B is more expensive this year.
C gets more expensive every year.

2 The greatest cost is for ...
A materials such as pens and exercise books.
B branded school uniform.
C textbooks.

3 Parents have to buy their children's school textbooks ...
A in some parts of Spain.
B unless they work for the government.
C no matter where they live.

4 Free after-school activities ...
A are readily available.
B are sometimes available.
C are rarely available.

5 Transport for students is ...
A also expensive.
B quite cheap for students.
C free for those who live far from school.

Leer 4 ***Extra-curricular activities.*** **Translate the following text into English.**

El martes voy a tocar en la orquesta del instituto.
Según mi profesor, hay que practicar cada día para mejorar.
También llevo dos años asistiendo al club de correr que es divertidísimo.
Acabamos de participar en un concurso donde gané el segundo premio.
Recomendaría este tipo de actividad si quieres hacer nuevos amigos.

Listening

Escuchar 1 **On Spanish TV, you listen to a student talk about opinions on uniforms. What is the opinion given on the following aspects of what the student says? Write down P if the opinion is positive, N if the opinion is negative or P+N for an opinion that is positive and negative.**

Answer both parts of question 1.
1.1 how it makes you feel
1.2 girls' uniform

Answer both parts of question 2.
2.1 getting dressed in the morning
2.2 wearing uniform

For this type of task, listen out for positive and negative phrases. Would each of the following suggest an advantage or a disadvantage?
desafortunadamente
lo bueno era que
lo que más me gustaba

Escuchar 2 **Manuel is talking to Ana. What do they say? Listen and complete the sentences. Write A, B or C for each question. Answer both parts of the question. (1–2)**

1 Manuel is talking about ...
A what he does at lunchtime.
B what clubs he would like to join.
C what he did yesterday.

Manuel goes to the running club when ...
A the weather is good.
B he has time.
C his friends are going.

2 Ana's school doesn't have ...
A a school orchestra.
B many sports activities.
C a technology club.

This year Ana is going to ...
A join the basketball team.
B attend the cookery club.
C help out with the film club.

For some of these questions you will hear more than one of the options mentioned. Distractors like these are designed to test your ability to listen for **detail** as well as gist. Take care with words which have more than one meaning (e.g. *tiempo*) and with 'false friends' (e.g. *asistir*).

Escuchar 3 **You will hear five short sentences. Listen carefully and, using your knowledge of Spanish sounds, write down in Spanish exactly what you hear for each sentence.**

Listen out for:
- ***ce***, ***ci***, ***z*** – which sound like 'th' in 'think' (Spain)
- ***r-*** (at the start of a word) and ***rr*** – which sound like an engine revving!
- ***ñ*** – which sounds like 'ny' in 'canyon'

Módulo 5

Prueba oral

Role play

Escribir 1

Look at the role play card and prepare what you are going to say.

> You are talking to your Argentinian friend about school. Your teacher will play the part of your friend and will speak first.
> You should address your friend using *tú*.
> When you see this – **?** – you will have to ask a question.
> **You must include at least one verb in your response to each point.**
> **Task:**
> **1** Say what subject you dislike and why. (Give one subject and one reason.)
> **2** Say why learning Spanish is important. (Give one reason.)
> **3** Say what you usually do at breaktime. (Give two details.)
> **4** **?** Ask a question about exams.
> **5** Say what you are going to do tomorrow at school. (Give two details.)

Remember to use the definite article (*el*/*la*/*los*/*las*) when giving your opinion of a noun.

Two details could be what you do and with whom.

Keep it simple – there are no extra marks for using complex language in the role play.

Use the word for 'exams' to ensure your answer is relevant.

You can use the near future or the simple future tense.

Escuchar 2

Practise what you have prepared. Then, using your notes, listen and respond to the teacher.

Escuchar 3

Now listen to Josh doing the role play task. In English, note down what he says for each of the points on the card, including the question he asks.

Reading aloud

Hablar 1

Look at this task. With a partner, read aloud the six sentences, paying attention to the underlined letters.

> No soy la alumna perfecta, pero hago mucho esfuerzo.
> Me interesan las ciencias.
> Creo que son útiles y el profesor es paciente.
> Una vez al día tengo español con la señora Ibañez que enseña muy bien.
> Siempre me corrige los errores.
> En el futuro querría desarrollar mi nivel de inglés.

Take extra care with how you pronounce:
- ***ce***, ***ci***, ***z***
- ***r-*** (at the start of a word) / ***rr***
- ***ñ***
- ***u***

Escuchar 2

Listen and check your pronunciation.

Hablar 3

Listen to the teacher asking four questions that relate to the topic of education and work. Translate each question into English and prepare your own answers in Spanish. Then listen again and respond to the teacher.

Focus on giving accurate answers to these questions. Each response should contain at least three verbs.

Photo card

Escuchar 1 **Look at the photos below and read the first part of the task card. Then listen to Szymon describing the photo.**

1 What does Szymon say about the person in the middle of the first photo? (Give two details.)
2 What does he say about the type of school in the first photo?
3 In his opinion, what are the pupils doing? Do you agree?
4 Szymon says ***está explicando***. Can you work out the infinitive of this verb and what it means?
5 What does Szymon say the people are doing in the second photo?
6 What does he say they are wearing?

Prepare your own description of the photos. Your teacher will ask you to talk about the content of these photos. You must include at least one detail about each photo.

After you have described the photos, your teacher will then ask you questions related to **People and lifestyle**.

Hablar 2 **Prepare your own description of the two photos. Then, with a partner, take turns to describe them.**

- *En la primera foto hay …*
- *En la segunda foto hay …*

Escuchar 3 **Read the second part of the task card. The teacher asks Szymon '*¿Cómo es tu instituto?*'. Listen and correct the six factual mistakes in the text below.**

Mi instituto es grande con más de mil alumnos y sesenta profesores. Tiene muchos edificios modernos pero las instalaciones son malas y no hay ni piscina ni gimnasio. No suelo comprar la comida en el instituto ya que el servicio es lentísimo.

la sala *room, hall*

Escuchar 4 **Listen to Szymon answering more questions: '*Describe una excursión escolar que hiciste en el pasado*' and '*¿Cómo cambiarías tu instituto?*'. Answer the questions.**

- For his first answer, note down:
  a what he did in the morning
  b his favourite part of the trip
  c what they didn't do and why.
- In his second answer, which of the following does he mention?
  A uniform **B** rules **C** the school day **D** facilities **E** meals
- Listen to both answers again. Write down eight examples of how he shows off a wide variety of language.

Examples of varied language could include:
- complex language
- different tenses and verb forms
- adverbs and negatives
- sequencers and time phrases
- a variety of vocabulary.

Hablar 5 **Prepare your own answers to Module 5 questions 1–10 on page 231. Then practise with your partner.**

Módulo 5

Prueba escrita

Translation

Escribir 1

Read the English text and Christina's translation of it. Fill in the gaps with the correct Spanish word(s).

My lessons start at eight o'clock. It is too early, in my opinion. I live quite far from the school and therefore I tend to go by bus if it's raining. Unfortunately, yesterday morning I arrived late. Tonight, I am going to prepare my things before going to bed.

Mis clases **1** a las ocho. Es **2** **3**, en mi opinión. Vivo bastante **4** del instituto y **5** suelo **6** en autobús **7** llueve. **8**, ayer por la mañana **9** tarde. Esta **10**, voy a preparar mis **11** antes de **12**.

Sometimes single words in English, such as 'therefore', may translate into Spanish as a short phrase.

Escribir 2

Translate the following sentences into Spanish.

I live near my school but I often arrive late.

Normally, my best friend and I go to school by bike.

After lessons, I study in the library if I have homework.

Last week, I got good marks in the history exam.

Tomorrow, I am going to visit the science museum with my class.

Spanish word order is often different to English when two nouns come together. For example:

- history exam = *examen* ***de*** *historia*
- science museum = ?

150-Word writing task

Escribir 1

Look at this writing task and then, <u>for each bullet point</u>:

1 Think about what vocabulary you have learned that you could use in your answer. For example:
- different **verbs** to give your opinion of school, and **adjectives** to explain your reasons
- language for **narrating a story** about what you did / where you went.

2 Write down <u>three or four</u> ideas for what you could write about.

3 Write down which tense(s) you will need to use in your answer.

Write a blog about your life at school. Write approximately **150** words in **Spanish** and say something about both bullet points.

Mention:
- the positive **and** negative aspects of your school
- what you did recently on a school trip.

Leer 2

Read Rishi's answer to the task. Answer the questions in the coloured shapes.

1 This is an example of **complex language**. What does it mean? Find two more examples from the text.

5 This phrase is followed by the infinitive. What does it mean? What other expressions could you use to talk about rules?

En mi opinión, hay muchas cosas positivas en el instituto. Primero, me encantan las asignaturas que estudio. Por ejemplo, llevo cuatro años aprendiendo español. Mis amigos dicen que las asignaturas prácticas son más útiles que los idiomas, pero no estoy de acuerdo. En el futuro, quiero sacar buenas notas en los exámenes y por eso voy a estudiar mucho.

Hay aspectos de las reglas en mi instituto que me gustan y otros que no me gustan. Por un lado, las reglas escolares te dan un sentimiento de seguridad. Por otro lado, hay otras reglas que no son necesarias. Por ejemplo, está prohibido tener el pelo muy corto.

Acabo de visitar Madrid con mi clase y fue increíble. El primer día visitamos el estadio de Real Madrid pero no saqué ninguna foto ya que perdí mi cámara. Lo que más me gustó fue cuando fuimos al Rastro, un mercado al aire libre donde compré un regalo para mi madre.

2 What does this **opinion phrase** mean? What other examples does he use?

3 Which **tense** is this? Which other tense could you use here to show variety?

4 This phrase shows a **variety of vocabulary**. Can you use context to work out its meaning?

Leer 3

Read Rishi's answer again. Answer the questions in English.

1. Why do his friends prefer practical subjects?
2. What is the benefit of school rules?
3. Which rule does he disagree with?
4. Why did he take no photographs of the stadium?
5. What is the *Rastro*?

Escribir 4

Prepare your own answer to the task.

- Think about how you can develop your answer for each bullet point.
- Look back at your notes from exercises 1 and 2.
- Look at the 'Challenge checklist' and consider how you can show off your Spanish!
- Write a brief plan and organise your answer into paragraphs.
- Write your answer and then carefully check the accuracy of what you have written.

Challenge checklist

	✓ Past, present and future time frames ✓ Connectives / time phrases / sequencers ✓ Extended sentences ✓ Different opinion phrases
	✓ A wider range of tenses (e.g. simple future) ✓ Opinions of others (e.g. *A … le gusta …*) ✓ A wide range of interesting vocabulary ✓ Adverbs (e.g. *desafortunadamente*) ✓ Negatives (e.g. *nadie, ningún, no … ni … ni …*)
	✓ Complex verb phrases (e.g. *llevar* + present participle) ✓ Other complex structures (e.g. *lo que más me gustó*, comparatives, superlatives) ✓ Verbs with an infinitive (e.g. *acabo de / se debe / hay que* + infinitive) ✓ Relative pronouns (e.g. *que, cuando, donde*)

Palabras

Key:
bold = this word will appear in higher exams only
* = this word is not on the vocabulary list, but you may use it in your own sentences

La vida escolar en España (pages 106–107):

¿Cómo es tu instituto?	*What's your high school like?*
el *curso/día *escolar	*school year/day*
el instituto / la escuela *primaria	*secondary school / primary school*
la escuela pública/**privada**	*state/private school*
los alumnos/estudios	*students/studies*
la **formación profesional** / el Bachillerato	*vocational training / baccalaureate (equivalent to A Levels)*
¿Qué ropa llevas en el insti?	*What clothes do you wear at school?*
Llevo ...	*I wear ...*
ropa deportiva / *un jersey	*sports clothes / a jumper*
un pantalón/uniforme	*trousers / a uniform*
una camisa/camiseta	*a shirt/T-shirt*
un vestido / una falda	*a dress/shirt*
*una chaqueta/*corbata	*a jacket/tie*
unos zapatos	*some shoes*
¿Cómo son las instalaciones?	*What are the facilities like?*
el edificio / la biblioteca	*building/library*
los campos deportivos	*sports pitches*
el gimnasio	*gym*
los laboratorios / **las aulas**	*laboratories / classrooms*
caro/a(s) / barato/a(s)	*expensive / cheap*
cómodo/a(s) / *incómodo/a(s)	*comfortable / uncomfortable*
bonito/a(s) / feo/a(s)	*beautiful/nice / ugly*
divertido/a(s) / excelente(s)	*funny/amusing / excellent*
viejo/a(s) / **decepcionante(s)**	*old / disappointing*
¿Cómo es el director / la directora?	*What is the headteacher like?*
El director / la directora ...	*The headteacher ...*
es alegre / buenísimo/a	*is happy/cheerful / very good*
tiene buen sentido del humor	*has a good sense of humour*
el nombre/apellido	*name/surname*
las cifras	*figures*

Un día en el insti (pages 108–109):

¿Cómo vas al instituto?	*How do you go to school?*
Voy (al insti) ...	*I go (to school) ...*
a pie / en coche/tren	*on foot / by car/train*
en autobús/bici	*by bus/bike*
¿Cómo es tu día *escolar?	*What is your school day like?*
Las clases empiezan/terminan a las ...	*Classes start/end at ...*
Cada clase dura una hora.	*Each class lasts an hour.*
Hay un recreo a las ...	*There is a break at ...*
¿Qué sueles hacer a la hora de comer?	*What do you usually do at lunchtime?*
Salgo al patio.	*I go out to the playground.*
Traigo un bocadillo.	*I bring a sandwich.*
Voy a la biblioteca/*cantina.	*I go to the library/canteen.*
¿Qué día de la semana prefieres?	*Which day of the week do you prefer?*
Prefiero los martes cuando tengo/tenemos ...	*I prefer Tuesdays when I/we have ...*
actividades *extraescolares.	*extracurricular activities.*
todas mis asignaturas favoritas.	*all my favourite subjects.*
¿Qué haces después del insti?	*What do you do after school?*
Soy miembro de un club.	*I am a member of a club.*
Ayudo con la **radio** *escolar.	*I help with the school radio.*
Me encantan *las artes escénicas.	*I like the performing arts.*
Juego con el equipo de mi insti.	*I play with my school team.*
¿Cuánto tiempo llevas ...?	*How long have you been ...?*
Llevo/Llevamos dos años ...	*I/We have been ... for two years.*
participando en el proyecto	*participating in the project*
asistiendo a clases de baile	*attending dance classes*
tocando la guitarra	*playing the guitar*
¿Por qué te gusta esta actividad?	*Why do you like this activity?*
Me encanta porque ...	*I love it because it...*
te ayuda a ...	*helps you to ...*
te da la oportunidad de ...	*gives you the opportunity to ...*
te anima a ... / te permite ...	*encourages/allows you to ...*
aprender cosas nuevas	*learn new things*
desarrollar tus **talentos**	*develop your talents*
hacer nuevos amigos	*make new friends*
te da ...	*gives you ...*
más confianza	*more confidence*
un sentimiento de éxito	*a sense of accomplishment*
te hace sentir **orgulloso/a**	*makes you feel proud*
te quita el estrés	*takes away stress*
¿Qué hiciste recientemente con el club/equipo?	*What did you do recently with the club/team?*
Organizamos un concurso ...	*We organised a competition ...*
Hicimos un espectáculo de ...	*We did a ... show*
Acabo de ganar un premio.	*I have just won a prize / an award.*

¿Qué tal tus estudios? (pages 110–111):

¿Cuál es tu asignatura favorita?	*What is your favourite subject?*
Mi asignatura favorita es ...	*My favourite subject is ...*
Lo que más/menos me gusta es ...	*What I like the most/least is ...*
Hago mucho esfuerzo en...	*I make a lot of effort in ...*
No aguanto ...	*I can't stand ...*
el alemán/dibujo/teatro	*German/Art/Drama*
el español/francés/inglés	*Spanish/French/English*
la geografía/historia	*Geography/History*
la **literatura**/música	*Literature/Music*
la religión/educación física	*Religion/PE*
la tecnología/informática	*Technology/IT*
las ciencias/matemáticas	*Science(s)/Maths*
los idiomas	*languages*
porque / ya que es/son ...	*because it is / they are ...*
aburrido/a(s) / difícil(es)	*boring / difficult*
divertido/a(s) / duro/a(s)	*fun/amusing / hard*
fácil(es) / importante(s)	*easy / important*
imposible(s) / interesante(s)	*impossible / interesting*
sencillo/a(s)	*simple/easy*
útil(es) / **práctico/a(s)**	*useful/practical*

complicado/a(s)	*difficult/complicated*
pesado/a(s)	*boring*
Me cuesta (mucho) …	*I find it very difficult to …*
recordar todas las fechas	*to remember all the dates*
resolver los problemas	*to resolve problems*

¿Qué vas a hacer para tener éxito? — *What are you going to do to be successful?*

Para aprobar mis exámenes, …	*To pass my exams, …*
Para mejorar mi **nivel**, …	*To improve my level, …*
Para sacar buenas/mejores notas, …	*To get good/better marks, …*
Para tener éxito en la prueba, …	*To be successful in the test, …*
aprenderé de mis errores	*I will learn from my mistakes*
participaré más en clase	*I will participate more in class*
preguntaré al profesor si no entiendo	*I will ask the teacher if I don't understand*
repasaré esta noche	*I will revise tonight*
dedicaré más tiempo a repasar	*I will spend more time revising*
asistiré a clases de *repaso	*I will attend revision classes*
No quiero volver a **suspender**.	*I don't want to fail again.*

¿Cómo cambiarías tu instituto? (pages 112–113):

¿Qué harías para mejorar tu instituto? — *What would you do to improve your school?*

Mejoraría la **calidad** de la comida.	*I would improve the quality of the food.*
Reduciría el precio del uniforme.	*I would reduce the price of the uniform.*
Permitiría el uso de los móviles en clase.	*I would allow the use of mobiles in class.*
Construiría un nuevo gimnasio.	*I would build a new gym.*
Ofrecería más actividades *extraescolares.	*I would offer more extracurricular activities.*

¿Qué es lo malo de tu instituto? — *What is the bad thing about your school?*

Lo malo de mi instituto es que …	*The bad thing about my school is that …*
las instalaciones deportivas son viejas / están en mal **estado** / **huelen** mal	*the sports facilities are old / are in a bad state / smell bad*
las reglas son demasiado **estrictas**	*the rules are too strict*
los teléfonos están prohibidos	*telephones are prohibited*
ciertos alumnos …	*certain students …*
son **violentos**	*are violent*
amenazan o **pegan** a **los demás**	*threaten or hit others*
Hay que …	*You have to …*
No se debe …	*You must (not) …*
No se permite / Está prohibido …	*You are (not) allowed to …*
llegar a tiempo	*arrive on time*
respetar a los alumnos/profesores	*respect students/teachers*
mantener limpio el patio	*keep the playground clean*
*quedarse sentado durante la clase	*stay seated during class*
traer **dispositivos** electrónicos personales	*bring personal electronic devices*
tirar basura al **suelo**	*throw rubbish on the floor*
comer/beber en **las aulas**	*eat/drink in classrooms*
ir al servicio sin **el permiso** del profesor	*go to the toilet without the teacher's permission*
(No) Estoy de acuerdo con esta regla porque …	*I (don't) agree with this rule because …*

La gente de mi insti (pages 114–115):

¿Qué tipo de alumno eres? — *What type of student are you?*

Soy muy/bastante/demasiado …	*I am very/quite/too …*
responsable/trabajador(a)	*responsible/hard-working*
independiente/perezoso/a	*independent/lazy*
Tengo ganas de tener éxito.	*I am keen to be successful.*
(No) Quiero / (No) Me gusta …	*I (don't) want / I (don't) like …*
aprender/aprobar	*to learn / to pass*
estudiar/repasar	*to study / to revise*

¿Cómo te preparas para el día *escolar? — *How do you prepare for a school day?*

(No/Nunca) Llego temprano / a tiempo.	*I (don't/never) arrive early / on time.*
¿Dónde sueles hacer los deberes?	*Where do you usually do your homework?*
Los hago en casa o en la biblioteca.	*I do it at home or in the library.*
No los hago **jamás**.	*I never do it.*
¿Aprendes mucho en clase?	*Do you learn a lot in class?*
(No) Escucho al profe / a nadie.	*I (don't) listen to the teacher / to anyone.*
(No) Hago todas las tareas.	*I (don't) do all the tasks.*
Suelo …	*I usually …*
sacar buenas notas	*get good marks*
recordar **lo que** necesito	*remember what I need*
Preparo mi mochila.	*I prepare my schoolbag.*
Mi compañero/a nunca se calla.	*My classmate never shuts up.*
Su comportamiento es malo.	*His/Her behaviour is bad.*

¿Cómo sería tu profesor(a) ideal? — *What would your ideal teacher be like?*

Mi profesor(a) ideal …	*My ideal teacher …*
haría mucho esfuerzo para …	*would make a lot of effort to …*
no gritaría nada	*wouldn't shout at all*
no **nos** pondría demasiados deberes	*wouldn't give us too much homework*
no sería demasiado **estricto/a**	*wouldn't be too strict*
nos dejaría usar el móvil	*would let us use our mobile*
nunca se pondría enojado/a	*would never get angry*
nunca nos **castigaría**	*would never punish us*
sería **comprensivo/a**	*would be understanding*

El viaje de fin de curso (pages 116–117):

¿Cómo fue el viaje? — *How was the trip?*

(des)afortunadamente	*(un)fortunately*
*especialmente	*especially*
*inmediatamente/rápidamente	*immediately/quickly*
*recientemente/**actualmente**	*recently/currently*
*seguramente/*verdaderamente	*surely/truly*
Hicimos un viaje de fin de *curso.	*We went on an end-of-year trip.*
El primer/segundo/tercer día …	*The first/second/third day …*
¿Visitaste algún lugar de interés?	*Did you visit any place of interest?*
Visitamos el parque **nacional** …	*We visited the … national park.*
Fuimos al parque temático …	*We went to the … theme park.*
Respiramos el aire **puro**.	*We breathed the pure air.*
Tuvimos una fiesta de disfraces.	*We had a fancy dress party.*
Hicimos actividades **distintas**.	*We did different activities.*
Las colas no eran largas.	*The queues weren't long.*
¡Qué vergüenza!	*How embarrassing!*

Módulos 1–5 Repaso de gramática

Using *ser*, *estar* and *tener* in the present tense (pages 58, 59 and 66)

Leer 1

Read the sentences. Copy and complete the table by categorising the underlined verb phrases. Then translate the sentences into English.

ser (description/nationality)	*estar* (location)	*estar* (feelings)	*tener* (age/possession)
es lista			

1 Mi mejor amiga es lista y siempre está contenta.
2 Mi hermano tiene once años. Nunca está enfermo.
3 Mi colegio tiene muchas instalaciones deportivas.
4 Ahora estoy en el instituto con mi grupo de teatro.
5 Estoy emocionado porque nuestra casa nueva es bonita y está en la costa.
6 Mis padres están enojados porque siempre me acuesto tarde.
7 Mis amigos y yo estamos en nuestro restaurante favorito. Es chileno.
8 Mis abuelos están en España porque tienen una casa de vacaciones allí.

Escribir 2

Fill in the gaps in the text below using the correct conjugated verb in the present tense of *ser*, *estar* or *tener*. Use exercise 1 to help you.

Mi familia **1** monoparental y pequeña. Me parezco a mi madre porque las dos **2** el pelo negro y los mismos ojos marrones. Sin embargo, **3** el pelo más largo que ella y llevo trenzas. También **4** más alta. Sonia **5** mi mejor amiga. **6** el pelo rubio y **7** muy lista y trabajadora. Me llevo bien con ella porque nunca **8** triste. Sonia **9** la misma edad que yo y **10** juntas en clase. Nuestro instituto **11** en una zona que **12** muy bonita. ***Gema***

Reflexive verbs in the present tense (pages 62, 84 and 85)

Escribir 3

Use the verbs in brackets to complete the sentences with the present tense or Spanish reflexive verbs. Then translate the sentences into English.

1 Por la mañana ___ temprano. Primero ___ y luego ___ para ir al colegio. (*I get up / I get dressed / I get ready*)
2 En las vacaciones ___ más tarde porque no tengo que ir al instituto. (*I go to bed*)
3 Mis amigas y yo ___ bien y casi nunca discutimos. (*we get on*)
4 Mi hermano ___ con sus amigos los fines de semana. (*he has fun*)
5 Mi mejor amiga está triste porque sus padres van a ___. (*to get divorced*)
6 Mi mejor amigo y yo ___ mucho cuando estamos juntos. (*we have fun*)
7 Mi tía ___ con su novio este sábado en una boda civil. (*she is getting married*)

divorciarse *to get divorced*

Using different tenses (Pages 58, 88, 90 and 112)

Leer 4

Read the text and complete the key for each tense (imperfect, preterite, present, simple future, conditional). Then translate the text into English.

Number	Tense
1	

En mi antiguo colegio la comida no **era**[1] sana ni fresca. Siempre **servían**[1] los mismos platos con patatas fritas y mucha grasa. Por eso no **tenía**[1] una dieta equilibrada y no **me sentía**[1] bien. Tampoco **había**[1] gimnasio, entonces no **practicaba**[1] deporte y no **estaba**[1] en forma. Ahora **voy**[2] a un instituto nuevo que **es**[2] mucho mejor porque **tiene**[2] muchas instalaciones deportivas. Ayer **jugué**[3] un partido de baloncesto y luego **comí**[3] el plato especial del día, pescado con verduras, que **me gustó**[3] mucho. Mañana **iré**[4] a clase de natación, y también **aprenderé**[4] a cuidar mi salud mental. En el futuro **me gustaría**[5] participar en el club de cocina porque **me encantaría**[5] aprender a preparar comida saludable, como ensaladas.

Escribir 5 **Translate these sentences into Spanish. Use the verbs and vocabulary from exercise 4 to help you. Then underline the Spanish verbs in your sentences and number them 1–5, using your key from exercise 4.**

1. I liked the food I ate at school yesterday because it was fresh and healthy.
2. At my old school I used to do a lot of sport every day and I was fit.
3. Tomorrow I will learn to cook healthy food with less oil, salt and fat in my cookery class.
4. Next month I would like to learn to reduce stress when I have exams because it's important to take care of my mental health.

Escribir 6 **Write seven sentences with 'if' clauses to say what will happen, using the phrases in each box. Then translate your sentences into English.**

Example: *Si me levanto más temprano, llegaré al instituto a tiempo. – If I get up earlier, I will arrive at school on time.*

> Remember the structure for 'if' clauses:
> *Si* + **present** + **simple future**
> *Si **estudio** más, **sacaré** mejores notas.*
> If **I study** more, **I will get** better grades.
>
> When the 'if' clause comes before the main verb, a comma is needed to separate the two clauses.

Si

~~me levanto más temprano,~~
no hago mis deberes,
los estudiantes aprenden a reducir el estrés,
dejamos de comer comida no saludable,
no discuto con mis padres,
pasas más tiempo al aire libre,
haces régimen y reduces el aceite y la grasa,

nos sentiremos más felices.
tendrás más energía.
mis profesores estarán enojados.
tendrán mejor salud mental.
~~llegaré al instituto a tiempo.~~
me llevaré mejor con ellos.
perderás peso.

Verbs and phrases followed by the infinitive (pages 87 and 113)

Escribir 7 **Write the words in the correct order to form sentences about healthy living and school rules. Then translate each sentence into English.**

Example: 1 *No se debe fumar ni beber alcohol. – You must not smoke or drink alcohol.*

1. se No ni beber debe alcohol fumar
2. Hay instalaciones cuidar las que
3. la se permite biblioteca No comer en
4. Está de llevar deporte prohibido zapatillas
5. sana debe llevar una comida dieta con fresca Se
6. de necesita consumo el Se reducir grasa
7. Siempre que los escuchar hay a profesores
8. falta dormir por bien la Hace noche

Using adjectives (pages 59, 82, 85 and 107)

Leer 8 **Read the text. Copy and complete the table by writing down the adjectives in Spanish in the correct column.**

Masculine singular	Masculine plural	Feminine singular	Feminine plural

Conocí a Pedro, mi mejor amigo, el primer día de instituto. Desde entonces siempre estamos juntos. Es trabajador y responsable, pero también divertido. Además, es el chico más positivo y optimista que conozco. Siempre me alegra estar con él. Su padre es inglés y su madre es española. Nos llevamos bien porque compartimos los mismos intereses. Aunque estudiamos las mismas asignaturas, estamos en distintas clases. Nunca sacamos malas notas porque somos buenísimos alumnos. Para la fiesta de fin de curso del año pasado, mi amigo preparó varios platos típicos españoles, que estaban riquísimos porque no tenían demasiada grasa ni sal. Mañana será un gran día porque celebraremos el final de los exámenes.

Módulos
1–5
Repaso de gramática

Using the conditional (page 112)

Escribir 1

Complete the sentences by translating the conditional verbs in brackets into Spanish. Then translate each sentence into English.

Don't forget to write the accent on the final ***í*** of the conditional ending.

En mi mundo ideal ...

1 ... ___ todo el tiempo con mis amigos. (*I would spend*)
2 ... los profesores no ___ deberes y tampoco ___ exámenes. (*they would not give / there would be*)
3 ... nunca ___ despertarme temprano. ___ dormir más y levantarme más tarde. (*I would have to / I would be able to*)
4 ... mis amigos y yo ___ mucho y siempre ___ juntos. (*we would have fun / we would be*)
5 ... ___ rico y ___ a gente famosa. También ___ a fiestas. (*I would be / I would meet / I would go*)
6 ... ___ muchos seguidores en mi canal de YouTube y ___ mucho dinero. (*I would have / I would earn*)

Escribir 2

Translate these sentences into Spanish using the conditional. You can use some of the language from exercise 1 to help you.

1 In my ideal school there would not be a uniform and students would be able to wear their own clothes.
2 Teachers would allow mobile phones in class and pupils would not have so many exams.
3 Students would also be able to choose only the subjects they prefer.
4 The quality of the food would be excellent, and they would offer options for different types of diets.
5 There would be many extra-curricular activities to choose, and the school would organise interesting trips abroad.

Using different tenses (pages 60, 88 and 109)

Leer 3

Fill in the gaps using verbs from the lists. Then translate both paragraphs into English.

Antes ...
... las familias **1** muchos hijos y los padres estaban casados y **2** heterosexuales.
... la gente **3** comida sana y fresca. Los niños **4** en la calle. Los jóvenes **5** una vida más activa y **6** solo cara a cara o por teléfono con sus amigos.
... las reglas escolares **7** más estrictas. Los alumnos **8** con libros, bolígrafos y papel.

Ahora ...
... las familias **1** más pequeñas. **2** más variedad en los tipos de familias y padres, que no siempre están casados.
... la gente **3** la comida ya preparada. Los niños y los jóvenes **4** en casa con juegos de ordenador.
... las personas **5** con móviles e Internet. Muchas personas **6** a los famosos en las redes sociales.
... los profesores **7** hablar y trabajar en equipo en clase. Los alumnos **8** con tecnología como tabletas, ordenadores y móviles.

jugaban
preparaba
tenían (x2)
eran (x2)
se comunicaban
estudiaban

permiten
compra
estudian
son
hay
se comunican
se divierten
siguen

Remember to use the **imperfect tense** to talk about what used to happen, and the **present tense** to talk about what happens now. The combination of both tenses allows you to compare and contrast how things have changed.

Escribir 4 **Rewrite the text about a student's plans, changing the near future tense to the simple future tense. Then translate the text in the simple future into English.**

Mañana **voy a empezar** mi nuevo plan para una vida más saludable.
Voy a hacer régimen y también **voy a dejar de** comer comida no saludable con demasiada grasa y sal. **Voy a hacer** deporte cuatro veces a la semana.
Voy a seguir los consejos de mis profesores y **ya no voy a usar** ni el móvil ni la tableta por la noche.
Además, **voy a cerrar** mis cuentas en todas las redes sociales. Esto **va a ayudarme** a mejorar mi salud mental y a estudiar mejor.
También **voy a tener** más tiempo para participar en las actividades que ofrece mi instituto.
El miércoles próximo **voy a ir** al campo en una excursión escolar. **Vamos a pasar** el día en contacto con la naturaleza. **Vamos a divertirnos** mucho. ¡Estoy emocionada!

Watch out for the position of **pronouns** when you change the text. Remember that they come before a conjugated verb.
*va a ayudar**me*** → ***me** ayudará*

Leer 5 **Read the sentences. Write down each verb and identify the tense (imperfect, preterite, present or simple future). Translate each verb into English.**

Example: Participé (preterite) – I participated

1 Participé en el club de baile por primera vez y me encantó.
2 En el pasado me llevaba mal con mis padres y discutíamos mucho. Siempre me castigaban. No me dejaban salir ni me permitían tener un móvil.
3 Haremos una excursión escolar y visitaremos los principales lugares de interés. Será divertido.
4 Siempre hago mis deberes y los entrego a tiempo. ¡Y nunca olvido mis libros!
5 Me acosté tardísimo y no dormí bien. Ahora estoy cansadísima y tengo poca energía. No quiero ir a clase de historia. ¡Es aburridísima!
6 Saqué muy malas notas porque no estudié nada. Mi profesor está enojado y dice que debo trabajar más.
7 Traigo mi propia comida de casa porque la que sirven en el colegio no suele ser ni sana ni fresca.
8 Probé la comida típica chilena. La compré en un mercado de la calle. Estaba riquísima.

Using adjectives (page 85)

Leer 6 **Read this text about young people and technology. Find and write down fifteen indefinite adjectives and their nouns. Then translate them into English.**

Example: algunos jóvenes – some young people

Actualmente algunos jóvenes no pueden vivir sin mirar las redes sociales cada día. Siguen a mucha gente famosa y pasan demasiado tiempo mirando los mismos canales de vídeos. Muchos chicos no tienen ningún interés en sus estudios. Solo piensan en ser ricos y famosos algún día porque quieren ser como sus personas famosas favoritas.

Muchos colegios prohíben a los estudiantes usar el móvil durante todo el horario escolar y castigan a los alumnos si los usan. No todos los padres apoyan esta regla nueva. Sin embargo otros padres ven demasiados ejemplos de acoso en los institutos y creen que prohibir los móviles podría ayudar. Todas las escuelas quieren tener estudiantes contentos, pero no pueden tener las mismas reglas que antes.

En Colombia todo es posible

- Finding out about Colombia
- Recognising demonstrative adjectives

Colombia: un país megadiverso

Colombia tiene una gran variedad de paisajes y climas y posee un gran número de plantas y animales que representan una cantidad enorme de la diversidad mundial de especies. Bogotá, la capital, es la ciudad más grande del país, con once millones de habitantes.*

Estas playas hermosas de arena blanca se encuentran en el norte del país. Con aguas claras y una selva tropical, el Caribe es un destino increíble para disfrutar de la naturaleza y la riqueza geográfica.

En el oeste se encuentra el Pacífico y el clima tropical aquí es húmedo. Esta región tiene muchos pájaros, una gran cantidad de ríos, varios volcanes y aproximadamente treinta mil especies de plantas.

Esta región, en el sur, es perfecta para animales como jaguares, anacondas y tucanes. La región Amazónica tiene una importante porción de la selva tropical más famosa del mundo, y aquí viven veintiséis comunidades indígenas.

La región Andina se encuentra en el centro del país. Es la región con la mayor cantidad de habitantes y actividad económica. Aquí hay muchas ciudades históricas como Bogotá y Medellín. Estas montañas famosas se llaman los Andes.

La Orinoquía, en el este del país, es conocida por su paisaje natural. Este paisaje tiene áreas de sabanas y bosques. Es una de las regiones más importantes del país gracias a sus reservas de gas natural y petróleo.

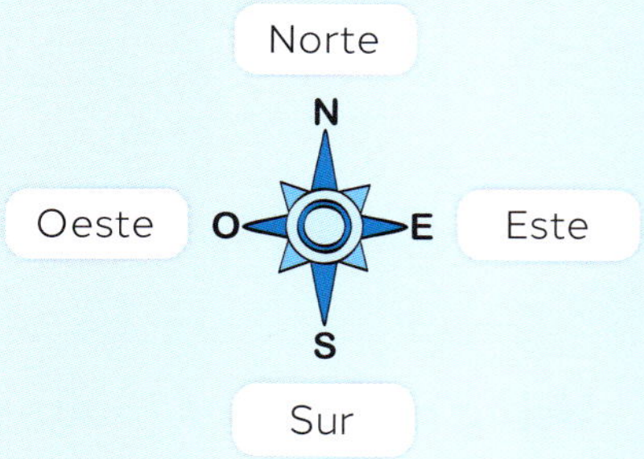

G

Demonstrative adjectives (like 'this' and 'these') are useful to emphasise something or to point out something. They need to agree with the noun they describe.

Este *pueblo es hermoso.*	**This** village is beautiful.
Esta *ciudad está en el sur.*	**This** city is in the south.
Estos *lugares son muy grandes.*	**These** places are very big.
Estas *montañas son increíbles.*	**These** mountains are incredible.

You will learn more about these in Unit 2.

*Statistics from World Population Review (2023).

la selva	*jungle, rainforest*
la sabana	*savannah (a grassland area with trees)*
el petróleo	*oil*

Escuchar 1 **Listen and read about the diverse geography of Colombia. Copy and complete the table in Spanish.**

Región	¿Dónde está?	Características
El Caribe	en el norte	playas hermosas de arena blanca, aguas claras, selva tropical

Leer 2 **Read about Colombia's regions again. For each text, find and copy the sentence that contains a demonstrative adjective, then translate it into English.**

Example: *Estas playas hermosas de arena blanca se encuentran en el norte del país.*
These beautiful white sand beaches are found in the north of the country.

Leer 3 **Read the texts (a–h) and match them to the photos of these famous Colombians. There are two extra texts; can you guess who they are talking about? Listen to check your answers. (1–8)**

1 
Luis Díaz

2 
Karol G

3 
Gabriel García Márquez

4 
María Isabel Urrutia

5 
J Balvin

6 
Shakira

a Esta cantante es del norte de Colombia. Es muy famosa, y también lleva muchos años ayudando a los niños pobres de Colombia con su fundación que se llama Pies Descalzos.

b Este famoso autor colombiano utiliza un estilo de escribir popular llamado realismo mágico, y siempre incluye elementos fantásticos en sus historias.

c Esta persona empezó su carrera en 2016 jugando en la segunda división del fútbol colombiano. Es de origen wayuu. Los wayuu son indígenas de la Península de la Guajira.

d Esta actriz y modelo es reconocida a nivel internacional. Es muy famosa por su papel como Gloria Delgado-Pritchett en la popular serie *Modern Family*.

e Esta rapera, cantante y compositora es una de las más famosas estrellas de reguetón. Nació bajo el nombre de Carolina Giraldo Navarro en Medellín.

f Este cantante popular de la música rap y reguetón canta en español e inglés. Le encanta colaborar con estrellas internacionales como Beyoncé y Ed Sheeran.

g Esta estrella colombiana de atletismo nació cerca de Medellín y comenzó a jugar al voleibol antes de practicar atletismo.

h Esta deportista y política obtuvo la primera medalla de oro en unos Juegos Olímpicos para Colombia e inspiró a muchas personas.

Escuchar 4 **Listen to some Colombians talking about their country. Then, in English, write down what they like about it. (1–5)**

Example: 1 *geographical diversity, the white sand beaches and big mountains*

Hablar 5 **In pairs, take turns to ask and answer questions about the geographical features where you live, using the points of the compass.**

- *¿Qué hay en tu región?*
- *En mi región tenemos ..., pero no hay ...*
- *¿Qué hay en el norte de tu país/región?*
- *En el norte hay ..., pero no tenemos ...*

En mi región ... En el [norte] de mi país ... (no) hay (no) tenemos	(un) río (un) paisaje (un) monte (una) costa (unos) bosques (unas) playas much**o** campo much**os** lagos much**os** pueblos much**as** ciudades much**as** montañas	hermos**o**/**a**(s). históric**o**/**a**(s). modern**o**/**a**(s). pequeñ**o**/**a**(s). suci**o**/**a**(s). limpi**o**/**a**(s). agradable(s). enorme(s). horrible(s). industrial(es).

1 Medellín, ciudad inteligente

- Describing cities
- Using the perfect tense
- Using prepositions of place for directions

Leer 1 **Read the travel webpage and translate the perfect tense phrases into English. Read the webpage again and find the phrases below in Spanish.**

¡48 horas en Medellín!

¿Has visto los grafitis de la Comuna 13?

Puedes ver el arte callejero con un guía local en un barrio joven y renovado.

Opiniones:

María Alejandra @213malejandrat
En las calles de la Comuna 13 **he descubierto** mucho arte innovador.

Tomás @tomás_aguilar15
Mis amigos y yo **hemos subido** las escaleras eléctricas para disfrutar de los grafitis.

¿Has ido a Pueblito Paisa?

Es un pueblo típico donde puedes comprar recuerdos de tu viaje. Es un entorno con árboles y montañas.

Opiniones:

Ismael @ismaelxr14
He viajado en Metrocable y **he visitado** el Pueblito Paisa. Las vistas son estupendas.

Ángela @xxgelarivera1
He visto las puertas de colores de las casas en Pueblito Paisa. ¡Qué lugar tan bonito!

¿Has visitado el Parque Explora?

Puedes hacer muchas cosas en el moderno Parque Explora: hay un museo de ciencias, un planetario y un acuario.

Opiniones:

Natalia @castillonatalia123
El acuario del Parque Explora es el más grande de Sudamérica. Ya **he aprendido** mucho sobre las pirañas. ¡Qué interesante!

Luis @luisssortiz98
Ya **hemos bebido** un café y **hemos probado** empanadas en la cafetería. **No hemos visto** el museo todavía.

la empanada — *stuffed pastry (pasty)*

1 You can do lots of things
2 in a young neighbourhood
3 you can buy souvenirs
4 an environment with trees
5 What a nice place!
6 coloured doors

Escuchar 2 **Listen to these young people talking about Medellín and complete the table in English. (1–6)**

	Have you …?	Two extra details
1	visited the …	It is very big and …

Escribir 3 **Imagine you are a tourist in your local area. Write about how you have spent the last 48 hours for a travel webpage.**

48 horas en …

Ya También Todavía no		he	visitado … viajado … comido … ido … visto … hecho …
Mis amigos y yo Mi familia y yo	ya todavía no	hemos	

When using the perfect tense, ***ya*** and ***todavía*** have different meanings.

*¿**Ya** has ido a la mezquita?*	Have you **already** been to the mosque?
*Sí, **ya** la he visitado.*	Yes, I've **already** visited it.
***Todavía** no hemos alquilado un coche.*	We haven't hired a car **yet**.

G

The **perfect tense** is used to talk about what you have done.
Use the present tense of *haber* + **past participle**.

(yo)	he	**visitado**
(tú)	has	**comido**
(él/ella/usted)	ha	**subido**
(nosotros/as)	hemos	
(vosotros/as)	habéis	
(ellos/ellas/ustedes)	han	

To form the **past participle**, take off the **-ar**, **-er** or **-ir** endings from the infinitive and add:
-ado (***-ar*** verbs) ***-ido*** (***-er***/***-ir*** verbs)

Some past participles are irregular:

abrir (to open) → ***abierto***
decir (to say) → ***dicho***
descubrir (to discover) → ***descubierto***
escribir (to write) → ***escrito***
hacer (to do/make) → ***hecho***
poner (to put) → ***puesto***
romper (to break) → ***roto***
ver (to see) → ***visto***
volver (to return) → ***vuelto***

Page 146

Hablar 4

Read the conversation. In pairs, use the information in the two boxes below to practise the dialogue, replacing the five underlined phrases.

- *¿Dónde está el centro comercial?*
- *Está cerca de la estación de metro, delante del ayuntamiento.*
- *¿Está lejos de aquí?*
- *No, está cerca. Mira el plano. Pasa el puente, toma la segunda calle a la izquierda y está a la derecha.*
- *Vale. Voy a ir al centro comercial esta tarde. ¿Qué hacemos mañana?*
- *¿Ya has ido a Pueblito Paisa?*
- *Todavía no. ¡Me encantaría ir!*

restaurant	the bull ring
behind the swimming pool	next to the bank
take the first street on the left	take the second street on the right
it is on the left	it is on the right
museum	park

G

Use ***estar*** + **preposition of place** to say where something is located.

Está *delante de ...*	**It is** in front of ...
detrás de ...	behind ...
al lado de ...	next to ...
cerca de ...	near ...
lejos de ...	far from ...

Remember that *a* + *el* becomes ***al*** and *de* + *el* becomes ***del***.

Page 146

Está		a la derecha.
Toma	la primera la segunda la tercera	a la izquierda.
Pasa		el puente. la fuente.
Cruza		la plaza (de toros).

Escuchar 5

Listen to the conversations about visiting Medellín. (1–4) Note down in English:

- the place they want to visit
- why they want to visit
- where it is located
- tomorrow's activity.

Leer 6

Read the interview with Salvador, a keen cyclist from Medellín, and answer the questions below.

Hola Salvador. ¿A quién admiras?

Me encanta montar en bici y por eso mi deportista favorita es Mariana Pajón, una ciclista increíble de BMX. La admiro por el talento que muestra. La velocidad y la altura de su bicicleta son impresionantes.

¿De dónde es y qué ha ganado durante su carerra?

Nació en Medellín, como yo, y todavía vive aquí. Empezó a practicar BMX a la edad de cuatro años. Su mayor logro es ser la única mujer sudamericana que ha ganado dos medallas de oro en deportes individuales en la historia de los Juegos Olímpicos.

Salvador, ¿ya has visitado todos los sitios turísticos de Medellín?

¡Ya he visitado muchos, pero todavía no he visitado todos! Mañana mi amigo y yo vamos a tomar un vuelo de quince minutos en parapente para disfrutar del paisaje desde el cielo. Será buenísimo.

Si tienes tiempo libre, ¿qué te gusta hacer?

Pues, me gusta mucho salir porque no quiero pasar demasiado tiempo en casa. Es difícil mantenerme tranquilo porque siempre tengo mucha energía. No puedo quejarme porque delante de mi casa hay un parque grande que está cerca de mi restaurante favorito.

el parapente	*paragliding*
el logro	*achievement*
la medalla de oro	*gold medal*

1. Why does Salvador admire Mariana Pajón? (Give one detail.)
2. When did Mariana first start riding a BMX?
3. What has been her biggest achievement?
4. What is Salvador going to do tomorrow? (Give two details.)
5. Why is it hard for him to stay at home?
6. Why is his house well situated?

Escribir 7

Write about where you live. Include:

- where you were born and live
- tourist sites you have visited
- somewhere you have not been yet
- what you like to do in your area
- what you are going to do in your area.

2 Medellín ahora y antes

- Describing how a city or town has changed
- Using demonstrative adjectives for descriptions
- Comparing now and then in the imperfect tense

Leer 1 **Read about Medellín's library parks and complete the sentences.**

Los Parques Biblioteca de Medellín

Medellín ha cambiado muchísimo en los últimos veinte años. Han renovado muchas zonas de la ciudad: han plantado más árboles, han creado muchas zonas verdes y han mejorado la red de transporte. Además, han abierto diez parques biblioteca donde se puede descansar, caminar, leer y aprender mucho.

1 **Aquellos** árboles del parque son muy bonitos. En **aquella** biblioteca hay varias salas de Internet.

2 **Esa** biblioteca es grande y tiene salas de lectura. **Esas** vistas desde el parque son increíbles.

3 **Este** lugar es muy acogedor y **esta** biblioteca es muy moderna – está hecha de bloques de concreto.

acogedor *welcoming*

1. Medellín has changed a lot in …
2. Many areas of the city have been …
3. The transport system has …
4. They have opened …
5. If you want to find a reading room, visit …
6. To see lots of trees, visit …

Listen and read. Remember that ***ll*** and ***rr*** are pronounced differently.
ll makes a 'y' sound: *calle, aquello, se llama*
rr is a rolled 'r' sound: *carretera, torre, arriba*

When the next word starts with ***i*** or ***hi***, the conjunction ***y*** (and) becomes ***e***.
*La ciudad es grande **e** industrial.*

When the next word starts with ***o*** or ***ho***, the conjunction ***o*** (or) becomes ***u***.
*Se puede visitar el castillo mañana **u** hoy.*

Leer 2 **Now translate texts 1–3 from exercise 1 into English.**

Hablar 3 **Read out the following text with your partner. Pay attention to your pronunciation of *ll* and *rr*.**

Aquellos edificios de mi ciudad son muy antiguos. Hay un castillo enorme y muchas calles bonitas. Esos edificios de allí son más modernos y las tiendas casi nunca cierran. Han renovado esta carretera y ahora está mucho mejor. También han construido aquellos parques grandes en el centro.

G **Demonstrative adjectives**

	singular		plural	
	masculine	**feminine**	**masculine**	**feminine**
this/these	est**e** edificio	est**a** calle	est**os** edificios	est**as** calles
that/those	es**e** espacio	es**a** carretera	es**os** espacios	es**as** carreteras
that/those … over there	aqu**el** barrio	aqu**ella** zona	aqu**ellos** barrios	aqu**ellas** zonas

Page 147

Escuchar 4 **Listen to some young people describing Medellín. What is it like now and what was it like before? Write the <u>two</u> correct letters for each person. (1–4)**

Ahora, ¿cómo es?

a La ciudad está limpia y hay más árboles.

b Su transporte es mejor.

c Es una ciudad digital.

d Las calles son más seguras y hay menos violencia.

Antes, ¿cómo era?

e La ciudad era más industrial y menos moderna.

f Había muchos delitos por todas partes.

g Se veían más drogas en las calles.

h Los niños de la calle sufrían mucho.

Escuchar 5 **Listen to the young people again. For each person note down <u>two</u> positives about the city now and <u>two</u> negatives from the past. (1–4)**

The **imperfect tense** is used when saying what places were like or what they 'used to' be like.

*La ciudad **era** más tranquila.*	The city **was / used to be** calmer.
***Había** menos edificios modernos.*	There **were / used to be** fewer modern buildings.

Leer 6 **Read about Medellín's development and history. Match each text with the descriptions of Medellín (a–h) from exercise 4.**

Thiago

Ahora Medellín es una ciudad vibrante e interesante, pero la imagen de la ciudad ha cambiado mucho. Antes era un lugar muy violento. En aquellos tiempos llegó a ser considerada como la ciudad más peligrosa del mundo. Ahora, con su servicio de Internet de alta velocidad y como hogar de cientos de empresas de tecnología e innovación, es conocida como una ciudad inteligente.

Lucía

Estoy muy orgullosa de ser de Medellín – una ciudad con tanto arte innovador que expresa nuestra cultura rica. La ciudad ha transformado la educación, y por lo tanto se ha convertido en un lugar más seguro. Antes se podían observar signos de consumo de drogas en las calles y en aquella época había tanta basura que generaba una atmósfera industrial y sucia. Ahora todo es completamente diferente.

Escribir 7 **Translate into Spanish this text about how Bogotá has changed.**

Bogotá is a city with lots of rich culture and lots of public spaces to enjoy. It is also a beautiful place with interesting buildings, such as castles. Before there used to be more rubbish on the streets and it was a lot dirtier. In those times the city was smaller. Now transport is better because there are more cyclists.

G

Use ***tan*** and ***tanto*** to write descriptively.
The word ***tan*** (so/such) is an adverb and therefore does not change.

*Las tiendas son **tan** caras.*
The shops are **so** expensive.

Tanto (so many/much) is an adjective and therefore has to agree with the noun it describes.

*Hay **tanta** cultura aquí.*
There is **so much** culture here.

*Hay **tantos** problemas en mi barrio.*
There are **so many** problems in my neighbourhood.

Escribir 8 **Write a paragraph about where you live. Use the present, imperfect and perfect tenses.**

- *Ahora es … / tiene …*
- *Antes era … / había …*
- *Han renovado … Han construido …*

3 ¡A comprar!

- Describing shopping preferences
- Revising direct object pronouns
- Practising key sounds

Escuchar 1 **Listen to and read these opinions about shopping from young people who live in Medellín. Copy and complete the table in English. (1–4)**

Name	Where they shop	Good points	Bad points
Claudia	Urban Outfitters online	Urban style	

¿Qué dicen estos jóvenes de Medellín de sus tiendas de ropa favoritas?

Claudia

Me encanta la ropa de *Urban Outfitters* porque, como su nombre, tiene un estilo urbano. Aquí en Medellín no tienen tienda, por lo tanto siempre compro su ropa por Internet. El único problema es que sus camisetas son muy caras.

Yamile

Pues prefiero llevar ropa bastante alternativa. *Seven Seven* es una marca de moda verde que nació en Colombia. Esto es muy importante para mí. Vende mucha ropa bonita, pero por lo general, no me gustan sus vestidos.

Andrés

Suelo comprar los pantalones y las camisas de *Pull&Bear*, la marca española. Creo que los precios son económicos y siempre se puede encontrar mucha variedad, pero vivo lejos de la tienda porque está en el centro de la ciudad.

Héctor

Mis amigos son fans de ir de compras, pero, ¡yo no! Por eso suelo usar apps como *Vinted* para buscar ropa de segunda mano porque es más barata y mejor para el planeta. Lo malo es que se necesita mucho tiempo para comprar o vender ropa.

Leer 2 **Read the texts from exercise 1 again. Then choose one to translate into English.**

Hablar 3 **Read out the text below, paying close attention to vowels with and without written accents. Then listen and check your pronunciation.**

Solemos comprar en l**í**nea, pero mis amigos y yo todav**ía** vamos a las tiendas f**í**sicas de mi barr**io**. Sin embargo, la semana próxima nos gustar**ía** ir al centro comercial porque reducen los prec**io**s en jun**io** y el horar**io** es mejor. Nos encantar**ía** estar en las tiendas hasta muy tarde y ¡sería incre**í**ble poder encontrar prec**io**s baj**í**simos!

Remember to pronounce each vowel sound carefully when two come together.
If a vowel has a written accent, stress this letter sound in the word. Listen and repeat.

í → *salí, aquí, día*
ía → *encantaría, alegría, mayoría*
io → *julio, radio, gimnasio*
ió → *región, bebió, acción*

Hablar 4 **In pairs, discuss your shopping habits.**

- *¿Prefieres ir al centro comercial o ir a las tiendas de tu barrio/ciudad?*
- *Suelo / Prefiero / No me gusta … porque … Por otro lado …*
- *¿Qué cosas te gusta comprar por Internet?*
- *Me gusta comprar … Por ejemplo, la semana pasada compré …*

<table>
<tr><td>(No) Suelo
(No) Me gusta
Prefiero/Odio</td><td colspan="3">ir a las tiendas [de mi barrio / de segunda mano]
ir al centro comercial
comprar por Internet</td></tr>
<tr><td rowspan="4">porque
ya que</td><td>es
son</td><td>más
menos
tan</td><td>barato/a(s).
caro/a(s).
económico/a(s).
práctico/a(s).
fácil(es).
verde(s).</td></tr>
<tr><td>(no) hay</td><td colspan="2">más/mucha variedad.
más/muchas ofertas.
tanta/demasiada gente.</td></tr>
<tr><td>(no) se puede</td><td colspan="2">comprar de todo.
probar la ropa.</td></tr>
<tr><td colspan="3">los precios son más bajos.
las tiendas son muy pequeñas.
(no) tengo que hacer cola.</td></tr>
</table>

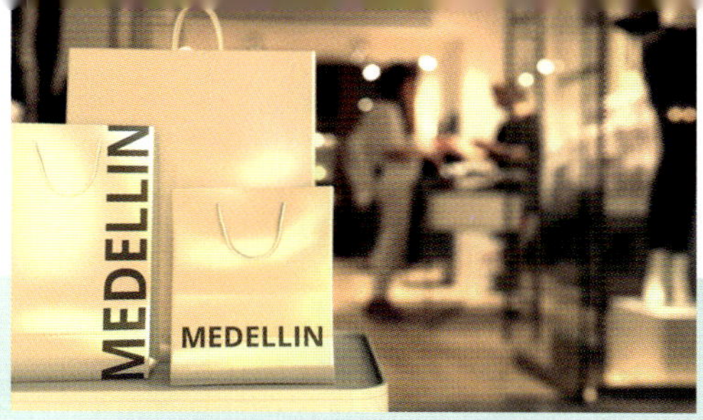

Leer 5 **Read this article about young people's shopping habits in Medellín. Then answer the questions below in English.**

¿Están muertos los centros comerciales?

Algunos jóvenes dicen que disfrutan de la experiencia de ir de compras porque prefieren ver los artículos antes de comprarlos. También piensan que es mucho más fácil devolver cosas en persona.

Por otro lado, hay quienes siempre vuelven a comprar en línea. Odian hacer cola y piensan que hay una mayor variedad de opciones online. También dicen que encuentran mejores descuentos en Internet. Más que nunca, muchos jóvenes suelen comprar ropa de segunda mano porque es sostenible, de buena calidad y puede estar de moda.

Algunas tiendas físicas han abierto espacios interactivos y han creado actividades para los jóvenes. Los centros comerciales y las calles principales no están muertos, pero sí están en constante cambio. Están en evolución.

sostenible	*sustainable*

1 What do young people like about going to physical shops? (Give two details.)
2 Why do some young people shop online? (Give three details.)
3 Why are so many youngsters buying second-hand clothes? (Give three details.)
4 What have some shops done to encourage young people? (Give two details.)
5 Are shopping centres and high street shops dead? Why (not)?

Escuchar 6 **Listen and read Alicia's and Gabriela's conversation about their *quinceañeras*. For each statement write (A) for Alicia, (G) for Gabriela or (A+G) for both girls.**

Gabriela: ¡Enhorabuena y feliz cumpleaños, Alicia! ¿Cómo vas a celebrar tu quinceañera esta tarde?

Alicia: ¡Lo voy a celebrar con una fiesta grande, como una reina! La vamos a celebrar en casa, después de asistir a una ceremonia religiosa en nuestra iglesia. ¿Y tú, Gabriela? ¿Qué vas a hacer?

Gabriela: Para mi quinceañera, quiero ir a un restaurante para una cena especial con todos mis vecinos. Mi padre va a cambiar mis zapatos por unos de tacón alto porque es una tradición. Ya tengo mi vestido azul claro y lo compré online. ¿Y tú? ¿Qué vas a llevar?

Alicia: Voy a llevar un traje blanco porque prefiero los pantalones. Lo compré en una tienda independiente. Prefiero este estilo más moderno en vez de un vestido tradicional.

Gabriela: Vas a estar muy guapa con tu traje, Alicia.

Alicia: ¡Ojalá!

de tacón alto	*high-heeled*

1 It's her birthday today.
2 She is sharing her celebration with neighbours.
3 She will eat a meal as part of her event.
4 She has something to wear to her celebration.
5 She is not dressing in a traditional way.
6 Her clothes were bought in a shop.

Many words contain ***cua*** or ***cue*** in Spanish. Listen and repeat.

cue → ***cue**sta, es**cue**la, des**cue**nto*
cua → *¿**Cuá**nto? ¿**Cuá**ndo? ¿**Cuá**l?*

G

Remember that **demonstrative adjectives** and direct object pronouns agree with the noun they describe.

*Compré **este** traje y **lo** quiero devolver.*
I bought **this** suit and I want to return it.

*Est**a** celebración es especial. Voy a compartir**la** con mi familia.*
This celebration is special. I am going to share it with my family.

Page 148

Escuchar 7 **Listen to these celebration descriptions. (1–3) Write (P) for a positive opinion, (N) for a negative opinion or (P+N) for a positive and negative opinion.**

Hablar 8 **Have a conversation about a birthday celebration.**

- *¿Cómo vas a celebrar tu cumpleaños?*
- *¿Qué vas a llevar? ¿Por qué?*

Quiero comprar Quiero devolver		est**e**	traje vestido reloj
		est**a**	falda camisa camiseta
		est**os**	pantalones zapatos
		est**as**	marcas
	es/son	precios**o**/**a**(s). fe**o**/**a**(s).	
porque	(no) es/son de buena calidad. está de moda. me gusta el estilo.		

Escribir 9 **Translate the text into Spanish.**

I usually go to the shopping centre with my friends on Saturdays. Last Saturday I bought some black shoes and my friend bought a blue shirt. Before, we used to find interesting clothing in second-hand shops, but now it is more difficult. Next Saturday I am going to return some trousers that I bought online because they are not good quality.

4 ¿Dónde prefieres vivir?

- Giving preferences about where you live
- Using the present subjunctive with *cuando*
- Revising comparisons

Escuchar 1 **Listen to and read statements from young people describing why they like living in Medellín or nearby. Then translate the phrases in bold into English.**

aburrirse	*to get bored*

¿Dónde prefieres vivir?

Prefiero vivir en Medellín porque **es más divertido que vivir en el campo**. Creo que **lo bueno de vivir en una ciudad es que siempre hay algo que hacer** y hay más cultura. **Es imposible aburrirse** con tantas tiendas en los alrededores.

Lo bueno de vivir en el campo es que hay más paisajes bonitos. Vivo en el campo, cerca de un pueblo que se llama San Carlos. Lo malo de vivir en el campo es que **no hay muchas posibilidades de trabajo**. Me encantaría vivir en una ciudad grande. ¡Sería fenomenal!

Yo vivo en un pueblo pequeño que se llama Santa Bárbara. Está a cincuenta kilómetros de Medellín. Vivir en un pueblo es preferible porque **hay menos contaminación que en una ciudad grande** y es más limpio. Además, **no hay tanta gente**.

Muchos dicen que en las ciudades la gente no se conoce, pero no es verdad. **Conozco a todos mis vecinos** y son tan agradables como los vecinos en el campo. Aquí el transporte es semejante y **hay una gran variedad de tiendas** a poca distancia.

Leer 2 **Read the text from exercise 1 again. Decide if the sentences below are true or false.**

1. Luciana prefers to live in the countryside.
2. She does not like the shops near her house.
3. There are lots of people where Samuel lives.
4. There are lots of jobs where Rosa lives.
5. Omar knows lots of people where he lives.
6. He thinks the transport system is good.

G

There are several ways to **compare** and **contrast**.

Use ***más/menos*** + **adjective/noun** + ***que*** (more/less ... than ...):
*Manchester es **más grande que** Medellín.*
*Medellín tiene **menos problemas que** muchas otras ciudades.*

Use ***tan*** + **adjective** + ***como*** (as ... as ...):
*Medellín es **tan bonito como** Nottingham.*

Use ***tanto/a(s)*** + **noun** + ***como*** (as much/many ... as ...):
*Mi barrio tiene **tantas tiendas como** un centro comercial.*

Hablar 3 **In pairs, talk about where you prefer to live. Use comparisons to give detailed answers.**

- *¿Dónde vives?*
- *Vivo en ...*
- *¿Prefieres vivir en el campo o en la ciudad?*
- *Prefiero vivir en ... porque es más/menos ... que ...*
- *¿Qué es lo bueno de vivir en ...?*
- *Lo bueno es que ...*
- *¿Qué es lo malo de vivir en ...?*
- *Lo malo es que ...*

Use the **conditional tense** to say what you would do in the future.
Mejoraría *los autobuses.*
I would improve the buses.
Construiría *más edificios.*
I would build more buildings.

Escuchar 4 **How would these young people improve public transport in their city? Listen and write two details for each person in Spanish. (1–3)**

la accesibilidad	*accessibility*
la movilidad reducida	*reduced mobility*

Lo bueno Lo malo Lo positivo Lo negativo Lo mejor Lo peor	de mi ... barrio ciudad pueblo zona	es que	tiene	mucha contaminación/gente.
			es	tranquilo/a. limpio/a. sucio/a.
			está	en la costa / las montañas / el campo.
			hay	más posibilidades de trabajo. tanto tráfico / tanta gente.
			la gente (no) se conoce.	

Leer 5

Read the newspaper article and identify the four correct statements. Then copy the sentences that contain a subjunctive verb and translate them into English.

Example: Cuando tenga más dinero, ... When I have more money, ...

los carros voladores	*flying cars*
los autopistas	*motorways*
las patinetas	*scooters*

¿Cómo deberían ser las ciudades del futuro?

La población de Colombia está creciendo rápidamente. Por eso si queremos tener un futuro habitable, hay que pensar en la cuestión de las ciudades. No habrá carros voladores, ni autopistas amplias, ni casas grandes porque ciudades grandes son peores por el planeta. Las ciudades del futuro serán pequeñas, bien planificadas y con transporte activo. Tendremos bicicletas y patinetas, o caminaremos en vez de usar carros modernos o eléctricos.

Pero, ¿qué piensan los jóvenes que viven en Medellín?

Luisa dice: En el futuro quiero escapar de Medellín y vivir en el campo, porque preferiría vivir en un lugar con el aire más limpio. Cuando tenga más dinero, compraré una casa pequeña para mí y para mi familia.

Emiliano dice: Cuando sea mayor, viviré aquí en Medellín. Pienso que la ciudad tendrá aun más espacios verdes y no habrá carros ni motocicletas porque todo el mundo viajará en bici o a pie. La ciudad será más tranquila y limpia.

Maya dice: En el futuro me gustaría seguir viviendo en esta ciudad fantástica. Cuando tenga dieciocho años, viviré con mi novio y sus padres, y cuando haga suficiente dinero, él y yo compartiremos un piso pequeño en los alrededores. Creo que el Medellín del futuro será más verde y con menos tráfico.

1 The Colombian population is getting bigger.
2 Future cities will be big and sustainable.
3 Flying cars may exist.
4 Future cities will have to be small and well designed.
5 Luisa thinks that there will be fewer green spaces.
6 Maya and Emiliano think Medellín will be greener.
7 Two young people want to buy somewhere to live in the future.
8 All three young people want to live in Medellín in the future.

There are many words that are different in Spain and Latin America, in the same way that there are differences between British English and American English. The most common differences are:

English	Spanish (Spain)	Spanish (Latin America)
car	*el coche*	*el carro/auto*
mobile phone	*el móvil*	*el celular*
computer	*el ordenador*	*la computadora*
potato	*la patata*	*la papa*
pen	*el bolígrafo/boli*	*la pluma*
pretty	*bonito*	*lindo/bello*

G

The **subjunctive** is a form of the verb that is used regularly in Spanish but only very rarely in English. You have to use the subjunctive when using ***cuando*** + future plans.

To form the present subjunctive in the first person singular, take the 'I' form of the present tense and remove the ***o***. For ***-ar*** verbs add ***e*** and for ***-er/-ir*** verbs add ***a***.

Infinitive	Present tense (*yo*)	Present subjunctive (*yo*)
tener	*tengo*	*tenga*
hacer	*hago*	*haga*
venir	*vengo*	*venga*

Ser and ***ir*** are irregular: *(yo) sea, (yo) vaya.*

*Cuando **sea** mayor, viviré en otro país.*
When **I am** older, I will live in another country.

*Cuando **vaya** al centro, tomaré un café.*
When **I go** to the centre, I will have a coffee.

*Cuando **haga** mis exámenes, estaré nervioso.*
When **I do** my exams, I will be nervous.

Page 148

Escribir 6

Write approximately 90 words about your city. Include:

- where you live and what your area is like — *Vivo en ... con ... Mi barrio es ... y ...*
- pros and cons of living in your area — *Lo bueno de vivir en ... / Lo malo es ...*
- something you did in your area last week — *La semana pasada fui ...*
- where you will live in the future and why — *Cuando sea mayor, viviré ... porque ...*
- what you would change about your area. — *Mejoraría ... Cambiaría ...*

5 Un intercambio cultural

- Talking about your area
- Using a variety of verb tenses
- Finding different ways to describe future plans

Leer **1** **Read the text conversation. Then copy and complete the statements in English.**

Hola, me llamo James y soy de Glasgow. ¿Cómo te llamas?

Me llamo Amira y vivo en Medellín. ¿Qué estás haciendo ahora?

Estoy escuchando música en mi piso. Te mando una foto. Mi piso tiene dos habitaciones y un balcón. Es cómodo y moderno. ¿Y tú, dónde vives?

Vivo en una casa de dos plantas. Arriba está mi habitación y abajo hay varios cuartos. Te puedes sentar fuera en el jardín. Me gusta mucho porque nuestros vecinos son nuestros amigos.

Me encanta tu casa. Es muy bonita. ¿Te gusta vivir en Medellín?

Sí. Me gusta mucho porque aquí hace buen tiempo casi todo el año y no llueve mucho. Agosto siempre es mi mes favorito en Medellín porque celebramos la Feria de las Flores que dura diez días. Visité la feria con mis amigos. Había muchos desfiles y las flores eran tan hermosas. ¿Y a ti? ¿Te gusta vivir en Glasgow?

¡Qué feria más impresionante! Sí, me gusta mucho Glasgow, aunque a menudo hace mal tiempo y llueve mucho. Es una ciudad muy dinámica y moderna. El fin de semana pasado tuvimos la oportunidad de ir al Parque Kelvingrove y quise caminar a lo largo del río con mi familia, pero no pude a causa de la lluvia. ¡Qué pena! Este fin de semana vamos a ir al Centro de Ciencias porque quiero ir al cine en 3D – será fenomenal.

1 James's flat in Glasgow is ... and it has ...
2 Amira likes her house because ...
3 The weather in Medellín is ...
4 The weather in Glasgow is ...
5 The Medellín Flower Festival takes place in ... and lasts ...
6 Amira went with ... to the festival last ...
7 Last weekend, James ...

Try to use a variety of tenses and give your opinion to create more detailed and complex answers.

Remember to use the **preterite tense** for completed actions in the past.

Visité *la feria con mis amigos.*
I visited the fair with my friends.

Use the **imperfect tense** to describe what something was like.

Las flores ***eran*** *tan hermosas.*
The flowers **were** so beautiful.

Escuchar **2** **Listen to some teenagers talking about where they live. Copy and complete the table in English. (1–5)**

	What they like	A recent activity	A future plan
1	Fun and young atmosphere ...	Rented a bike and went to ...	...

Hablar **3** **In pairs, talk about your area. Answer the following questions.**

- *¿Dónde vives?*
- *Vivo en ...*
- *¿Qué es lo bueno/mejor de tu ciudad/pueblo/zona?*
- *Lo bueno/mejor es ...*
- *¿Cuál es tu lugar favorito de tu ciudad/pueblo/zona?*
- *Mi lugar favorito es ...*
- *¿Qué hiciste la semana pasada / ayer?*
- *La semana pasada / Ayer fui a ...*
- *¿Qué vas a hacer en tu ciudad/pueblo/zona el fin de semana próximo?*
- *Voy/Vamos a ...*

G

Some verbs in the **preterite tense** are completely irregular (*ser*, *ir*, *dar* and *ver*).

Other preterite verbs have **irregular stems**, but their endings follow similar patterns.

For example:

tener → *tuve, tuviste, tuvo, tuvimos, tuvisteis, tuvieron*
estar → *estuve, estuviste, estuvo, estuvimos, estuvisteis, estuvieron*
hacer → *hice, hiciste, hi**z**o, hicimos, hicisteis, hicieron*
poder → *pude, pudiste, pudo, pudimos, pudisteis, pudieron*

Page 149

Escuchar 4 **Listen to and read about the flower festival in Medellín. Identify the three correct statements below.**

La Feria de las Flores

Medellín está listo para recibir uno de los eventos más esperados del año, que se celebra del 5 al 14 de agosto, y promete sorprender a todos con su belleza y alegría.

Durante la feria, las calles van a llenarse de desfiles y carrozas con las flores más hermosas. Los visitantes tendrán la oportunidad de ver los jardines flotantes que pasan por el río Medellín y de disfrutar de los distintos espectáculos artísticos en los parques.

Habrá conciertos, exposiciones de arte floral y una gran variedad de eventos culturales. Además, todos podrán participar en clases de arte floral y aprender sobre las tradiciones locales. Si quieres comer algo, en la feria habrá muchos platos típicos de la región con sabores auténticos, hechos con ingredientes frescos.

Este evento es estupendo para los que se interesan por la naturaleza y la cultura. ¡No te lo pierdas!

las carrozas *floats*

1 La feria se celebra en agosto.
2 Durante la feria, las calles estarán decoradas con flores.
3 No habrá desfiles en las calles.
4 La feria va a incluir música y muchas cosas que hacer.
5 Las clases de arte floral son para niños.
6 La comida nunca forma parte de la feria.

Leer 5 **Translate the third paragraph of the text in exercise 4 into English.**

Escuchar 6 **Listen to some young people talking about their plans and write down each sentence you hear. Then translate the sentences into English. (1–5)**

Hablar 7 **In pairs, create dialogues about your weekend plans. Try to use different ways of saying what you will do. Then use the present subjunctive to say what you will do when you have more money. Complete the example dialogue, using the pictures below. (1–3)**

- *¿Qué vas a hacer este fin de semana?*
- *Primero, iré a la playa para tomar el sol. Luego, jugaré al fútbol porque es divertido, y después mis amigos y yo vamos a …*
- *Cuando tenga más dinero, iré a …*

1

2

3

G

There are several ways you can describe future events or plans.

1 Use the **near future tense** (present of ***ir*** + ***a*** + infinitive):
*Los niños **van a** comprar helados.*
The children **are going to** buy ice-creams.

2 Use the **future tense**:
*Mi amigo **irá** a la playa.*
My friend **will go** to the beach.
***Podremos** disfrutar de muchos eventos.*
We will be able to enjoy lots of events.

3 Use the **conditional tense** of ***gustar***.
***Nos gustaría** visitar (los) sitios históricos.*
We would like to visit (the) historic sites.

Escribir 8 **Research a city you would like to visit in Spain or Latin America. Look online to find three or four things you could do there. Then imagine you have visited this city and write about your trip.**

- Write about the city and what you like about it (present tense).
  Medellín es una ciudad preciosa con mucha cultura y lo que más me gusta es …
- Write about what you did in the city (preterite and imperfect tenses).
  El año pasado visité [Medellín] con mis padres donde … La ciudad era …
- Write about what you will do the next time you visit (future tense or future phrases).
  La próxima vez visitaré … y … Cuando tenga más dinero/tiempo, visitaré …

Gramática 1

The perfect tense (Unit 1, page 136)

Escribir 1 **Write the jumbled words below in the correct order to form sentences about travel. Then translate each one into English.**

1 en · viajado · han · tren

2 he · increíbles · visitado · mezquitas · dos

3 ¿ · la · de · probado · región · comida · has · la · ?

4 típicos · y · mis · yo · hemos · platos · amigos · comido

5 alrededores · nuevas · abierto · los · tiendas · han · muchas · en

Use the **perfect tense** to talk about what you have done. The perfect tense is formed by using the verb ***haber*** in the present and the **past participle**.

To form the past participle, remove the ***-ar***, ***-er***/***-ir*** endings from <u>infinitive</u> verbs and add:
-ado for ***-ar*** verbs and ***-ido*** for ***-er*** / ***-ir*** verbs.

Refer to the grammar box on page 136 for information on irregular verbs.

He comido empanadas.
¿Has viajado a Medellín?
Hemos salido al parque este fin de semana.

When saying what someone **has just done**, you do not use the perfect tense. Instead, you use the present tense of
acabar + ***de*** + <u>infinitive</u>.

Acaban de *<u>descubrir</u> una tienda nueva en las afueras.*
They have just discovered a new shop in the suburbs.

Hablar 2 **In pairs, use the word wheel of <u>infinitives</u> to make sentences in the perfect tense about what you have already done (or have not done yet) in your area.**

Example: Todavía no he visto el castillo. Ya he visitado la oficina de correos.

¿Qué has hecho en tu zona?

Prepositions of place (Unit 1, page 137)

Escribir 3 **Translate these sentences into Spanish.**

1 The tree is behind the house.
2 The bus station is in front of the library.
3 The museum is through the square, next to the park.
4 The bank is on the left, near the swimming pool.
5 The keys are on the table.
6 The restaurants are behind the shopping centre.
7 There is an old church on top of the mountain.
8 I found my phone under the bed.

Prepositions of place are useful to help us say where something is situated.

As in English, they are used before a noun.

Remember to use the contractions ***al*** and ***del*** when *a* or *de* are followed by *el*.

El banco está ***debajo del*** *árbol.*
The bench is **underneath** the tree.

al lado de	next to / beside
bajo	under/underneath
delante de	in front of
detrás de	behind
cerca de	near/close to
encima de	above / on (top of)
hacia	towards
sobre	on (top of)
través, a través de	through, across

Demonstrative adjectives (Unit 2, page 138)

Leer 4

Match the sentence halves, ensuring your demonstrative adjectives agree. Then write out the sentences and translate them into English.

1 En mi ciudad, esta
2 Los paisajes son bonitos con esas
3 Quiero devolver este
4 Me gustaría visitar aquella
5 En mi barrio, aquel

a ayuntamiento es muy famoso.
b calle tiene muchas tiendas populares.
c playas limpias.
d traje porque es demasiado grande.
e plaza de toros.

Escribir 5

Read the sentences and write a list of the possible demonstrative adjectives for each gap. Then listen and circle the demonstrative adjective used. (1–6)

Example: 1 *este, ese, aquel*

1 ___ fin de semana vamos a visitar el castillo.
2 ¿Has viajado en tren para ver ___ vistas bonitas?
3 Ya hemos comido unos platos típicos en ___ restaurante.
4 En ___ plaza hay muchos árboles y una fuente grande.
5 Hay una gran variedad de edificios en ___ pueblo.
6 Es bueno porque ___ tiendas casi nunca cierran.

Demonstrative adjectives are words like 'this', 'that', 'these' and 'those'.

They are used to identify things.

They are positioned before the noun and must agree with the noun.

*Est**e** rincón*	This corner
*Es**a** playa*	That beach
*Aquell**as** pinturas*	Those paintings (over there)

Refer to the grammar box on page 138 for more examples.

There are three neuter demonstrative pronouns: *esto, eso* and *aquello*. They are often used to describe abstract ideas, when we don't know the gender of the word, and to make general statements.

***Esto** es bueno.*	**This** is good.
*¿Qué es **eso**?*	What is **that**?
***Aquello** fue horrible.*	**That** was awful.

The imperfect tense (Unit 2, page 139)

Escuchar 6

Listen to the statements about people's towns and fill in the gaps with the imperfect tense verbs. (1–4)

1 En los alrededores de mi ciudad ___ más casas y los parques ___ más árboles.

2 Antes no ___ mi ciudad de forma positiva porque mucha gente ___ más violenta.

3 En aquella época, las afueras ___ menos industriales y en el centro ___ seguridad.

4 Hace diez años, cuando mis abuelos ___ en la ciudad, los niños pobres ___ las calles y los delitos ___ a menudo.

Gramática 2

Direct object pronouns (Unit 3, page 141)

Escribir 1 **Use direct object pronouns to write a second sentence about these items, saying why you bought them or why you want to return them. Then translate each sentence into English.**

Example: 1 *Los quiero llevar a una fiesta esta noche.*
I want to wear them to a party tonight.

1. La semana pasada compré estos pantalones.
2. Compré esta falda en el centro comercial.
3. El fin de semana pasado compré este traje.
4. Ayer compré este reloj.
5. Quiero quejarme de esta camiseta.
6. Hace dos días compré estos zapatos.
7. Mi madre me compró este regalo, pero no me gusta.
8. Compré esta camisa esta mañana.

Hablar 2 **In pairs, read out your Spanish sentences from exercise 1. Pay close attention to your pronunciation. Then translate your partner's sentences into English.**

Direct object pronouns are used to replace something that has already been mentioned.

me	me	***nos***	us
te	you	***os***	you
lo/la	it	***los/las***	them

Remember to position direct object pronouns correctly.

- Before the conjugated verb:
  *¿**Lo** has visto?* — Have you seen **it**?
  ***La** quiero comprar.* — I want to buy **it**.
- Attached to the end of the infinitive or gerund:
  *Voy a devolver**los**.*
  I am going to return **them**.
  *Estamos comprándo**las**.*
  We are buying **them**.
- After a negative:
  *Nunca **los** compro.* — I never buy **them**.
  *No **la** uso.* — I don't use **it**.

The present subjunctive (Unit 4, page 143)

Escribir 3 **Fill in the gaps with the correct present subjunctive form of each of the five key verbs. Then translate each sentence into English.**

Example: 1 *Cuando tenga dinero, ...*
When I have money, ...

1. Cuando ___ dinero, me compraré un reloj nuevo.
2. Cuando mi amigo ___ mayor, viajará a Sudamérica.
3. Cuando ___ a mi casa, conocerás a mi nuevo perro.
4. Cuando mi hermana ___ al centro, tomará un café.
5. Cuando ___ sol, mis amigos y yo iremos a la playa para descansar.

Escribir 4 **Write about your future plans using *cuando* and the present subjunctive. Write a sentence for each bullet point:**

- Say what you will do when you have money.
- Say what you will do when you are older.
- Say what a family member will do when they go to the town centre.
- Say what you and your friends will do when it is sunny.
- Finish this sentence to your friend: *Cuando vengas a mi casa, ...*

The **present subjunctive** is a form of the verb that is used regularly in Spanish but only very rarely in English. You use it after the word ***cuando***, when talking about the future.

To form the present subjunctive, take the 'I' form of the present tense and remove the ***o***. Add the endings -***a***, -***as***, -***a*** to -***er***/-***ir*** verbs, and add the endings -***e***, -***es***, -***e*** to -***ar*** verbs.

	hacer	**tener**	**venir**
(yo)	haga	tenga	venga
(tú)	hagas	tengas	vengas
(él/ella/usted)	haga	tenga	venga

Ser and *ir* are irregular:
ser → *sea, seas, sea*
ir → *vaya, vayas, vaya*

There are only five key verbs you will be tested on in the subjunctive form. They are *hacer, ir, ser, tener* and *venir*.

You also use the present subjunctive after verbs of wishing, command, request and emotion and after *para que*.

Verbs in the preterite tense (Unit 5, page 144)

Escuchar **5** **Listen to Malek and Fátima talking about a visit to Cali, in Colombia. Fill in the gaps with the missing verbs in the preterite tense.**

Hola, Fátima, ¿cómo estás?

Estoy muy contenta. **1** la suerte de visitar Cali la semana pasada con mis padres. ¿Has tenido la oportunidad de visitar Cali, Malek?

Sí, **2** a Cali el mes pasado. A mí, me **3** también. ¿Qué cosas **4** hacer mientras **5** en Cali, Fátima?

6 al Parque del Gato de Tejada. Era muy bonito y estaba lleno de esculturas de gatos diferentes.

7 ir a ese parque, pero no pude porque **8** un accidente en la carretera.

También **9** mucha comida típica de la región en un restaurante en el centro.

Yo también. ¡ **10** mucho en Cali!

Some verbs in the **preterite tense** have irregular stems but their endings follow mainly familiar patterns.

Verbs with *u*	Verbs with *i*	Verbs with *j*
andar (*to walk*)	**querer** (*to want*)	**decir** (*to say*)
anduve anduviste anduvo anduvimos anduvisteis anduvieron	quise quisiste quiso quisimos quisisteis quisieron	dije dijiste dijo dijimos dijisteis dijeron
estar: estuve, ... **tener:** tuve, ... **poder:** pude, ... **poner:** puse, ... **saber:** supe, ...	**venir:** vine, ... **hacer:** hice, ... (hi**z**o *for he/she/it form*)	**traer:** traje, ...

Mi amiga ***vino*** *a visitarme.* — My friend **came** to visit me.
No ***dije*** *nada.* — I **said** nothing.

Other verbs are completely irregular (*ser, ir, dar, ver*).

Notice that there are no written accents on any of the endings for these irregular preterite verbs.

dar → *di, diste, dio, dimos, disteis, dieron*
ver → *vi, viste, vio, vimos, visteis, vieron*

Conducir and *reducir* follow the same *j* stem and ending pattern as *decir* and *traer*. These verbs end in *-eron* and not *-ieron* for the third person plural.

conducir → *conduje, condujiste, condujo*
reducir → *reduje, redujiste, redujo*

Escribir **6** **Write out the complete paradigm for the following verbs in the preterite tense. Pay careful attention to your spelling and watch out for irregular verbs.**

Example:	*beber* (to drink)
(I)	*bebí*
(you sing.)	*bebiste*
(he/she/it)	*bebió*
(we)	*bebimos*
(you pl.)	*bebisteis*
(they)	*bebieron*

~~beber~~ hacer salir traer poder escuchar estar ir

¡En marcha! (Units 1–5)

Escribir **7** **Translate the travel blog into Spanish. Make sure you use the correct tense for each verb in bold.**

Colombia **is** a country with some beautiful woods and lots of diversity. **Have you seen** the beaches in the north? **Have you** already **been** to Medellín with its spectacular views? Last weekend, **I visited** the city and **my friends and I had** the opportunity to go to Plaza Botero. **I wanted to go** to the Antioquia museum, which **is** behind the metro station, but **there wasn't** time. **I bought** a present for my father, but **I would like to return** it because it is not good quality. When **I have** the opportunity, **I will return** to Medellín.

Hablar **8** **Name the tenses you have used for each bold verb in exercise 7 and discuss why they are used. Then read out your text, paying attention to your pronunciation and using intonation to make it clear which sentences are questions.**

Example: es = present tense (this is a description of a place now)

Leer y escuchar

Reading

Leer 1

***Travel adverts.* You read these adverts in a travel magazine for travel destinations in Colombia. Write the correct letter (A–F) for each question. (1–4)**

A El Caribe. Si quieres disfrutar de aguas claras y playas hermosas de arena blanca, es el lugar perfecto para ti.

B La Orinoquía. Este lugar es muy importante para la industria, pero también cuenta con paisajes preciosos y muchos bosques altos.

C La región Amazónica. Cuando llegues a esta región, verás muchos animales en peligro de desaparecer y pequeñas comunidades de gente que viven en los bosques.

D El Pacífico. Llueve mucho en esta parte del país pero este clima es ideal para muchos tipos de pájaros y especies de plantas.

E La región Andina. Se encuentra en el centro del país. Aquí, encontrarás las mejores vistas de las montañas.

F Bogotá. Una de las ciudades más altas del mundo con una economía importante, te sorprenderá el tamaño de esta ciudad colombiana.

la industria	*industry*
la economía	*economy*
sorprender	*to surprise*

Landscape and views are very similar. Be sure to pick the option that relates to mountains.

1 Where will you have spectacular mountain views?
2 Where will you see endangered wildlife?
3 Where will you be at high altitude?
4 Where will you be able to relax on a beach?

Two options mention wildlife, but which one specifies that animals are at risk?

Alto is mentioned twice, but which option is implying you will be at a high level?

The word 'relax' is not mentioned, but which option implies that you could do so on a beach?

Leer 2

***Party preparations.* You read a blog about Andrea's birthday party. Which statements (1–5) are correct? Write A if only statement A is correct, B if only statement B is correct or A+B if both statements A and B are correct.**

1 A Andrea invited a lot of people to her birthday celebration.
B Andrea only invited close friends and family to her birthday celebration.

2 A Andrea normally shops online.
B Andrea often goes shopping with her friends.

3 A There was a selection of shops at the shopping centre.
B The selection of shops online is better.

4 A Andrea's friends bought dresses.
B Andrea's style is modern.

5 A Andrea is going to buy used clothes.
B Sustainability is important for Andrea.

Ayer fue mi cumpleaños. No lo celebré con una fiesta enorme, sino que solo asistieron mis mejores amigos y mi familia.

Hice compras para prepararme para el día. Suelo hacer las compras online porque normalmente es más fácil, pero mis amigos me llevaron al centro comercial. Aunque hay una gran variedad de tiendas, la selección de ropa en las tiendas en Internet es mejor.

Mis amigas compraron unos vestidos pero no me van bien y compré un traje blanco. Los vestidos eran muy modernos y yo prefiero algo más tradicional y de mejor calidad.

Para la próxima fiesta, voy a ir a una tienda de ropa de segunda mano. A mí me importa ser más verde pero para mis amigas las marcas son más importantes.

Some of the ideas in the answer options are expressed using different words in the text.

Leer 3

Translation. Translate the following sentences into English.

How could you translate *gran* in this instance to make the translation sound more natural?

The infinitive *asistir* usually translates as '**to** attend', but after *después de*, it changes to 'attend**ing**'.

Watch out for little words such as *más* that can easily be missed when translating quickly.

1 Habrá una gran variedad de eventos culturales en el centro.
2 Después de asistir a la iglesia, mi hermano celebró la ocasión con sus amigos.
3 Ayer compré esta falda en el mercado pero quiero devolverla.
4 Cuando tenga más dinero, lo compartiré con otras personas.
5 Lo mejor es que la estación de autobuses está cerca del centro histórico.

Check verb endings carefully to ensure you spot tense changes in translation tasks.

Watch out for expressions that use different prepositions in English to those that are used in Spanish.

Listening

Escuchar 1

A travel report. You listen to a travel reporter talk about her recent trip to Colombia in her podcast. What is her opinion of these aspects of her trip? Answer both parts of each question. (1–2)
Write (**P**) for a **positive** opinion, (**N**) for a **negative** opinion or (**P+N**) for a **positive and negative** opinion.

1 **A** the city **B** the buildings
2 **A** the culture **B** the people

Escuchar 2

Making travel plans. Vicente is talking to his friend Sofía. Listen and complete the sentences. Answer both parts of each question. (1–2)

1 Vicente asks about ...
A a birthday party.
B a food festival.
C a traditional parade.

It takes place ...
A in front of the main square.
B inside the town hall.
C behind the bullring.

2 The food is ...
A eaten by the locals.
B eaten by everyone.
C prepared by the locals.

Sofía's favourite thing is ...
A the atmosphere.
B the economic benefit.
C the drinks.

Escuchar 3

You will hear <u>five</u> short sentences. Listen carefully and, using your knowledge of Spanish sounds, write down in Spanish exactly what you hear for each sentence.

Prueba oral

Role play

Hablar 1 **Look at the role play card and prepare what you are going to say.**

You are talking to your Mexican friend about your local area.

Your teacher will play the part of your friend and will speak first.

You should address your friend as *tú*. When you see this – **?** – you will have to ask a question.

You must include at least one verb in your response to each bullet point.

Task:

1. Say what there is for tourists where you live. (Give two details.)
2. Say what the weather is like in your area. (Give two details.)
3. **?** Ask your friend a question about their local area.
4. Say what you are going to do in your local area this weekend. (Give two details.)
5. Give one disadvantage of your town/city.

This is a two-part task; don't forget to give two pieces of information.

Remember that most weather expressions use ***hace***.

An easy way to ask a question is to ask if someone likes or dislikes something.

Use the near future tense.

Keep it simple – there are no extra marks for using complex language in the role play task.

Hablar 2 **Practise your role play answers. Listen and respond to the questions.**

Escuchar 3 **Now listen to Robert doing the role play task. In English, note down what he says for each of the points on the card, including the question he asks.**

Reading aloud

Hablar 1 **When your teacher/partner asks you, read aloud the following text in Spanish:**

Ayer mi madre me compró un nuevo reloj en el centro comercial.

No me gustó y lo devolví.

Las tiendas estaban llenas de gente.

Después, fuimos al mercado local donde compré unos zapatos negros.

Esta noche, vamos a una fiesta de cumpleaños.

Voy a llevarlos con un traje azul y una camisa blanca.

Pay particular attention to *j*, *ge* and *gi* – pronounce these from the back of your throat.

Pronounce *ll* like the *y* in 'yellow'.

Remember to stress any letters with accents on them. Try clicking your fingers as you read to help you get the stress right.

If you talk about something you like, mention something you don't like to help you develop your responses easily.

Escuchar 2 **Listen and check your pronunciation.**

Hablar 3 **Listen to the teacher asking four questions that relate to the topic of customs, festivals and traditions. Translate each question into English and prepare your own answers in Spanish. Then listen again and respond to the teacher.**

Photo card

Escuchar 1

Look at the photos below and read the task. Then listen to Nadya describing the photos.

1 How does Nadya describe the appearance of the people in the first photo?
2 How does she think the adults are related to the young girls in the first photo?
3 What does Nadya say about the relationship of the people in the second photo?
4 What does she say the people are doing in the second photo?

Prepare your own description of the photos. Your teacher will ask you to talk about the content of these photos. You must include at least one detail about each photo.

After you have described the content of the photos, your teacher will then ask you questions related to any of the topics within the theme of **Communication and the world around us**.

Remember, you **must** describe both photos to be able to score full marks. Introduce each photo by using '*En la primera foto …*' '*En la otra foto …*' to signpost this to an examiner.

Use the present tense or present continuous to say what people are doing.

Hablar 2

Prepare your own description of the two photos. Then, with a partner, take turns to describe them.

- *En la primera foto hay …*
- *En la otra foto hay …*

Escuchar 3

Now listen to Nadya responding to the second part of the task card and the conversation questions asked by her teacher. Write down the missing word(s) for each gap. (1–9)

¿Qué hay para turistas en tu zona?
Hay muchas **1** para turistas en mi zona. Primero, los turistas **2** disfrutar de muchos platos tradicionales que **3** los restaurantes locales. Si quieren hacer algo más **4**, pueden nadar en el lago en las afueras. Mi ciudad tiene mucho que ofrecer a todos.

¿Qué has hecho recientemente en tu zona?
Recientemente, he **5** muchos monumentos y sitios de interés en mi barrio. La semana pasada, mis amigos y yo decidimos ir al museo de **6** en el centro. Las exposiciones eran estupendas y **7** mucho sobre el arte y la cultura de mi país. Lo **8** fue que no tuve que pagar para entrar. Cuando **9** mis exámenes, quiero visitar más museos en mi ciudad.

Escuchar 4

Listen to Nadya answering more conversation questions. Note down, in English, the three questions she is asked by the teacher. Next, write down the verbs in the past time frame and the future time frame that she uses.

Hablar 5

Prepare your own answers to Module 6 questions 1–10 on page 231. Then practise with your partner.

If you are asked what you like to do, give an example of when you last did that activity using the preterite tense to demonstrate your knowledge of tenses.

Use a variety of structures that are followed by the infinitive to add complexity to your work.

Prueba escrita

Translation

Escribir 1

Read the English text and Komal's translation of it. Write down the missing word for each gap. (1–7)

She started her career in 2016 in the national football team. She was born in the north of the country. In this region, you can find loads of beaches with white sand and clear waters. Also, you should visit the natural forests in the mountains if you want to enjoy nature. I have visited them and they are beautiful. When I visit the country in the summer, I am going to spend more time in the south.

Empezó su carrera en 2016 en el equipo de fútbol **1** . **2** en el norte del país. En **3** región, se puede encontrar un montón de playas con arena **4** y aguas claras. También, **5** visitar los bosques naturales en las montañas si quieres disfrutar de la naturaleza. Los he **6** y son hermosos. Cuando **7** el país en el verano, voy a pasar más tiempo en el sur.

Escribir 2

Translate the sentences into Spanish.

He started his journey in the south of the country.

You should visit the brilliant lakes in the summer.

I have bought a dress, but my friend wants a suit.

The city had a lot of industry and fewer trees in the past.

They have just gone to the forest.

To say someone has done something, use the perfect tense.
To say someone has just done something, use *acabar de* + infinitive.

150-Word writing task

Escribir 1

Look at this writing task and then, for each bullet point, consider:

- what examples of **complex language** you could use to impress the examiner
- how you could use a **variety of vocabulary** to avoid repetition
- **which tense(s)** you will need to use in your answer.

You are writing a post about your local area.

Write approximately **150** words in **Spanish**. You must include something about each bullet point.

Mention:

- the positive aspects of your region
- something you did recently in your local area.

Leer 2 **Read Beth's answer to the task. Answer questions 1–5 in the coloured shapes.**

1 Justify your opinions to say why you feel a certain way. Find one other opinion and justification in Beth's response.

2 Use *acabar de* + infinitive to say what you have just done. Find one more example of *acabar de* in the text.

3 Which tense has Beth used here to show that she can use more complex Spanish?

4 Use the perfect tense to say that something has happened. Find one other example of the perfect tense in the text.

5 Use the preterite tense to narrate in the past. Pick out six further examples of the preterite tense from the text.

Hay muchos aspectos positivos de mi región y por eso, me encanta vivir aquí. Vivo en una ciudad enorme y siempre hay algo que hacer. Acabo de visitar el museo de ciencias y me encantó porque vi muchas exposiciones interesantes. Hay más museos aquí, y cuando termine mis exámenes, voy a visitarlos. Otro aspecto positivo son las vistas hermosas de la ciudad y de los edificios modernos. En el pasado, había muchas industrias y los edificios eran feos, pero acaban de construir edificios modernos que son maravillosos. En mi opinión, esta región ha cambiado mucho y ahora es un buen lugar para vivir.

Mis amigos y yo hemos decidido descubrir más sobre nuestra ciudad y ayer, fuimos al centro para aprender sobre la historia. Primero, cogimos el tren y luego anduvimos por las calles históricas. Debajo de un puente encontramos unos monumentos del pasado. Después de caminar por la ciudad, tuvimos hambre y comimos en un restaurante barato. Lo pasamos guay.

Leer 3 **Read Beth's text again and finish the sentences.**

1 Beth loves living in her region because ...
2 Beth loved the science museum because ...
3 In the past, in her city, there used to be ...
4 Now her city is ...
5 She and her friends have ...
6 Under a bridge, they found ...
7 After walking through the city ...

Escribir 4 **Prepare your own answer to the task.**

- Think about how you can develop your answer for each bullet point.
- Look back at your notes from exercises 1 and 2.
- Look at the 'Challenge checklist' and consider how you can show off your Spanish!
- Write a brief plan and organise your answer into paragraphs.
- Write your answer and then carefully check the accuracy of what you have written.

Challenge checklist

	✓ Past, present and future time frames ✓ Connectives / time phrases / sequencers ✓ A range of adjectives
	✓ The perfect tense to say what you have done ✓ Different persons of the verbs ✓ Opinions in the past (e.g. *Fue* ...)
	✓ The present subjunctive with *cuando* (e.g. *Cuando termine mis exámenes, voy a* ...) ✓ *Acabar de* + infinitive to say what you have just done ✓ Direct object pronouns (e.g. *Me encantan los monumentos. Los visitaré* ...)

Módulo 6 Palabras

Key:
bold = this word will appear in higher exams only
* = this word is not on the vocabulary list, but you may use it in your own sentences

En Colombia todo es posible (pages 134–135):

¿Qué hay en tu país?	*What is there in your country?*
En (el norte de) mi país/ región ...	*In (the north of) my country/ region ...*
(no) hay ...	*there are / there aren't ...*
(no) tenemos ...	*we (don't) have ...*
mucho campo	*lots of countryside*
muchos **lagos**	*lots of lakes*
unos bosques / unas playas	*some forests/beaches*
un paisaje/río/**monte** espectacular	*a spectacular landscape/ river/hill*
comunidades *indígenas	*indigenous communities*
mucha **riqueza**	*lots of wealth*
*selva tropical / *volcanes	*rainforest/volcanoes*
Se encuentra(n) en ...	*It is / They are found in ...*
Está(n) en ...	*It is / They are in ...*
el norte/sur	*the north/south*
el este/oeste	*the east/west*
el centro	*the centre*

Medellín, ciudad inteligente (pages 136-137):

¿Has visitado ...?	*Have you visited ...?*
(Ya) He/Has/Hemos ...	*I/You/We have (already)...*
También he/has/hemos ...	*I/You/We have also ...*
Todavía no he/has/hemos ...	*I/You/We haven't ... yet.*
alquilado/probado ...	*rented/tried ...*
bebido/comido ...	*drunk/eaten ...*
ido (al museo)	*been (to the museum)*
abierto/**dicho**/subido / visto ...	*opened / said / gone up / seen ...*
descubierto (el **entorno**) ...	*discovered (the surroundings) ...*
viajado (en metro)	*travelled (by underground)*
visitado (el parque famoso)	*visited (the famous park)*
¿Dónde está el centro comercial más cercano?	*Where is the nearest shopping centre?*
Está ...	*It is ...*
al lado de ...	*next to ...*
delante de / detrás de ...	*in front of / behind ...*
cerca de / lejos de ...	*close to / far from ...*
la estación (de metro)	*the (underground) station*
el banco	*the bank*
Mira el plano.	*Look at the map.*
Pasa / **Cruza** ...	*Go past / Cross ...*
el puente / la plaza / la mezquita	*the bridge/square/mosque*
Toma la primera/segunda/ tercera calle ...	*Take the first/second/third street ...*
a la derecha/izquierda	*on the right/left*
Está a la derecha/izquierda.	*It is on the right/left.*
¿Qué hacemos mañana?	*What are we doing tomorrow?*
Me encantaría / Quiero ...	*I would love to / I want to ...*
Podemos ...	*We could ...*
Voy/Vamos a ...	*I am / We are going to ...*
ir de excursion	*go on an outing*
tomar el metro	*take the underground*

Medellín ahora y antes (pages 138–139):

¿Cómo es?	*What is it like?*
este lugar / esta calle	*this place/street*
estos árboles / estas tiendas	*these trees/shops*
ese espacio (público)	*that (public) space*
esa carretera	*that road*
esos parques / esas zonas	*those parks/areas*
aquel barrio	*that neighbourhood (over there)*
aquella biblioteca	*that library (over there)*
aquellos castillos	*those castles (over there)*
aquellas vistas	*those views (over there)*
En **aquellos** tiempos ...	*In those days ...*
Ahora, ¿cómo es?	*What is it like now?*
Ahora ...	*Now ...*
está limpio/a / sucio/a	*it is clean/dirty*
Hay / Tiene ...	*there is/are / it has ...*
más árboles / menos violencia	*more trees / less violence*
tanto arte / tanta cultura	*so much culture/art*
tantos problemas	*so many problems*
es ...	*it is ...*
más *acogedor (a) / seguro/a	*more welcoming / safer*
completamente diferente	*completely different*
tan caro/a	*so expensive*
Antes, ¿cómo era?	*What was it like before?*
Antes había ...	*Before there was/were ...*
muchos delitos.	*lots of criminal offences*
menos edificios modernos.	*fewer modern buildings*
mucha/tanta basura.	*lots of/so much rubbish*
Antes era ...	*Before it was ...*
más pequeño/a / tranquilo/a / **violento/a**	*smaller / quieter / more violent*
menos moderno/a	*less modern*
más industrial / peligroso/a	*more industrial/dangerous*
Ha cambiado mucho porque ...	*It has changed a lot because ...*
han abierto/creado ...	*they have opened/created ...*
han limpiado/mejorado ...	*they have cleaned/improved ...*
han construido ...	*they have built ...*
*han plantado ...	*they have planted ...*
*han renovado ...	*they have renovated ...*

¡A comprar! (pages 140–141):

¿Dónde prefieres ir de compras?	*Where do you prefer to go shopping?*
Por un lado, ...	*On one hand, ...*
Por otro lado, ...	*On the other hand, ...*
(No) Me gusta / Me encanta ...	*I (don't) like / I love ...*
Prefiero / Odio ...	*I prefer / I hate ...*
Suelo/**Solemos**/**Suelen** ...	*I/We/They usually ...*
ir a las tiendas de mi barrio	*go to the shops in my neighbourhood*
comprar ropa de segunda mano	*buy secondhand clothes*
comprar por Internet/online	*buy on the internet/online*

ir al centro comercial.	*go to shopping centre.*
Es/Son ...	*It is / They are ...*
menos/tan ...	*less/so ...*
barato/a(s)	*cheap*
económico/a(s)	*cheap*
caro/a(s) / fácil(es)	*expensive / easy*
práctico/a(s)	*practical*
*sostenible(s)	*sustainable*
más barato/a(s) / caro/a(s)	*cheaper / more expensive*
Hay más ofertas.	*There are more offers.*
Hay tanta/demasiada gente.	*There are so/too many people.*
(No) Se puede probar la ropa.	*You can/can't try on the clothes.*
Los precios son más bajos.	*Prices are lower.*
Las tiendas son muy pequeñas.	*The shops are very small.*
(No) tengo que hacer **cola**.	*I (don't) have to queue.*

¿En qué puedo servirle?	*How may I help you?*
Ayer / Hace una semana compré ...	*Yesterday / A week ago I bought ...*
Quiero **devolver**/cambiar ...	*I want to return/exchange ...*
este reloj/vestido/traje	*this watch/jumper/dress/suit*
esta camisa/camiseta/falda	*this shirt/T-shirt/skirt*
estos pantalones/zapatos	*these trousers/shoes*
estas marcas	*these brands*
porque es/son demasiado ...	*because it is / they are too ...*
pequeño/a(s)	*small*
largo/a(s)	*long*
grande(s)	*big*
porque es/son de mala **calidad**	*because it is / they are poor quality*
porque no me gusta el color/ **estilo**	*because I don't like the colour/ style*

¿Dónde prefieres vivir? (pages 142–143):

¿Prefieres vivir en el campo o en la ciudad?	*Do you prefer to live in the country or in the city?*
Prefiero vivir en la ciudad/ el campo porque ...	*I prefer to live in the city/ countryside because ...*
es más/menos ... que ...	*it is more/less ... than ...*
hay más/menos ... que ...	*there is more/less ... than ...*
es imposible *aburrirse	*it is impossible to be bored*

¿Qué es lo bueno/malo de vivir en ...?	*What is the good/bad thing about living in ...?*
Lo bueno/malo de mi pueblo es que ...	*The good/bad thing about my town is that ...*
Lo positivo/negativo de mi ciudad es que ...	*The positive/negative thing about my city is that ...*
tiene mucha contaminación/ gente	*it has a lot of pollution/ people*
(no) es ...	*it is (not) ...*
divertido/a / tranquilo/a	*fun / quiet*
está en la costa / las montañas	*it is on the coast / in the mountains*
no hay más **posibilidades** de trabajo	*there aren't more job prospects*
hay tanto tráfico	*there is so much traffic*
hay tanta gente	*there are so many people*
la gente (no) se conoce	*people (don't) know each other*
conozco a todos mis vecinos	*I know all my neighbours*
hay una gran variedad de tiendas en los **alrededores**	*there is a large variety of shops in the surrounding area*
siempre hay algo que hacer	*there is always something to do*

Cuando **tenga** más dinero, ...	*When I have more money, ...*
Cuando **sea** mayor, ...	*When I am older, ...*
Cuando **tenga** dieciocho años, ...	*When I am eighteen, ...*
compraré una casa pequeña	*I will buy a small house*
viviré con mi novio/a	*I will live with my boyfriend/ girlfriend*
compartiremos un piso	*we will share a flat*

¿Cambiarías algo de tu zona?	*Would you change anything about your area?*
Cambiaría/Mejoraría ...	*I would change/improve ...*
Me encantaría/gustaría ...	*I would love/like ...*
Preferiría / Construiría ...	*I would prefer/build ...*
semejante	*similar*

Un intercambio cultural (pages 144–145):

¿Qué es lo mejor de tu pueblo/ciudad?	*What is the best thing about your town/city?*
Vivo en una casa de dos plantas.	*I live in a two storey house.*
No llueve mucho.	*It doesn't rain much.*
Tiene mucha cultura.	*It has a lot of culture.*
Hay una *feria.	*There is a fair.*
Lo bueno/mejor es ...	*The good/best thing is ...*
la gente/comida	*the people/food*
¿Cuál es tu lugar favorito de tu pueblo/ciudad/zona?	*What is your favourite place in your town/city/area?*
Mi lugar favorito es el mercado/ parque/museo.	*My favourite place is the market/ park/museum.*

¿Qué hiciste ayer / la semana pasada?	*What did you do yesterday / last week?*
Ayer / La semana pasada ...	*Yesterday / Last week ...*
alquilamos unas bicicletas	*we rented some bicycles*
compré ...	*I bought ...*
mucha fruta	*lots of fruit*
unos zapatos nuevos	*some new shoes*
fui ...	*I went ...*
a la playa / al estadio	*to the beach/stadium*
a un concierto/restaurante	*to a concert/restaurant*

¿Qué vas a hacer este fin de semana?	*What are you going to go this weekend?*
Primero/Luego ...	*First / Later/Afterwards ...*
Me/**Nos** gustaría ...	*I/We would like to ...*
Podremos ...	*We could/will be able to ...*
Quiero/Queremos ...	*I/We want to ...*
Voy/Vamos a ...	*I am / We are going to ...*
salir a comer / ir de compras	*go out to eat / go shopping*
ir a la playa	*go to the beach*
visitar la plaza de toros / sitios históricos	*visit the bullring / historic places*
comprar *helados	*buy ice creams*
participar en muchos **eventos**	*participate in lots of events*
Jugaré a ...	*I will play ...*
Iré (a la playa) para ...	*I will go (to the beach) (in order) ...*
celebrar / disfrutar de ...	*to celebrate/enjoy ...*
tomar el sol	*to sunbathe*

Módulo **7**

Un mundo mejor para todos

Espacios naturales maravillosos

- Learning about natural wonders of Spanish-speaking countries
- Using pronouns after prepositions

¡Descubre los paisajes más increíbles!

En América Latina y España, hay numerosos lugares naturales que son maravillosos y te dejarán con la boca abierta. Unos jóvenes explican cuál es para ellos su lugar favorito.

1 Para nosotros los colombianos, este es el río más hermoso del mundo. Tiene colores amarillos, azules, verdes, rojos y negros. Durante los meses de julio a noviembre, sus aguas se convierten en una vista increíble, con colores que contrastan con el paisaje de los alrededores. ¿A ti qué te parece? **Leticia**

2 Puedes verlo desde el cielo. Para mí, es el lugar más bonito y único del planeta. Tiene una forma circular perfecta y es de color azul. Está en medio del mar y es muy profundo: tiene más de 120 metros. A mí me gusta porque es un lugar lleno de sorpresas con varias especies de peces. **Félix**

3 Es la cascada natural más alta del planeta, con casi mil metros de altura. ¿Te atreverías a saltar desde ella? En los alrededores se encuentran valles y bosques. ¿Quieres descubrirla conmigo? Es increíble verla en los meses húmedos (agosto y septiembre), aunque hay que ir cuando hace buen tiempo porque las nubes y la lluvia esconden las vistas. **Laura**

4 Si eres aficionado al buceo, es el lugar ideal para ti. Está cerca de Isla Mujeres. Fue creado en 2009 para luchar contra los peligros que amenazan la vida marina. Un artista británico construyó figuras hechas con un material que ha permitido crear corales en ellas. ¿Te gustaría visitarlo con nosotros? **Julián y Rosario**

los peces	*fish*	***húmedo***	*humid*
la cascada	*waterfall*	***el buceo***	*diving*

a El Gran Agujero Azul (Belice)

b El Museo Subacuático de Arte (México)

c Caño Cristales (Colombia), un río de cinco colores

d Salto Ángel (Venezuela), en el Parque Nacional Canaima

Leer 1 **Read the texts above and look at the photos. Match each text with the correct photo (a–d).**

Leer 2 **Read the texts above again and find these expressions in Spanish.**

1 Do you want to discover it with me?
2 full of surprises
3 Would you dare to jump from it?
4 For us Colombians
5 Would you like to visit it with us?
6 What do you think?
7 which has allowed corals to be created in them
8 it's the ideal place for you

Leer 3 **Read the sentences below and write which place from exercise 1 they relate to.**

1 A mí me interesan las experiencias únicas. Prefiero ver la vida marina porque me encantan los animales que viven en el mar. ***Samuel***

2 No tengo miedo de nada. A mí me gustan las experiencias y las emociones fuertes. ***Agustín***

3 A mí me preocupa la protección de las especies marinas. También me gusta el arte y sacar fotos bajo el agua. ***Amelia***

4 Para mí, lo más interesante es mirar los colores increíbles de la naturaleza y las imágenes hermosas de sus paisajes naturales. ***Rita***

Escuchar 4 **Listen. Fill in the gaps in Spanish with the preposition and pronoun you hear. (1–6) Then translate the sentences into English.**

Cómo proteger nuestros paisajes increíbles:

1 Reciclar papel tiene beneficios ______ ______.
2 El agua es esencial. ______ ______ no es posible la vida en nuestro planeta.
3 El plástico causa mucha basura. Debido ______ ______ hay mucha contaminación.
4 Es importante proteger los bosques. Gracias ______ ______ hay diversidad.
5 Confiamos ______ ______ para participar en este proyecto sobre el medioambiente.
6 Mañana voy a participar en una manifestación a favor de la protección de los animales. ¡Piensa ______ ______!

G

Prepositional pronouns are pronouns used after prepositions such as *a, de, en, para* and *sin*. They are the same as the subject pronouns, except for the forms *mí* (me) and *ti* (you).

Note that *mí* and *él* have an accent, to distinguish them from *mi* (my) and *el* (the), but there is no accent on *ti*.

There are two irregular forms: *conmigo* (with me) and *contigo* (with you).

The use of pronouns after ***a*** is to add emphasis:
***A mí** me encanta este museo.* — **I** love this museum.
*¿**A ti** te gusta?* — Do **you** like it?

Singular		Plural	
me	**mí**	*us*	**nosotros/as**
you	**ti**	*you*	**vosotros/as**
him	**él**	*them (masc.)*	**ellos**
her	**ella**	*them (fem.)*	**ellas**
you (formal)	**usted**	*you (formal)*	**ustedes**

Page 170

Hablar 5 **In pairs, take turns to ask and answer the questions.**

- *¿A ti qué lugar te gustaría/interesaría visitar?*
- *A mí me gustaría/interesaría visitar el Museo Subacuático de Arte / el río Caño Cristales …*
- *¿Por qué te gustaría/interesaría visitarlo?*
- *(A mí) me gustaría visitarlo porque parece interesante/increíble/emocionante y (a mí) me gusta(n)/encanta(n) …*

Hablar 6 **Read out the following text. Take care to pronounce words correctly, focusing on the sounds in bold. Then listen to check your pronunciation.**

El Parque Nacional del Teide

El Parque Na**ci**onal del Teide se en**cu**entra en la hermosa isla de Tenerife, que es parte de las Islas **Ca**narias. Es famoso por su **v**ol**cá**n, el Teide, que es el pi**co** más alto de España y uno de los más altos de Europa.

Este parque es una mara**v**illa natural úni**ca**, ya que tiene paisajes vol**cá**nicos increíbles. Si **v**as allí podrás disfrutar de bonitas **v**istas de ro**ca**s y piedras vol**cá**nicas y tierras se**ca**s, **co**n **co**lores que **v**an desde el negro hasta los tonos rojos. Es popular entre los turistas que bus**ca**n experien**ci**as diferentes.

se encuentra	*is located*
el volcán	*volcano*
el pico	*peak*
las rocas	*rocks*

- ***ci*** is pronounced like 'th' in 'think' and 'thing' in most of Spain
- ***ca, co, cu*** are pronounced like 'k', similar to English words like 'cake' and 'cold'
- ***v*** sounds the same as b

1 ¡Actúa ya!

- Talking about how you help in your community
- Using the imperative
- Using *falta, hace falta, vale la pena, basta*

Escuchar 1 **Listen to and read the slogans. Match them to their English equivalent. Then, in pairs, take turns to read them out in Spanish, paying attention to correct pronunciation.**

1 ¡Respeta la igualdad!
2 ¡Vota por un futuro mejor!
3 ¡Lucha contra la discriminación!
4 ¡Protege el futuro del planeta!
5 ¡Exige más seguridad y medidas fuertes contra los delitos!
6 ¡Lucha por la libertad de expresión!
7 ¡Rechaza la violencia y levanta tu voz contra ella!
8 ¡Apoya la huelga!

a Support the strike!
b Vote for a better future!
c Fight for freedom of expression!
d Fight against discrimination!
e Reject violence and raise your voice against it!
f Respect equality!
g Protect the future of the planet!
h Demand more security and strong measures against crime!

G

The **imperative** is used to give instructions.
The singular (*tú*) positive imperative is formed by removing the -s from the *tú* form of the verb. This is the same as the 'he/she/it' form in the present tense.

votar	→ (*tú*) ***votas***	→ ***¡Vota!***	Vote!
proteger	→ (*tú*) ***proteges***	→ ***¡Protege!***	Protect!
pedir	→ (*tú*) ***pides***	→ ***¡Pide!***	Ask!

With imperatives, **pronouns** are attached to the end of the verb to become a single word.
*Haz**lo***. Do **it**.

If the imperative verb has two syllables or more, an accent is placed on the second-to-last syllable, not counting the pronoun.
Protégelos. Protect them. *¡Ayúdame!* Help me!

Page 170

Leer 2 **Read the opinions and write the correct name for each question below. Then translate Camila's and Guadalupe's texts into English.**

Who ...
1 says that young people must set up organisations?
2 says that the action of young people is key to change things?
3 says that we need to avoid harming the environment?
4 supports women's rights?
5 is asking us to support good causes?
6 demands equality for all?

Es importante hacer manifestaciones para tener una sociedad mejor para todos nosotros. Los jóvenes somos importantes en el mundo actual. Nuestra acción es clave para cambiar las cosas. Ayuda con tus acciones y haz todo lo posible para apoyar buenas causas sociales. ***Shafful***

La igualdad es un derecho. ¿Por qué tratarnos de forma diferente a los hombres? Debemos ayudar y fundar organizaciones. ¡Reconoce y respeta los derechos de las mujeres! ¿Qué haría la sociedad sin ellas? ***Camila***

No es justo discriminar a las personas por su sexo o religión. Todos merecemos tener las mismas oportunidades. Si quieres una sociedad más justa, ¡pide igualdad para todos! ***Guadalupe***

El futuro del planeta es nuestro, por eso es importante actuar contra los peligros que lo amenazan. Necesitamos tener cuidado con nuestras acciones y evitar hacer más daño al medioambiente. ¡Lucha por protegerlo! ***Radhika***

Escuchar 3 **Listen to and complete the sentences with the missing words.**

1 Haz trabajo ____ en tu comunidad.
2 Sé amigo del planeta y ____
3 Pide una ____ más justa para todos.
4 ____ los mensajes de la naturaleza y ...

Leer 4 **Read what some young people do to help in their community. Copy and complete the table with the correct paragraph numbers. Then find (a) six verbs in the preterite tense, (b) five verbs in the future tense and (c) one verb in the conditional tense.**

Action(s) in the past	Action(s) now	Action(s) in the future

¿Y tú? ¿Cómo ayudas en la sociedad?

1 Ayudo en proyectos sociales en mi comunidad. Me hace sentir bien y es algo que vale la pena hacer. Si quieres participar en ellos, contacta conmigo y te daré toda la información que necesitas.

2 Compraré ropa de segunda mano online. Será más económico y ahorraré dinero. Faltan recursos en el planeta y hace falta dar una segunda oportunidad a las cosas. Elegiré productos de comercio justo también. Hace falta ser responsable con nuestras opciones de compra.

3 Ayudé en un hogar de ancianos. Ofrecí apoyo y cariño a personas mayores. Para mí, valió la pena hacerlo. Siempre hacen falta personas para ayudar. ¿Te gustaría venir conmigo la próxima vez?

4 Soy miembro de una organización que apoya a las personas pobres sin hogar. Si quieres ayudar, basta con dar comida o ropa y zapatos que ya no usas. ¡Participa en esta buena causa!

5 Di dinero para apoyar buenas causas. También llevé comida a los bancos de alimentos. Lo hice porque hay muchas personas que no tienen trabajo ni dinero. Hace falta ser comprensivo y generoso.

Escuchar 5 **Listen to two young people and for each person write down one detail about each of the following. (1–2)**

- What they do to help in society or their community.
- What they have done in the past.
- What they will/would like to do in the future.

G

These **impersonal verbs** can be used alone or followed by an infinitive:

vale la pena	it's worth it / it's worth (doing something)
basta (con) / (de)	it's enough (to)
hace falta	it's necessary (to)
falta	is lacking

***Vale la pena** apoyar buenas causas.*
It's worth supporting good causes.

Page 170

Hablar 6 **In pairs, take turns to answer these questions. Use the language you have learned so far in this unit to help you.**

- *¿Qué haces para ayudar en tu comunidad o en la sociedad? ¿Por qué lo haces?*
- *¿Y qué hiciste en el pasado para ayudar a otras personas?*
- *¿Qué más te gustaría hacer en el futuro?*

Para ayudar en mi comunidad	compro ropa de segunda mano. doy/llevo comida a ... ayudo en proyectos sociales. hago campañas para ...	
Es importante hacerlo porque	vale la pena apoyar buenas causas. hace falta ayudar / ser responsable.	
La semana pasada El mes pasado El fin de semana pasado	participé/ayudé en ... ayudé a personas sin hogar. organicé/compré/hice ... di dinero a ...	
En el futuro El próximo verano El próximo año	haré/daré ... participaré/ayudaré en un proyecto de protección ... compraré productos de comercio justo.	
	me gustaría ...	dar/recoger ... ayudar/participar en ...

Escribir 7 **Write about how you help in your community for a volunteering blog. Include:**

- what you normally do to help others / your community
- your opinion about why it is important
- something that you did in the past to help and your opinion
- an activity you will do or would like to do in the future and why.

2 El planeta en peligro

- Talking about climate change
- Using the passive
- Using the imperfect continuous tense

Hablar 1 **In pairs, take turns to read out the following headlines. What do you think each headline means?**

1. El hambre aumenta a nivel mundial
2. Emergencia: ¡América Latina tiene sed!
3. Contaminación del aire: un peligro para la salud
4. El invierno con más calor del siglo en España
5. Cambio climático: una carrera contra el reloj
6. ¡Alerta roja! Los glaciares están desapareciendo

Leer 2 **Find headlines in exercise 1 to match the articles. Then match the Spanish passive verbs in purple to the English phrases below. Finally, translate text C into English.**

A ______

Perú tiene alrededor del 70% de los glaciares tropicales del mundo, pero muchos kilómetros de esos glaciares **han sido destruidos** por el aumento de la temperatura del planeta. A nivel mundial, millones de personas del planeta **serán amenazadas** por el agua derretida, no solo porque aumentará el nivel del mar sino también porque muchos desastres **serán causados** por el agua de los lagos glaciares, lo que causará la muerte de mucha gente y animales.

B ______

La falta de agua es el principal problema en muchos países de Latinoamérica. El agua **es usada** por las empresas, pero la cantidad para los ciudadanos **es controlada y limitada** a unos pocos litros. Incluso **fue cortada** durante meses en los barrios de algunas ciudades. En el futuro, una de cada cuatro personas de estos países **será afectada** por este problema. Es una cuestión muy grave que mata a mucha gente cada año.

C ______

En España, el invierno de 2022 fue el quinto invierno más caliente desde que empezó este siglo. Es un ejemplo de cómo el clima global **ha sido afectado** por los cambios. Las temperaturas **fueron investigadas** por los científicos. Ese año, la producción de alimentos también cayó porque los cultivos **fueron afectados** por la falta de lluvia.

derretido/a *melted*

1 is controlled and limited
2 will be caused
3 were researched
4 is used
5 have been destroyed
6 has been affected
7 was cut off
8 will be affected
9 will be threatened
10 were affected

Escuchar 3 **Listen to some young people discussing environmental problems. Copy and complete the table in English. (1–5)**

	Biggest problem or issue	Reason
1	(huge amount of) food waste	people are hungry / not enough food.

G

The **passive** is used to say what is / was / will be done to something or someone. To form it, use the correct person and tense of ***ser*** followed by the **past participle**, which must agree.

*El problema **es investigado** por los científicos.*
*Los campos **son afectados** por la falta de lluvias.*
*La casa **fue destruida** por los vientos fuertes.*

Page 171

Hablar 4 **In pairs, talk about the biggest problem facing the planet and give reasons. Use the language from previous exercises to help you.**

- *Para ti, ¿cuál es la cuestión más grave? ¿Por qué?*

Para mí, el problema / la cuestión más grave es		el hambre la contaminación	el cambio climático la falta de agua/comida
porque	creo que pienso que me parece que	afecta a nuestro planeta / nuestra salud. hay personas que no tienen comida. no se puede vivir sin agua limpia. mata a mucha gente.	

Leer 5 **Read about one of the most important climate events in recent years in Spain. Answer the questions in English.**

www.lasnoticiasdelplaneta.es

Filomena, la peor tormenta del siglo

La tormenta Filomena dejó un profundo impacto en España. Muchas ciudades españolas fueron afectadas por la nieve y aguantaron temperaturas bajo cero.

Los aeropuertos, las carreteras y el transporte público fueron cortados por la cantidad enorme de nieve que cayó, lo que hizo difícil el tráfico e incluso el acceso a los hospitales.

Como la electricidad también fue cortada y no había calefacción, el gobierno y las autoridades tuvieron que introducir planes de emergencia para ayudar a los ciudadanos.

Aunque hubo dificultades, mucha gente ayudó a limpiar las calles de nieve, dar alimentos y medicinas, y salvar a aquellos que no podían salir de sus coches. Las redes sociales fueron importantísimas para organizar las tareas de ayuda y compartir información útil sobre la situación.

Además, la tormenta Filomena también dejó muchas imágenes hermosas en todo el país, con los monumentos más famosos de España cubiertos de nieve.

Filomena: hermosa, pero peligrosa

la tormenta	*storm*
la nieve	*snow*

1 How did the snow affect transport?
2 Why did the government implement emergency plans?
3 How did the community come together to help? (Give two details.)
4 Why is social media mentioned? (Give two reasons.)

Leer 6 **Read the accounts of these young people and focus on the imperfect continuous phrases in purple. Write down the following information in English.**

- What they were doing when the natural disaster happened.
- What they say about the natural disaster, and/or its consequences.

¿Qué **estabas haciendo** cuando ocurrió el desastre natural?

1 Ese día, mi padre **estaba durmiendo** y yo **estaba ayudando** a mi madre en el jardín. Empezó a llover fuerte y lo llenó todo de agua. Llovió durante 36 horas sin parar. El ejército tuvo que venir a ayudarnos. ***Eduardo***

2 Mis amigos y yo **estábamos jugando** un partido de fútbol en el estadio con nuestro equipo. Pero con el viento tuvimos que parar porque era imposible continuar con el partido. ***Rubén***

3 **Estaba viendo** una película mientras mis hermanos **estaban escuchando** un pódcast. Miré por la ventana y todos los árboles y los coches estaban rotos debido al viento fuerte. ¡Qué miedo! ***Gonzalo***

4 Cuando empezó el desastre mi amiga y yo **estábamos paseando** a su perro. Sin embargo, tuvimos que volver a casa rápidamente porque era peligroso estar en la calle. ***Valentina***

Escuchar 7 **Listen. Copy and complete the table in English. (1–4)**

	Weather event	Activity	Problems (mention two)
1	sandstorm	eating a sandwich, ...	had to leave quickly, ...

G

The **imperfect continuous** is used to describe what people were doing.

Estaba corriendo *en el parque cuando empezó a llover.*
I was running in the park when it started to rain.

To form this tense, use the imperfect of ***estar*** and the **present participle**.

Page 172

Escribir 8 **Translate these sentences into Spanish. Use the vocabulary from exercise 6 to help you.**

1 I was studying in the school library.
2 My friends and I were playing a basketball match.
3 I was going to school by bike.
4 I was buying a gift for my friend's birthday in a market.
5 My best friend and I were walking in the park.
6 My younger sister was sleeping while I was preparing dinner.

3 Protegemos el planeta

- Talking about actions to help the environment
- Avoiding the passive
- Practising negatives

Leer 1 **Write the correct letter for each sentence.**

¿Qué haces en casa para cuidar el medioambiente?

Para cuidar el medioambiente, en mi casa, ...

1 apago o no enciendo la luz para ahorrar energía.
2 separo la basura.
3 voy en bicicleta o a pie con frecuencia.
4 reciclamos el papel, las botellas de plástico y el vidrio.
5 usamos el agua de lluvia en el jardín para ahorrar agua.
6 uso el transporte público.
7 tratamos de no tirar los alimentos a la basura.
8 intentamos no usar bolsas de plástico.

a 
b 
c 
d 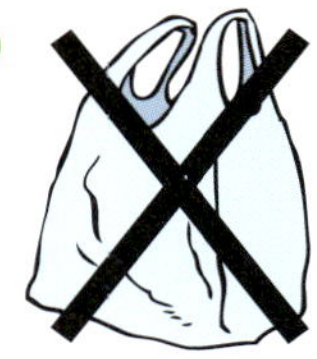
e 
f 
g 
h 

Escuchar 2 **Listen to and read this entry on an eco-school blog. Then copy and complete the passive phrases below in English, selecting the correct words from the box.**

Un colegio verde

En nuestra comunidad escolar trabajamos juntos para crear un colegio verde. Queremos dejar un legado positivo para las futuras generaciones.

En nuestro colegio **se piensa** que el cuidado del medioambiente es importantísimo. Por eso, regularmente **se organizan** actividades educativas para ayudar a protegerlo y conservarlo, y **se sigue** la regla de 'las tres erres': reducir, reciclar y reusar. A menudo **se hacen** campañas para reciclar que tienen mucho éxito para controlar y reducir la cantidad de basura que producimos. Además, al final del día **se apagan** todas las luces, los ordenadores y las pantallas porque no son necesarios. Así **se ahorra** energía.

Nuestro colegio tiene zonas verdes para jugar y jardines llenos de árboles y plantas que **se mantienen** limpios con la ayuda de todos. Además, nunca **se tira** la comida a la basura, sino que **se recicla** y **se usa** para hacer compost para la tierra.

el legado *legacy*

Examples: **1** *In our school* ***it is thought*** *...*
2 *Educational activities* ***are organised*** *...*

3 The rule of the three Rs ...
4 Recycling campaigns ...
5 At the end of the day the lights ...
6 Energy ...
7 Green zones ... clean.
8 Food is never ... It is ...

thrown away	are kept
are switched off	is followed
recycled and used	is saved
are organised	are held
it is thought	are switched on

Escribir 3 **Translate these sentences into Spanish. Use the vocabulary from exercise 2 to help you.**

1 Campaigns to recycle are organised every month.
2 Water is saved and green areas are kept clean.
3 To help the environment in my school, the rule of the three Rs is followed.
4 Food is recycled, it is not thrown away; it is used to create compost for the garden.

G

In Spanish the **passive** is often avoided by using the reflexive pronoun **se**.
*En mi colegio **se recicla** el papel.*
In my school, paper **is recycled**.

Sometimes the subject of the verb comes after the verb.
Se organizan actividades.
Activities **are organised**.

Page 172

Escuchar 4 **Listen to Joaquín, Almudena and Rosario talking about what they do for the environment. For each person, write down one detail in English for the following:**

1 what they do at home
2 what they do at school
3 what they did in the past
4 what they'd like to do in the future.

Use ***no solo ... sino también*** as an alternative to using *y*.

No solo *es malo para la salud* ***sino también*** *para el planeta.*
It's **not only** bad for your health **but also** for the planet.

Hablar 5 **In pairs, take turns to answer questions about the environment.**

- *¿Qué haces para cuidar el medioambiente en casa?*
- *¿Y en tu colegio? ¿Qué cosas hacéis para ayudar?*
- *¿Qué hiciste en el pasado para ayudar al medioambiente?*
- *¿Y en el futuro? ¿Qué más te gustaría hacer para ayudar?*

En Barcelona tienen supermanzanas. Esta iniciativa quiere transformar los espacios de la ciudad en zonas para andar con menos tráfico y más espacios verdes. Quieren que las calles sean más seguras para los ciudadanos y tengan menos contaminación.

la supermanzana	*superblock*

Escribir 6 **Write a blog in Spanish for your school's eco council on what you do to help the environment. Include:**

- what you do to help the environment at home/school
- your opinion on how you are making a difference
- something you did last month for the environment
- what you would like to do in the future to help.

Para ayudar al medioambiente,	en casa	reciclo / separo la basura. no uso bolsas/botellas de plástico. uso botellas de vidrio. trato de / intento reducir/controlar el uso de ... viajo en ...
	en el colegio	se sigue la regla de 'las tres erres'. se apagan las luces / se ahorra energía. se recicla el papel/vidrio. se organizan ... reciclamos/apagamos/usamos ...
La semana pasada El mes/año/verano pasado El fin de semana pasado		participé en ... organicé ... ahorré ... hice ... viajé en ... ayudé a ... aprendí a ... usé ...
En el futuro El verano/año próximo	me gustaría	ayudar a los animales en peligro. aprender a arreglar/reciclar la ropa. organizar campañas para reciclar. organizar un mercado para vender/comprar ropa y objetos de segunda mano.

4 Nuestro mundo, nuestra responsabilidad

- Talking about solutions
- Using the present subjunctive to give opinions
- Translating more complex texts

Escuchar 1 **Listen and read. Write the correct letter for each person. (1–5) Can you find the verbs in the subjunctive?**

Jóvenes con causa

1 Recomiendo que la gente haga una lista de la compra cuando vaya al supermercado. Quiero que sea más responsable para evitar tirar la comida y crear más basura. **Fátima**

2 Me pone triste que mucha gente en nuestra sociedad no tenga suficiente para comer. **Carla**

3 Odio que la gente vaya a los parques y a las playas y no tenga cuidado con la basura que produce. ¡No se puede aguantar! **Paula**

4 Me preocupa que la gente sea víctima de la violencia y la discriminación. En el futuro, espero que la sociedad sea más justa. **Julián**

5 Quiero que más gente haga sus compras en tiendas de comercio justo. Animo a la gente a apoyar esta iniciativa. **Guillermo**

a

b

c

d

e

Leer 2 **Translate these phrases into English.**

1. Recomiendo que vengas a mi casa en bicicleta o en transporte público.
2. Me preocupa que la sociedad no sea justa.
3. Odio que la gente no tenga cuidado con la basura.
4. Quiero que cada niño tenga suficientes alimentos para comer.
5. Espero que la gente vaya a comprar a las tiendas de comercio justo.
6. Me pone triste que el gobierno no haga más para evitar las consecuencias del cambio climático.

Escuchar 3 **Listen to the interviews and select the correct option. (1–2)**

a Emilio believes that **discrimination** / **gender violence** / **problems with animal rights** still exist(s).

b He wants **schools to teach families** / **women to show respect** / **schools and families to teach children**.

c His call to action is for **violence against sexism** / **men to respect women's rights** / **women to be included in protests**.

d Julia is annoyed about **the pollution of mountains** / **food waste** / **supermarkets selling too many clothes**.

e Her solution is **for shops to be more responsible** / **that unsold food go to the hungry** / **to stop using a shopping list**.

G

You have already learned to use the **subjunctive** with *cuando*. It is also used after verbs of wishing, command, request and emotion, such as ***recomendar***, ***esperar***, ***querer*** and ***odiar***.

Remember that to form the present subjunctive in the first person singular, take the 'I' form of the present tense and remove the ***-o***. For ***-ar*** verbs add ***-e***, and for ***-er*** and ***-ir*** verbs add ***-a***.

*Odio que mucha gente no **tenga** comida.*
I hate that lots of people don't have food.

Only use the subjunctive when there is a change of subject in the sentence.

*Quiero que la gente **sea** más responsable con sus costumbres de compra.*
I want people **to be** more responsible with their shopping habits.

Irregular verbs in the present subjunctive include:

ser → *sea*   *ir* → *vaya*

Page 173

Leer 4 **Read about the actions of Sam, an activist dog, and answer the questions in English.**

Conoce a Sam, un perro activista y superhéroe

Sam es un perro que lucha contra la basura en un parque de Santiago de Chile. A Sam y a su dueño, Gonzalo, les encantaba pasear por el parque, pero siempre tenían que parar en el camino para recoger basura, como botellas de plástico, cajas de alimentos, ropa y otros materiales, que la gente tiraba.

Los responsables de Parquemet, un hermoso parque en la capital chilena, decidieron usar su imagen y sus acciones para mandar un mensaje positivo de protección del medioambiente. Ahora, Sam es el personaje de un cómic educativo, *Sam, el superhéroe de Parquemet*, que se ha utilizado para la presentación de una campaña. Esta iniciativa pide que la gente tenga cuidado con la basura para no tirarla por todas partes. Quiere que la gente haga un esfuerzo para ponerla en un punto de reciclaje.

La campaña fue un éxito y rápidamente recibió buenos comentarios de los usuarios. A Sam le gusta pasarlo bien en el parque, pero quiere que la gente sea más responsable.

1 What did Gonzalo and Sam have to do on their walks?
2 What is Parquemet and where is it?
3 What does the campaign want visitors to do with their rubbish? (Give two details.)
4 What are we told about the impact of the campaign?

Escuchar 5 **Listen and fill in the gaps in Spanish. Then take turns to read out the sentences with your partner.**

1 A Sam le gusta ir de ___ en Parquemet.
2 Las personas que visitan el parque necesitan recibir ___ sobre el medioambiente.
3 La ___ de Parquemet tomó una buena ___.
4 La campaña busca la ___ positiva de los ciudadanos de la capital de Chile.
5 Los directores de Parquemet esperan mejorar la ___ de la basura en el parque.

Words ending in the suffixes ***-ción*** and ***-sión*** are usually cognates for English words ending in '-tion' or '-sion' and are always **feminine**. Pay attention to the difference in pronunciation.

*celebra**ción*** celebration
*impre**sión*** impression

Hablar 6 **In pairs, take turns to talk about your opinion on social and environmental problems. Include your ideas for solutions and actions.**

- *¿Qué problema te preocupa más?*
- *¿Por qué?*
- *¿Qué acción quieres ver?*

(A mí) Me preocupa(n) ...
la contaminación de los bosques/mares ... la falta de agua ...
la violencia contra las mujeres / personas transgénero ...

porque	muchas personas muchos animales	no tienen suficiente comida. sufren. son afectad**os**/**as**.
Odio que Me pone triste que Espero que Quiero que Recomiendo que	el gobierno la gente la juventud la sociedad	(no) haga acciones positivas ... (no) haga campañas contra ... (no) tenga cuidado con ... (no) sea responsable. (no) vaya a manifestaciones contra ...

Escribir 7 **Translate the text into Spanish.**

The problem that worries me is the pollution of forests, rivers and seas. I hate that people are not careful with their rubbish. I want people to be more responsible because the environment and animals are affected by it. We must act and make an effort. More campaigns on social media are needed. My message is: respect nature, look after and protect our beautiful planet!

The present subjunctive
The passive
The imperative
Prepositional pronoun
Avoiding the passive

5 El futuro está en nuestras manos

- Developing effective comprehension skills
- Using *(no) se debería* + infinitive
- Understanding multiple tenses

Leer 1 **Read the texts. Write *Jesús*, *Joaquín*, or both names, for each sentence below. Then translate the last paragraph from both texts.**

Jóvenes en acción

Texto 1

Mi modelo a seguir es Jesús Morales. Durante la pandemia perdió su trabajo y tuvo la feliz idea de utilizar su canal para ayudar a la gente usando su popularidad en TikTok.

Primero Jesús subió vídeos graciosos a la red social y sus seguidores dieron dinero, el cual usó para ayudar a otros ciudadanos sin suerte. Salió a la calle y empezó a dar el dinero recibido a los vendedores de la calle en San Diego y Los Ángeles. Al mismo tiempo, grabó las imágenes en vídeos para compartir en la red social, los cuales tuvieron muchísimo éxito. Gracias a la fama que consiguió, pudo seguir con su proyecto social.

A mí me parece que a Jesús le pone triste que su comunidad latina sea víctima de las consecuencias de la crisis económica; por lo tanto, quiere apoyarla. Yo estoy de acuerdo con sus acciones porque creo que se debería ayudar a resolver los problemas sociales.

Alejandro

Texto 2

Mi modelo a seguir es Joaquín Verdeja. Cuando tenía 16 años, decidió ayudar a niños vulnerables que vivían en hogares sin su familia.

Su mejor amigo, Augusto, y él trabajaron juntos y crearon el proyecto Undood Argentina. Con la ayuda de grupos de amigos del colegio, recogieron juegos y otros objetos que la gente ya no usaba. Así comenzaron a hacer actividades sociales y culturales en los hogares de los chicos.

Creo que a estos jóvenes voluntarios no les gusta que un niño sin padres no tenga compañía y quieren asegurarse de que cada niño sea feliz. Por eso desean prestar una mano y dar cariño a estos chicos. Yo pienso que se debería hacer todo lo posible por apoyar proyectos como este en nuestra comunidad.

Joaquín Verdeja

Emiliana

1 His project had a positive influence in the community.
2 He shared videos of his actions on social media.
3 His project helped people down on their luck.
4 He organised activities and games for the people he helped.
5 He received support from others to carry out the project.
6 He wanted to help children living in homes without their family.
7 He used his fame on social media to help people in his community.

los vendedores de la calle	*street vendors*
los voluntarios	*volunteers*
prestar una mano	*to lend a hand*

The **relative pronouns** *el cual*, *la cual*, *los cuales*, *las cuales* are another way to say 'who', 'which' or 'that' in Spanish. They can refer to people and things and change according to gender and number. Sometimes we can just use ***que*** instead.

*Sus seguidores dieron dinero, **el cual** utilizó para ayudar a otros.*

His followers gave money, **which** he used to help others.

Hablar 2 **In pairs, take turns to ask and answer the questions.**

- *¿Quién es tu modelo a seguir favorito?*
- *Mi modelo a seguir favorito es … porque usa su popularidad en TikTok para … / ayuda a mucha gente …*
- *¿Te gustaría hacer trabajo voluntario? ¿Por qué?*
- *Sí, me gustaría hacer … Creo que es importante ayudar/participar en …*
  No, me gustaría hacer … porque …
- *¿Qué se debería hacer para ser un buen voluntario?*
- *Para ser un buen voluntario, se debería ayudar a resolver …*

G Use ***(no) se debería*** + infinitive to say what should or shouldn't be done.

***Se debería** hacer todo lo posible para ayudar a otros.*

Everything possible **should** be done to help others.

Escuchar 3 **Listen to an extract in two parts about Olivia Mandle, a Spanish teen, and her activism. Choose one correct answer in part 1 and two correct answers in part 2.**

Part 1

1. Olivia's interest in the sea started when she was a child.
2. She campaigns against overfishing.
3. She has a house near the sea.
4. She thinks that people buying too much plastic is not sustainable.

Part 2

5. She wants the government to make laws to protect her favourite animal.
6. Through social media she encourages people to act.
7. She is looking for support from scientists and other organisations.
8. Her book was published a few months ago.

Leer 4 **Read the text and select the correct option in the sentences below. Then translate the last two sentences in the third paragraph into English.**

Yalitza Aparicio, una actriz que defiende los derechos humanos

Esta actriz mexicana fue una de las dos protagonistas de la película *Roma*, la cual tuvo mucho éxito porque ganó el premio *Oscar* como mejor película de lengua no inglesa. También fue nominada como mejor actriz en estos premios. Además, fue elegida Embajadora de Buena Voluntad por la UNESCO por su lucha para defender los derechos de los pueblos indígenas.

Yalitza habló en contra del racismo en las redes sociales y también escribió un artículo para un periódico sobre el racismo y la discriminación. En él habló de la importancia del arte para denunciar los problemas sociales, ayudar a ser conscientes de ellos y causar un cambio.

En 2020 Yalitza fue elegida miembro de la Academia de Artes y Ciencias Cinematográficas de Hollywood, y ese mismo año presentó los premios *Latin Grammy*. Los seguidores de sus redes sociales y su canal de YouTube mencionan que ella es un buen ejemplo para México, porque apoya a quienes más lo necesitan. Siempre da mensajes positivos y se siente orgullosa de su cultura.

Yalitza Aparicio

la Embajadora de Buena Voluntad	*Goodwill Ambassador*
denunciar	*to denounce*

1. Yalitza starred in a film that **won a prize** / **was nominated for a prize** / **had some success.**
2. Yalitza was chosen as Goodwill Ambassador by UNESCO **to defend the homes of Indigenous People** / **because she was the best actress** / **for her activism**.
3. She wrote about racism and discrimination **on social media** / **in an article and on social media** / **in her artwork**.
4. Yalitza thinks that art **reflects social problems** / **is important in social problems** / **can help create awareness and promote change**.
5. She also **won** / **presented** / **was chosen to represent** the Latin Grammy awards.
6. Her followers on social media think she **is proud of her success** / **is an example of Mexican culture** / **supports those who need it most**.

To develop effective comprehension skills:
- read or listen for gist first
- match sections to questions
- identify verb tenses
- watch out for distractors in questions
- pay attention to information around the key words.

Gramática 1

Prepositional pronouns (Zona de cultura, page 159)

Escribir 1 **Read the grammar box on page 159. Fill in the gaps using the phrases from the list. Then translate the completed sentences into English.**

Para ti | conmigo | a ella | sin ellos | con él | A mí | contigo

1 Mañana participaré en una manifestación. ¿Te gustaría venir ___?
2 Debemos cuidar los bosques y los árboles porque no podemos vivir ___.
3 ___, ¿cuál sería la mejor solución a este problema? ___ me parece que lo mejor sería prohibir el uso del plástico.
4 Víctor, me gustaría ir ___ al banco de alimentos para llevar comida.
5 El sábado mi primo organizará un evento y yo quisiera participar ___.
6 Mi hermana no usa bolsas de plástico porque ___ le preocupa mucho el medioambiente.

The imperative (Unit 1, page 160)

Escuchar 2 **Complete the sentences with the correct form of the imperative. Listen and check your answers. Then translate the sentences into English.**

Example: 1 <u>*Poned*</u> *atención a la situación ...*
Pay attention to the situation ...

1 **(poner, vosotros)** atención a la situación y **(escuchar, vosotros)** la voz de los jóvenes.
2 **(tener, tú)** cuidado con tus acciones. **(apoyar, tú)** este proyecto sobre el medioambiente y **(protegerlo, tú)**.
3 **(poner, tú)** la basura en el lugar correcto para reciclarla. **(ser, tú)** responsable con lo que haces.
4 ¡**(venir, tú)** a la manifestación! **(ayudar, tú)** a luchar contra la discriminación y **(defender, tú)** lo que es justo.
5 ¡**(hacer, tú)** compost con la basura de los alimentos y **(usarlo, tú)** en tu jardín!

The singular (*tú*) positive **imperative** is formed by removing the **-s** from the *tú* form of the verb.
The positive command is the same as the 'he/she/it' form in the present tense.

Da *dinero para causas importantes.*
Give money for important causes.

These verbs are **irregular** in the *tú* form:

ser (be)	→ *sé*	***hacer*** (do/make)	→ *haz*
ir (go)	→ *ve*	***poner*** (put)	→ *pon*
tener (have)	→ *ten*	***salir*** (go out/leave)	→ *sal*
venir (come)	→ *ven*	***decir*** (to say / to tell)	→ *di*

To form the **plural** (*vosotros/as*) positive command, use the <u>infinitive</u> and change the **-r** to a **-d**.

*participa**r*** → *¡Participa**d** en la manifestación!*
*pedi**r*** → *¡Pedi**d** justicia!*

Remember that **object** and **reflexive pronouns** are attached to the end of the imperative to become a single word.
*Pon**lo** aquí.* Put **it** here.

If the command has two syllables or more, put a written accent on the second-to-last syllable, before adding the pronoun.
*Píde**la**.* Ask for **it**. *Reláj**ate**.* Relax.

Impersonal verbs (Unit 1, page 161)

Leer 3 **Read the grammar box on page 161 and then translate these sentences into English.**

Parece is another impersonal verb meaning 'it seems'.

1 Hace falta producir menos basura. ¡Piensa antes de comprar!
2 Ya he tirado la basura. Solo falta reciclar el papel y las botellas de vidrio.
3 Todo está listo. Ahora falta decidir quién llevará la comida al banco de alimentos.
4 Parece que algunas personas creen que reciclar no es necesario.

The passive (Unit 2, page 162)

The passive is used to say what is / was / will be done to something or someone. To form it, use the correct person and tense of ***ser*** followed by the **past participle**, which must agree in number and gender with the object. The **object** becomes the **subject** of the sentence. Remember that the past participle is formed by removing the ***-ar***, ***-er*** or ***-ir*** from the infinitive and adding ***-ado***, ***-ido*** or ***-ido***.

Active		Passive
El viento fuerte (subject) *destruyó* ***las casas*** (object).	→	***Las casas*** (subject) *fueron* ***destruidas*** *por* ***el viento fuerte***.
The strong wind destroyed **the houses**.	→	**The houses** were **destroyed** by **the strong wind**.
La situación ***ha sido causada*** *por la falta de lluvias.*		The situation **has been caused** by the lack of rain.
El agua ***será limitada*** *a diez litros por ciudadano.*		Water **will be restricted** to ten litres per citizen.

Leer 4 **Read and select the correct form of the passive. Remember to check if the object/subject is masculine/feminine and singular/plural. Also check for clues such as time expressions. Then translate the sentences into English.**

1. El debate sobre el cambio climático no para. Este proceso **ha sido estudiado** / **fue estudiada** / **serán estudiadas** por los científicos durante décadas.
2. Sus consecuencias **son discutidos** / **son discutidas** / **es discutido** en todos los medios de comunicación.
3. Los mares y las temperaturas **son afectados** / **fueron afectadas** / **es afectado** por este cambio.
4. En el siglo pasado muchos bosques **fueron destruidas** / **son destruidos** / **fueron destruidos**.
5. La calidad del aire **fue afectado** / **fue afectada** / **es afectado** por el aumento de las fábricas.
6. En las próximas décadas, la biodiversidad del planeta **es reducida** / **serán reducidas** / **será reducida** seriamente por las consecuencias que trae el cambio climático.
7. Los recursos del planeta **fueron limitados** / **serán limitados** / **serán limitadas** por los efectos del cambio climático.

Escribir 5 **Complete the sentences with the indicated form of the passive. Then translate each one into English.**

1. El bosque (*was destroyed*) por el fuego.
2. Los campos (*are affected*) por la falta de agua y lluvia.
3. La información (*was shared*) rápidamente en las redes sociales.
4. Las carreteras (*were closed*) debido a la lluvia y el viento fuertes.
5. Algunos objetos (*are not recycled*) por la gente.
6. El aumento del hambre (*is caused*) por los cambios rápidos en el clima.

Hablar 6 **Read out the text in pairs, paying attention to correct pronunciation.**

Reciclar tiene muchas ventajas y beneficios no solo para el planeta sino también para la sociedad y la economía. Hace falta reducir la cantidad de basura que producimos. También vale la pena reciclar porque ayuda a reducir la contaminación del aire, del agua y de la tierra. Si reciclamos más, ayudaremos a conservar la diversidad de la naturaleza y el medioambiente porque usaremos menos recursos naturales. Por lo tanto, ¡sé responsable y recicla!

Gramática 2

The imperfect continuous (Unit 2, page 163)

Escribir 1

Fill in the gaps with the correct form of the imperfect continuous. Then translate the sentences into English.

1. ¿Te acuerdas de qué ___ ___ aquel día? **(tú, hacer)**
2. ___ ___ en coche cuando comenzó la lluvia fuerte. **(yo, viajar)**
3. Cuando empezó el incendio mis amigos y yo ___ ___. **(nosotros, estudiar)**
4. Los niños ___ ___ en la calle cuando empezó el viento fuerte. **(ellos, jugar)**
5. Ese día mi primo y yo ___ ___ un partido de baloncesto en el estadio. **(nosotros, ver)**
6. Mi hermano ___ ___ cuando llegaron mis abuelos. **(él, dormir)**
7. ___ ___ al colegio cuando vi el accidente. **(yo, caminar)**

The **imperfect continuous** is used to describe what people were doing and translates as 'was/were ...ing'. Use the imperfect of *estar* and the **present participle**. Remember to remove the ***-ar***, ***-er*** and ***-ir*** of the infinitive and add the ending ***-ando*** (for *-ar* verbs) or ***-iendo*** (for *-er*/*-ir* verbs).

	estar (*to be*)	**present participle**
(yo)	estaba	
(tú)	estabas	jug**ando**
(él/ella/usted)	estaba	v**iendo**
(nosotros/as)	estábamos	escrib**iendo**
(vosotros/as)	estabais	
(ellos/ellas/ustedes)	estaban	

Verbs with **irregular** present participles include:
leer → *le**y**endo* (reading)
dormir → *d**u**rmiendo* (sleeping)

You can also use the imperfect tense to talk about continuous actions in the past.

Avoiding the passive (Unit 3, page 164)

Escuchar 2

Listen to the announcements. Write down the letter of the correct picture and the verbs used (to avoid the passive). Then translate the verbs into English. (1–6)

Example: 1 *f, se esperan – are expected*

a

b

c

d

e

f

Read the grammar box on page 164. In Spanish the **passive** is often avoided by using the reflexive pronoun **se** and the third person singular (he/she/it) or plural (they) forms of the verb. Use this construction when you don't know who or what has done the action.

Se esperan *muchas lluvias y vientos fuertes este fin de semana.*
A lot of rain and strong winds **are expected** this weekend.

Notice the different word order in Spanish and English in these types of sentences.

Se prohíbe *el uso del plástico.*
The use of plastic **is banned**.
Se construyen *muchos edificios en mi ciudad.*
Many buildings **are constructed** in my city.

The present subjunctive to give opinions (Unit 4, page 166)

Remember that to form the present subjunctive, take the 'I' form of the present tense and remove the ***-o***. Add the endings ***-a***, ***-as***, ***-a*** to ***-er/-ir*** verbs, and add the endings ***-e***, ***-es***, ***-e*** to ***-ar*** verbs. Some verbs (like *ir* and *ser*) are irregular and do not follow this pattern.

ser (to be) → *sea, seas, sea* ***ir*** (to go) → *vaya, vayas, vaya*

	hacer	tener	venir
(yo)	haga	tenga	venga
(tú)	hagas	tengas	vengas
(él/ella/usted)	haga	tenga	venga

Use the subjunctive after verbs of wishing, command, request and emotion such as ***recomendar***, ***esperar***, ***preferir***, ***querer*** and ***odiar***.

It is also used after the conjunction ***que*** with verbs such as ***gustar*** and ***encantar*** when there is a change of subject in the sentence.

Me gusta que *la gente* ***sea*** *generosa.* I like people being generous.

Escuchar 3 **Listen and correct the underlined mistakes in each sentence. (1–6) Then translate the corrected sentences into English.**

1 Quiero que vengas conmigo al hogar de ancianos.
2 El gobierno recomienda que la gente no tenga coches.
3 Espero que en el futuro la sociedad haga más para proteger el planeta.
4 Me pone triste que la gente no haga todo lo posible con sus acciones.
5 Me gusta que seas responsable con el medioambiente.
6 A mí me molesta que la mayoría de la gente vaya en coche por la ciudad.

Hablar 4 **In pairs, take turns to build sentences containing one element from each column, taking care with your pronunciation. Your partner translates the sentence into English.**

Example: Me gusta que vayas en transporte público. – I like that you go on public transport.

Odio Me gusta Me encanta Me preocupa Espero Recomiendo Quiero Me pone triste No aguanto	que	la gente el gobierno tú el mundo/planeta mi familia la sociedad la gente famosa la juventud	(no) haga(s) (no) sea(s) (no) vaya(s) (no) venga(s) (no) tenga(s)	a las manifestaciones. cuidado con la basura. acciones positivas para el medioambiente. en transporte público. afectado por el cambio climático. leyes para proteger el planeta. un buen modelo de comportamiento para otros. víctima de la discriminación.

¡En marcha! (Units 1–5)

Leer 5 **Read the text and translate the bold phrases into English. Write down the tense or grammar point and the infinitive form of the verb.**

Example: estaba caminando – I was walking (imperfect continuous, caminar)

Me acuerdo que, ese día, yo **estaba caminando** por el bosque cuando **empezó** el fuego. Un grupo de jóvenes **estaba celebrando** una fiesta allí. Rápidamente **llamé** a los servicios de emergencia, pero todos los árboles **fueron destruidos**. Se piensa que el fuego **fue causado** porque aquellas personas **estaban fumando**. ¡Odio que la gente **no sea responsable** y **no tenga cuidado**. **Hace falta castigar** a quienes **cometen estos delitos**. Tres semanas después, muchas casas y edificios de mi pueblo **fueron afectados** por las lluvias fuertes que **causaron** graves problemas en la zona.

Leer y escuchar

Reading

Leer 1

The environment. **You read these comments from some Spanish teenagers about the environment. Then match the correct person to each question below (1–4) by choosing the correct letter. (A–F)**

A ALBERTA
Creo que no deberíamos usar productos de plástico, pero mis padres siempre los compran porque dicen que son más baratos.

B BERNARDO
Hoy en día, mis padres y yo estamos usando cada vez menos plástico en casa. Intentamos comprar productos verdes.

C CLARA
Lo que no me gusta es que mis amigos siempre tiran las botellas al suelo. Deberían hacer más para proteger el planeta.

D DIEGO
Yo diría que podríamos organizar más manifestaciones para promover la importancia de cuidar el medioambiente en las próximas generaciones.

E ELENA
Aunque mis amigos todavía usan botellas de plástico, lo bueno es que siempre reciclan el papel.

F FEDERICO
Hay muchas cosas que podrías hacer en el colegio. En nuestro instituto se apagan las luces para ahorrar energía.

1 Who says saving energy is important to help the environment?
2 Who feels their parents could do more to help the environment?
3 Who says it's important to think about future generations?
4 Who does not like their friends' attitude towards the environment?

There may be more than one option which makes reference to the general theme of a question. For example, two of the texts mention 'parents' but which one contains the correct answer to question 2?

Leer 2

Environmental problems. **Read Andrea's report about the environment.**

Hoy en día hay cada vez más problemas que afectan el medioambiente en toda Latinoamérica. Por ejemplo, el hambre afecta a muchas personas y hay más condiciones climáticas extremas. Sin embargo, los científicos consideran que el problema principal en esta región es la falta de agua.

En España también hay falta de agua. Este problema no ha sido causado por empresas que usan demasiada agua, sino que ha sido producido por el calor. Lo que a los científicos les preocupa es que el cambio climático va a crear condiciones extremas en muchos países.

las condiciones climáticas *weather conditions*

Complete the sentences by choosing the correct letter **A**, **B** or **C**.

1 There are increasing problems affecting ...
A some Latin American countries.
B food production in Latin America.
C the environment throughout Latin America.

2 The main problem according to scientists is ...
A the lack of water.
B a lack of food.
C the heat.

3 Spain's climate problems have been caused ...
A by large companies.
B by floods.
C by heat.

4 Scientists are worried about the effects of ...
A extreme conditions in Spain.
B climate change in many countries.
C drought worldwide.

Avoid jumping to conclusions and beware of distractors . For example, why are the phrases *cada vez más* and *el problema principal* important in the first paragraph?

In this type of task the answers are given in the text in the same order as the questions. Watch out for negatives and connectives that might affect the meaning.

Leer 3

Social problems. **Translate the following sentences into English.**

Actualmente hay muchos problemas en mi ciudad.

En el futuro nos gustaría hacer más para ayudar a nuestra comunidad.

Participar en proyectos sociales te permite conocer a nueva gente en tu barrio.

El año pasado, muchas personas fueron afectadas por temperaturas muy bajas.

Espero que más gente tome acción para crear una sociedad mejor.

A translation may contain words that you don't know. Try to translate the rest of the sentence in your head and work out how to replace the missing word or words from the context.

Listening

Escuchar 1

Weather events. **David is talking to his friend Julio. Listen and complete the sentences. (1–2) Answer both parts of the question.**

1 David was ...

A having a great day with his team.
B caught in a large storm.
C playing football with his family.

David was disappointed because ...

A the game was tough.
B it was impossible to continue the game.
C he had to go home.

2 Julio ...

A was at home.
B thought the storm was amazing.
C went to visit his grandmother.

David ...

A likes being with his family.
B doesn't see his friends a lot.
C is afraid of storms.

Look at the answer options carefully. When listening, pay attention to small details which contradict what is written (e.g. adjectives, people, locations).

All of the options may be mentioned. Listen out for the specific reason he gives for feeling **disappointed**.

Listen carefully as an event may be mentioned but does it match the answer options?

Listen for words that convey the same meaning and for wording that contradicts the options given.

Escuchar 2

Helping the environment. **You are listening to a Spanish podcast. Two people are talking about helping the environment. Which aspect is good? Which aspect needs to improve? Choose the correct letter. (A–F)**

A	making small changes
B	being a student
C	being able to attend protests
D	price of ecological products
E	buying used clothes
F	being fashionable

	Good:	Needs to improve:
1	☐	☐
2	☐	☐

You won't hear the Spanish words *bueno* and *mejorar*. You need to concentrate on positive or negative opinion phrases or adjectives linked to the answer options on the left.

Listen out for:

- ***qu*** – which has a hard sound like the English 'k'
- ***i*** – which sounds like 'ee' in English
- ***ge / gi / j*** – which sound like a stronger version of 'h' in English.

Focus, too, on words that need a **written accent** on the stressed vowel.

Escuchar 3

Dictation. **You will hear <u>five</u> short sentences. Listen carefully and, using your knowledge of Spanish sounds, write down in Spanish exactly what you hear for each sentence.**

Prueba oral

Role play

Hablar 1 **Look at the role play card and prepare what you are going to say.**

You are talking to your Chilean friend about your local area.

Your teacher will play the part of your friend and will speak first.

You should address your friend as *tú*.

When you see this – **?** – you will have to ask a question.

You must include at least one verb in your response to each bullet point.

Task:

1 Say what you think of your local area and why. (Give one opinion and one reason.)
2 Say what the weather is like in your area. (Give two details.)
3 **?** Ask your friend a question about their town/city.
4 Say what you do to help others in your area. (Give one detail.)
5 Say what you are going to do to protect the environment. (Give two details.)

Use an opinion phrase to introduce your opinion and follow with *porque* to make your reason clearer.

Remember that weather phrases often start with *hace* in Spanish.

You could ask if they like their town/city.

Any 'I' form verb connected with helping can be used.

Use the near future tense (*ir* + *a* + infinitive) to say what you are going to do.

Escuchar 2 **Practise what you have prepared. Then, using your notes, listen and respond to the teacher.**

Escuchar 3 **Now listen to Jess doing the role play task. In English, note down what she says for each of the points on the card, including the question she asks.**

Use intonation to make it clear that you are asking a question: raise the tone of your voice at the end of the question.

Reading aloud

Hablar 1 **Look at this task. With a partner, read aloud the six sentences, paying particular attention to the underlined letters.**

Antonio, your Spanish friend, has written a letter about the environment.

Read out the text below to your partner.

Mucha gente piensa que vale la pena cuidar el medioambiente.
Limita el uso de plástico e intenta reciclar.
En el colegio, se apagan las luces para ahorrar energía.
Creo que se debería hacer más para proteger el medioambiente.
Voy a vender objetos de segunda mano.
Será divertido participar en este proyecto.

Take extra care with how you pronounce the underlined sounds:

- ***j*** and ***ge*** / ***gi*** produce a sound like English 'h'.
- both ***b*** and ***v*** are pronounced like 'b' in English
- when the word ***y*** (meaning 'and') is followed by a word beginning with ***i*** or ***hi***, ***y*** changes to

Escuchar 2 **Listen and check your pronunciation.**

Hablar 3 **Listen to the teacher asking <u>four</u> questions that relate to the topic of the environment and where people live. Translate each question into English and prepare your own answers in Spanish. Then listen again and respond to the teacher.**

If you are unsure of a further question or want to check that you heard it correctly, ask your teacher to repeat it (*¿Puedes repetir por favor?*).

Photo card

Escuchar 1 **Look at the photos below and read the first part of the task card. Then listen to Oliver describing the photos.**

1 Where does Oliver say the two people in the first photo are?
2 What does he say the two people in the first photo are doing? (Give <u>two</u> details.)
3 What does he say about their mood? Why does he think this?
4 How does he describe their appearance? (Give <u>two</u> details.)
5 Where does Oliver say the person in the second photo is?
6 What does Oliver say the person in the second photo is doing?

Describe these photos.

Your teacher will ask you to talk about the content of these photos. You must include at least one detail about each photo.

After you have described the photos, your teacher will then ask you questions related to **Communication and the world around us**.

Hablar 2 **Prepare your own description of the two photos. Then, with a partner, take turns to read it aloud.**

- *En la primera foto hay ...*
- *En la segunda foto hay ...*

In the wider conversation, try to combine past tenses to extend your answer and show off your knowledge. Think about using the imperfect continuous (for example, *Estaba comiendo*) followed by *cuando* and the preterite tense (for example, *cuando vi ...*).

Escuchar 3 **Read the second part of the task card and listen to the first question in the wider conversation. The teacher asks: *'¿Qué hiciste recientemente para ayudar a otros?'* Note down <u>five</u> examples of language that Oliver uses to give a strong response.**

Escuchar 4 **Listen to the next part of the wider conversation. Answer the questions in English.**

1 What does Oliver's class use instead of paper?
2 What happens in the evening?
3 How has the amount of food thrown away changed?
4 Why does Oliver want to attend protests?
5 What does he want to talk to others about?
6 What does he hope for in the future?

Hablar 5 **Prepare your own answers to Module 7 questions 1–10 on page 231. Then practise with your partner.**

Prueba escrita

Translation

Escribir 1

Read the English text and Karim's translation of it. Fill in the gaps with the correct missing Spanish word(s).

I like to look after the environment. It is necessary to recycle plastic and glass. My parents and I always separate the rubbish and we never throw food into the waste. Yesterday, I was helping in the local food bank. I hope that in the future it will be easier to look after the environment.

Me gusta **1** el medioambiente. Es necesario **2** el plástico y el vidrio. Mis padres y yo siempre **3** la basura y **4** tiramos comida a la basura. Ayer, estaba **5** en el banco de alimentos local. **6** que en el futuro sea más fácil cuidar el medioambiente.

Take care with verbs. Decide whether you need to use the infinitive form or a conjugated verb using the correct person and tense.
With the imperfect continuous tense, which form of the verb do you need to use after *estar*?

Escribir 2

Translate the following text into Spanish.

It is important to look after the environment.
I used to separate glass and plastic.
My friends and I always recycle our clothes and turn off the lights.
Last week, we watched a very educational film about the lack of water in Spain.
I hope that in the future the situation will be better.

Remember to use the 'we' form of the verb after 'my friends and I'.

Look out for the small words that can be missed in translations, such as 'very' and 'always'.

Think carefully about the translation of the tense here. Do you need to use the simple future tense or the subjunctive after verbs that express a wish?

150-Word writing task

Escribir 1

Look at this writing task and then, <u>for each bullet point, consider</u>:

- what examples of **complex language** you could use to impress the examiner
- how you could use a **variety of vocabulary** to avoid repetition
- **which tense(s)** you will need to use in your answer.

You are writing an article about your local area and your local community.
Write approximately **150** words in **Spanish**.
You should write something about both bullet points.

Mention:
- the importance of looking after the environment
- something you did recently to help in your local community.

Leer **2** **Read Hope's answer to the task. Answer the questions in the coloured shapes.**

1 Use *para mí* as an alternative way to introduce an opinion. Find two other ways opinions are given in the response.

2 Use direct object pronouns to replace nouns and avoid repetition. Find one more example in the text.

4 Use *por eso* and *por lo tanto* as different ways to introduce reasons. Find one other expression used to introduce reasons in the text.

Para mí, se debería ayudar a mejorar el medioambiente porque se necesita proteger el futuro del planeta. Por eso, vale la pena hacer cosas fáciles para cuidarlo. Por ejemplo, yo ya no uso tanta agua como usaba en el pasado e intento usar más mi portátil cuando hago mis deberes para gastar menos papel. Además, quiero que la gente sea más responsable con lo que compra. Sin embargo, lo negativo es que comprar productos verdes puede ser muy caro y por eso no los compro.

Para ayudar a la comunidad, la semana pasada mis amigos y yo trabajamos en un banco de alimentos. Dimos a la gente la comida que fue entregada al banco de alimentos. Me gustó mucho la experiencia porque conocí a mucha gente nueva. Después de mis exámenes este año, quisiera participar en más proyectos sociales porque diría que es una experiencia muy útil.

3 Which form of the verb do you need after *quiero que*?

5 Which grammatical structure is this an example of?

Leer **3** **Read Hope's answer again and answer the questions in English.**

1 What does Hope do to help the environment?
2 What does she say about buying green products?
3 What did she do last week to help the community? (Give two details.)
4 How did she find the experience? (Give two details.)
5 Note down five different infinitive expressions that Hope uses. Translate each one into English.

Escribir **4** **Prepare your own answer to the task.**

- Think about how you can develop your answer for each bullet point.
- Look back at your notes from exercises 1 and 2.
- Look at the 'Challenge checklist' and consider how you can show off your Spanish!
- Write a brief plan and organise your answer into paragraphs.
- Write your answer and then carefully check the accuracy of what you have written.

Challenge checklist	
	✓ Past, present and future time frames ✓ Different persons of the verb ✓ Extended sentences
	✓ Phrases to introduce reasons (e.g. *por lo tanto, por eso*) ✓ *Se debería* + infinitive to say what people should do (e.g. *Se debería reciclar …*) ✓ Impersonal verbs (e.g. *vale la pena, hace falta*)
	✓ Present subjunctive to give opinions (e.g. *Me gusta que la gente sea …*) ✓ Passive verb forms (e.g. *La comida fue entegrada.*) ✓ Imperfect continuous followed by the preterite (e.g. *Estaba ayudando cuando vi a Lionel Messi.*)

Módulo **7**

Palabras

Key:
bold = this word will appear in higher exams only
* = this word is not on the vocabulary list, but you may use it in your own sentences

Espacios naturales maravillosos (pages 158–159):

¿A ti qué te parece?	*What do you think?*
A mí me gusta(n) / me encanta(n) ...	*I like / I love ...*
A mí me interesa(n) ...	*I am interested in ...*
A mí me parece(n) ...	*It seems / They seem ... to me*
¿**A ti** qué lugar te gustaría / te interesaría visitar?	*Which place would you like to visit / be interested in visiting?*
A mí me interesaría / me gustaría visitar ...	*I would be interested in visiting / I would like to visit ...*
¿Por qué te gustaría/interesaría visitarlo?	*Why would you like to visit / be interested in visiting it?*
(**A mí**) Me gustaría visitarlo porque parece ...	*I would like to visit it because it seems ...*
increíble/emocionante/ **maravilloso/a**	*incredible/exciting/ marvellous*
Hay que ir ...	*You have to / One has to go ...*
cuando hace buen tiempo	*when it is good weather*
durante el mes de (julio)	*during the month of (July)*
El sitio más hermoso/alto del mundo está en ...	*The prettiest/highest place in the world is in ...*
*América Latina / España	*Latin America / Spain*
el medio del mar	*the middle of the sea*
la isla hermosa de ...	*the beautiful island of ...*
un lugar lleno de sorpresas	*a place full of surprises*
el medioambiente	*the environment*
la lluvia / las **nubes**	*rain / clouds*
amenazar / **atreverse a**	*to threaten / to dare to*
esconder / *saltar	*to hide / to jump*
A/Para/Sin ...	*To/For/Without ...*
mí / ti / él/ella	*me / you / him/her*
nosotros/as / vosotros/as	*us/you (plural)*
ellos/ellas	*them*

¡Actúa ya! (pages 160–161):

¡Respeta **la igualdad**!	*Respect equality!*
¡**Exige medidas** fuertes contra los delitos!	*Demand strong measures against crime!*
¡**Lucha** por **la libertad** de **expresión**!	*Fight for freedom of expression!*
¿Qué haces para ayudar ... ?	*What do you do to help ...?*
en tu comunidad / la sociedad	*in your community / society*
Para ayudar en mi comunidad / la sociedad,	*To help in my community / society,*
compro ...	*I buy ...*
ropa de segunda mano	*secondhand clothes*
productos de **comercio** justo	*fairtrade products*
ayudo/participo en proyectos sociales	*I help/participate in social projects*
doy/llevo comida a los bancos de **alimentos**	*I give/take food to food banks*
hago **campañas** para apoyar a las personas sin **hogar**/trabajo	*I do campaigns to support homeless people / unemployed people*
Es importante hacerlo porque ...	*It is important to do it because ...*
vale la pena apoyar buenas causas	*it is worth supporting good causes*
hace falta ayudar / ser responsable	*it is necessary to help / be responsible*
todos **merecemos** tener las mismas oportunidades	*we all deserve to have the same opportunities*
¿Qué hiciste en el pasado para ayudar a otras personas?	*What did you do in the past to help other people?*
El mes/año/verano pasado ...	*Last month/year/summer ...*
di dinero a ...	*I gave money to ...*
organicé / compré / hice ...	*I organised / I bought / I did/ made ...*
ayudé en un **hogar** de **ancianos**	*I helped in a care home*
¿Qué más te gustaría hacer en el futuro?	*What else would you like to do in the future?*
El próximo verano/año ...	*Next summer/year ...*
haré/daré ...	*I will do/make / I will give ...*
ayudaré / participaré en ...	*I will help / participate in ...*
un proyecto / una **campaña**	*a project / a campaign*
me gustaría ...	*I would like to ...*
ayudar / participar en ...	*help / participate in ...*
dar/recoger ropa	*give/collect clothes*

El planeta en peligro (pages 162–163):

¿Cuál es el problema más grave para el planeta?	*What is the most serious problem for the planet?*
Para mí, el problema / la **cuestión** más grave es ...	*For me, the most serious problem/issue is ...*
el hambre / la contaminación	*hunger/pollution*
el cambio climático	*climate change*
la falta de agua/comida	*the lack of water/food*
porque **me parece** que ...	*because it seems to me that ...*
afecta a nuestro **planeta** / nuestra salud	*it affects our planet / our health*
hay personas que no tienen *acceso a comida	*there are people who don't have access to food*
no se puede vivir sin agua limpia	*you/one can't live without clean water*
¿Qué estabas haciendo cuando ocurrió el desastre natural?	*What were you doing when the natural disaster happened?*
Estaba ayudando a mi madre.	*I was helping my mother.*
Estaba viendo una película.	*I was watching a film.*
Mi amiga y yo estábamos **paseando** a su perro.	*My friend and I were walking her dog.*
Mis amigos y yo estábamos jugando un partido de fútbol.	*My friends and I were playing a football match.*
Estaban escuchando un *pódcast.	*They were listening to a podcast.*
Los **cultivos** fueron afectados.	*The crops were affected.*
llover/*nevar	*to rain / to snow*
mientras	*while*

Protegemos el planeta (pages 164–165):

¿Qué haces para cuidar el medioambiente en casa?	*What do you do to look after the environment at home?*
Para ayudar al medioambiente, en casa ...	*To help the environment, at home ...*
no uso bolsas/botellas de plástico	*I don't use plastic bags/ bottles*
trato de / intento controlar el uso de ...	*I try to control the use of ...*

viajo en ...	*I travel by ...*
reciclo/separo la basura	*I recycle/separate the rubbish*
utilizo botellas de **vidrio**	*I use glass bottles*
¿Y en tu colegio? ¿Qué cosas hacéis para ayudar?	*What about at your school? What do you do to help?*
Para ayudar al medioambiente en el colegio ...	*To help the environment, at school ...*
se sigue la regla de 'las tres erres'	*the 'three Rs' rule is followed*
se recicla el papel/**vidrio**	*paper/glass is recycled*
se ahorra energía/agua	*energy/water is saved*
se organizan/hacen **campañas** de *reciclaje ...	*recycling campaigns are organised/done ...*
se mantienen limpias las zonas verdes	*green spaces are kept clean*
la comida se recicla, no se tira	*food is recycled, it isn't thrown away*
se usa para crear *compost para el jardín	*it is used to create compost for the garden*
se apagan los ordenadores, las pantallas y las luces	*computers, screens and lights are switched off*
¿Qué hiciste en el pasado para ayudar?	*What did you do in the past to help?*
El mes/año/verano pasado ...	*Last month/year/summer ...*
El fin de semana pasado ...	*Last weekend ...*
aprendí/ayudé a ...	*I learned/helped to ...*
hice ...	*I did/made ...*
ahorré/organicé ...	*I saved/organised ...*
participé en ...	*I participated in ...*
viajé en ...	*I travelled by ...*
¿Qué más te gustaría hacer para ayudar?	*What else would you like to do to help?*
El verano/año próximo ...	*Next summer/year ...*
me gustaría ...	*I would like ...*
ayudar a los animales en peligro	*to help animals at risk*
reciclar la ropa	*to recycle clothes*
organizar un mercado para comprar/vender ropa y **objetos** de segunda mano	*to organise a market to buy/sell secondhand clothes and objects*
aprender a **arreglar portátiles**/ropa	*to learn to fix laptops/clothes*
organizar **campañas**	*to organise campaigns*
No solo es malo para la salud **sino** también para el **planeta**.	*It's not only bad for your health but also for the planet.*

Nuestro mundo, nuestra responsabilidad (pages 166–167):

¿Qué problema(s) te preocupa(n) más?	*Which problem(s) worry/worries you the most?*
(**A mí**) me preocupa(n) ...	*I worry about ...*
la discriminación	*discrimination*
la contaminación de los bosques/mares	*pollution of forests/seas*
la violencia contra ...	*violence against ...*
las mujeres	*women*
las personas transgénero	*transgender people*
la falta de agua	*lack of water*
debido a que ...	*due to (the fact that) ...*
muchos animales ...	*many / lots of animals ...*
muchas personas ...	*many / lots of people ...*
no tienen suficiente comida	*don't have enough food*
son afectados/as	*are affected*
sufren	*suffer*
¿Qué acción quieres ver?	*What action do you want to see?*
Quiero/Espero que ...	*I want/hope (that) ...*
Recomiendo que ...	*I recommend (that) ...*
Odio que ...	*I hate that ...*
Me pone triste que ...	*It makes me sad that ...*
el **gobierno** ...	*government ...*
la gente/sociedad	*people/society*
la juventud	*youth / young people*
haga acciones positivas ...	*do(es) positive actions*
haga campañas contra ...	*do(es) campaigns against*
sea responsable	*is/are responsible*
tenga cuidado con ...	*is/are careful with ...*
vaya a **manifestaciones** contra ...	*go(es) to demonstrations against ...*
no **haga** acciones positivas	*do(es) not do positive actions*
no **haga campañas**	*do(es) not do campaigns*
no **sea** responsable	*is/are not responsible*
no **tenga** cuidado con ...	*is/are not careful with ...*
hacer un esfuerzo	*to make an effort*
proteger/cuidar	*to protect / to look after*
preocupar(se)	*to worry*
tener cuidado	*to be careful*
parar / recoger	*to stop / to pick up*
el **camino**	*route/path*
el **comentario**	*comment*

El futuro está en nuestras manos (pages 168–169):

Jóvenes en acción	*Young people in action*
Se debería ayudar a resolver los problemas sociales.	*You/One should help to solve social problems.*
¿Quién es tu modelo a seguir favorito?	*Who is your favourite role model?*
Mi modelo a seguir favorito es ...	*My favourite role model is ...*
porque ...	*because ...*
usa su *popularidad en TikTok para ...	*he/she uses his/her popularity on TikTok to ...*
ayuda a mucha gente	*he/she helps a lot of people*
¿Te gustaría hacer trabajo *voluntario? ¿Por qué (no)?	*Would you like to do volunteer work? Why (not)?*
(No) Me gustaría hacer ...	*I would (not) like to do ...*
Creo que es importante ayudar / participar en ...	*I think it is important to help / participate in ...*
Para ser un buen *voluntario, se debería ayudar a resolver ...	*To be a good volunteer, you/one should help to solve ...*
Yo pienso que se debería hacer todo lo posible ...	*I think that you/one should do everything ...*
Yo estoy de acuerdo con sus acciones porque ...	*I agree with his/her actions because ...*
(no) se debería	*you/one should (not)*
gracias a / **igual** que	*thanks to / the same as*
el/la **protagonista**	*protagonist, main character*
prestar	*to lend*
dar **cariño** a	*to give affection to*
haz/pon/sal	*do/put/go out*
sé/ten/ve/ven/di	*be/have/go/come/tell*

Pioneros latinos

- Learning about Latino trailblazers
- Using Spanish stress patterns correctly

Pioneros en sus campos

Algunos son conocidos por el desarrollo científico. Otros por la cultura, la política o los negocios. Lo que todos tienen en común es su éxito en sus campos respectivos.

A

Carlos Acosta

- Bailarín y coreógrafo
- Nació en 1973 en La Habana (Cuba).

Cuando era niño, vivía en uno de los barrios más pobres de la capital cubana, pero su padre lo animó a estudiar en la Escuela Nacional de Ballet de Cuba.

En 1991, a la edad de 18 años, llegó a ser el bailarín principal más joven de la historia del Ballet Nacional de Inglaterra, y entre 1998 y 2015 fue miembro del Ballet Real.

Desde entonces ha montado su propia compañía de ballet.

Carolina Herrera

- Empresaria y diseñadora de moda
- Nació en 1939 en Caracas (Venezuela).

Pasó su juventud en Venezuela donde, a la edad de trece años, su abuela la llevó a un desfile de moda del diseñador español Balenciaga.

Empezó su carrera en 1965, y en 1981 decidió abandonar Venezuela para fundar su propia casa de moda en Nueva York, donde presentó su primera colección de moda.

Desde 1988 también es conocida por su colección de perfumes famosos.

B

Ellen Ochoa

- Astronauta e ingeniera de la NASA
- Nació en 1958 en California (Estados Unidos).

Aunque sus padres nacieron en Estados Unidos, sus abuelos eran mexicanos.

En 1993, fue la primera latina del mundo en viajar al espacio. Desde entonces, ha participado en tres vuelos espaciales más.

En 2013, se convirtió en la primera directora latina del Centro Espacial Johnson en Houston.

Benito Antonio Martínez Ocasio

- Rapero y cantante
- Nació en 1994 en Vega Baja (Puerto Rico).

Es mejor conocido como Bad Bunny, el rapero que ha ganado varios premios por su música, incluidos tres premios Grammy.

En 2018, creó la Fundación Good Bunny para dar apoyo a los jóvenes latinos. Cada año, entrega regalos de Navidad a los niños de Puerto Rico para animarlos a participar en las artes, la música y el deporte.

C

Jordi Muñoz

- Empresario e **1**
- Nació en 1986 en Ensenada (**2**).

De niño, era un gran aficionado a los ordenadores y los aviones, y su **3** era ser piloto.

En 2009, **4** estas dos pasiones, abrió una **5** de drones con el empresario y **6** Chris Anderson, con la creación de la empresa 3DR. Actualmente, se destaca por ser una de las **7** más importantes del mundo en ese sector.

convertirse en	*to become*
apenas	*scarcely, barely*

Alexandria Ocasio-Cortez

- **8** y activista
- Nació en 1989 en Nueva York (Estados Unidos).

Hasta los cinco años, **9** con su familia en un piso en el Bronx. Mientras estaba estudiando en la **10**, su **11** murió. Después de terminar sus estudios **12** empleo como camarera para ayudar a mantener a su familia.

En 2018, con apenas 29 años, fue la mujer más joven en ser elegida para el Congreso de los Estados Unidos. Se **13** por asuntos como el medioambiente y la **14**.

Hablar 1

In pairs, take turns to read out part A of the text, taking care to use correct stress patterns. Then find these phrases in Spanish.

1 his father encouraged him to study
2 he became the youngest principal dancer
3 since then he has set up
4 she spent her youth
5 she decided to leave
6 she is also known for

To talk about a specific year, just say it like any other number.

mil ochocientos cincuenta ***y*** *cinco* 1855
*dos mil veint**i**dós* 2022

Note that 700 (*setecientos*) and 900 (*novecientos*) are irregular.

When reading something out, it is important to use **correct stress patterns**. Pay attention to the final letter of each word and any letters with a written accent.

If the word:

- contains a vowel with a written accent, stress that vowel (***fá**cil*, ***rá**pido*).
- ends in a vowel, *n* or *s*, stress the second-to-last syllable (***a**ños*, *in**dus**tria*), unless it has a written accent (*ma**má***, *na**ció***).
- ends in any other letter, stress the final syllable (*apo**yar***, *juven**tud***).

Leer 2

Read part B of the text and select the four correct statements.

1 Ellen Ochoa was born in the same country as her parents.
2 She was the second Latina to travel into space.
3 She has made three more space flights since then.
4 She was the first woman to become director of the Johnson Space Station.
5 Bad Bunny has won three awards in total.
6 The Good Bunny Foundation supports young people.
7 Each year it gives out Christmas presents to children.
8 Children have to be good at sport, music or art to receive a gift.

Escuchar 3

Read part C of the text. Listen and fill in the gaps.

Escuchar 4

Listen to an extract from a podcast about four other trailblazers from the Spanish-speaking world. Copy and complete the table in English. (1–4)

1 Guillermo González Camarena
2 Rita Moreno
3 Lin-Manuel Miranda
4 Domingo Liotta

	Occupation	Date and country of birth	Known for (one detail)
1			

inventar	*to invent*
sustituir	*to replace*
un(a) compositor(a)	*composer*
el corazón	*heart*

Escribir 5

Translate the text into Spanish using vocabulary from page 182. Then take turns to read out your text with your partner.

Beto Pérez is a dancer, choreographer and entrepreneur. He was born in 1970 in Colombia and is known as the man who invented Zumba. When he was younger, his passion was dancing, but dance lessons were too expensive. In 1999, he decided to leave Colombia to live in Miami, where he set up his own company. Latin music has become more popular across the world thanks to Zumba.

a través de *across*

When transcribing spoken Spanish (i.e. writing down what you hear), only write an accent on the stressed vowel …

for words stressed on	where the word ends in
• the final syllable	• a vowel, *n* or *s* (*cre**ó***, *coraz**ó**n*)
• the second-to-last syllable	• a consonant except *n* or *s* (***ú**til*, *d**ó**lar*)
• the third-to-last syllable	• any letter (***j**ó**venes***, *pel**í**cula*)

1 Sueños y esperanzas

- Talking about plans for the future
- Using *seguir/continuar* + present participle
- Transcribing unfamiliar words

Leer 1 **Read about the plans that these young people have for the future. Then write the correct name for each statement below.**

a 

b 

No tengo ganas de casarme, pero me gustaría tener hijos algún día. ***Rubén***

c 

d 

Voy a estudiar Formación Profesional porque quiero entrar en el mundo laboral lo antes posible. También compartiré piso con mi novio, Nacho. ***David***

e 

f 

Tengo la intención de hacer una carrera universitaria, y luego buscaré un empleo con un buen salario. ***Sonia***

g 

h 

El año próximo tengo ganas de aprender a conducir. Cuando sea mayor, voy a ser empresaria. ***Cristina***

i 

j 

Me gustaría luchar por un mundo más justo. Más que nada, espero ser feliz en el futuro. ***Nilam***

k 

l 

Espero conseguir un trabajo como actor. Cuando tenga bastante dinero, quiero viajar por el mundo. ***Ibai***

1 Quiero probar la vida en otros países.
2 Me gustaría montar mi propio negocio.
3 Voy a ganar mucho dinero.
4 Si apruebo mis exámenes, iré a la universidad.
5 Tengo ganas de vivir con mi pareja.
6 Me importa la vida familiar y me encantan los niños.
7 Quiero poner fin a la discriminación.
8 Tengo la intención de comprarme un coche.

Remember to use the **present subjunctive** after the word *cuando* when talking about future plans.

*Cuando **sea** mayor, ...*	*When I'm older, ...*
*Cuando **tenga** bastante dinero, ...*	*When I have enough money, ...*

G

To talk about **future plans** you can use a variety of phrases followed by the infinitive:

espero	I hope to
me gustaría	I would like to
quiero	I want to
tengo ganas de	I am keen to
tengo la intención de	I intend to
voy a	I am going to

Espero tener hijos. I hope to have children.

You can also use the **simple future tense**. For most verbs this is also formed using the infinitive, although some verbs have an **irregular stem**.

*Me casaré, pero no **tendr**é hijos.*
I'll get married, but I won't have children.

Page 196

Escuchar 2 **Look back at pictures a–l in exercise 1 and listen to Sergio discussing his future plans. Copy and complete the table. (1–6)**

	When	Plan	Future time phrase(s) used
1	next year	c	me gustaria

Escribir 3 **Translate these sentences into Spanish. Use vocabulary from exercises 1 and 2 to help you.**

1 I would like to buy a car and therefore I hope to get a job with a good salary.
2 When I'm older, I'm keen to share a flat with my partner, but I don't want to get married.
3 If I pass my exams, I will study abroad because I would like to try university life in another country.

Spanish often uses an **adjective** where English uses a **noun**.

*la vida **familiar***	**family** life
*una carrera **universitaria***	a **university** degree
*las prácticas **laborales***	**work** experience

Leer 4

Read this article. Match each statement to the correct post-16 pathway. Write B (*Bachillerato*), FP (*Formación Profesional*) or B + FP (both). Then translate the second text (FP) into English.

Seguir estudiando – ¿Bachillerato o Formación Profesional?

Después de terminar la ESO (Educación Secundaria Obligatoria), en España la mayoría de los jóvenes decide continuar estudiando. Las dos opciones principales son:

Bachillerato

- ✓ Los estudios de Bachillerato tienen una duración de dos años.
- ✓ Te permiten continuar aumentando los conocimientos académicos.
- ✓ Vale la pena hacer el Bachillerato si quieres una educación más general.
- ✓ El Bachillerato es ideal para los que todavía no están seguros de lo que quieren hacer como trabajo en el futuro.
- ✓ Se estudian varias asignaturas generales junto con algunas asignaturas específicas.
- ✓ Ofrece el camino ideal para los que quieren hacer una carrera universitaria después.

Formación Profesional (FP)

- ✓ Los cursos de FP duran dos años.
- ✓ Te enseñan las capacidades necesarias para un campo específico (por ejemplo, la construcción).
- ✓ La FP ofrece una formación más especializada y práctica.
- ✓ Es ideal para los que ya han decidido lo que quieren hacer en el futuro.
- ✓ Te permite hacer prácticas laborales para descubrir el mundo laboral de primera mano.
- ✓ Incluso podrías ganar un salario al mismo tiempo.
- ✓ Ofrece la posibilidad de hacer una carrera universitaria en el futuro, pero tarda más tiempo.

Estudios superiores o Entrada directa al mercado laboral

1 The course lasts two years.
2 It is more focused on increasing knowledge than practical skills.
3 It provides more specialised training.
4 It is a good option if you don't know what job you want to do.
5 It includes work experience.
6 You could even earn money while studying.
7 It provides a route to future university study.

G

Seguir/Continuar + **present participle** is used to mean 'carry on' or 'continue' doing something.

*Voy a **continuar estudiando**.*
I'm going to **carry on studying**.

You can also use these verbs to say that you are still doing something.

***Sigo viviendo** con mis padres.*
I'm still living with my parents.

Page 196

Escuchar 5

Listen and look at some of the different categories of *Formación Profesional* courses available. Fill in the gaps with the missing information. Then listen again and note down Alicia's opinion of each one in English. (1–5)

Títulos de Formación Profesional

1 Actividades Físicas y ____
2 Informática y ____
3 ____ y Turismo
4 ____ y Marketing
5 Seguridad y ____ ____

When transcribing words you don't recognise, pay attention to:
- **vowels** (as these appear in every word)
- letters that share the same or similar sounds:
  j/ge/gi ***z/ce/ci*** ***y/ll*** ***b/v*** ***ca/co/cu/que/qui***
- your knowledge of Spanish spelling and grammar.

Hablar 6

In pairs, take turns to ask and answer these questions. Use a range of different phrases for talking about future plans.

- ¿Qué planes tienes para el año próximo?
- ¿Qué vas a hacer después?
- ¿Qué otros planes tienes?

- *El año próximo quiero seguir estudiando en mi insti porque …*
- *Después, tengo la intención de …*
- *Cuando tenga … años, me gustaría … También espero …*

Escribir 7

Write a text about your future plans. Include:

- a range of verb phrases for talking about the future
- one or two examples of the present subjunctive
- whether you would prefer to take the *Bachillerato* (equivalent to A-Levels) or a vocational course, and why
- your other hopes and ambitions for the future.

2 ¡A trabajar!

- Talking about getting a job
- Using possessive pronouns
- Using prepositions followed by the infinitive

Escuchar 1 **Listen to three dialogues about earning money. For each person, write the four or five correct letters. Then listen again and note down two extra details in English. (1–3)**

¿Qué haces para ganar dinero?
Para ganar dinero, ...
a trabajo en la caja de una tienda.
b trabajo en un bar de pinchos.
c cuido a los niños de mis vecinos.
d hago cosas y las vendo en línea.

¿Cuánto dinero ganas?
Gano ...
i diez euros por hora.
j quinientos pesos por día.
k cien libras por semana.
l poco, pero no me importa.

¿Cuándo lo haces?
Lo hago ...
e los fines de semana.
f cuando necesito dinero.
g cuando me necesitan.
h en las vacaciones.

¿Qué tal tu trabajo?
m Me llevo bien con mi jefe.
n Mis compañeros son agradables.
o Me encanta, ya que ¡no tengo jefe!
p Lo odio y quiero dejarlo.

la libra *pound*

San Sebastián (en la costa norte de España) es muy conocido por sus bares de pinchos. Con una gran variedad de sabores, olores y colores, los pinchos (o *pintxos*) son semejantes a las tapas, pero de tamaño más pequeño. Se sirven fríos o calientes, y es costumbre ir de bar en bar para tomar un pincho (¡o más!) en cada uno.

Hablar 2 **In pairs, take turns to ask and answer the four questions from exercise 1. Use the examples given and your imagination to develop your own answers fully.**

- *¿Qué haces para ganar dinero?*
- *Cuido los perros de mis abuelos. Es aburridísimo.*
- *¿Cuándo ...?*

G **Possessive pronouns** ('mine', 'hers', etc.) are used to avoid repetition. They must agree with the noun they are replacing.

singular	plural
el mío / la mía	los míos / las mías
el tuyo / la tuya	los tuyos / las tuyas
el suyo / la suya	los suyos / las suyas
el nuestro / la nuestra	los nuestros / las nuestras
el vuestro / la vuestra	los vuestros / las vuestras
el suyo / la suya	los suyos / las suyas

Page 197

Leer 3 **Read the messages and translate the phrases in purple. Then answer the questions in English.**

Almudena FJ
¡Basta! Me niego a seguir trabajando en ese restaurante. He tenido otro día fatal!

María Alegre
¿De qué te quejas? La tienda de moda donde trabajo yo es peor y **mi jefa es más estricta que la tuya**.

Almudena FJ
Sí, pero **la mía siempre me echa la culpa** cuando hay un problema. Y tú tienes suerte porque tus compañeros son simpáticos – **los míos no me hablan**.

María Alegre
Pero los clientes en tu restaurante **no son tan extraños como los nuestros**. Y si quieres hablar de trabajos malísimos, pregúntale a Silvia. **El suyo es el peor**.

Silvia Marco
Chicas, no sabéis lo que es un trabajo duro – **los vuestros son facilísimos comparados con el mío** en el centro deportivo. Paso el día limpiando las duchas y recogiendo ropa sucia. Es asqueroso.

1 How do we know that Almudena doesn't like her job?
2 Where does María work?
3 Why does Almudena think that María is lucky?
4 In María's opinion, who has the worst job?
5 Why doesn't Silvia like working at the sports centre?
6 Which of these is the best translation of the word ***asqueroso***?
   a tasty
   b educational
   c disgusting

negarse a	*to refuse to*
echar la culpa	*to blame*

Leer **4** **Read these tips on how to get a job. Write the correct letter to complete each one. Listen to check your answers. Then translate tips 1–4 into English.**

Ocho consejos para conseguir un trabajo

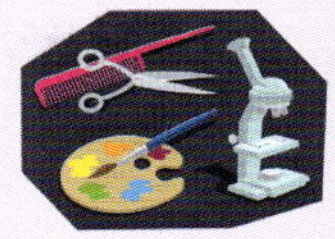

1 Para lograr un trabajo, tienes que saber qué tipo de profesión te interesa. Por lo tanto, …

2 Es importante saber tus capacidades y las cosas que necesitas mejorar. Antes de buscar un trabajo, …

3 Después de recibir tu solicitud de empleo, ciertas empresas buscarán tu nombre en la red. Por eso, …

4 Es más difícil obtener un empleo sin tener la experiencia relevante. Si no la tienes, …

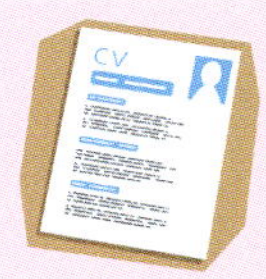

5 Si ves un anuncio que te interesa, antes de solicitar el puesto, …

6 Hay que tener un buen CV. Si el tuyo no contiene información actual, …

7 Antes de ir a la entrevista (¡si consigues una!), …

8 Después de la entrevista, ten paciencia. Si no consigues el trabajo, …

a considera cuáles son tus puntos fuertes y tus puntos más débiles.

b busca una oportunidad para hacer prácticas laborales.

c pregúntate si tus cuentas en las redes sociales dan una buena primera impresión de ti.

d empieza por preguntarte lo que quieres hacer de verdad.

e prepárate bien. El día de la entrevista, lleva ropa apropiada … ¡y llega a tiempo!

f escribe una versión nueva con los detalles de tu experiencia y tus títulos.

g considera si tienes las capacidades necesarias para hacer el trabajo.

h decide lo que podrías hacer mejor la próxima vez.

la solicitud de empleo *job application*

Remember that the **imperative** is used to give instructions. Remove the -*s* from the *tú* form of the verb.

*(tú) busca**s*** ⟶ ***Busca** una oportunidad.*
Look for an opportunity.

See page 236 for irregular imperative verbs.

G

Prepositions are sometimes followed by the infinitive.

para + infinitive	in order to (do)
sin + infinitive	without (doing)
antes de + infinitive	before (doing)
después de + infinitive	after (doing)

***Antes de** solicitar un puesto, …*

Page 197

Escuchar **5** **Read this interview for a summer job in Spain. Listen to both versions and fill in the gaps with the correct words in Spanish. Then listen again and write down five extra details in English. (1–2)**

Una entrevista de trabajo

- *¿Por qué le interesa este puesto?*
- *Me interesa este trabajo porque me encanta* **a** .
- *¿Qué experiencia laboral tiene?*
- *Llevo* **b** *trabajando* **c** .
  También he trabajado **d** .
- *¿Cuáles son sus puntos positivos?*
- *Soy una persona* **e** .
- *¿Qué otras capacidades tiene?*
- *Tengo* **f** .
- *¿Qué planes tiene para el futuro?*
- *El año próximo espero* **g** .

He trabajado Llevo (un año) trabajando	en	un café. un gimnasio.	una fábrica. una tienda.
	para	mi madre.	mis vecinos.
Soy una persona		activa. ambiciosa. artística. fuerte. independiente.	lista. organizada. práctica. responsable. trabajadora.
Tengo	buen sentido del humor. buenos conocimientos [de informática]. buenas capacidades [de comunicación].		

Hablar **6** **In pairs, take turns to ask and answer the questions from exercise 5.**

Escribir **7** **Write a letter of application for a summer job in Spain. Use exercise 5 to help you.**

- *Me gustaría solicitar el puesto anunciado online. Me interesa este trabajo porque … Además …*

3 Un trabajo para todos

- Talking about future career intentions
- Using masculine and feminine nouns for jobs
- Using and understanding the suffix *-dad/-idad*

Leer 1 **Read what jobs these young people wanted to do when they were younger and what they want to do now. Answer the questions below in English.**

Hassan

Antes me interesaba ser abogado, pero ya no quiero tener un trabajo con tanta responsabilidad. Ahora quiero hacer un trabajo al aire libre.

Nadia

En el pasado quería ser actriz. Todavía espero hacer un trabajo artístico, pero creo que preferiría ser directora de cine.

Eduardo

Cuando era más joven, quería ser soldado en el Ejército. Sin embargo, quiero ser policía desde hace un par de años.

Toni

Todavía tengo ganas de trabajar en otro país, pero acabo de decidir que no quiero trabajar en una empresa multinacional.

Gabriela

De niña, mi sueño era trabajar como médica, ya que me gustaba la idea de ayudar a otra gente. Sin embargo, recientemente he decidido que me gustaría más trabajar con los animales enfermos.

G

Some **nouns** have different masculine and feminine forms.

*secretar**io*** → *secretar**ia***
*profes**or*** → *profes**ora***

Nouns ending in ***-e*** or ***-ista*** are usually **invariable**. For example, *cantant**e*** and *art**ista***.

Other invariable nouns include *modelo*, *soldado* and *policía*.

Page 198

When saying what job someone does, you don't use the indefinite article unless adding specific details.

*Soy científic**o/a**.*
I am **a** scientist.

*Es **una** científic**a** muy conocida.*
She's **a** very well-known scientist.

1 Why does Hassan no longer want to be a lawyer?
2 How have Nadia's career plans changed?
3 For how long has Eduardo wanted to be a police officer?
4 Where does Toni not want to work?
5 Why did Gabriela use to dream of becoming a doctor?
6 Who wants to work abroad?

Escuchar 2 **Read the texts in exercise 1 again and listen to the summary. In English, write down the two mistakes for each person. Note: you will hear all verbs in the 'he/she' form.**

Hablar 3 **In pairs, take turns to ask and answer the following questions:**

- *¿Qué tipo de trabajo querías hacer en el pasado?*
- *Cuando era más joven, me gustaba la idea de ... También quería ... porque ...*
- *¿Todavía te interesa el mismo trabajo?*
- ✓ *Sí, todavía quiero ... porque ...*
- ✗ *No, he decidido que ya no quiero ... Ahora mi sueño es ..., ya que ...*

Antes De niño/a, Cuando era más joven, En el pasado	querían ... me gustaba la idea de ... mi sueño era ...			
Ahora He decidido que Todavía Ya no	quiero ... me gusta la idea de ... mi sueño (ya no) es ...			
ser	científico/a. médico/a.	profesor(a). pintor(a).	policía. modelo.	
trabajar	al aire libre.	desde casa.	solo/a.	
	en	el extranjero. una oficina. un hogar de ancianos.	la enseñanza. una empresa.	
	con	los animales. los ordenadores.	los niños. otra gente.	
hacer un trabajo	artístico.	práctico.	seguro.	
	con	responsabilidad. un buen salario.	variedad. flexibilidad.	

Leer 4 **Read the text and use the four Cs (Clues, Cognates, Context and Common sense) to help you work out the meaning of the jobs in bold. Then, in pairs, take turns to read out the text.**

Mi hermano, Hugo, tiene ganas de trabajar en un hospital infantil como **enfermero**, pero a mí no me interesa – ¡es que no aguanto ver sangre! Tampoco me gustaría atender a los pasajeros en un avión como mi madre, que es **auxiliar de vuelo**.

Mi madrastra es **periodista** y escribe para un periódico local, pero no me interesa trabajar en la prensa. Mi hermana Julia era **camarera** en un restaurante, pero no le gustaba servir comida y bebida. Ahora es **peluquera** – ¡aunque le gusta incluso menos cortar el pelo!

Creo que sería genial trabajar en el extranjero, quizás haciendo excursiones con los turistas como **guía turístico**. ***Miguel***

Remember that the letter ***g*** has a hard sound (like 'g' in 'gate' in English) when followed by ***a***, ***o*** or ***u***.
When followed by ***e*** or ***i***, it is pronounced like a stronger version of English 'h'. The Spanish letter ***j*** also produces this same sound.

Listen and read.

*A mi ami**go** ar**ge**ntino*
*Mi**gu**el le **gu**staría*
*se**gu**ir traba**ja**ndo*
*como in**ge**niero.*

Escuchar 5 **Read the results of a survey about what young people in Latin America consider most when looking for a job. Then listen and identify the <u>two</u> criteria that each person mentions. Indicate whether each one is important (✓) or not important (✗) to them. (1–4)**

¿Qué les importa más a los jóvenes latinos a la hora de buscar un trabajo?

Según un informe, estos son los factores de más importancia que exigen los jóvenes de Sudamérica a la hora de buscar un empleo:

a la flexibilidad horaria
b la posibilidad de trabajar desde casa
c la oportunidad de seguir desarrollándose
d la igualdad en el lugar de trabajo
e un buen ambiente de trabajo
f la estabilidad y la seguridad
g la cantidad de dinero que ganarán
h la variedad

exigir	*to demand*
el teletrabajo	*remote working*

The suffix ***-dad*** or ***-idad*** is often added to a Spanish adjective to form a noun. In English, the equivalent word usually ends in '-ty' or '-ity'.
seguro ⟶ *segur**idad*** (security/safety) *igual* ⟶ *igual**dad*** (equality)
Words ending in ***-dad***/***-idad*** are always feminine.

Escribir 6 **Translate this text into Spanish.**

When I was younger, I used to like the idea of being a police officer. However, now I intend to do a university degree when I am eighteen and then I hope to apply for a job abroad. My best friend and I have been working in a shopping centre for almost a year. My boss is really nice, but his is very serious.

You only need one word here.

Use the subjunctive of *tener*.

Use the imperfect tense.

These phrases are followed by the infinitive.

Use *llevamos* + time period + present participle, or use present tense + *desde hace* + time period.

Which possessive pronoun do you need?

4 Las lenguas te abren las puertas

- Talking about the importance of learning languages
- Using modal verbs
- Using different verb forms

Leer 1 **Read the texts. Answer the questions below and then translate the phrases in purple into English.**

Maite
Vivo en Bilbao y hablo castellano y euskera en casa. Si sabes hablar idiomas distintos **puedes conocer a más gente**, y por eso he estudiado inglés, alemán e italiano. Aprender idiomas **te permite descubrir otras culturas**.

Carlos
Trabajo en un bar en California donde tengo que hablar tanto inglés como español. Para poder comunicarte con todos los clientes, **debes saber hablar ambos idiomas**. También, **puedes estudiar o trabajar en el extranjero** si hablas otras lenguas.

Amy
Nací en Manchester, pero llevo cinco años trabajando como cuidadora de ancianos en México. En mi opinión, **si quieres tener éxito en otro país, tienes que aprender la lengua**. Aprender otras lenguas **mejora tus oportunidades laborales** y también **te abre la mente**.

Víctor
Tu lengua materna refleja una parte de tu identidad, pero **no basta con hablar una sola lengua**. Mi primera lengua es el quechua, pero también hablo español e inglés. Y si quieres viajar al extranjero, **debes poder comprender las señales de tráfico**, etc.

Who ...

1 uses language skills to communicate with customers?
2 has moved abroad to work?
3 speaks two different languages at home?
4 thinks that your first language is part of who you are?
5 can speak more languages than the others?

G

Modal verbs are followed by the infinitive.
They include:

deber (debo)	to have to / must
poder (puedo)	to be able to / can
querer (quiero)	to want to
saber (sé)	to know (how to)
tener que (tengo que)	to have to

Page 198

En España, mucha gente habla otro idioma oficial aparte del castellano. Por ejemplo, más de la mitad de los habitantes de Galicia elige hablar gallego cada día, y más del noventa por ciento de la población de Cataluña entiende el catalán.

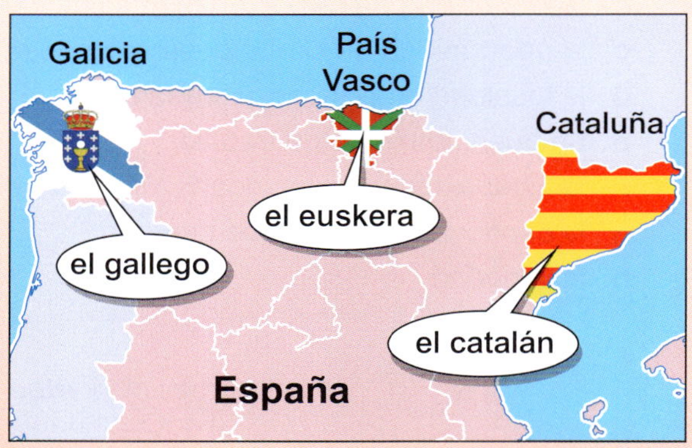

Escuchar 2 **Listen. Copy and complete the table in English. (1–4)**

	Language skills	Importance	Future plans
1			

saber	to know (information), to know how to
conocer	to know (a person/place), to meet / get to know

***Conozco** a Yoli, pero **no sé** donde está.*
I know Yoli, but **I don't know** where she is.

Hablar 3 **In pairs, take turns to ask and answer the following questions.**

- *¿Qué idiomas hablas?*
- *¿Por qué es importante aprender otras lenguas, en tu opinión?*
- *¿Qué otros idiomas te gustaría aprender?*

- *Hablo ... y llevo ... estudiando ...*
- *Si sabes hablar otro idioma, ... Además, ...*
- *En el futuro me gustaría aprender ...*

Escribir **4** **Write the correct form of the verbs in brackets. Then find the phrases below in Spanish.**

Abriendo puertas y fronteras

Ser capaz de hablar lenguas distintas es importantísimo. Soy británica, pero llevo ocho años **1 (vivir)** en Barcelona donde trabajo para una empresa de diseño. Cuando era más joven, **2 (escoger)** el español como asignatura optativa en el insti. Por lo tanto, antes de **3 (venir)** a España, ya lo hablaba bastante bien.

Sin embargo, hoy todavía **4 (acordarse)** de cómo me sentía cuando llegué. Al principio, no **5 (atreverse)** a hablar porque pensaba que todo el mundo se reiría de mí. En realidad, no fue así y pronto me acostumbré a pasar el día hablando español.

Ahora puedo **6 (charlar)** en español o en catalán - no me importa. Aunque todavía **7 (equivocarse)** a veces, me alegra usar ambos idiomas cada día - escribo correos, hago traducciones, **8 (producir)** documentos ...

Agradezco mucho las oportunidades que tengo de **9 (viajar)** con mi trabajo. Si tengo que asistir a una reunión con clientes en otra ciudad, siempre **10 (coger)** el AVE (el tren español superrápido), excepto cuando necesito ir a otro país.

Para mí, aprender idiomas te abre no solo las puertas, sino también las fronteras.

G

The infinitive can be used as a **noun** where English uses a word ending in *-ing*.
Aprender idiomas te abre la mente.
Learning languages opens your mind.
Creo que viajar es más fácil ahora.
I think **travelling** is easier now.

Page 199

a I chose Spanish as an optional subject
b I still remember how I felt
c At the start, I didn't dare speak
d in reality, it wasn't like that
e although I still make a mistake
f I'm very grateful for the opportunities
g If I have to attend a meeting
h not only ..., but also ...

Decide whether you need to use:

- the infinitive (*-ar/-er/-ir*)
- the present participle (*-ando/-iendo*)
- a conjugated verb (in the correct person/tense).

Remember that you cannot have two conjugated verbs together.

Take care with reflexive verbs (e.g. ***me** equivoco*).

Verbs ending in ***-ger*** or ***-cer/-cir*** have an irregular 'I' form in the present tense.

*co**ger*** (to get/take) → *co**jo***
*esco**ger*** (to choose) → *esco**jo***
*agrade**cer*** (to be grateful for) → *agrade**zco***
*cono**cer*** (to know/meet) → *cono**zco***
*produ**cir*** (to produce) → *produ**zco***
*condu**cir*** (to drive) → *condu**zco***

Escuchar **5** **Listen to check your answers.**

Leer **6** **Read the text again and decide which of the following statements are correct. For each question, write A if only statement A is correct, B if only statement B is correct, A+B if both statements A and B are correct.**

1

A	Katelyn currently lives in Barcelona.
B	She set up her own design company eight years ago.

2

A	Katelyn started learning Spanish when she was at school.
B	She moved to Spain to improve her Spanish.

3

A	Other people used to laugh at Katelyn when she made mistakes.
B	She quickly got used to speaking Spanish all day.

4

A	Katelyn now uses both Spanish and Catalan every day.
B	She doesn't mind which of these two languages she uses.

5

A	Katelyn enjoys travelling for work.
B	She always catches the train when meeting clients.

In this task, you may need to read the whole paragraph to check whether the statement is correct.
Pay attention to the precise wording of the Spanish text and English statements and look out for distractors.

5 El trabajo antes, ahora ... y mañana

- Talking about changes in the world of work
- Understanding more complex texts
- Listening for percentages

¿Cómo ha cambiado nuestra forma de vivir y trabajar?

Siglo dieciocho

Trabajo
En muchos países, la mayoría de las personas todavía trabajaba en la tierra. En la segunda mitad del siglo, la Revolución Industrial en el Reino Unido trajo varios desarrollos tecnológicos.

Sociedad
La gran mayoría de la población vivía en el campo, donde las condiciones de vida eran duras y el día laboral era largo.

Fecha clave
1775 – el barco de vapor fue inventado, haciendo más fácil el transporte de productos.

Siglo diecinueve

Trabajo
En España, la agricultura siguió siendo el sector que empleaba a más gente, mientras que, en el Reino Unido, más personas estaban encontrando empleo como obreros en las fábricas. En la década de **a**, solo el **b** por ciento estaba trabajando en la agricultura, comparado con el **c** por ciento en la industria.

Sociedad
Había una falta de igualdad social por todo el mundo. A las mujeres les faltaban derechos fundamentales.
En España, la esperanza de vida media apenas alcanzaba los **d** años. La mitad de los bebés que nacían no sobrevivían hasta los **e** años.

Fechas claves
f – el primer tren de la historia fue inventado por un ingeniero inglés.
g – un pueblo del norte de España fue el primero en instalar luz eléctrica en sus calles.

el Reino Unido *United Kingdom*

1700

1800

Hablar 1 **In pairs, read out the *Siglo dieciocho* section, paying attention to your pronunciation of *r*/*rr*.**

Escuchar 2 **Listen to and read the *Siglo diecinueve* section. Fill in the missing figures. Then read the text again and find these phrases in Spanish.**

1. continued to be
2. were finding work
3. Women lacked fundamental rights
4. average life expectancy barely reached
5. Half of the babies who were born

Percentages are often preceded by *un* or *el*.
For numbers above 30, listen out for *y*. Take care with 60 and 70.
el sesenta y siete por ciento 67%
un setenta y seis por ciento 76%

Leer 3 **Read the *Siglo veinte* section on page 193 and answer the questions in English.**

1. Name one new product which started to be produced.
2. What happened in the second half of the century?
3. Name four areas that form part of the service sector.
4. Which device revolutionised the workplace?
5. What was the consequence of increased access to the internet?
6. Give one example of how gender equality improved.

When reading more complex texts, use **Clues**, **Cognates**, **Context**, and **Common sense**, and then focus on:

1. your own general knowledge
   - *el barco de vapor* – consider what type of *barco* might have been invented in 1775. Think of a synonym for the cognate 'vapour'.
2. words that look similar
   - *los ciudadanos* – what does *ciudad* mean? Translate the rest of the sentence in your head: 'all cit ______ over 21 obtained the right to vote'.
3. word order
   - *la esperanza de vida* – Spanish often reverses the word order and uses ***de*** where English has two nouns together: 'life ______'.

Siglo veinte

Trabajo
Empezaron a fabricarse nuevos productos como coches y dispositivos electrónicos.
En la segunda mitad del siglo, creció la popularidad de las oficinas como lugar de trabajo, con más gente trabajando en el 'sector servicios' (el comercio, el turismo, la cultura, los medios de comunicación, la salud y la educación).
El uso de ordenadores revolucionó el mundo laboral.

Sociedad
En la última década del siglo, el aumento del acceso a Internet cambió para siempre nuestra vida diaria, no solo en el trabajo, sino también en el hogar.

Fechas claves
1928 – en el Reino Unido, todos los ciudadanos y todas las ciudadanas mayores de 21 años consiguieron el derecho a votar.
1970 – se aprobó una ley para asegurar la igualdad de salarios entre hombres y mujeres.

Siglo veintiuno

Trabajo
Muchos lugares de trabajo tradicionales (tiendas, cines, restaurantes) se han cerrado debido a las compras en línea y la posibilidad de pedir comida con entrega a casa.
Desde la pandemia del coronavirus, muchos empleados se han acostumbrado a trabajar desde casa.

Sociedad
En muchos casos, las redes sociales han sustituido el uso de los correos electrónicos.
Más gente es consciente de la importancia de tener una vida equilibrada.
Nos preocupamos más por temas como el cambio climático.

Fechas claves
2006 – se prohibió fumar en el lugar de trabajo en España.
2022 – se publicó la app ChatGTP, un sistema de inteligencia artificial.

1900

2000

2100

¿Y en el futuro?

¿Cómo cambiará nuestra sociedad?

¿Cómo será el mundo laboral?

Leer **4** **Read the *Siglo veintiuno* section and translate it into English.**

Leer **5** **Read the whole timeline again. Find <u>two or three</u> examples of each tense. Then translate each example into English.**

1 the present tense
2 the preterite tense
3 the imperfect tense
4 the imperfect continuous tense
5 the perfect tense

Escuchar **6** **Listen to and read the text below. Select the correct words.**

En la próxima década creo que el trabajo será **más / menos / tan** importante y la gente pasará **más / menos / tanto** tiempo disfrutando de la vida y cuidando su salud **física / mental / general**.
Viajaremos / Compraremos / Comeremos menos porque querremos ahorrar **recursos / dinero / tiempo** y salvar el medio ambiente. Por lo tanto, habrá menos **bancos / tráfico / tiendas**.
En el mundo laboral, muchos de los trabajos de hoy **cambiarán / seguirán siendo importantes / ya no existirán**, y casi nadie trabajará en **una oficina / una tienda / casa**.

los recursos	*resources*

Escribir **7** **Use language from exercise 6 to write your own text using the prompts below. Include:**

- how things will be different — *En mi opinión, en la próxima década habrá más/menos ... que hoy.*
- what people will spend time doing — *La gente pasará más/menos tiempo ...*
- what the world of work will be like. — *En el mundo laboral ...*

6 El futuro sin límites

- Talking about the impact of artificial intelligence
- Using *para que* + present subjunctive
- Working out the infinitive of a conjugated verb

Escuchar **1** **Listen and read. Then copy and complete the sentences below in English.**

¿Estás de acuerdo con el uso de la inteligencia artificial (IA)?

Estoy a favor de la inteligencia artificial y creo que podremos usarla para que todo el mundo haga menos horas de trabajo en el futuro. Necesitamos la IA para que el mundo sea más seguro – por ejemplo, las cámaras de tráfico podrán identificar a gente que usa el móvil cuando está conduciendo. La IA podría resolver problemas como el hambre, la pobreza y la soledad, y ayudar a salvar vidas. ¡Ojalá! **Isabel**

Estoy en contra de la inteligencia artificial porque es peligrosa y, en mi opinión, empezaremos a depender demasiado de la IA. Creo que nos robará la imaginación y ya no habrá ni escritores ni artistas ni músicos. Además, los ordenadores no tienen cerebro verdadero y no comprenden sentimientos como el miedo. Tampoco son capaces de sentir dolor, de enamorarse, etc. **Juan**

1 According to Isabel, AI will allow people to work …
2 She says that it will make the world …
3 Traffic cameras will be able to identify …
4 AI could solve … and help to …
5 Juan thinks that AI is …
6 He thinks that we will start to …
7 There will no longer be any …
8 Computers don't understand …

G

Use the **present subjunctive** after ***para que*** ('so that', 'in order that') to express the purpose of an action where the subject of the verb changes.
Podemos usarla ***para que*** *todo el mundo* ***haga*** *…*
We can use it **so that** everyone **does** …

Where the subject of the verb is the same in both parts of the sentence, simply use ***para*** + infinitive.
Las cámaras usarán la IA ***para*** *identificar …*
Cameras will use AI in order to identify …

Page 199

Leer **2** **Read these replies to the posts in exercise 1. Who does each person agree with? For each one, write *I* (Isabel) or *J* (Juan). Then choose the correct summary (a–f) for each one.**

Los expertos advierten que la IA amenaza con aumentar la tasa de paro porque muchos empleos desaparecerán. Va a destruir la economía (¡los ordenadores no pagan impuestos!). **Conchita**

No entiendo por qué la gente teme a las nuevas tecnologías y rechaza desarrollos como la IA. ¡No podemos impedirlos! Yo creo que la IA será muy útil para la educación. **Carlos**

El desarrollo de la IA es carísimo, pero vale la pena. Y si las grandes empresas están dispuestas a gastar millones de dólares para que yo tenga una vida más fácil en el futuro, ¡no me quejaré! **Merche**

Deberíamos destacar los riesgos y asegurarnos de la seguridad, sí, pero los peligros son evitables si tenemos cuidado. Y ya llevamos muchos años usando la IA con apps que reconocen la voz. **Sebastián**

Me niego a confiar en la IA. Pienso que tendrá muchas consecuencias desconocidas y perderemos la capacidad de tomar nuestras propias decisiones. **Raúl**

Yo tengo dudas sobre la IA y creo que nos estamos equivocando. Los ordenadores nos cuentan mentiras y nos engañan. Podrían tomar el control del mundo. **Luisa**

a A worthwhile investment.
b We can avoid the risks if we are careful.
c Computers could take over the world.
d A big threat to employment.
e Why do people fear new technologies?
f AI isn't to be trusted.

The suffix ***-able*** can sometimes be added to a verb stem to create an adjective.

*evit**ar***	→	*evit**able***	(avoidable)
*compar**ar***	→	*compar**able***	(comparable)

Escribir 3 **Read the opinions in exercise 2 again. Write down the <u>infinitive</u> for each of the following verbs.**

1 to disappear
2 to make a mistake
3 to spend
4 to complain
5 to trust
6 to recognise
7 to reject
8 to threaten
9 to destroy/ruin
10 to ensure
11 to trick/deceive
12 to prevent

If it has been used as a conjugated verb in the text, look closely at the verb ending to work out the <u>infinitive</u> form.

desaparecerán → *<u>desaparec**er**</u>*
(they will disappear)
nos estamos equivocando → *<u>equivoc**arse**</u>*
(we are making a mistake)

Escuchar 4 **Listen to these four teenagers talking about artificial intelligence. Then copy and complete the table in English. (1–4)**

	In favour?	Opinion	Reasons (<u>two</u> details)
1	✓	AI is necessary	it will help to ...

Escribir 5 **Write a sentence for each picture to give an argument for or against AI. Use vocabulary from exercises 1–4 to help you.**

1

2

3

4

5

6

Estoy	a favor de en contra de de acuerdo con	la IA, ya que	(no) es	necesaria. útil. peligrosa. cara. segura.
			(no) vale la pena.	
Creo que la IA	podría ayudar a		evitar la discriminación. reducir las horas de trabajo. resolver problemas. salvar vidas.	
	amenaza con		robar la imaginación. destruir la economía. tomar el control del mundo.	
(No) Deberíamos	asegurarnos de la seguridad de la IA. confiar en la IA. tener cuidado para evitar los riesgos. destacar los peligros.			

Hablar 6 **In pairs, debate the pros and cons of artificial intelligence.**

- *¿Cuál es tu opinión de la inteligencia artificial?*
- *Estoy a favor de la inteligencia artificial porque ...*
- *No estoy de acuerdo con ella. Yo estoy en contra, ya que ...*
- *Sí, es verdad, pero ...*

Escribir 7 **Write your own entry for a discussion forum on artificial intelligence. Include reasons for and against the use of AI.**

- *Por un lado, estoy a favor de la inteligencia artificial. Creo que es ... porque ...*
- *También, ...*
- *Por otro lado, estoy en contra porque ...*
- *Además, ...*

Gramática 1

Expressing future plans (Unit 1, page 184)

Leer 1 **Read the grammar box on page 184. Then read the text and answer the questions in English. Pay attention to the phrases in bold; these appear in a different order in the text.**

El año próximo voy a cambiar de instituto porque quiero sacar buenas notas. Espero ser abogado en el futuro, y por eso me gustaría hacer una carrera universitaria cuando tenga dieciocho años. Estudiaré mucho porque sé que no será fácil. Después, tengo ganas de trabajar en otro país (¡con más sol y menos lluvia!), y por lo tanto creo que buscaré un empleo en el extranjero. También, tengo la intención de comprar un coche porque voy a aprender a conducir.

According to Daniel, what …

1 would he **like to** do?
2 does he **intend to** do?
3 does he **want to** do?
4 does he **hope to** do?
5 is he **keen to** do?
6 is he **going to** do? (two details)
7 **will** he do? (two details)

Escribir 2 **Re-write these sentences using a range of phrases followed by the infinitive to express future plans. Take care with reflexive verbs and those with an irregular stem in the future tense. Then translate your sentences into English.**

Example: *1 Me gustaría tener dos o tres hijos. – I would like to have two or three children.*

1 Tendré dos o tres hijos.
2 Compraré una casa en el campo.
3 Cuando tenga bastante dinero, compartiré piso con mis amigos.
4 Haré una carrera universitaria en España.
5 Me enamoraré y luego me casaré.
6 Si apruebo mis exámenes, iré a la universidad.
7 Lucharé contra la discriminación.
8 Montaré mi propio negocio porque seré empresaria.

Seguir/Continuar + present participle (Unit 1, page 185)

Escribir 3 **Fill in the gaps with the present participle of an appropriate verb from the word box. Then translate each sentence into English.**

Example: *1 estudiando – I want to carry on studying at my school next year.*

aprender buscar compartir servir
estudiar leer trabajar vivir

1 Quiero seguir ___ en mi insti el año próximo.
2 Mi hermana sigue ___ en la empresa de mi madre.
3 ¿Vas a continuar ___ alemán cuando seas mayor?
4 Ricardo siguió ___ en Madrid después de terminar sus estudios.
5 Continuaré ___ piso con mi amiga porque es más barato.
6 No voy a continuar ___ esta novela porque es tan aburrida.
7 Todavía no he encontrado un trabajo, y por eso tengo que seguir ___.
8 No quiero seguir ___ a los clientes en el restaurante.

Seguir/Continuar + **present participle** is used to mean 'to carry on' or 'to continue' doing something.

Voy a ***continuar estudiando****.* I'm going **to carry on studying**.

You can also use these verbs to say that you are still doing something.

Sigo viviendo *con mis padres.* **I'm still living** with my parents.

To form the **present participle**, remove the ***-ar***, ***-er*** or ***-ir*** from the infinitive and add ***-ando*** (for ***-ar*** verbs) or ***-iendo*** (for ***-er/-ir*** verbs).

Irregular present participles include:

leer → leyendo *dormir → durmiendo* *servir → sirviendo*

Seguir is an ***e > i*** stem-changing verb in the **present tense** (like *pedir* and *servir*).
sigo, sigues, sigue, seguimos, seguís, siguen

In the **preterite tense**, it has a spelling change in the 'he/she' form (*siguió*) and 'they' form (*siguieron*).

Possessive pronouns (Unit 2, page 186)

Escribir 4

Fill in the gaps with the correct possessive pronoun. Then translate each sentence into English.

1 Sus compañeros son más serios que ___. (*mine*)
2 Nuestra jefa es más estricta que ___. (*theirs*)
3 Mi gimnasio es más pequeño que ___. (*yours, sing.*)
4 Tus compañeros son más agradables que ___. (*his*)
5 Su entrevista era más larga que ___. (*yours, plur.*)
6 Vuestras condiciones laborales son peores que ___. (*ours*)

Possessive pronouns ('mine', 'hers', etc.) are used to avoid repetition. They must agree with the noun they are replacing.

	singular		plural	
mine	el mío	la mía	los míos	las mías
yours	el tuyo	la tuya	los tuyos	las tuyas
his/hers/its	el suyo	la suya	los suyos	las suyas
ours	el nuestro	la nuestra	los nuestros	las nuestras
yours	el vuestro	la vuestra	los vuestros	las vuestras
theirs	el suyo	la suya	los suyos	las suyas

Unlike possessive adjectives (*mi*, *tu*, etc.), **possessive pronouns** can never be followed directly by a noun.
Mi jefe es más agradable que ***el tuyo***.
My boss is nicer than **yours**.

Hablar 5

In pairs, take turns to make a comparative sentence that includes a possessive pronoun. Your partner translates your sentence into English.

Example:

- *Vuestra empresa es más pequeña que* ***la nuestra***.
- *Your company is smaller than ours.*

vuestra empresa | sus tareas | su horario laboral | nuestros clientes | tu trabajo | nuestra tienda

- Make the adjective agree with the noun.
- Do you need ***es*** ('is') or ***son*** ('are')?

Useful adjectives

aburrido alegre alto barato difícil duro fácil listo moderno pequeño

Prepositions followed by the infinitive (Unit 2, page 187)

Leer 6

Read the grammar box on page 187. Then read this account and select the correct options.

Antes de la entrevista, compré un traje nuevo **1 después de / para / sin** dar una buena impresión. La noche anterior, pasé tres horas preparándome para la entrevista **2 antes de / después de / para** acostarme. Me acosté temprano **3 antes de / para / sin** dormir bien.

Sin embargo, pasé la noche **4 sin / después de / para** dormir, ya que había mucho ruido en la calle. Por eso, al día siguiente me desperté muy tarde.

5 Sin / Antes de / Después de levantarme, fui enseguida al baño **6 después de / sin / para** ducharme, pero me caí en la ducha. Luego, noté que ¡mi perro se estaba comiendo mi traje! No tenía tiempo para tomar el desayuno **7 para / sin / antes de** salir de casa y, por lo tanto, tuve que ir a la entrevista **8 sin / para / después de** comer nada.

Desafortunadamente, al final llegué muy tarde ¡y no conseguí el trabajo!

el traje *suit, costume*

Escuchar 7

Read the sentences and then listen. Correct the mistake(s) in each sentence.

1 Héctor wants to buy a car in order to learn to drive.
2 Sonia is going to look for a summer job after finishing her university degree.
3 Felipe worked in his mum's company for a month to earn some money.
4 Marina hopes to get a good job after travelling around the world.

Gramática 2

Masculine and feminine nouns (Unit 3, page 188)

Escribir 1 **Fill in the gaps with the correct words from the word box below, paying attention to the gender of the nouns. Then translate each sentence into English.**

1 Me duelen los dientes. Afortunadamente, mi padre es ___.
2 No me cuesta nada cortarme el pelo – ¡mi marido es ___!
3 A mi amiga Pilar le interesa la medicina. Quiere ser ___.
4 Mi prima es ___ del Ejército Mexicano.
5 Estas dos ___ merecen ganar un premio por la película – son buenísimas.
6 Mi hermana espera ser ___ porque le encantan las ciencias.
7 Mi tía es ___ profesional y tiene una voz preciosa.

actor	científico	peluquero
soldado	dentista	
cantante	médico	

merecer *to deserve*

Some **nouns** have different masculine and feminine forms:

- those ending in ***-o***, including
  *médic**o*** → *médic**a***
- those ending in ***-or***, including
  *escrit**or*** → *escrit**ora***

Nouns ending in ***-e*** or ***-ista*** are usually **invariable**.

*estudi**ante*** → *estudi**ante***
*art**ista*** → *art**ista***

Exceptions include:

*jef**e*** → *jef**a***

The words *modelo*, *soldado* and *policía* are also invariable.

Some job nouns have completely different masculine and feminine words.
actor → ***actriz***

To form a plural noun:

- if it ends in a vowel, add **-s**
- if it ends in a consonant, add **-es**
- if it ends in **-z**, change to **-ces**.

Modal verbs (Unit 4, page 190)

Escuchar 2 **Listen to this podcast about learning languages. For each speaker (1–6), write down the letter of the photo and the <u>two</u> modal verbs you hear. Then translate the verbs into English.**

Example: 1 *b, sabes – you know, puedes – you can*

a

b

c

d

e

f

Escribir 3 **Translate these questions into Spanish using the correct form of the appropriate modal verb.**

Example: 1 *¿Cuándo **puedo** aprender a conducir?*

1 When can I learn to drive?
2 What do you want to study in the future?
3 Why do we have to get a job?
4 What must I do in order to pass my exams?
5 How many languages do you (know how to) speak?

Hablar 4 **In pairs, take turns to ask and answer your questions from exercise 3. Remember to change the modal verbs to the correct form in your answers.**

Example:

- *¿Cuándo **puedo** aprender a conducir?*
- ***Puedes** aprender a conducir (a la edad de) …*

Modal verbs are followed by the <u>infinitive</u> and include:

deber	to have to / must
poder	to be able to / can
querer	to want to
saber	to know
tener que	to have to

- ***poder*** (*p<u>ue</u>do*, etc.) and ***querer*** (*qu<u>ie</u>ro*, etc.) are stem-changing in the present tense and have an irregular stem in the future/conditional tenses (see page 236)
- ***tener*** is an irregular verb
- ***saber*** is irregular in the 'I' form of the present tense (***sé***, *sabes*, …)

Saber is used to mean 'to know how to'

*¿**Sabes** cocinar?* **Do you know how** to cook?

Using the infinitive as a noun (Unit 4, page 191)

Escribir 5 **Read the grammar box on page 191 and write six logical sentences using the phrases below. Then translate your partner's sentences into English.**

Example: 1 *Según mi madre, viajar en tren no es barato.*
According to my mum, travelling by train isn't cheap.

Para mí, En mi opinión, Creo que Pienso que He decidido que Según mi madre, Mi padre dice que	aprender compartir hacer prepararse solicitar tener trabajar viajar	en el extranjero en tren hijos y casarse otros idiomas para una entrevista de trabajo piso con tus amigos un trabajo con un buen salario una carrera universitaria	(no) es barato. (no) es fácil. (no) es importante. (no) sería bastante útil. (no) sería muy divertido. (no) vale la pena. no importa.

Para que + present subjunctive (Unit 6, page 194)

Leer 6 **Translate these sentences into English. Then take turns to read out the Spanish sentences with a partner, taking care with pronunciation.**

1 Quiero hacer una carrera universitaria para que sea más fácil conseguir un trabajo.
2 Necesitamos hacer más para que los niños de todo el mundo vayan al colegio.
3 Voy a comprarte un billete de tren para que vengas conmigo a Madrid.
4 Voy a enseñarte un poco de inglés para que seas capaz de comunicarte en las tiendas y en los restaurantes durante tu viaje.

Use the present subjunctive after ***para que*** ('so that', 'in order that') to express purpose, when the subject changes.
*Podemos usar la IA **para que** el mundo **sea** ...*
We can use AI **so that** the world **is / may be** ...

To form the subjunctive, take the 'I' form of the present tense, remove the ***-o*** and add ***-e***, ***-es*** or ***-e*** for ***-ar*** verbs, and ***-a***, ***-as*** or ***-a*** for ***-er/-ir*** verbs.
- ***hacer*** → *haga, hagas, haga*
- ***tener*** → *tenga, tengas, tenga*
- ***venir*** → *venga, vengas, venga*

Ir (*vaya, vayas, vaya*) and ***ser*** (*sea, seas, sea*) are irregular.

Where the subject of the verb is the same in both parts of the sentence, use ***para*** + infinitive.
*Quiero viajar **para** conocer a gente nueva.*
I want to travel **in order to** meet new people.

¡En marcha!

Escuchar 7 **Listen and fill in the gaps with the correct word(s) in Spanish. Then translate the text into English.**

Mi novio **1** hacer una carrera universitaria porque **2** ser **3**. Sin embargo, he decidido que **4** hacer un trabajo práctico **5** tener que ir a la universidad. Por eso, **6** terminar mis exámenes, **7** Formación Profesional **8** trabajar como ingeniera.

El año próximo **9** continuar **10** con mis padres porque **11** un piso es carísimo. No me importa porque me llevo bien con mis padres, aunque mi novio se pelea mucho con **12**.

Escribir 8 **Match the sentence halves. Then translate the completed sentences into English.**

1 Si me enamoro algún día, ...
2 Debes preguntar por el salario ...
3 Quiero conseguir un buen trabajo para ...
4 Creo que los ordenadores seguirán ...
5 Mis padres se niegan a prestarme el coche ...

que mi familia tenga bastante dinero.
porque dicen que conduzco mal.
robando nuestros trabajos en el futuro.
espero casarme.
antes de solicitar el trabajo.

prestar *to lend*

Reading

Leer 1 ***University study.*** **Read Emilio's blog about going to university. What does he say about each aspect? (1–4) Write (P) for something that happened in the past; (N) for something happening now; (F) for something that will happen in the future.**

Mi hermana mayor acaba de terminar la carrera universitaria y ahora está buscando trabajo en una empresa de marketing. Disfrutó mucho del tiempo que pasó estudiando en Buenos Aires porque conoció a mucha gente nueva y le encantó compartir piso con sus amigos. Lo único malo fue que era carísimo vivir en la capital.

A mí me gustaría ir a la universidad si apruebo los exámenes, aunque hay que pensarlo con cuidado. Mucha gente se equivoca cuando elige la universidad y luego decide dejarla porque no le gusta. Todavía no he decidido lo que quiero estudiar.

1 looking for a job
2 sharing a flat with friends
3 living in a big city
4 deciding what to study

Leer 2 ***Working from home.*** **Read this news article about the pros and cons of working from home. Answer the following questions in English.**

When reading a Spanish text, look for common suffixes. For example, words ending in ***-dad/-idad*** almost always end in '-ty'/'-ity' in English.

La popularidad del trabajo a distancia ha aumentado enormemente en años recientes gracias a los desarrollos en las Tecnologías de la Información y la Comunicación (TIC), y también debido a situaciones como la pandemia.

Este modelo de trabajo ofrece más flexibilidad porque no hay horario estricto – se puede escoger la hora de empezar y terminar el trabajo, y puede permitir un mejor equilibrio entre la vida laboral y la vida familiar.

Los beneficios para la sociedad también son importantísimos. Causa menos contaminación y reduce los accidentes de tráfico porque hay menos personas que viajan diariamente al trabajo. Además, las empresas ahorran dinero porque no necesitan tanto espacio si hay menos gente trabajando en la oficina.

Sin embargo, hay desventajas. Pasar el día entero delante del ordenador puede causar dolor de ojos. Además, puede llevar a una falta de contacto social.

Adverbs ending in ***-mente*** usually end in '-ly' in English.

-ísimo is added to an adjective to mean 'really' or 'extremely'.

Also look out for words beginning with ***es-*** + consonant. Remove the ***e*** to identify words that are similar to English more easily.

1 According to the article, why has remote working become more popular in recent years?
2 In what way does remote working offer more flexibility?
3 How does society benefit from remote working?
4 How does remote working enable companies to save money?
5 According to the article, what are the two disadvantages of spending the day in front of a computer?

xla pandemia	*pandemic*
la flexibilidad	*flexibility*
el equilibrio	*balance*

Leer 3

My part-time job. **Translate the following paragraph into English.**

Los fines de semana trabajo en el centro deportivo.
Lo hago desde hace un año y es divertidísimo.
Los clientes suelen ser agradables y me llevo bien con mis compañeros.
Ayer llegué tarde y por eso mi jefa no estaba contenta.
Después de terminar mis estudios, buscaré un empleo como profesor de natación.

Leer 4

A Latin American trailblazer. **You read the following article about Omara Portuondo, an artist from the Latin American country of Cuba. Write (P) for something that happened in the past; (N) for something happening now; (F) for something that will happen in the future.**

Buena Vista Social Club es uno de los grupos musicales más populares de Cuba. Uno de los cantantes principales es Omara Portuondo, una persona con mucho talento. Ahora, tiene 93 años de edad y no tiene la intención de parar – quiere cantar en otros países.

Omara no comenzó su carrera como cantante. Antes de cantar, bailaba en clubs de música en la ciudad de la Habana. Ha ganado varios premios, que incluyen Latin Grammys – unos de los premios más importantes en la industria musical en América Latina.

1 Popularity of Vista Social Club
2 Singing throughout the world
3 Dance performances
4 Winning awards

Listening

Escuchar 1

Part-time job and future plans. **Fatima is talking about working in a café and her future career plans. What does she think of the following aspects? Write (P) for a positive opinion, (N) for a negative opinion or (P+N) for a positive and negative opinion.**

1.1 the location
1.2 the tasks
2.1 going to university
2.2 a physical job

Escuchar 2

The world of work. **You hear a report about how workplaces are changing. Listen and answer the following questions in English.**

1 How have new technologies made teamwork easier?
2 What can you now do without leaving the house?
3 What sort of benefits do many companies offer?
4 Who are companies hoping to attract?

In this task, which Spanish words (for example, *equipo*) might help you to spot where the relevant information is given?

Escuchar 3

Dictation. **You will hear five short sentences. Listen carefully and using your knowledge of Spanish sounds, write down in Spanish exactly what you hear for each sentence.**

Listen out for:

- ***ca / co / cu / que / qui*** – which have a hard sound like 'k' in English
- ***ga / go / gu*** – which have a hard sound like 'gate' in English
- ***ge / gi / j*** – which sound like a stronger version of 'h' in English

Focus, too, on words that need a **written accent** on the stressed vowel.

Módulo 8

Prueba oral

Role play

Escribir 1

Look at the role play card and prepare what you are going to say.

You are talking to your Colombian friend about education and work. Your teacher will play the part of your friend and will speak first. You should address your friend as *tú*.

When you see this – **?** – you will have to ask a question.

You must include at least one verb in your response to each bullet point.

1 Say what you normally do in class. (Give one detail.)
2 Give two advantages of speaking a foreign language.
3 Say what you think about university study. (Give one opinion and one reason.)
4 Say what you are going to do in the future and why. (Give two details.)
5 **?** Ask a question about your studies.

Keep your answer short and simple.

Pay attention to how many advantages you need to give.

You could use the near future or simple future tense here.

Start with an appropriate question word, such as '**What** (do you like to study)'?

Escuchar 2

Practise what you have prepared. Then, using your notes, listen and respond to the teacher.

Escuchar 3

Now listen to Hussain doing the role play task. In English, note down what he says for each of the points on the card, including the question he asks.

Reading aloud

Hablar 1

Look at this task. With a partner, read aloud the six sentences, paying particular attention to the underlined letters.

Monika, your Peruvian friend, has written this post on social media about learning languages.

Read out the text below to your partner.

Hay que saber otras lenguas si quieres trabajar en el extranjero.

Te permite viajar, conocer otros países y descubrir culturas distintas.

Tengo ganas de aprender a hablar mandarín y árabe.

Creo que estos idiomas son muy antiguos.

La capacidad de comprender y comunicarse con la gente es útil.

Te ayuda a apreciar la riqueza del mundo.

Take extra care with how you pronounce the underlined sounds:

- ***ca / co / cu / que / qu*** – which produce a hard 'k' sound
- ***ga / go / gu*** – which at the beginning of a word produce a hard sound as in 'gate' in English
- ***ge / gi*** and ***j*** – which produce a 'huh' sound from the back of your throat

Also, pay attention to **written accents** and be sure to use correct **stress patterns**.

Escuchar 2

Listen and check your pronunciation.

Hablar 3

Listen to the teacher asking four questions that relate to the topic of education and work. Translate each question into English and prepare your own answers in Spanish. Then listen again and respond to the teacher.

For these four questions, you will score marks for developing your answers and for using clear, accurate language.

Photo card

Escuchar 1 **Look at the two photos below and read the first part of the task card. Then listen to Piotr describing the photos.**

1 Piotr uses the adverb ***solamente***. What does it mean?
2 What two mistakes does he make when talking about the people in the first photo?
3 He uses the phrase ***hacer la compra*** instead of ***ir de compras***. What do you think is the slight difference in meaning between these two phrases?
4 What time of day does he think it is in the first photo and why?
5 Where does he think the people are in the second photo?
6 What does he think the people are doing in the second photo?

Prepare your own description of the photos. Your teacher will ask you to talk about the content of these photos. You must include at least one detail about each photo.

After you have described the photos, your teacher will then ask you questions related to **People and lifestyle**.

Hablar 2 **Prepare your own description of the two photos. Then, with a partner, take turns to describe them.**

- *En la primera foto hay …*
- *En la segunda foto hay …*

Escuchar 3 **Read the second part of the task card and listen to the first question in the wider conversation. The teacher asks Piotr *'En tu opinión, ¿es importante para los jóvenes tener un pequeño trabajo?'* Listen and write down the missing word(s) for each gap.**

¡ **1** ! Tener un trabajo te **2** a ser más **3** y te da más **4** . Además, te **5** cosas nuevas. Yo llevo cinco meses trabajando en el **6** local donde **7** las entradas y sirvo comida y **8** . Lo hago los **9** y es divertidísimo porque me llevo bien con **10** .

Escuchar 4 **Listen to Piotr answering two more questions: *'Háblame de un problema que tuviste recientemente en tu trabajo'* and *'¿En qué te gustaría trabajar en el futuro?'*. Answer the questions in English.**

1 For his first answer, write down the order in which he mentions the following:
A my boss was angry **B** I fell **C** I got the schedule wrong **D** I missed the bus

2 For his second answer, write down:
a why he no longer wants to be a doctor
b what he now hopes to do and why
c why his stepmum's job isn't a good option for him.

3 Listen to both answers again. Write down examples of verbs in each of the following past tenses:
- preterite
- imperfect
- imperfect continuous
- perfect.

Listen out for how Piotr shows off an example of a possessive pronoun.

Hablar 5 **Prepare your own answers to Module 8 questions 1–10 on page 231. Then practise with your partner.**

Módulo
8 Prueba escrita

Translation

Escribir 1

Read the English text and Riley's translation of it. Correct the ten mistakes in the Spanish translation. (Be careful: they are not grammatical mistakes, just mistakes of meaning.)

I am hardworking and I like working in a team. I work in a pharmacy where I have to help the customers and give information. Today I am tired because I finished very late yesterday. In the future I will look for a different job because I don't earn enough money.

Soy perezosa y me gusta trabajar en casa. Trabajo en una oficina donde tengo que ayudar a los niños y pedir información. Hoy estoy enferma porque empecé muy temprano ayer. En el futuro encontraré un trabajo diferente porque no gasto suficiente dinero.

Escribir 2

Translate the following text into Spanish.

Remember to use the infinitive form after 'I love'.

Remember, the structure 'to have to' is different to the English.

My job is fun because I love being outdoors.
At weekends, I sell food in the local park.
Sometimes my cousin helps and we have to make coffee, too.
Last week, he only worked on Saturday because he was ill.
I would like to live in another country and meet new people.

Take care with the word order in these phrases.

Think carefully about the translation of these past tenses. You will need to decide between using the preterite or the imperfect for each one.

Never use the word *un/una* before *otro/otra*.
'another' = ~~*un*~~ *otro* / ~~*una*~~ *otra*

150-Word writing task

Escribir 1

Look at this writing task and then, for each bullet point, consider:

- what examples of **complex language** you could use to impress the examiner
- how you could use a **variety of vocabulary** to avoid repetition
- **which tense(s)** you will need to use in your answer.

You are writing a blog about future study and work.
Write approximately **150** words in **Spanish**.
You should write something about both bullet points.

Mention:
- the positive and negative aspects of going to university
- your ambitions for the future.

Leer 2

Read Joe's answer to the task. Answer the questions in the coloured shapes.

1 These are examples of a verb + infinitive or verb phrase + infinitive. What do they mean? Find two more examples from the text.

2 These are examples of **complex language**. What do they mean? Find two more examples from the text.

Por un lado, vale la pena hacer una carrera universitaria porque te permite conocer a gente nueva. Además, puede mejorar tus posibilidades de conseguir tu puesto ideal. Por otro lado, lo malo es que suele ser carísimo y no es necesario para todos los empleos. Por ejemplo, para encontrar un buen trabajo hace falta tener buena comunicación y poder tomar riesgos. Sin embargo, lo más importante es saber resolver problemas. No es necesario ir a la universidad para aprender estas cosas.

Después de terminar mis exámenes seguiré estudiando. Si saco buenas notas, haré una carrera universitaria porque mi sueño es ser abogado. Espero ser unos de los mejores abogados del mundo. Además, quiero mejorar mi nivel de español para que sea más fácil comunicarme cuando vaya a España el año próximo. Acabo de descargar una app e intento usarla todos los días. También, he empezado a ver programas en Netflix (u otro servicio semejante) con el sonido en español.

3 Which two synonyms does Joe use in the text to avoid repeating this word?

4 What do these phrases mean? What do we call this verb form?

5 Why have the Spanish words for 'and' / 'or' changed their spelling here?

Leer 3

Read Joe's answer again. Copy and complete the sentences.

1 Going to university can improve your chances of ...
2 According to Joe, you need to be able to take ...
3 The most important thing is ...
4 Joe hopes to be one of the ... in ...
5 He wants to improve his Spanish so that ... when ...
6 He has started to watch programmes with ...

Escribir 4

Prepare your own answer to the task.

- Think about how you can develop your answer for each bullet point.
- Look back at your notes from exercises 1 and 2.
- Look at the 'Challenge checklist' and consider how you can show off your Spanish!
- Write a brief plan and organise your answer into paragraphs.
- Write your answer and then carefully check the accuracy of what you have written.

Challenge checklist	
	✓ Past, present and future time frames ✓ Connectives / time phrases / sequencers ✓ Extended sentences ✓ Different opinion phrases
	✓ A wider range of tenses (e.g. perfect, simple future) ✓ 'If' clauses (e.g. *Si* + present + future) ✓ A wide range of interesting vocabulary ✓ Adverbs (e.g. *probablemente*)
	✓ Verbs / verb phrases with an infinitive (e.g. *vale la pena* + infinitive) ✓ Other complex structures (e.g. *Lo malo es que*) ✓ Present subjunctive (e.g. *cuando vaya, para que sea*) ✓ Relative pronouns (*que, el/la cual, cuando, donde*)

Módulo 8 Palabras

Key:
bold = this word will appear in higher exams only
* = this word is not on the vocabulary list, but you may use it in your own sentences

Pioneros latinos (pages 182–183):

Pioneros en sus campos	*Pioneers in their fields*
*el/la bailarín(a)	*dancer*
el/la médico/a	*doctor*
a la edad de ... años	*at the age of ... years old*
nació en ...	*he/she was born in ...*
es conocido/a por ...	*he/she is known for ...*
cuando era niño/a / más joven ...	*when he/she was a child / younger ...*
apenas	*hardly/barely*
llegar a ser / **convertirse en**	*to become*
encontrar (un trabajo/empleo)	*to find (a job)*
apoyar/mantener	*to support / to maintain*
montar/**fundar**	*to set up*
crear/**desarrollar**	*to create / to develop*
abandonar/**animar**	*to leave / to encourage*
destacar/**entregar**	*to stand out / to deliver*
elegir	*to choose/elect*

Sueños y esperanzas (pages 184–185):

¿Qué planes tienes para el año próximo?	*What plans have you got for next year?*
El año próximo ...	*Next year ...*
quiero **seguir estudiando** en mi insti porque ...	*I want to continue studying at my (high) school because ...*
Seguiré/Continuaré ...	*I will keep/continue ...*
estudiando/trabajando en ...	*studying/working in ...*
Voy a ...	*I am going to ...*
Me gustaría ...	*I would like to ...*
Espero ...	*I hope to ...*
Tengo ganas de ...	*I am keen to ...*
Tengo la intención de ...	*I intend to ...*
casarme / tener hijos	*get married / have children*
aprender a conducir	*learn to drive*
compartir piso con ...	*share a flat with ...*
ir a la universidad	*go to university*
hacer una carrera **universitaria**	*do a university degree*
conseguir un buen trabajo	*obtain/get a good job*
buscar un puesto con un buen salario	*find a position with a good salary*
ser **empresario/a**	*to be an entrepreneur*
montar mi **propio** negocio	*to set up my own business*
¿Qué vas a hacer después?	*What are you going to do afterwards?*
Después, tengo la intención de ...	*Afterwards, I intend to ...*
¿Qué otros planes tienes?	*What other plans do you have?*
Cuando **tenga** ... años, me gustaría ...	*When I am ... years old, I would like to ...*
Cuando **sea** mayor ...	*When I am older ...*
Cuando **tenga** bastante dinero ...	*When I have enough money ...*

¡A trabajar! (pages 186–187):

¿Qué haces para ganar dinero?	*What do you do to earn money?*
Para ganar dinero ...	*To earn money ...*
hago cosas y las vendo	*I make things and sell them*
trabajo en ...	*I work in/at ...*
cuido a los niños de mis vecinos	*I look after my neighbours' children*
¿Cuánto dinero ganas?	*How much money do you earn?*
Gano ... euros/pesos/*libras por hora/día/semana	*I earn ... euros/pesos/pounds per hour/day/week*
Gano poco, pero no me importa.	*I don't earn much, but I don't mind.*
¿Cuándo lo haces?	*When do you do it?*
Lo hago ...	*I do it ...*
los fines de semana	*at weekends*
cuando necesito dinero	*when I need money*
cuando me necesitan	*when they need me*
en las vacaciones	*during holidays*
¿Qué tal tu trabajo?	*How is your job?*
Me llevo bien con mi jefe.	*I get on (well) with my boss.*
Mis compañeros son agradables.	*My colleagues are nice.*
Lo odio y quiero dejarlo.	*I hate it and I want to leave it.*
¿Qué experiencia laboral tiene?	*What work experience do you have?*
Llevo (un año) trabajando en ...	*I have been working in/at ... (for a year)*
He trabajado en ...	*I have worked in/at ...*
una tienda/fábrica	*a shop/factory*
un café/gimnasio	*a café/gym*
¿Cuáles son sus **puntos** positivos?	*What are your good points?*
Soy una persona ...	*I am a(n) ... person*
activa/fuerte	*active/strong*
*organizada/responsable	*organised/responsible*
trabajadora/artística	*hard-working/artistic*
independiente/lista	*independent/clever*
práctica/**ambiciosa**	*practical/ambitious*
Tengo ...	*I have ...*
buen sentido del humor	*a good sense of humour*
buenos **conocimientos** de ...	*good knowledge of ...*
buenas *capacidades (de comunicación)	*good (communication) skills*
antes de solicitar un puesto	*before applying for a post*
después de ir a la entrevista	*after going to the interview*
para **lograr** ...	*in order to achieve, get*
sin tener experiencia.	*without having experience*

Un trabajo para todos (pages 188–189):

¿Qué tipo de trabajo querías hacer en el pasado?	*What type of job did you want to do in the past?*
Cuando era más joven, me gustaba la idea de ...	*When I was younger, I liked the idea of ...*
También quería ... porque ...	*I also wanted to ... because ...*
Todavía quiero ... porque ...	*I still want ... because ...*
He decidido que **ya no** quiero ...	*I have decided that I no longer want ...*
Antes / De niño/a ...	*Before / As a child ...*
Cuando era más joven ...	*When I was younger ...*
era mi sueño ...	*it was my dream ...*
quería ...	*I wanted ...*
me gustaba la idea de ...	*I liked the idea of ...*

Ahora / He decidido que ...	*Now / I have decided that ...*
(**todavía** / **ya no**) quiero ...	*I (still / no longer) want ...*
me gusta la idea de ...	*I like the idea of ...*
es mi sueño ...	*it is my dream ...*
ser ...	*to be (a/an) ...*
abogado/a	*lawyer*
actor/actriz	*actor/actress*
camarero/a	*waiter/waitress*
director(a) de cine/teatro	*film/theatre director*
enfermero/a / ingeniero/a	*nurse / engineer*
guía *turístico	*tour guide*
modelo / científico/a	*model/scientist*
peluquero/a	*hairdresser*
pintor(a) / periodista	*painter/journalist*
policía / profesor(a)	*police officer / teacher*
soldado (en el Ejército)	*soldier (in the Army)*
trabajar ...	*to work ...*
al aire libre / desde casa	*outdoors / from home*
solo/a / en el extranjero	*alone / abroad*
en **la enseñanza** / la prensa	*in teaching / the press*
en un hospital (**infantil**)	*in a (children's) hospital*
en un **hogar** de **ancianos**	*at a care home*
en una empresa/oficina	*in a business/office*
con los ordenadores	*with computers*
con otra gente	*with other people*
hacer un trabajo ...	*to do a(n) ... job*
seguro / práctico	*safe/secure / practical/useful*
con **responsabilidad**	*with responsibility*
con un buen salario	*with a good salary*
con variedad/*flexibilidad	*with variety/flexibility*
atender/**exigir**	*to serve / to demand*
la **sangre**	*blood*

Las lenguas te abren las puertas (pages 190–191):

¿Qué idiomas hablas?	*What languages do you speak?*
Hablo ... y **llevo** ... estudiando ...	*I speak ... and I have been studying ... for ...*
También he aprendido ...	*I have also learned ...*
¿Por qué es importante aprender otras lenguas?	*Why is it important to learn other languages?*
Si sabes hablar otro idioma, ...	*If you know how to speak another language, ...*
puedes estudiar o trabajar en el extranjero	*you can study or work abroad*
puedes descubrir otros países	*you can discover other countries*
puedes conocer a más gente	*you can meet more people*
te permite descubrir otras culturas	*it allows you to discover other cultures*
mejora tus oportunidades laborales	*it improves your job opportunities*
te abre **la mente**	*it opens your mind*
No **basta** con hablar una sola lengua.	*It's not enough to speak only one language.*
Debes poder **comprender** las **señales** de tráfico.	*You must be able to understand traffic signs.*
Agradezco las oportunidades.	*I'm grateful for the opportunities.*
Me alegra usar **ambos** idiomas.	*It makes me happy to use both languages.*
En el futuro me gustaría aprender ...	*In the future I would like to learn ...*
español/francés/inglés	*Spanish/French/English*
castellano	*(Castilian) Spanish*
*catalán/*euskera/*gallego	*Catalan/Basque/Galician*
saber	*to know (how to)*
conocer	*to know, meet*
escoger / acordarse	*to choose / to remember*
atreverse/**acostumbrarse**	*to dare / to get used to*
producir / **sorprender**	*to produce / to surprise*
equivocarse	*to be wrong / make a mistake*
conducir	*to drive*
ser **capaz** de ...	*to be capable of ..*
así	*like this, like that*
el/la cuidador(a)	*carer*
la mitad	*half*
la **traducción**	*translation*

El trabajo antes, ahora ... y mañana (pages 192–193):

¿Cómo será el mundo laboral?	*What will the world of work be like?*
En la *década próxima habrá más/menos ... que hoy.	*In the next decade there will be more/less ... than today.*
La gente pasará más/menos tiempo ...	*People will spend more/less time ...*
la tierra	*earth/land*
el/la **obrero/a**	*worker/labourer*
alcanzar/**asegurar**	*to reach / to ensure*

El futuro sin límites (pages 194–195):

¿Cuál es tu opinión de la inteligencia *artificial?	*What is your opinion of artificial intelligence?*
Estoy a favor de ...	*I am for / in favour of ...*
Estoy de acuerdo con ...	*I agree with ...*
Estoy en contra de ...	*I am against ...*
la **inteligencia** *artificial	*artificial intelligence*
porque / ya que es ...	*because / as it is ...*
cara/necesaria	*expensive/necessary*
peligrosa/útil	*dangerous/useful*
segura	*secure/safe*
porque **vale la pena**	*because it is worth it*
La *IA podría ayudar a ...	*AI could help ...*
reducir las horas de trabajo	*to reduce working hours*
resolver problemas	*to resolve problems*
salvar vidas	*to save lives*
Podemos usarla **para que** ...	*We can use it so that ...*
el mundo **sea** más seguro	*the world is safer*
todo el mundo **haga** menos horas de trabajo	*the whole world does fewer working hours*
Creo que la *IA **amenaza** con ...	*I think AI threatens ...*
robar **la imaginación**	*to steal imagination*
destruir la economía	*to destroy the economy*
Además (no) deberíamos ...	*Besides, we should (not) ...*
asegurarnos de la seguridad de la *IA	*ensure the safety of AI*
confiarnos en la *IA	*trust AI*
tener cuidado para evitar los riesgos	*be careful to avoid risks*
destacar los peligros	*emphasise the dangers*
advertir/**enamorarse**	*to warn / to fall in love*
engañar/**impedir**	*to trick / to prevent*
negarse a	*to refuse to*
rechazar/**temer**	*to reject / to fear*

Repaso de gramática

Using suffixes (pages 107, 167, 189 and 194)

Escribir 1 **Rewrite each sentence to include an absolute superlative by adding the correct form of the superlative suffix *-ísimo* to each adjective in bold. Then translate your sentences into English.**

Example: En el norte del país tenemos una costa ***hermosísima****. –*
In the north of the country we have a ***very beautiful*** *coast.*

1 En el norte del país tenemos una costa **hermosa**.
2 Mi amigo trabaja en la caja de una tienda, pero dice que es **aburrido**.
3 Es **fácil** buscar trabajo online. Sin embargo, conseguir un empleo bueno es duro.
4 Cuando tenga más dinero, me gustaría comprar un piso **moderno**.
5 A mí me pone **triste** que nuestra comunidad tenga tanta pobreza.
6 Trabajo en un restaurante donde se puede comer muchos platos **ricos**.
7 La educación es **importante** para luchar contra la discriminación.
8 En mi zona, aquellas torres son **famosas** y muchos turistas vienen a verlas.

If an adjective has a hard **c** sound, like *ri**c**o*, the **c** changes to a ***qu*** to keep this sound in an absolute superlative.
*La comida es ri**c**a.* → *La comida es ri**qu**ísima.*

Escribir 2 **The suffix *-mente* can be added to many (feminine) adjectives to create adverbs. Someone has translated this text, but they have forgotten to change the adjectives into adverbs. Rewrite the Spanish text, correcting the mistakes.**

On Saturdays, I normally work in a clothes shop in the centre of Madrid. It is difficult, as I don't speak much Spanish. Generally the people in the shop speak slowly and I understand perfectly. Naturally, if I have a problem my boss can help me and I am going to learn more Spanish quickly.

Los sábados, normal trabajo en una tienda de ropa en el centro de Madrid. Es difícil porque no hablo mucho español. General la gente en la tienda habla lento y entiendo perfecto. Natural, si tengo un problema mi jefe me puede ayudar y voy a aprender más español rápido.

Other suffixes that can be added to some Spanish verbs and nouns include ***-able*** and ***-ito***:
-able is added to a verb to create an adjective: *evitar* (to avoid) → *evit**able*** (avoidable)
-ito is added to a noun and must agree with the noun (*-it**o**/**a**/**os**/**as***). If the noun ends in *-**o**/**a***, remove it first. This is called a diminutive, as it describes something as being small.
It can also be used to show something is precious or loved.
mi perrito blanco my dear/little white dog

Escribir 3 **Change each adjective into a noun by adding the suffix *-idad*. Then use each noun in a sentence.**

*Example: 1 nacional → la naciona**lidad***
Soy orgulloso de poder hablar con gente de nacionalidades distintas.

1 nacional
2 real
3 personal
4 activo
5 feliz
6 seguro

With the suffix ***-idad***, if the adjective ends in a vowel, you need to remove it. Also, if the adjective ends in **-z**, this will change to **-c** when the suffix is added.

Different types of adjectives (Pages 106, 117, 134 and 138)

Escribir 4

Complete the sentences with the correct possessive adjective (*mi, tu, su* etc.) or with the correct demonstrative adjective (*este, ese, aquel* etc.).

1 El mejor aspecto de ___ trabajo en el hotel es que es fácil conocer a gente de otros países. (*this*)
2 Admiro a varias personas famosas, pero ___ verdadero modelo a seguir es ___ madre. (*my, my*)
3 En mi pueblo ___ tiendas aquí son mejores que ___ tiendas. (*these, those … over there*)
4 El gobierno debe utilizar ___ poder para mejorar la sociedad para todos. (*its*)
5 La violencia y la discriminación son unos problemas graves para nosotros y ___ hijos. (*our*)
6 A veces la moda es increíble. Por ejemplo, ___ zapatos cuestan más que ___ móvil. (*those, your*)

Escribir 5

Copy and complete the text in Spanish, by translating the English adjectives in the box.

Vivo en Cádiz desde hace cinco meses. Es una ciudad muy **1** con unas calles **2** y muchos lugares **3**. Para mí, vivir en una ciudad **4** y **5** es **6**. **7** amigas **8** dicen que soy muy **9** y **10**, y creo que soy una persona muy **11**. Me encanta vivir en esta ciudad **12**.

1 pretty	**4** open	**7** numerous	**10** optimistic
2 old	**5** safe	**8** Spanish	**11** loyal
3 historic	**6** extremely important	**9** hard-working	**12** exciting

Using pronouns (pages 141, 159, 160 and 186)

Escribir 6

Complete the sentences using the pronouns in brackets. Then translate each sentence into English.

1 Para ___, es importantísimo nadar en los ríos y los mares limpios. (*us*)
2 En la foto se puede ver mucha basura en las calles y los animales están encima de ___. (*it*)
3 A ___ me preocupa mucho la contaminación que existe en nuestras ciudades. (*me*)
4 Si te gusta la naturaleza, la amenaza de los cambios climáticos es un problema muy grave para ___. (*you*)
5 Los árboles nos ayudan a respirar. Sin ___ nuestro planeta estará en aun más peligro. (*them*)
6 La discriminación afecta a todas nosotras y por eso todos debemos hacer algo si vamos a luchar contra ___. (*it*)

Emphatic pronouns (*mí/ti/él/ella* etc.) are used after prepositions.

Leer 7

Read the dialogue. Find the <u>six</u> possessive pronouns and translate them into English. Then write <u>six</u> new sentences using the possessive pronouns in Spanish.

Example: el tuyo – yours → *Pienso que mi pueblo es muy tranquilo, pero* ***el tuyo*** *tiene muchos parques.*

- *Creo que mi barrio es bastante seguro, pero el tuyo todavía tiene muchos delitos.*
- *Sí. Las cifras muestran esto. Pero lo bueno es que mi comunidad hace mucho más que la tuya. Por ejemplo, tenemos muchas celebraciones en las calles.*
- *También tenemos fiestas en mi zona y creo que las mías son más divertidas.*
- *¿Qué piensas del centro comercial nuevo que han construido en el centro?*
- *Este centro comercial es enorme, pero el nuestro, que está cerca de nuestras dos casas, es mejor porque tiene más tiendas de ropa.*
- *Estoy de acuerdo. Las nuestras son mejores porque son independientes.*
- *Sí, y también las suyas son muy caras.*

Escribir 8

Rewrite the sentences using direct or indirect object pronouns.

Example: 1 Siempre ***lo*** *cuido.*

1 Siempre cuido al perro de mis abuelos.
2 ¿A ti te gustaría visitar el museo?
3 ¡Protege a los animales en peligro!
4 ¿Ya has comido los caramelos?
5 Ese día estaba ayudando a mi madre en la cocina.
6 Quiero ayudar a los niños pobres.

Repaso de gramática

Verbs and phrases followed by infinitives (pages 161, 168, 184 and 187)

Leer 1 **Match up the sentences. Then make a list of the verbs with infinitives (from statements a–g) that express obligation or possibility.**

1. He trabajado todo el día y estoy muy cansada.
2. Quiero visitar a mis abuelos que viven lejos de aquí.
3. Mi actividad favorita es ir de compras.
4. Los cambios climáticos afectan a todos nosotros.
5. Para mí es importante comprar productos verdes.
6. Ayudo en un banco de alimentos.
7. Me gustaría viajar a varios países y descubrir otras culturas.

- **a** Siempre vale la pena ayudar a otros si puedes.
- **b** Hay que visitar las tiendas independientes en la plaza.
- **c** Se puede viajar en tren porque es más rápido.
- **d** Tienes que aprender otras lenguas.
- **e** Hace falta ser responsable con nuestras opciones de compra.
- **f** Debes descansar e ir a la cama temprano.
- **g** Se debería ahorrar energía y limitar nuestro uso de plástico.

Escribir 2 **Fill in the gaps with the correct infinitive from the box. There are more infinitives than gaps.**

1. Hay que ___ mucho si quieres tener éxito.
2. Necesitamos ___ cuidado con el lenguaje que usamos en las redes sociales.
3. Se debería ___ más si queremos reducir la cantidad de basura que producimos.
4. Vale la pena ___ buenas causas y tomar acción en nuestra comunidad.
5. Si quieres conseguir un empleo, tienes que ___ un CV con los detalles de tu experiencia.
6. Se debería ___ por la igualdad y participar en huelga.
7. Andrea tiene la intención de ___ bien antes de su entrevista.
8. En el futuro, espera ___ una carrera y también le gustaría ___.

luchar	casarse	trabajar	escribir	hacer
tener	apoyar	viajar	reciclar	prepararse

Escribir 3 **Complete each sentence with some advice for a friend about school. Don't forget to use an infinitive!**

Example: 1 *Vale la pena estudiar idiomas porque te permite descubrir otras culturas.*

1. Vale la pena …
2. Se puede …
3. Debes …
4. Tienes que …
5. Hace falta …
6. Se debería …

Se debería is the conditional impersonal form of the verb *deber*. It is used to give advice and means 'you should' or 'one should'.

Se debería *ahorrar energía.* — **You/One should** save energy.

To translate 'you must', use the present tense of *deber* in the second person singular, or use the present tense of ***deber*** with the impersonal ***se***.

Debes *prepararte para una entrevista.* — **You must** prepare for an interview.
Se debe *beber más agua.* — **You/One must** drink more water.

Talking about the past (pages 134, 137, 142 and 161)

Leer 4

Read the sentences and note down the verbs used. Label them: perfect, imperfect, preterite, imperfect continuous or passive voice.

Example: 1 vivía (imperfect), viajaba (imperfect)

1 Cuando vivía en el campo, siempre viajaba en coche, pero ahora no.
2 Mi abuela me dijo que la ciudad tenía más espacios verdes y que había menos gente y por lo tanto menos ruido.
3 Aquella plaza de toros fue visitada por cientos de turistas el mes pasado, pero todavía no he tenido la oportunidad de ir a una corrida de toros.
4 Cuando era más jóven, me gustaba la idea de hacer un trabajo artístico, pero ahora he decidido ser científica.
5 Estábamos viendo la televisión cuando el sol salió y salimos rápidamente para jugar en el jardín.
6 En mi familia nadie ha perdido su trabajo durante esta crisis económica, pero el padre de mi novio no ha podido encontrar un empleo nuevo en los últimos diez meses.
7 Ese día mis amigos y yo estábamos participando en un proyecto de conservación cuando vino una tormenta fuertísima y tuvimos que volver a casa sin terminarlo.
8 Aunque él ha participado en varios proyectos sociales, el premio fue ganado por una joven que se ha atrevido a luchar contra las empresas multinacionales.

To identify the passive voice, remember that the verb ***ser*** will be used with a past participle, which has to agree with the object. It will often be followed by ***por*** and the person who has done the action.

Escribir 5

Complete these sentences by changing the infinitives in brackets into the correct past tense verbs.

1 Antes mi amigo (*trabajar*) en una tienda y (*vender*) ropa para niños, pero ahora no tiene empleo.
2 El sábado pasado mis padres (*ir*) al museo y luego (*tomar*) un café.
3 Todavía yo no (*visitar*) todos los sitios turísticos de mi ciudad que aparecen en el sitio web.
4 Ayer mis amigos y yo (*decidir*) hacer un vídeo sobre el uso de plástico para nuestro proyecto escolar.
5 Cuando (*ser*) más joven, (*querer*) trabajar con animales y mi sueño (*ser*) trabajar al aire libre con ellos.
6 Los alumnos de mi clase (*organizar*) una campaña contra el plástico y (*tener*) mucho éxito, no solo en el instituto sino también en la comunidad.
7 En aquellos tiempos mi pueblo (*ser*) más tranquilo y pequeño, aunque recientemente (*mejorar*) mucho porque han limpiado las calles y (*construir*) una biblioteca nueva.
8 Hace dos meses mi amigo Diego (*ir*) a un hogar de ancianos, donde (*ofrecer*) apoyo a personas mayores, y él (*decidir*) que (*ser*) una experiencia muy especial.

Escribir 6

Rewrite the following text in the past. Change all the present tense verbs into the preterite, imperfect or imperfect continuous tenses.

Voy al cine para trabajar. Tengo que recoger la basura y luego paso dos horas en la caja. Yo bebo agua, pero mi amiga no bebe nada porque nunca tiene sed. Luego, mi amiga y yo decidimos ir al centro comercial. Cuando estoy comprando un regalo para el cumpleaños de mi madre, empieza a llover y tenemos que ir a una cafetería para esperar. La cafetería es bastante grande y hay mucha gente allí a causa de la lluvia. Después, vuelvo a casa y hago mis tareas. Luego, leo y escucho música.

Remember to use the imperfect tense for descriptions in the past, but the preterite tense for completed actions in the past.

Remember that ***y*** ('and') has to change to ***e*** before words beginning with *hi*, such as the preterite forms *hice* and *hizo*.

Repaso de gramática

Using the present subjunctive (pages 143, 166 and 194)

Leer 1 **Identify the present subjunctive verb in each sentence. Then write the correct letter to explain why the present subjunctive has to be used.**

a After ***cuando***, when talking about the future

b After ***para que***, when expressing purpose

c After a verb of wishing, command, request or emotion

d To express feelings with the structure ***es* + adjective + *que***

1. Necesitamos luchar contra la pobreza para que el mundo sea mejor para todos.
2. Cuando vengas a mi casa, estudiaremos juntos para los exámenes.
3. Me pone triste que todavía mucha gente no tenga suficiente comida.
4. Utilizo mucho mi móvil para que mi vida sea más fácil.
5. Cuando sea mayor, experimentaré la vida de otros países.
6. Odio que la gente no haga más para mantener las playas limpias.
7. Es esencial que seas honesto en una entrevista de trabajo.
8. Me preocupa que mi amigo no venga nunca al colegio.
9. Es necesario que todo el mundo sea responsable de sus acciones.
10. La inteligencia artificial se utiliza para que la gente tenga más tiempo para hacer otras cosas.

Leer 2 **Read and match the sentence halves. Then translate the completed sentences into English.**

1. Cuando tenga más dinero,
2. Cuando sea mayor,
3. Me pone triste que
4. Recomiendo que
5. Debemos reducir el uso de las redes sociales

a nuestro gobierno no haga más contra el racismo.
b compartiré un piso con mi novia.
c para hablar más cara a cara.
d la juventud vaya a manifestaciones.
e iré de vacaciones a España.

Escribir 3 **Fill in the gaps with the correct form of the present subjunctive, using a suitable verb from the box.**

1. Cuando mi mejor amigo ___ mayor, irá a la universidad.
2. Cuando (yo) ___ más tiempo, buscaré un trabajo nuevo.
3. Cuando ___ el verano, aprenderé otro idioma.
4. Cuando (yo) ___ a la universidad, estudiaré matemáticas.
5. Cuando (tú) ___ deporte a menudo, mejorarás tu salud física y mental.

hacer
ir
venir
ser
tener

Escribir 4 **Write <u>four</u> sentences about your future plans. Use the sentences from exercise 3 as a model, and make sure you include a present subjunctive verb after *cuando* for each one.**

Try to learn some key phrases in the present subjunctive that you can add into your speaking or writing answers. These will add complexity and, if used correctly, may enable you to score more highly.

Combining tenses (page 144)

(page 144)

Leer 5 **Complete the text by adding in the correct verbs from the box.**

Mi familia y yo **1** en un pueblo pequeño en el norte de nuestro país. Antes **2** en la capital, pero hace dos años **3** de casa. En aquel tiempo, en la capital, **4** mucha violencia en los barrios. Ahora **5** vivir en el campo porque **6** un lugar seguro y tranquilo. Anoche **7** la oportunidad de ir a un concierto de música clásica y **8** una experiencia emocionante y divertida. Sin embargo, si **9** vivir en el campo, es importante que **10** paciencia, ¡porque el transporte es bastante lento!

había fue quieres tengas vivimos es
vivíamos cambiamos tuve prefiero

It is important to invest time in learning verbs and endings for different tenses:

- write out the verb conjugations on flashcards or a computer
- focus on the tenses that you find trickier or know less well
- practise using the verbs in different sentences to help memorise them
- remember to test yourself – or ask someone to test you regularly – to see if you are retaining the knowledge in your long-term memory.

Escribir 6 **For each question, note down the tense used. Then write your own answer to the question, using the correct tense(s).**

Example: 1 present – Normalmente me gusta descansar un poco, pero también suelo organizar una fiesta grande.

1. ¿Qué sueles hacer en las vacaciones de invierno?
2. ¿Qué has hecho en tu zona recientemente?
3. Cuando tengas dieciocho años, ¿qué harás?
4. En tu opinión, ¿cómo es un buen amigo?
5. ¿Qué idiomas hablas?
6. ¿Qué costumbres no saludables tenías antes?
7. ¿Qué haces para proteger el medioambiente?
8. ¿Cómo cambiarías tu instituto?
9. ¿Qué problema mundial te preocupa más?
10. ¿Cómo será el mundo laboral en el futuro?

Use the words in the question to help you formulate the start of your answer each time. However, be careful with the verb endings and pronouns.

Escribir 7 **Translate the following text into Spanish.**

Take care with the word 'have' in this past tense phrase.

Can you remember the expression with *tener* for this? It is followed by an infinitive!

I think that I have learned a lot at school and I am looking forward to finishing my studies. I hope to continue studying, but I will need to find a job as well. I am interested in working in mental health as, for me, it is extremely important. I would also like to travel to different countries because I love learning about other cultures. When I am older, I intend to live abroad.

Verb forms ending in '-ing' (present participle) are used after the verbs *estar*, *llevar*, *seguir* and *continuar*.

Can you use an absolute superlative here?

Which tense is used after *cuando* when it refers to the future?

Módulo 1 ¡A repasar!

Escribir 1

Refresh your memory! **Look back through Module 1 and note down five nouns under each of these categories. Then write a sentence for each noun identified.**

Example: *el fútbol* → *Soy aficionado al fútbol porque es un deporte divertido.*

- los deportes (el fútbol, ...)
- las actividades (la música, ...)
- películas y programas de televisión (las series, ...)

Escuchar 2

Refresh your memory! **Listen to Ana describing her hobbies and note down the following:**

1. her favourite hobbies and how often she does each one
2. what she likes to do on her computer
3. what she did last weekend.

Leer 3

Refresh your memory! **Match up these sentence halves about the advantages and disadvantages of using mobile phones.**

1. Uso muchas apps ...
2. Mi móvil es práctico y ...
3. Algunos usuarios dicen que ...
4. Utilizo mi teléfono para ...
5. Es fácil pasar demasiadas ...
6. Muchas apps ...

a son aficionados a los videojuegos.
b lo uso para leer noticias.
c horas delante de una pantalla.
d no son privadas.
e para estar en contacto con mi familia.
f buscar información por Internet.

Escuchar 4

On Spanish TV, you listen to a young person talking about spending time online. What is his opinion of these aspects of technology? Choose P for a positive opinion, N for a negative opinion or P+N for a positive and negative opinion. (1–2)

1.1 screen time
1.2 video games

2.1 online shopping
2.2 using apps

When listening out for positive and negative opinions, adjectives are important. However, it is also important to pay close attention to the preceding words too, e.g. *nunca es fácil*. *Fácil* is normally associated with a positive opinion but it can also be used to give a negative opinion.

Escuchar **5**

You are going to hear <u>five</u> short sentences about hobbies. Listen carefully and, using your knowledge of Spanish sounds, write down in Spanish exactly what you hear for each sentence.

Use your knowledge of the vowel sounds to help you transcribe words correctly. Remember that each vowel sound is always pronounced the same way and usually each vowel is pronounced separately. Practise saying these words:

gui**ta**rr**a** **e**sc**e**n**a** v**i**dr**i**o **o**rgull**o**s**o** **ju**vent**u**d

These dictation tasks are worth ten marks and you will need to transcribe words with a high level of accuracy to score this top mark.

Leer **6**

Read Luis's review of a music concert.

El mes pasado compré tres entradas online para ver a mi banda favorita, y finalmente ayer mis amigos y yo fuimos al concierto en Girona. Fue un espectáculo increíble de esta nueva banda de rock española.

Comenzaron con una canción nueva y luego tocaron su canción más famosa y popular sobre los deportes. La guitarra en esta canción fue maravillosa y me gustó mucho. Luego tocaron muchas canciones con mucha energía y por eso lo grabé todo en mi móvil.

Complete the sentences. Choose the correct letter, **A**, **B** or **C**, for each question.

1 The concert took place ...
A last month.
B yesterday.
C three days ago.

2 The event started with ...
A their most popular song.
B a guitar solo.
C a new song.

3 Their popular song was about ...
A sport.
B love.
C fame.

4 Luis liked the concert so he ...
A took photos.
B recorded it.
C sang the songs.

Leer **7**

Translate these sentences into English.

1 Hago muchas actividades y me encanta la tecnología.
2 Para subir vídeos, muchas veces utilizo apps seguras en mi móvil.
3 La semana pasada vi una película y luego jugué al fútbol en el parque.
4 Disfrutar de música en vivo es divertido y también nos gusta la lectura.
5 Mañana voy a charlar con mis amigos y vamos a ver una telenovela.

Escribir **8**

Write an email to your friend about how you use technology. Write approximately 90 words in Spanish. You must write something about each bullet point.

Mention:

- what you like about technology
- what you used your phone for last week
- how you would like to use technology in the future.

To say what you *are going to do*, use ***ir*** + infinitive (the near future): ***Voy a compartir*** *fotos.* (**I am going to share** photos.)

To impress in your writing, aim to use a **direct object pronoun** to give further details about what you did on your phone.

Example: La semana pasada vi un documental en mi móvil. ***Lo*** *vi con mi novio.*

Módulo 2 ¡A repasar!

Leer 1 ***Refresh your memory!* Unjumble these sentences and then translate them into English. Remember to add the correct punctuation too.**

Example: en/ porque/ rápido/ prefiero/ es/ viajar/ tren/ más/
Prefiero viajar en tren porque es más rápido.
I prefer to travel by train as it is quicker.

1 te/vacaciones?/ir/gustaría/de/¿Adónde
2 favor/una/para/Quisiera/por/cinco/mesa/personas
3 estaba/y/Me/hotel/limpio/todo/quedé/en/un/muy
4 a/familia/verano/con/En/playa/ir/suelo/la/mi
5 semana/visitar/donde/una/Acabamos/Valencia/de/pasamos
6 ir/con/próximo/a/El/novia/al/extranjero/año/voy/mi

Escuchar 2 ***Refresh your memory!* Listen to Karima talking about a recent holiday. What does she say about the campsite?**

Note down:

★★★★ four facilities at the campsite
★★★ three points about the location
★★ two problems she had
★ one fact about the cost

Escribir 3 ***Refresh your memory!* Divide your page into <u>four</u> different sections with the following verb-tense headings. Write <u>four</u> example sentences for each tense. Look back at Module 2 to help you.**

- **Present tense**
  Se puede probar platos típicos.
- **Preterite tense**
  El primer día tomé el sol porque hizo buen tiempo.
- **Imperfect tense**
  El apartamento estaba en el centro y las habitaciones eran grandes.
- **Near future tense**
  Mañana vamos a sacar fotos de la arquitectura famosa.

Escuchar 4 **Indra is talking about her holidays. What does she say? Listen to the recording and choose A, B or C for each question. (1–4)**

1 Yesterday, Indra ...
A stayed in a country hotel.
B went for walks.
C learnt a lot.

2 First Indra ...
A learnt about the area.
B met new people.
C went to the beach.

3 In the hotel restaurant ...
A her mother had a bad experience.
B her mother ate a lot.
C the food was delicious.

4 Next year, Indra would prefer to ...
A relax on beaches.
B be outside.
C go skiing.

Prepare for this listening task by thinking about key vocabulary and tenses you will need to listen out for to pick the correct answer. You would expect to hear *el campo* for the first option of question 1.

Leer 5

Read Antonio's description of a Mexican festival. Answer the following questions in English.

Ayer mi familia celebró el Día de Muertos y lo pasamos bien. Primero mi padre y yo fuimos al cementerio donde pusimos muchas flores en las tumbas y luego vimos los desfiles en las calles. Normalmente también preparamos muchos platos típicos para celebrar a los muertos, pero este año mi abuela cocinó todo en su casa.

Aunque es un festival mexicano también es popular en muchos países donde se habla el español. Muchos jóvenes creen que esta celebración es la mejor porque les encantan los desfiles en ese día. Es imposible asistir a esta fiesta emocionante sin divertirse mucho y lo más importante es recordar a los ***parientes*** que han muerto.

el cementerio	*cemetery*
las tumbas	*graves*

1. What did Antonio and his family think about the recent celebration?
2. What did Antonio do first?
3. Why did they not prepare food this year?
4. Why do young people love this festival in particular?
5. What does the word ***parientes*** mean? Choose the correct letter:

A parents **B** relatives **C** costumes

Hablar 6

Look at the role play card and prepare what you are going to say.

You are talking to your Spanish friend about your holiday.
Your teacher will play the part of your friend and will speak first.
You should address your friend as *tú*.
When you see this – **?** – you will have to ask a question.
You must include at least one verb in your response to each bullet point.
Task:

1. Say what you did during your last school holiday. (Give two details.)
2. Say what you normally like to do. (Give two details.)
3. Give two advantages of staying at a campsite.
4. Say what you want to do next holiday. (Give one detail.)
5. **?** Ask your friend a question about their holiday preferences.

Don't overcomplicate your answers by trying to translate text from the instructions exactly. For example, when giving two advantages of camping, you don't have to use the word 'advantage'. Instead, you could start your answer: *Me gusta mucho el camping porque ...*

Hablar 7

Practise what you have prepared. Then, using your notes, listen and respond to the teacher.

Hablar 8

Paula, your friend, has contributed to a blog about Spanish New Year. With a partner, read aloud the following text in Spanish.

La Nochevieja es una celebración maravillosa.
Suelo ver los fuegos artificiales porque es una tradición genial.
Cada año mis vecinos salen a las calles y llevan comida para celebrar.
Mucha gente prefiere disfrutar de una fiesta en un bar o restaurante antes de volver a casa.
El año pasado lo pasamos muy bien en el piso de mi primo.

Pay particular attention to these words in the reading aloud task.

Take extra care with how you pronounce the underlined sounds above:

- ***ll*** sounds like English y
- ***j***, ***ge*** and ***gi*** sound like English 'h'.

Escuchar 9

Listen and check your pronunciation. What questions were asked after the reading aloud task? Write these questions down in Spanish.

Hablar 10

Prepare your own answers to the questions from exercise 9 and read them aloud to a partner.

Escribir 11

Translate the following sentences into Spanish.

1. Every summer I usually visit different places.
2. Normally we don't stay in a hotel because it is expensive.
3. I like to travel by train because it is safer.
4. I have just returned from the coast but I broke my camera.
5. Next month, we will go to a historic city.

Módulo 3

¡A repasar!

Escuchar **1** ***Refresh your memory!*** **Listen to five people describing themselves. Copy and complete the table in Spanish. Use the Module 3 vocabulary pages to check your spelling. (1–5)**

	El pelo y los ojos	Descripción física	Carácter	Se parece a ...
1	los ojos azules el pelo corto y marrón	alto	serio	su abuelo

Leer **2** ***Refresh your memory!*** **Match the questions to the answers. Then translate each question and answer into English.**

1 ¿Cómo es un buen amigo?
2 ¿Cómo es tu mejor amigo o tu mejor amiga físicamente?
3 ¿Desde cuándo sois amigos?
4 ¿Qué actividades hiciste la semana pasada con tu mejor amigo o amiga?
5 ¿A quién admiras?
6 ¿Desde hace cuánto tiempo?

a Desde hace mucho tiempo.
b Somos amigos desde hace tres años.
c Vimos una película buena y luego fuimos a la fiesta de un amigo.
d Sigo a la cantante Olivia Rodrigo en las redes y la admiro mucho porque escribe sus propias canciones.
e Se llama Isabel, tiene el pelo largo, es morena y lleva gafas.
f Para mí te apoya en lo bueno y lo malo y te hace reír.

Escribir **3** ***Refresh your memory!*** **Write your own answers to the questions in exercise 2. Look back at Module 3 for ideas.**

When revising, build up a bank of questions on each theme. Questions are very important for your speaking assessment. You will need to ask a question as part of your role play task; for the reading aloud task you will need to answer four questions, and after the photo card task you will need to participate in a conversation.

Escuchar **4** **You are listening to a young person talk about being online. (1–2)**

Choose the correct **number** of the activity he mentions.

Choose the correct **letter** for when it takes place.

Activity

1	Reading the news
2	Learning new games
3	Posting comments
4	Finding role models

When

P	Past
N	Now
F	Future

Escuchar **5** **You are going to hear five short sentences about relationships and identity. Listen carefully and, using your knowledge of Spanish sounds, write down in Spanish exactly what you hear for each sentence.**

Remember that ***ga***, ***go*** and ***gu*** are hard 'g' sounds, similar to 'g' in English but ***j***, ***ge*** and ***gi*** sound like a stronger version of 'h' in English. Watch out for these sounds in dictation tasks.

Leer 6 **Read these posts about mental health. Which post matches which description? Choose the correct letter.**

A La juventud de hoy sufre mucho de problemas mentales que le afectan.
B Muchos jóvenes sienten mucha presión de grupo o sufren acoso escolar.
C El uso excesivo de las redes sociales puede hacerte daño.
D Es muy común sentirse muy solos aunque pasan mucho tiempo en Internet.
E Evitar el estrés es muy importante en la época de exámenes.

1 addiction to social media **2** loneliness **3** peer pressure

When matching descriptions to statements, think about the Spanish for different types of words. For example, when thinking about the noun 'loneliness', you may need to look for the adjective 'alone' or 'isolated'.

Leer 7 **Translate the following sentences into English.**

1 Mi mejor amiga Nadia y yo siempre estamos juntas.
2 Nos llevamos bien y yo sé que puedo contar con ella.
3 La conocí en el colegio hace siete años.
4 Creo que soy bastante seria y Nadia es más abierta, pero nos preocupan las mismas cosas.
5 Hace tres días, paseamos al perro de mi abuelo en el parque.

Escribir 8 **You are writing a blog about friendship. Write approximately 150 words in Spanish. You must write something about both bullet points.**

Mention:

- the positive **and** negative aspects of having a best friend
- the last time you went out with a friend or a group of friends.

To answer the first bullet point, look back at Module 3 and revise phrases about friendships. For example, to discuss the positive aspects of having a best friend, you could say, 'A best friend supports you and knows you well.' To discuss the negative aspects, you could explain the advantages of having lots of friends instead. For example, 'A group of friends can give you better advice.'

Módulo 4 ¡A repasar!

Leer 1 ***Refresh your memory!*** **Put the following sentences describing healthy or unhealthy habits into a table with the column headings *costumbres saludables* and *costumbres malas*.**

Suelo comer verduras, pescado y arroz.

Me acuesto demasiado tarde.

Como carne roja todos los días.

Hago yoga o meditación antes de dormir.

Como muchos caramelos.

Me encantan las bebidas con azúcar.

Después de levantarme, voy al gimnasio.

Para el desayuno tomo un café y alguna fruta.

Mi dieta es sana y equilibrada.

Evito la comida con mucho azúcar.

Si tengo sed, siempre bebo agua.

Si tengo hambre, siempre como chocolate.

Escribir 2 ***Refresh your memory!*** **Create a short paragraph about your own healthy or unhealthy habits by copying or amending the sentences from exercise 1. Use time references to add detail to your answer.**

- ✓ Siempre / todos los días
- ✓ Algunas tardes/noches
- ✓ Nunca / casi nunca

Escuchar 3 ***Refresh your memory!*** **Listen to these young people talking about their meals. For each person, note down the time they eat and what they usually eat. (1–5)**

When listening for times, remember the word order is different: listen out for the hour first and then for ***y*** (minutes past) or ***menos*** (minutes to).

Escuchar 4 **Your Spanish friend Amira is talking about healthy habits. What does she say? Choose A if only statement A is correct. Choose B if only statement B is correct. Choose A+B if both statements A and B are correct. (1–4)**

1 Amira always ...
  A gets up before seven o'clock every day.
  B eats breakfast before exercising.

2 To look after her mental health ...
  A she reads before doing her homework.
  B she plays sport after doing her homework.

3 With regards to food ...
  A she is careful with what she eats.
  B she eats lots of fresh vegetables.

4 Amira has a healthy diet as ...
  A she avoids sugary drinks.
  B she does not want to get ill.

Escribir 5 **Translate the following sentences into Spanish.**

1 I have a healthy routine and I take care of my diet.
2 During the week, I wake up early and I have breakfast.
3 I am always hungry but I am never thirsty.
4 Two weeks ago, I broke my leg when I fell off my bicycle.
5 Now my leg hurts and I will rest a lot.

Leer 6 **You read these comments from some Spanish young people about eating out in Spain. Match the correct person to each question by choosing the correct letter. (A–F)**

A Alberto
España está experimentando una emocionante revolución gastronómica. En todo el país, numerosos restaurantes han empezado a ofrecer una variedad de opciones para cada gusto.

B Bartolo
Lo bueno es que ahora muchos restaurantes ofrecen muchos platos ideales para la dieta vegana, que está muy de moda.

C Carolina
Sobre todo los clientes quieren comida buena y sana a un buen precio. Esto es posible en muchas ciudades grandes, pero es más difícil encontrar comida saludable en los pueblos pequeños.

D Daniela
Existen muchos lugares innovadores en Madrid, como una cafetería donde puedes tomar un café o una merienda con gatos. Esta idea nació en Japón.

E Eduardo
Lo mejor de los restaurantes españoles es la variedad de la comida. En la mayoría de los lugares tradicionales, la cocina española es muy rica con un gran uso de productos frescos y saludables.

F Francisca
Prefiero la comida de otros países y lo bueno es que nunca te aburres en una ciudad como Valencia, donde yo vivo, porque puedes hacer una gira gastronómica mundial sin salir de la ciudad.

1 Who says that finding healthy food outside cities is tricky?
2 Who mentions the fact that restaurants cater for non-meat-based diets?
3 Who likes the fact that there are some unusual places to eat?
4 Who is pleased that they can try food from different places?

una gira gastronómica	*a gastronomic tour*
aburrirse	*to get bored*

Hablar 7 **Alejandro, your Venezuelan friend, has contributed to a blog about wellbeing. With a partner, read aloud the following text in Spanish.**

Afortunadamente ahora nun<u>ca</u> estoy <u>ca</u>nsado.
Antes no tenía energía porque bebía demasiadas bebidas <u>co</u>n azú<u>ca</u>r.
Mientras que ahora siempre bebo muchísima agua.
También <u>ca</u>si siempre evito la <u>co</u>mida mala.
Para mejorar la salud física y mental hay que aumentar el nivel de ejer<u>cici</u>o.

Take extra care with how you pronounce the underlined sounds when reading aloud the text in exercise 6. Remember that:
- ***ce*** and ***ci*** are pronounced like 'th' in most of Spain
- ***ca*** is a hard 'k' sound.

Escuchar 8 **Listen and check your pronunciation.**

Hablar 9 **Now answer these <u>four</u> follow-up questions related to the topic of Healthy living and lifestyle.**

- ¿Cómo es tu dieta?
- ¿Qué costumbres saludables tienes?
- ¿A qué hora te levantas y te acuestas?
- ¿Qué haces para estar en forma?

Hablar 10 **Prepare and practise this photo card. Your description could cover details such as people/things, location and activities.**

Photo 1

Photo 2

- During your preparation time, look at the two photos. You may make as many notes as you wish on an Additional Answer Sheet and use these notes during the test.
- Your teacher will ask you to talk about the content of these photos. The recommended time is approximately <u>one</u> minute. You must say at least one thing about each photo.
- After you have finished describing the photos, your teacher will then ask you questions related to any of the topics within the theme of **People and lifestyle**.

Módulo 5

¡A repasar!

Escribir 1

***Refresh your memory!* Use these sentence starters to write eight sentences about your school life. Look back through Module 5, and the vocabulary pages, for ideas.**

a Para ir al instituto llevo ___.
b Normalmente voy al instituto ___ porque ___.
c Mis clases empiezan ___ y terminan ___.
d En la hora de comer suelo ___ o ___.
e Mi asignatura favorita es ___ porque ___.
f Sin embargo, odio ___ porque ___.
g Hay unas instalaciones buenas en mi colegio como ___ y ___.
h Llevo ___ participando en ___ y me gusta porque te permite ___.

Leer 2

***Refresh your memory!* Write down the word for the gap in each sentence, using a verb from the box. Then match each question to your answers for exercise 1.**

Example: 1 *vas b*

1 ¿Cómo ___ al colegio?
2 ¿Qué ropa ___ en el insti?
3 ¿Qué asignaturas ___?
4 ¿Cuánto tiempo llevas ___ en el club?
5 ¿Cómo ___ las instalaciones?
6 ¿Qué ___ hacer en la hora de comer?
7 ¿Cómo ___ tu día en el instituto?
8 ¿Qué asignaturas te ___?

son gustan es participando
odias sueles llevas vas

Escuchar 3

***Refresh your memory!* For each person, note down what they like and what they don't like about their school. (1–5)**

Escuchar 4

Alba and Iván are talking about their schools. What do they say? Listen and choose A, B or C for each question. (1–2) Answer both parts of the question.

1 Alba's school has ...
A few rules.
B bullying.
C no uniform.

Alba would like to have ...
A more teachers.
B phones in class.
C better geography lessons.

2 Iván describes the school trips as ...
A expensive.
B badly organised.
C good value for money.

Last year Iván preferred ...
A the local cuisine.
B the beautiful views.
C doing sport.

Remember that there will be distractors, so you will need to understand full sentences rather than pick out single words.

Escuchar
5

You are going to hear <u>five</u> short sentences about life at school. Listen carefully and, using your knowledge of Spanish sounds, write down in Spanish exactly what you hear for each sentence.

Remember that the ***ce***, ***ci*** and ***z*** sounds often sound like 'th' in 'thin' (in Spain) and 's' in 'sit' (in Latin America).
Be careful to transcribe these sounds correctly in exercise 5.

Leer
6

You see a website where Spanish people talk about tests and exams. What are their opinions? Choose P for a positive opinion, N for a negative opinion or P+N for a positive and negative opinion for each person.

Marcos
La temporada de exámenes es la temporada de pánico para algunos alumnos en el instituto pero no para mí. Entiendo que son necesarios. Creo que ayudan a los alumnos a desarrollar su confianza y su interés en los estudios.

Elena
Soy consciente de que hay que trabajar duro para sacar buenas notas en las pruebas. Por eso estudio mucho. Este verano asistiré a más clases de repaso para mejorar mi nivel. Tengo ganas de hacerlas.

Maite
Mis amigas siempre tienen éxito, pero a mí me cuesta leer y entender las preguntas. No comprendo a los alumnos a los que les gustan los exámenes.

Karima
Siempre paso mucho tiempo repasando e intento dormir bien antes de una prueba y normalmente saco buenas notas, aunque las pruebas de matemáticas son fatales.

Leer
7

Translate these sentences into English.

1. Mi asignatura favorita es el inglés porque me encanta la lectura.
2. Mis amigos y yo sacábamos buenas notas en dibujo y música.
3. El año pasado no tenía mucha confianza en las ciencias.
4. Sin embargo, este año el profesor me escucha y me explica las cosas muy bien.
5. En junio, tengo una prueba y repasaré mucho porque quiero aprobar.

When translating, remember to read all the sentences first, before you start, as you will often not need to translate every single word. For example, you will often need to leave out articles ('a', 'the', 'some'), as English does not use them as much as Spanish, and you will also need to look out for set phrases that cannot be translated word for word.

Escribir
8

You are writing a post for a Spanish website about your school. Write approximately 90 words in Spanish. You must write something about each bullet point.

Mention:

- what your school facilities are like
- a club or extracurricular activity you did at school recently
- a school trip that you will take this year.

¡A repasar!

Escuchar 1 ***Refresh your memory!*** **Where is ...? Listen to the directions and use the map to write down the name of the place. (1–6)**

Example: 1 *el museo*

Directions are often included in lists with prepositions, as they are key to saying where something is located. You use the **imperative** to give directions:

gira *a la izquierda*	**turn** left
toma *la segunda calle a la derecha*	**take** the second street on the right
pasa *el puente*	**pass** the bridge
cruza *la plaza*	**cross** the square

Leer 2 ***Refresh your memory!*** **Change these infinitive verbs into the perfect tense to create sentences about how Barcelona has changed. Then translate the sentences into English.**

1 Barcelona (cambiar) muchísimo en los últimos diez años.
2 Muchas calles (cerrar) el paso a los coches en varios barrios.
3 Muchas tiendas nuevas de ropa (abrir).
4 Lo bueno es que (construir) más edificios modernos.
5 También (crear) más espacios verdes con muchos árboles.
6 La ciudad (ponerse) más limpia y más segura.

Escribir 3 ***Refresh your memory!*** **In pairs, choose two of the following questions and create a vocabulary mind map for each one. Make sure each mind map contains at least ten words or phrases.**

- ¿Qué hay en tu región?
- ¿Te gusta ir de compras?
- ¿Qué es mejor, vivir en el campo o en la ciudad?
- ¿Cómo era tu zona antes y cómo es ahora?
- ¿Qué hiciste recientemente en tu zona?
- ¿Cómo cambiarías tu zona?

¿Qué hay en tu región?
- Hay dos ríos hermosos.
- No hay montañas.
- Es una región perfecta para disfrutar de la naturaleza.
- En mi pueblo tenemos tres parques enormes.

Escuchar 4 **Gaby is talking about her city. What does she say? Answer the questions in English. (1–4)**

1 What did her city not use to have?
2 Why is shopping in the city better now?
3 What do most tourists come to do in the city?
4 Why did the tourists not see the fireworks last year?

Leer 5 **Read Luis's article for a school newspaper about the singer Juanes. Complete the sentences by choosing the correct letter.**

Juanes es un famoso cantante colombiano de Medellín que canta tanto sobre el amor como sobre las dificultades. Aprendió la guitarra escuchando música latinoamericana. Ha ganado muchos premios y mucha gente lo considera como uno de los artistas más influyentes de América Latina.

Durante su carrera, Juanes ha utilizado su fama para luchar por la paz en Colombia. Tiene un amor profundo por Medellín y aún tiene una casa en esa ciudad, aunque vive en Miami.

Medellín es la segunda ciudad más grande de Colombia y es famosa por su clima agradable. Ahora es un lugar creativo con mucha tecnología moderna. Sin embargo, en el pasado, había más violencia y además en las calles faltaba seguridad.

influyente *influential*

1 Juanes mainly sings about ...
- **A** crime and problems.
- **B** positive and negative aspects of life.
- **C** Medellín.

2 Juanes has ...
- **A** won many awards.
- **B** met lots of influential people.
- **C** stopped playing guitar.

3 As well as music, Juanes is interested in ...
- **A** living in Miami.
- **B** travelling around Colombia.
- **C** fighting for peace in Colombia.

4 Medellín is famous for its ...
- **A** pleasant climate.
- **B** lack of good technology.
- **C** unsafe streets.

Hablar 6 **Marta, your Colombian friend, has contributed to a blog about Medellín. With a partner, read aloud the following text in Spanish.**

Medellín se encuentra en Latinoamérica.

La mejor época para visitar es diciembre.

Han desarrollado mi barrio y ahora tenemos más posibilidades de trabajo.

Los habitantes se sienten orgullosos de vivir en esta región del país.

Muchos jóvenes salen a las calles para comer algo sencillo y barato.

Take extra care with how you pronounce the underlined sounds when reading aloud the text in exercise 6. Remember to
- pronounce each vowel carefully when two come together
- pronounce ***ll*** like English 'y'
- roll the 'r' when you pronounce ***rr***.

Practise saying the word *desarrollado* to make sure you are saying each sound correctly.

Escuchar 7 **Listen and check your pronunciation. Write down the four follow-up questions the teacher asks after the reading aloud task. Make notes in English on the answers that you hear. Then prepare your own answers to the questions.**

Escribir 8 **Look at the role play card and write done notes about what you are going to say.**

For the question about shopping, you could ask 'Do you like shopping?' Or 'What are the shops like in your area?' Or even 'Do you have a shopping centre near your house?'

You are talking to your Colombian friend about where you live.

Your teacher will play the part of your friend and speak first.

You should address your friend as *tú*.

When you see this – **?** – you will have to ask a question.

You must include at least one verb in your response to each bullet point.

Task:

1 Say what you think about where you live. (Give two details.)

2 Give your opinion of shops in your area. (Give one detail.)

3 **?** Ask your friend a question about shopping.

4 Say what you did in your area last week. (Give two details.)

5 Say if you prefer to go shopping or buy things online. (Give one opinion and one reason.)

Hablar 9 **Practise what you have prepared. Then, using your notes, listen and respond to the teacher.**

¡A repasar!

Leer 1

Refresh your memory! **What's the problem? Match the issue to the definition.**

1 la discriminación
2 el hambre
3 el cambio climático
4 la contaminación
5 la falta de agua
6 la igualdad

a la falta de suficiente comida que afecta a millones de personas a nivel mundial
b el aumento de la temperatura del planeta causado por las actividades del ser humano
c el derecho que tenemos a ser iguales y a ser tratados con respeto, independientemente de nuestra nacionalidad, color, sexo, idioma, religión u opinión política
d el odio o la exclusión de una persona debido a su color de piel, origen étnico o lengua
e afecta la calidad del aire o del agua y causa daño al medioambiente y a las personas
f un problema grave cuando la gente no tiene acceso a este recurso esencial

Escribir 2

Refresh your memory! **Complete the sentences with an appropriate phrase. Watch out for one that needs the present subjunctive. Use the vocabulary pages from Module 7 to help you get ideas.**

1 El plástico causa ...
2 Es importante proteger los bosques porque ...
3 Se debería participar en ...
4 El gobierno quiere que la gente ...
5 Para ayudar al medioambiente en el colegio ...
6 Ayudar en tu comunidad es ...

Escuchar 3

Refresh your memory! **Listen to these young people describing different events. (1–5) Note down what they were doing at the time.**

Escuchar 4

Listen to Manat and Enrique talking about the advantages and disadvantages of protesting. What do they say? Choose the correct letter to complete the sentences. (1–2)

1 Manat thinks that ...
  A protesting can lead to violence.
  B we should protest more often.
  C society is taking away our right to protest.

2 Enrique believes that ...
  A protests are bad for the environment.
  B protesting against companies is key.
  C governments are listening.

Escuchar 5

You are going to hear <u>five</u> short sentences about the environment. Listen carefully and, using your knowledge of Spanish sounds, write down in Spanish exactly what you hear for each sentence.

Remember, the letter 'v' is pronounced the same as 'b' in Spanish. Therefore, for dictation tasks with words containing these letters, you need to think carefully about their spelling.

Leer 6

Read this blog about community action, written by Natalia in Ecuador. Answer the questions in English.

Tanto los jóvenes como los ancianos son claves para mejorar sus comunidades. En la costa ecuatoriana, limpiar los manglares no solo ayuda a proteger las plantas y los animales sino también contribuye a calmar los efectos del cambio climático. Desde los años ochenta se ha perdido más de ochenta por ciento de los manglares.

Participé en un proyecto social organizado por un colectivo de mujeres que tomó acción contra la continua pérdida de los manglares preciosos con resultados positivos. Limpiamos la gran cantidad de basura que se encuentra en los manglares, como plástico, metal y caucho. Pronto comenzaremos una campaña educativa en las redes sociales y seguiremos recogiendo para que los manglares puedan sobrevivir en el futuro.

los manglares	*mangroves (trees or shrubs growing in coastal areas)*
el caucho	*rubber*

1 According to the blog, which groups of people are key for helping their communities?
2 What helps prevent more climate change?
3 Who organised the project that Natalia participated in?
4 What was the aim of the project?
5 What <u>two</u> things will the project do next?

When you see the reflexive pronoun ***se***, you need to decide if it is used with a reflexive verb or whether it is being used to avoid the passive. If it is avoiding the passive, you should translate the sentence into the passive voice in English, e.g. ***se apagan las luces*** (the lights are turned off).

Leer 7

Translate the following sentences into English.

1 En nuestro colegio, pensamos que el cuidado del medioambiente es importante.
2 Siempre seguimos la regla de reducir, reutilizar y reciclar.
3 El mes pasado, participé en una campaña para ahorrar energía.
4 Piensa dos veces antes de comprar productos plásticos y evítalos si puedes.
5 Se separa y se tira la basura pero también debemos reducir la cantidad que producimos.

Hablar 8

Prepare and perform this photo card. Your description could cover details such as people/things, location and activities.

- During your preparation time, look at the two photos. You may make as many notes as you wish on an Additional Answer Sheet and use these notes during the test.
- Your teacher will ask you to talk about the content of these photos. The recommended time is approximately <u>one</u> minute. You must say at least one thing about each photo.
- After you have finished describing the photos, your teacher will then ask you questions related to any of the topics within the theme of **Communication and the world around us**.

Photo 1

Photo 2

Try not to translate whole phrases word for word in the preparation time for speaking tasks but instead start by thinking of what you **can** say. For these photos, as a starting point, you could write down words and phrases that come to mind about helping in a food bank, and then write down words related to recycling or clearing rubbish.

Módulo 8 ¡A repasar!

Escuchar 1 ***Refresh your memory!*** **Listen to the interview for a summer job. Write down, in Spanish, the five questions the candidate is asked. Then note down, in English, his replies.**

Escribir 2 ***Refresh your memory!*** **Look back at Module 8, then write out and complete these sentences about studying, work and the future.**

1. Vale la pena hacer el bachillerato si ___.
2. La formación profesional ofrece la posibilidad de ___.
3. Para ganar dinero ___.
4. Para lograr un trabajo tienes que ___.
5. Antes me interesaba ___ pero ahora quiero ___.
6. Es importante aprender otros idiomas porque ___.
7. En la próxima década creo que el trabajo ___.
8. En mi opinión la inteligencia artificial ___.

Leer 3 ***Refresh your memory!*** **With a partner, read aloud your sentences from exercise 2 to each other. Then translate your partner's sentences into English.**

Escuchar 4 **Listen to the voicemail message that Alba leaves. Complete the sentences by choosing the correct letter.**

1. Alba has ...
   - **A** learnt to drive.
   - **B** passed her exams.
   - **C** moved to the countryside.
2. She plans to ...
   - **A** go to university.
   - **B** travel with her friends.
   - **C** do a vocational course.

In this task, you need to listen carefully to the meaning of the whole sentence before choosing an answer. Before starting, use the answer options to help you think about the key vocabulary you need to listen out for.

Escuchar 5 **Someone is giving their views about jobs and the future. For each gap, write the correct word in English. (1–2)**

Example: The speaker says he is going to study ***languages*** *and he wants to be a* ***lawyer****.*

1. Students often work in ___ rather than ___.
2. When looking for jobs, young people should consider the ___ and ___.

Pay attention to the stress patterns of words and any accents. Remember that, for words with an accented vowel, you will stress the vowel sound (*prácticas*). Words ending in a vowel, 'n' or 's' will be stressed on the second-to-last syllable (*trabajado*) and words ending in any other letter are stressed on the final syllable (*aprender*).

Hablar 6 **Javier, your Colombian friend, writes tips on job-hunting for an online newspaper. With a partner, read out the text below, paying attention to the stress patterns of the words.**

Considera cuáles son tus puntos débiles.

Hay que buscar oportunidades para solicitar prácticas laborales.

He trabajado en una fábrica enorme donde aprendí mucho.

Aprender idiomas distintos te permite descubrir otras culturas.

Para tener éxito, es importante estudiar otras lenguas.

Escuchar 7 **Listen and check your pronunciation.**

Hablar 8 **Practise your answers to these four follow-up questions to the reading aloud task that relate to the topic of education and work.**

- ¿Qué haces ahora para ganar dinero?
- ¿Qué quieres hacer?
- ¿Qué tipo de trabajo te interesa?
- ¿Qué piensas de aprender idiomas?

Leer 9 **Read this article about part-time work in Spain.**

Desafortunadamente, son los jóvenes quienes sufren el impacto más alto del paro. Según el Ministerio de Trabajo, más del cuarenta por ciento de los jóvenes españoles menores de veinticinco años trabajan a tiempo parcial y las mujeres de esta edad son las que trabajan más de esta manera: una de cada dos mujeres entre dieciséis y veinticuatro años trabaja a tiempo parcial. Estos jóvenes ganarán salarios más bajos y muchas veces trabajan más horas de las que se les pagan. Es una situación ***inquietante***.

El motivo de trabajar a tiempo parcial depende de la edad de la persona. Por un lado, es una manera efectiva de poder seguir estudiando, y por otro lado, en muchos casos la gente lo hace porque no ha podido encontrar un trabajo a tiempo completo.

tiempo parcial/completo *part-time/full-time*

Complete the sentences below. Choose the correct letter, **A**, **B** or **C**, for each question.

1 Young people are more likely to …
A want to work part-time.
B be working full-time.
C be unemployed.

2 Those young people who work part-time are mostly …
A studying.
B women.
C under twenty.

3 The proportion of young females who work part-time is …
A one in four.
B one in two.
C one in forty.

4 One problem with working part-time is …
A you work more hours than you are paid for.
B the contracts are temporary.
C you miss out on training.

5 Read the first paragraph again. What is the meaning of ***inquietante***?
A quiet
B curious
C troubling

Escribir 10 **Translate the following sentences into Spanish.**

1 This job interests me as I love to meet new people.
2 I have work experience because I have been working for six months in a cafe.
3 In addition, I believe I am a practical and hard-working person.
4 Before, I wanted to work in a shop but now I want to do a job outside.
5 I have decided that it is my dream to be a nurse.

Escribir 11 **You are writing a blog about learning languages. Write approximately 150 words in Spanish. You must write something about both bullet points.**

Mention:

- the positive aspects of learning a language
- when you last spoke in a different language.

Look back at Unit 4 of Module 8 to gather vocabulary for this task. Remember that you do not need to be truthful! For the second bullet, you can say you last spoke Spanish on holiday or with a Spanish friend, even if you can't think of when you last spoke Spanish, or another language, outside the classroom!

Conversation questions

You can use these questions to help you prepare for two different sections of the speaking test:

- the questions that follow on from the **reading aloud task**
- the questions that you will be asked during the **photo card task**.

In the **reading aloud task** there is a short, unprepared conversation on the topic of the text, after you read the text out loud. This will include four compulsory questions.

In the **photo card task** you will have to describe two photos from one of the three themes. Afterwards, there will be a more general conversation in which you have the opportunity to show that you know a range of structures and tenses in Spanish.

Módulo 1 (pages 6–29)

Theme 3: Communication and the world around us

1 ¿Qué haces en tu móvil normalmente?
2 ¿Qué vas a hacer en tu móvil mañana?
3 ¿Qué hiciste en tu móvil ayer?
4 ¿Cuánto tiempo pasas en tu móvil/dispositivo?
5 ¿Qué piensas de las redes sociales?

Theme 2: Popular Culture

6 ¿Qué actividades te gusta hacer en tu tiempo libre?
7 ¿Qué deportes haces?
8 ¿Eres miembro de un club o equipo?
9 ¿Qué haces normalmente los fines de semana?
10 ¿Qué vas a hacer este fin de semana?
11 ¿Qué hiciste el fin de semana pasado?
12 Describe un día fatal. ¿Qué pasó?

Módulo 2 (pages 30–53)

Theme 2: Popular culture
Theme 3: Communication and the world around us

1 ¿Adónde te gustaría ir de vacaciones?
2 ¿Qué te gustaría hacer allí?
3 ¿Cómo te gustaría viajar? ¿Por qué?
4 ¿Cuál es la fiesta más divertida? ¿Por qué?
5 ¿Qué comida te gusta comer cuando vas a un restaurante?
6 ¿Qué sueles hacer en verano?
7 ¿Qué tal tus últimas vacaciones?
8 ¿Qué hiciste?
9 ¿Qué fue lo mejor de tus vacaciones?
10 ¿Dónde te quedaste?
11 ¿Cómo era el pueblo / la ciudad?
12 ¿Adónde vas a ir de vacaciones el año próximo?

Módulo 3 (pages 56–81)

Theme 1: People and lifestyle
Theme 2: Popular culture
Theme 3: Communication and the world around us

1 ¿A quién sigues en las redes sociales? ¿Por qué?
2 Describe a tu persona famosa favorita. ¿Por qué te gusta?
3 ¿Qué te gusta hacer con la tecnología / en las redes sociales? ¿Por qué?
4 ¿Para qué usaste la tecnología/las redes sociales la semana pasada?
5 ¿Cómo eres físicamente?
6 ¿Cómo es tu familia? Describe una celebración reciente con tu familia.
7 ¿Cómo es tu relación con tus amigos?
8 ¿Cómo es un buen amigo?
9 ¿Qué actividades hiciste con tu mejor amigo/a el fin de semana pasado?
10 ¿Qué cosas te preocupan? ¿Cuál es tu sueño?

Módulo 4 (pages 82–105)

Theme 1: People and lifestyle

1 ¿Qué plato de España o Sudamérica te gustaría probar? ¿Por qué?
2 ¿Cómo es tu día típico?
3 ¿Tienes costumbres no saludables?
4 ¿Qué tomas para el desayuno/la comida/la cena?
5 ¿Cómo es tu dieta?
6 ¿Qué hay que hacer para tener una dieta sana?
7 ¿Cómo era tu vida cuando tenías [seis] años? ¿Cómo es tu vida ahora?
8 ¿Qué te gustaba comer y beber cuando eras niño/a?
9 ¿Qué hacías en tu tiempo libre cuando eras pequeño?
10 ¿Qué harás para mejorar tu salud y evitar problemas en el futuro?

How to prepare:
- Read through the questions to check you understand them. Focus on the question words (*¿Qué? ¿Cómo? ¿Dónde?* etc.).
- Check the verbs and time phrases to understand which time frame the questions are about.
- Then practise answering the questions using full sentences.
- Think about how you could extend your answers using more complex structures, particularly for answering questions during the **photo card task** conversation.

Ways to extend your answers:
- Join together ideas with connectives (*y, pero, también* etc.)
- Add in opinions and justify them: *me gusta / odio … porque …*
- Use opposing arguments: *Por un lado, … Por otro lado, … Sin embargo, …*
- Add in examples of recent activities in the past tenses.
- Add in examples of future plans using a future tense.

Módulo 5 (pages 106–129)

Theme 1: People and lifestyle

1. ¿Cómo es tu instituto?
2. ¿Cómo es tu día escolar?
3. ¿Qué actividades extraescolares haces?
4. ¿Qué hiciste recientemente con el club/equipo?
5. ¿Qué asignaturas te gustan y no te gustan? ¿Por qué (no)?
6. ¿Qué harás para tener éxito en el futuro?
7. ¿Qué es lo bueno y lo malo de tu instituto?
8. ¿Cómo cambiarías tu instituto?
9. ¿Cómo sería tu profesor(a) ideal?
10. ¿Adónde fuiste de viaje con tu instituto el año pasado? ¿Qué hiciste?

Módulo 7 (pages 158–181)

Theme 3: Communication and the world around us

1. ¿Qué haces para ayudar en tu comunidad o en la sociedad? ¿Por qué lo haces?
2. ¿Qué hiciste en el pasado para ayudar a otras personas?
3. ¿Qué más te gustaría hacer en el futuro para ayudar en tu comunidad o en la sociedad?
4. Para ti, ¿cuál es el problema o la cuestión más grave que afecta al planeta? ¿Por qué?
5. ¿Qué haces para cuidar el medioambiente en casa?
6. ¿Y en tu colegio? ¿Qué cosas hacéis para ayudar?
7. ¿Qué hiciste en el pasado para ayudar al medioambiente?
8. ¿Y en el futuro? ¿Qué más te gustaría hacer para ayudar?
9. ¿Qué problema {del mundo} te preocupa más y qué acción quieres ver?
10. ¿Quién es tu modelo favorito a seguir?

Módulo 6 (pages 134–157)

Theme 3: Communication and the world around us

1. ¿Qué hay en tu región?
2. ¿Cómo es tu pueblo/ciudad?
3. ¿Cómo ha cambiado tu pueblo/ciudad recientemente?
4. ¿Prefieres vivir en el campo o en una ciudad? ¿Por qué?
5. ¿Qué es lo bueno / lo malo de vivir en tu zona?
6. ¿Prefieres ir al centro comercial o a las tiendas de tu barrio? ¿Por qué?
7. ¿Qué cosas te gusta comprar online y por qué?
8. ¿Cómo era tu zona/ciudad/pueblo antes?
9. ¿Cómo es [tu zona] ahora?
10. ¿Cómo cambiarías [tu zona]?
11. ¿Qué hiciste en [tu zona] la semana pasada?
12. ¿Qué vas a hacer en [tu zona] el fin de semana próximo?

Módulo 8 (pages 182–207)

Theme 1: People and lifestyle

1. ¿Qué planes tienes para el año próximo?
2. ¿Qué otros planes tienes para el futuro?
3. ¿Qué haces para ganar dinero?
4. ¿Cuáles son tus puntos positivos?
5. ¿Qué tipo de trabajo querías hacer en el pasado?
6. ¿Todavía te interesa hacer el mismo trabajo?
7. ¿Qué idiomas hablas?
8. ¿Por qué es importante aprender otras lenguas, en tu opinión?
9. ¿Cómo será el mundo laboral en el futuro?
10. ¿Cuál es tu opinión de la inteligencia artificial?

Spanish phonics

Here is a list of all the sounds that you need to understand and produce.
The **SSCs** (Sound Symbol Correspondences) will be assessed in the **reading aloud** and **dictation** tasks.

The **reading aloud** task will be the second task in your speaking test. You will have **15** minutes' preparation time for the whole speaking test, including this task. The task will be a short text of a minimum of 50 words on a topic from one of the themes.

The **dictation task** will form part of your listening paper. You will have to transcribe a minimum of 30 words in short spoken extracts. Two of the words will not be on the vocabulary lists. Practising the sounds on these pages will help with both the **reading aloud** and **dictation** tasks.

Sounds	Key words and other examples	Pages with a focus on this sound	Further examples to practise
a	nada amiga	page 7 page 185 page 215	Me gusta la natación al aire libre. Soy alta y simpática y llevo gafas. ¿Has apagado las luces?
o	no dos	page 7 page 185 page 215	Estos museos son modernos. Esos periódicos son buenos. No nos gustan los sitios peligrosos.
e	este españoles	page 7 page 185 page 215	Es una serie europea y diferente. Es heterosexual y vive en Sudamérica. Hemos celebrado una cena especial.
i	divertido interesante	page 7 page 185 page 215	Es una tradición histórica e increíble. Mi libro tiene ciento diecisiete páginas. Recibí mi primer mensaje de mi tío.
u	uno instituto	page 7 page 115 page 185 page 215	Disfruto mucho de la música popular. Algunos estudiantes discuten mucho. Lucho por un mundo justo y cultural.
ll	llevar calle	page 35 page 138 page 217 page 225	Es una silla amarilla. El castillo tiene detalles bonitos. Los caballos llegan a las calles.
ch	escuchar chicos	page 14 page 83	Como chocolate y bebo leche por la noche. Estas chicas luchan por sus derechos. Escuchamos canciones y charlamos.
ca	casa cara	page 14 page 91 page 159 page 221	Cada día tomo un café en el campo. En la caja puedes cambiar la camisa. Cerca del camping había un castillo.
co	como coche	page 14 page 91 page 159	Como comida rica en el colegio. Fui a un concierto clásico en la costa. Puedes contar con tus amigos simpáticos.
cu	cultura película	page 14 page 91 page 159	Para mi cumpleaños voy de excursión. Me encanta descubrir películas cubanas. Me preocupo si no escucho en clase.
cu + *vowel*	cuando recuerdo	page 14 page 91 page 141	¿Cuántos cuartos hay en tu casa? Estoy de acuerdo con cuarenta personas. La comida cuesta cincuenta y cuatro euros.
ce	centro cerca	page 14 page 83 page 106 page 221 page 223	A veces hay que celebrar o hacer una fiesta. Las tiendas cercanas están cerradas. Entonces tomamos la cena en el centro.
ci	gracias concierto	page 14 page 83 page 106 page 221 page 223	En la oficina fue fácil reciclar todo. Los edificios en la ciudad están sucios. No es difícil encontrar el cine en la ciudad.

Sounds	Key words and other examples	Pages with a focus on this sound	Further examples to practise
z	cabe**z**a **z**ona	page 106 page 223	Me duelen la cabe**z**a y el bra**z**o. En mi **z**ona hay una pla**z**a. Soy feli**z** porque compré **z**apatos a**z**ules.
que	por**que** **que**dar	page 39	¿**Que**damos en el bos**que** pe**que**ño? ¿Por **qué que**das a las dos? **Que**remos comer **que**so por**que** es rico.
qui	e**qui**po tran**qui**lo	page 39	A**quí** hay **qui**nce e**qui**pos. **Qui**ero vivir en una es**qui**na tran**qui**la. ¿**Qui**én **qui**ere al**qui**lar un coche?
ga	**ga**nar lle**ga**r	page 189 page 218	Mi ami**ga**, que es ve**ga**na, lle**ga** ahora. Pueden ju**ga**r en este lu**ga**r. Mi madre va a lle**ga**r con el re**ga**lo.
go	ten**go** lue**go**	page 189 page 218	El domin**go** ha**go** al**go** con mi familia. Lue**go** jue**go** a los videojue**go**s. En a**go**sto los días son más lar**go**s.
gu	al**gu**no **gu**star	page 189 page 218	Me **gu**sta tu casa anti**gu**a y se**gu**ra. Todos tus seguidores no son i**gu**ales. **Gu**stavo responde a al**gu**nas pre**gu**ntas.
ge	**ge**nte ima**ge**n	page 36 page 57 page 189 page 217–218	Es trans**gé**nero como mucha **ge**nte. **Ge**neralmente subo imá**ge**nes. Vamos a esco**ge**r platos ve**ge**tarianos.
gi	re**gi**ón cole**gi**o	page 36 page 57 page 189 page 217–218	En mi re**gi**ón somos reli**gi**osos. La tecnolo**gí**a ahorra ener**gí**a. Vir**gi**nia estudia en el cole**gi**o.
gue	hambur**gue**sa ju**gué**	page 189	Ju**gué** con Mi**gue**l y Á**gue**da. Apa**gué** el ordenador. Pa**gué** mucho por una hambur**gue**sa.
gui	al**gui**en se**gui**r	page 189	Se**gui**mos a al**gui**en famoso. ¿Tienes muchos se**gui**dores?
j	mu**j**er traba**j**o	page 36 page 57 page 217	En **j**ulio más **j**óvenes traba**j**an **j**untos. Es pelirro**j**o con los me**j**ores o**j**os azules. Durante el via**j**e **j**ugaron con sus hi**j**os.
ñ	monta**ñ**a espa**ñ**ol	page 115	Ma**ñ**ana vamos a Espa**ñ**a. El gato del se**ñ**or es peque**ñ**o. Al ni**ñ**o le gustaría tomar un ba**ñ**o.
v	**v**ida **v**erdad	page 57 page 159 page 226	Prefiero las **v**acaciones de prima**v**era. Los hue**v**os y las **v**erduras son sanos. **V**amos a **v**isitar a nuestros **v**ecinos.
-r- / -r	pe**r**o pensa**r**	page 83 page 111	Lee**r** y p**r**onuncia**r** las palab**r**as es du**r**o. No**r**malmente recue**r**do mi**r**a**r** mis co**r**reos. Quie**r**o rese**r**va**r** una mesa pa**r**a t**r**es.
rr / r- / -r- *(after* n, l *or* s*)*	ce**rr**ar son**r**eír	page 83 page 111 page 138 page 225	Mi pe**rr**o me hace son**r**eír. En el **r**estaurante el a**rr**oz está **r**ico. En los al**r**ededores la tie**rr**a es verde.
silent **h**	**h**ola **h**acer	page 57	Mis **h**ermanos tienen **h**ambre. **H**e **h**echo una tortilla con ocho **h**uevos. **H**emos **h**ablado y **h**emos comido **h**elados.
Stress patterns (Higher tier only)	f**á**cil r**á**pido sal**i**r ingl**é**s probl**e**ma	page 140 page 183 page 228	Las matem**á**ticas son **ú**tiles pero dif**í**ciles. Ant**o**nio hace su ex**a**men sin probl**e**mas. Dec**i**r la verd**a**d es tom**a**r responsabilid**a**d.

Escuchar 1 **Listen to and repeat each sound, example word and practice phrase. Make a list of the sounds or words you find most challenging and keep practising them. Then find other words for each sound to test your pronunciation.**

Role play skills

What do I need to know about the role play?

- It is an imagined conversation with a friend about a topic.
- It is the first part of the speaking test (**reading aloud** and **photo card** tasks follow).
- It is worth **ten** marks.
- Speak in the present tense except for one of the task points when you will need to answer in the past or near future tense.
- You will need to ask **one** question.
- Three of the task points will require: **two** details, **two** pieces of information or an opinion and a reason.
- To score full marks, you will need to include a verb in your answer.

Themes and topics

There are three themes and each theme has three topics. You will find examples of role plays in core modules, test practice pages and the revision module.

Module	Themes and topics
	Theme 1 – People and lifestyle
3, 4	**1** Identity and relationships with others
4	**2** Healthy living and lifestyle
5, 8	**3** Education and work
	Theme 2 – Popular culture
1	**1** Free-time activities
2, 4	**2** Customs, festivals and celebrations
1, 3, 6	**3** Celebrity culture
	Theme 3 – Communication and the world around us
2, 6	**1** Travel and tourism, including places of interest
1, 3, 8	**2** Media and technology
6, 7	**3** The environment and where people live

In order to score full marks, you will need to give a verb in your answer. Also, don't forget to ensure you answer both parts of the task. For example: If you are asked to **say what subject you prefer and why**

✗ don't say: Las matemáticas
✓ instead say: Prefiero las matemáticas porque me gusta el profesor.

Questions

These are a key part of role plays. You will need to ask **one** question. When it comes to your numbered item telling you to ask a question, it will be indicated with a '?' in front of it. Here are some examples.

Role play question tasks	Example questions
Ask your friend a question about where they live.	¿**Hay** una piscina en tu región?
Ask your friend a question about school.	¿**Te gusta** tu colegio / el inglés?
Ask your friend a question about food.	¿**A qué hora** cenas?
Ask your friend a question about celebrations.	¿**Qué** piensas de las fiestas españolas?
Ask your friend a question about free time.	¿**Qué** haces en tu tiempo libre?
Ask your friend a question about social media.	¿**A quién** sigues?

Learn these key question words and phrases:

¿A qué hora?	At what time?	*¿Dónde?*	Where?
¿Cómo?	How?	*¿Qué?*	What?
¿Cómo es ...?	What is ... like?	*¿Quién?*	Who?
¿Cuándo?	When?	*¿Cuál?*	Which?

Example role play

Scenario:
- You are talking to your Spanish friend.
- Your teacher will play the part of the friend and will speak first.
- You should address your friend as tú.
- When you see this - **?** – you will need to ask a question

You must include at least one verb in your response to each task point.

Task:
1. Say what you like about your best friend. (Give <u>two</u> details.)
2. Say what you like to do when you are with them. (Give <u>two</u> details.)
3. Say what you did last week with your friends. (Give <u>two</u> details.)
4. Say when you prefer to see your friends. (Give <u>one</u> detail.)
5. **?** Ask your friend a question about hobbies.

Teacher: ¿Qué te gusta de tu mejor amigo?
Student: Es simpático y me hace reír.
Teacher: ¿Qué te gusta hacer con tu mejor amigo?
Student: Nos gusta ir al cine o escuchar música.
Teacher: ¿Qué hiciste la semana pasada?
Student: La semana pasada fui al parque y jugué al fútbol con mis amigos.
Teacher: ¿Cuándo prefieres ver a tus amigos?
Student: Prefiero ver a mis amigos los sábados.
Teacher: De acuerdo.
Student: ¿Te gusta el fútbol?
Teacher: Sí, me encanta.

Filler words give you time to think (and stop you saying the English filler 'um'). They also make you sound more Spanish!

pues well/um
bueno well/um
a ver let's see/um

Top tips for the role play

Make sure you engage with your teacher by greeting them and saying goodbye.

Hola	Hello
Adiós	Goodbye
Gracias	Thank you
¡Hasta luego/pronto!	See you later/soon!

If you don't understand what your teacher is asking, you can ask them to repeat the question.
¿Puedes repetir la pregunta, por favor?
Can you repeat the question, please?

Remember these key tenses and opinion verbs when answering questions:
Prefiero - I prefer

Me gusta(n)	I like
Me encanta(n)	I love
Creo que / Pienso que	I think that
Fui	I went
Voy a (hacer)	I am going (to do)

- Remember to try and stay as calm as possible during this first part of your speaking test, even though it can feel like a challenging situation.
- Take some deep breaths, check your card as you go through and remember to try and say something for all 5 task points.
- Keep it simple and don't expand your answers once you have answered each task point in full.
- Aim to use accurate rather than complex language. The time to expand your answers and show off complex language will come later on in your speaking test, in the unprepared conversation after the photo card description.

Speaking: Photo card task

The **photo card task** is the final part of your speaking test and is made up of **two** parts:

The photo card contains **two** photos relating to one of the three themes:

- Theme 1 - People and lifestyle
- Theme 2 - Popular culture
- Theme 3 - Communication and the world around us

Each theme is made up of three topics (see page 234).

1 Response to the two photos
(one to one and a half minutes)
Give a detailed description of both photos on the photo card.

2 Unprepared conversation
(four to five and a half minutes)
Take part in a conversation on one or more topics from the theme specified on the photo card.

Response to the two photos

During your preparation time, **PLAN** how you are going to respond to the content of the two photos. Prepare a detailed description of both photos. This could include, for example, **People/things**, **Location** and **Activities**.

People/things
Who/What can you see?

Location
Where are they?

Activities
What are they doing?

Now check your accuracy carefully.

En la primera foto En la segunda foto En el fondo En el centro A la derecha A la izquierda	hay veo se puede(n) ver	un chico / una chica / un bebé. un hombre / una mujer. un coche / una mesa / comida. tres [personas/jóvenes/mujeres]. mucho tráfico / mucha gente. muchos [alumnos/árboles/edificios]. muchas [niñas/casas/tiendas].	
Creo que es	una familia / una pareja / un grupo de [amigos]. el padre / la madre / el mayor / la menor.		
[El hombre]	es [alto/a] y tiene el pelo [largo].		→ *page 59*
[La chica]	lleva [una camiseta] y ...		→ *page 125*
[La comida]	es/parece	antiguo/a(s) rico/a(s) estupendo/a(s).	
[Los edificios]	son/parecen	divertido/a(s) caro/a(s) agradable(s).	

Creo que Pienso que Me parece que Diría que	está están	en	casa/clase. el campo/instituto/parque/trabajo. la calle/ciudad/playa. un bosque / centro comercial. una oficina/plaza/tienda.
		al aire libre / de vacaciones.	
	es verano/invierno, ya que [hace sol]. → *page 30*		

El [chico en el centro] La [profesora]	está	aprendiendo ... comiendo ... escuchando ...	jugando ... leyendo ... trabajando ...
Los [dos clientes] Las [tres personas]	están	haciendo ... divirtiéndose. hablando.	usando ... sonriendo. paseando.

Check:
- verbs
  - regular or irregular?
  - 'he/she' or 'they'?
  - *ser* or *estar*?
- indefinite articles (**un**/**una**/**unos**/**unas**)
- definite articles (**el**/**la**/**los**/**las**)
- adjective agreements.

To say what people are doing, use the **present continuous tense**. (***estar*** + present participle). Alternatively, use the **present tense**.
está(n) bailando → *baila(n)*
está(n) bebiendo → *bebe(n)*

To gain top marks you must give a full, detailed description of both photos using **accurate language** and **correct pronunciation**.

Example photo card
(Theme 3: Communication and the world around us)

During your preparation time, look at the two photos. You may make as many notes as you wish and use these notes during the test.

Your teacher will ask you to talk about the content of these photos. The recommended time is approximately <u>one and a half</u> minutes. You must say at least <u>one</u> thing about each photo. (Please note that the photos in the test will be in **black and white** as shown in this example photo card.)

After you have spoken about the content of the photos, you will take part in an **unprepared conversation**, where your teacher will ask you questions related to any of the topics within the theme of **Communication and the world around us**.

Photo 1

Photo 2

Háblame de las fotos.

Example answer

En la primera foto hay cinco personas. Creo que es un grupo de amigos. La chica a la derecha tiene el pelo largo y lleva gafas de sol. En el fondo a la izquierda hay un edificio. Están en un autobús y me parece que están de vacaciones. Diría que es verano ya que hace buen tiempo. Están sonriendo y por eso creo que están disfrutando de las vistas de la ciudad. La chica a la derecha también está mirando un plano de la ciudad.

En la segunda foto ...

Unprepared conversation

For the unprepared conversation section of the photo card task, your teacher will ask you questions related to any or all of the three topics within the stipulated theme on the photo card you discussed.

Listen carefully to the questions and take care with how you start each answer. Are you using the correct tense?

If you make a mistake, just correct yourself. If you want the teacher to repeat a question, ask *¿Puedes repetir, por favor?*

During your course, you may be asked to prepare and practise answers to a wide range of questions (see examples on pages 230-231). This is an opportunity to show off your Spanish!

In the speaking test, an '**extended response**' is one which contains at least <u>three</u> clauses, each with a **verb**.
For example:
<u>***Fui** al centro deportivo con mi mejor amigo donde **nadamos** en la piscina. **Me encanta** la natación.*</u>

Examples of complex language include:
- a wide range of tenses
- impersonal verbs + infinitive
- the present subjunctive
- relative pronouns *que, cuando, donde*
- *si* clauses
- negatives
- comparatives/superlatives
- the absolute superlative (*-ísimo/a*)

How can I do my best in the unprepared conversation?

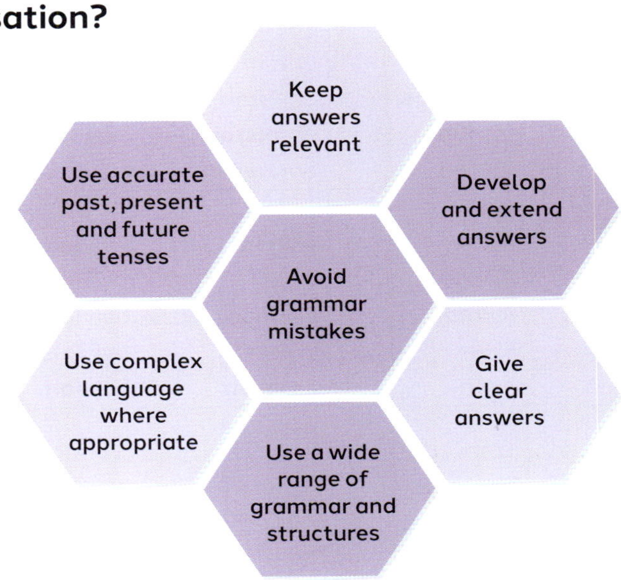

Verb tables

Tenses

See the following pages for more details on each tense:

- **the present tense** → page 18
- **the preterite tense** → page 20
- **the imperfect tense** → pages 44 and 88
- **the simple future tense** → page 92
- **the conditional tense** → page 120

To form the **near future tense**, use the present tense of *ir* + *a* + infinitive → page 20

Subject pronouns are normally only used for emphasis in Spanish, because the verb ending usually shows who is doing the action:

yo	*I*
tú	*you*
él/ella/usted	*he/she/you (polite singular)*
nosotros/as	*we*
vosotros/as	*you (plural)*
ellos/ellas/ustedes	*they/you (polite plural)*

Other verb forms

The **present participle** is used:

- after the present tense of *estar* to form the **present continuous tense** → page 58
- after the verb *llevar* → page 119
- after the imperfect tense of *estar* to form the **imperfect continuous tense** → page 172
- after the verb *seguir* or *continuar* → page 196

The **past participle** is used after the verb *haber* to form the **perfect tense** → page 136

See page 170 for details on the **imperative** (for giving instructions).

Regular verbs

Infinitive	Present tense	Preterite tense	Imperfect tense	Simple future tense	Conditional tense	Present participle Past participle
hablar *to speak* *(regular* **-ar** *verb)*	habl**o** habl**as** habl**a** habl**amos** habl**áis** habl**an**	habl**é** habl**aste** habl**ó** habl**amos** habl**asteis** habl**aron**	habl**aba** habl**abas** habl**aba** habl**ábamos** habl**abais** habl**aban**	hablar**é** hablar**ás** hablar**á** hablar**emos** hablar**éis** hablar**án**	hablar**ía** hablar**ías** hablar**ía** hablar**íamos** hablar**íais** hablar**ían**	(e.g. estoy) habl**ando** (e.g. he) habl**ado**
comer *to eat* *(regular* **-er** *verb)*	com**o** com**es** com**e** com**emos** com**éis** com**en**	com**í** com**iste** com**ió** com**imos** com**isteis** com**ieron**	com**ía** com**ías** com**ía** com**íamos** com**íais** com**ían**	comer**é** comer**ás** comer**á** comer**emos** comer**éis** comer**án**	comer**ía** comer**ías** comer**ía** comer**íamos** comer**íais** comer**ían**	(e.g. estoy) com**iendo** (e.g. he) com**ido**
vivir *to live* *(regular* **-ir** *verb)*	viv**o** viv**es** viv**e** viv**imos** viv**ís** viv**en**	viv**í** viv**iste** viv**ió** viv**imos** viv**isteis** viv**ieron**	viv**ía** viv**ías** viv**ía** viv**íamos** viv**íais** viv**ían**	vivir**é** vivir**ás** vivir**á** vivir**emos** vivir**éis** vivir**án**	vivir**ía** vivir**ías** vivir**ía** vivir**íamos** vivir**íais** vivir**ían**	(e.g. estoy) viv**iendo** (e.g. he) viv**ido**

Irregular verbs / Verbs with spelling changes

Infinitive	Present tense	Preterite tense	Imperfect tense	Simple future tense	Conditional tense	Present participle Past participle
dar	**doy**	**di**	daba	daré	daría	(e.g. estoy)
to give	das	**diste**	dabas	darás	darías	dando
	da	**dio**	daba	dará	daría	
	damos	**dimos**	dábamos	daremos	daríamos	(e.g. he)
	dais	**disteis**	dabais	daréis	daríais	dado
	dan	**dieron**	daban	darán	darían	
decir	**digo**	**dije**	decía	**diré**	**diría**	(e.g. estoy)
to say	**dices**	**dijiste**	decías	**dirás**	**dirías**	diciendo
	dice	**dijo**	decía	**dirá**	**diría**	
	decimos	**dijimos**	decíamos	**diremos**	**diríamos**	(e.g. he)
	decís	**dijisteis**	decíais	**diréis**	**diríais**	**dicho**
	dicen	**dijeron**	decían	**dirán**	**dirían**	
estar	**estoy**	**estuve**	estaba	estaré	estaría	(e.g. estoy)
to be	**estás**	**estuviste**	estabas	estarás	estarías	estando
	está	**estuvo**	estaba	estará	estaría	
	estamos	**estuvimos**	estábamos	estaremos	estaríamos	(e.g. he)
	estáis	**estuvisteis**	estabais	estaréis	estaríais	estado
	están	**estuvieron**	estaban	estarán	estarían	
***hacer**	**hago**	**hice**	hacía	**haré**	**haría**	(e.g. estoy)
to do/make	haces	**hiciste**	hacías	**harás**	**harías**	haciendo
	hace	**hizo**	hacía	**hará**	**haría**	
	hacemos	**hicimos**	hacíamos	**haremos**	**haríamos**	(e.g. he)
	hacéis	**hicisteis**	hacíais	**haréis**	**haríais**	**hecho**
	hacen	**hicieron**	hacían	**harán**	**harían**	
***ir**	**voy**	**fui**	**iba**	iré	iría	(e.g. estoy)
to go	**vas**	**fuiste**	**ibas**	irás	irías	**yendo**
	va	**fue**	**iba**	irá	iría	
	vamos	**fuimos**	**íbamos**	iremos	iríamos	(e.g. he)
	vais	**fuisteis**	**ibais**	iréis	iríais	**ido**
	van	**fueron**	**iban**	irán	irían	
pedir	**pido**	pedí	pedía	pediré	pediría	(e.g. estoy)
to ask for / order	**pides**	pediste	pedías	pedirás	pedirías	**pidiendo**
	pide	**pidió**	pedía	pedirá	pediría	
	pedimos	pedimos	pedíamos	pediremos	pediríamos	(e.g. he)
	pedís	pedisteis	pedíais	pediréis	pediríais	pedido
	piden	**pidieron**	pedían	pedirán	pedirían	
poder	**puedo**	**pude**	podía	**podré**	**podría**	(e.g. estoy)
to be able (can)	**puedes**	**pudiste**	podías	**podrás**	**podrías**	**pudiendo**
	puede	**pudo**	podía	**podrá**	**podría**	
	podemos	**pudimos**	podíamos	**podremos**	**podríamos**	(e.g. he)
	podéis	**pudisteis**	podíais	**podréis**	**podríais**	podido
	pueden	**pudieron**	podían	**podrán**	**podrían**	
poner	**pongo**	**puse**	ponía	**pondré**	**pondría**	(e.g. estoy)
to put	pones	**pusiste**	ponías	**pondrás**	**pondrías**	poniendo
	pone	**puso**	ponía	**pondrá**	**pondría**	
	ponemos	**pusimos**	poníamos	**pondremos**	**pondríamos**	(e.g. he)
	ponéis	**pusisteis**	poníais	**pondréis**	**pondríais**	**puesto**
	ponen	**pusieron**	ponían	**pondrán**	**pondrían**	

*See page 148 for the **present subjunctive** of this verb.

Verb tables

Infinitive	**Present tense**	**Preterite tense**	**Imperfect tense**	**Simple future tense**	**Conditional tense**	**Present participle** **Past participle**
querer *to want/love*	**quiero** **quieres** **quiere** queremos queréis **quieren**	**quise** **quisiste** **quiso** **quisimos** **quisisteis** **quisieron**	quería querías quería queríamos queríais querían	**querré** **querrás** **querrá** **querremos** **querréis** **querrán**	**querría** **querrías** **querría** **querríamos** **querríais** **querrían**	(e.g. estoy) queriendo (e.g. he) querido
saber *to know*	**sé** sabes sabe sabemos sabéis saben	**supe** **supiste** **supo** **supimos** **supisteis** **supieron**	sabía sabías sabía sabíamos sabíais sabían	**sabré** **sabrás** **sabrá** **sabremos** **sabréis** **sabrán**	**sabría** **sabrías** **sabría** **sabríamos** **sabríais** **sabrían**	(e.g. estoy) sabiendo (e.g. he) sabido
salir *to go out / leave*	**salgo** sales sale salimos salís salen	salí saliste salió salimos salisteis salieron	salía salías salía salíamos salíais salían	**saldré** **saldrás** **saldrá** **saldremos** **saldréis** **saldrán**	**saldría** **saldrías** **saldría** **saldríamos** **saldríais** **saldrían**	(e.g. estoy) saliendo (e.g. he) salido
***ser** *to be*	**soy** **eres** **es** **somos** **sois** **son**	**fui** **fuiste** **fue** **fuimos** **fuisteis** **fueron**	**era** **eras** **era** **éramos** **erais** **eran**	seré serás será seremos seréis serán	sería serías sería seríamos seríais serían	(e.g. estoy) siendo (e.g. he) sido
***tener** *to have*	**tengo** **tienes** **tiene** tenemos tenéis **tienen**	**tuve** **tuviste** **tuvo** **tuvimos** **tuvisteis** **tuvieron**	tenía tenías tenía teníamos teníais tenían	**tendré** **tendrás** **tendrá** **tendremos** **tendréis** **tendrán**	**tendría** **tendrías** **tendría** **tendríamos** **tendríais** **tendrían**	(e.g. estoy) teniendo (e.g. he) tenido
traer *to bring*	**traigo** traes trae traemos traéis traen	**traje** **trajiste** **trajo** **trajimos** **trajisteis** **trajeron**	traía traías traía traíamos traíais traían	traeré traerás traerá traeremos traeréis traerán	traería traerías traería traeríamos traeríais traerían	(e.g. estoy) **trayendo** (e.g. he) **traído**
***venir** *to come*	**vengo** **vienes** **viene** venimos venís **vienen**	**vine** **viniste** **vino** **vinimos** **vinisteis** **vinieron**	venía venías venía veníamos veníais venían	**vendré** **vendrás** **vendrá** **vendremos** **vendréis** **vendrán**	**vendría** **vendrías** **vendría** **vendríamos** **vendríais** **vendrían**	(e.g. estoy) **viniendo** (e.g. he) venido
ver *to see/watch*	**veo** ves ve vemos veis ven	**vi** viste **vio** vimos visteis vieron	**veía** **veías** **veía** **veíamos** **veíais** **veían**	veré verás verá veremos veréis verán	vería verías vería veríamos veríais verían	(e.g. estoy) viendo (e.g. he) **visto**

*See page 148 for the **present subjunctive** of this verb.